# Motivation

## Mechanisms of the Mind and their Quest for Expression

Introduction to a Study on a Theoretical Model of the Process of Motivation

# Motivation

## Mechanisms of the Mind and their Quest for Expression

Introduction to a Study on a Theoretical Model of the Process of Motivation

Menno A. Mennes

Volume I

Series on Motivation

The Institute for Studies in Motivation and Development of Human Potential
Leiden, the Netherlands

Routledge
Taylor & Francis Group
LONDON AND NEW YORK

First published in 2023 by Amsterdam University Press Ltd.

Published 2025 by Routledge
4 Park Square, Milton Park, Abingdon, Oxon OX14 4RN
605 Third Avenue, New York, NY 10158

*Routledge is an imprint of the Taylor & Francis Group, an informa business*



ISBN: 9789463727648 (pbk)
ISBN: 9781003700111 (ebk)

Cover design: Gijs Mathijs Klunder, *Gijs Mathijs Ontwerpers, Amsterdam*

Motivation - Mechanisms of the Mind and their Quest for Expression: Introduction to a Study on a Theoretical Model of the Process of Motivation.

For Product Safety Concerns and Information please contact our EU representative: GPSR@taylorandfrancis.com
Taylor & Francis Verlag GmbH, Kaufingerstraße 24, 80331 München, Germany.

# Series on Motivation
## Volume I

The 'Series on Motivation' provides background information following the publication of the dissertation *'De Theatro Motivarum - Motivation: In Search of Essentials* - Research on a Theoretical Model of the Process of Motivation and on Critical Determinants of Interference', which appeared in 2016. In the dissertation a summarized overview was presented of findings from a study that had covered almost 30 years of research on motivation.

The 'Series on Motivation' is intended to provide a comprehensive coverage of the study, and of findings obtained from empirical research during those years.

The Series will consist of several Volumes. The present Volume, Volume I of the Series, provides a general introduction to a theoretical 'Model of Motivation'. Using various levels of detail in separate Sections throughout the text, this introductory Volume is intended for an audience including the casual reader, the student and those already familiar with the subject from an academic perspective.

# *A Note to the Reader*

This first Volume in a 'Series on Motivation' provides an introduction of a theoretical Model describing the process of motivation. Its presentation needs an introduction to clarify the approach that has been chosen in this first comprehensive overview.

Why a 'Series on Motivation', and why an 'introductory Volume'?

In 2016 a dissertation was published, that contained a summarized overview of findings from a study that had covered almost 30 years of research on motivation. It appeared a new 'Model of Motivation' had emerged that was in need of a more elaborate and in-depth coverage, not only of its findings obtained from empirical research, but also of its theoretical foundations and inferences.

Amsterdam University Press kindly agreed to provide a podium, and in close consultation it was decided to cover this new approach on motivation in a number of separate publications, which was to be presented as a 'Series on Motivation'.

At this point in time, two options emerged: to either publish the Series in full, or in a sequence of separate Volumes as they were to appear over successive years of writing. The first approach would favor comprehensiveness, but would take years to complete. The second would provide a means of direct access to the reader, at the expense, however, of being 'fragmentary'.

In an intent to compromise between both options, I was called to meet the challenge of providing an 'introductory Volume' first, thereby provided with the opportunity of informing the academia at an early stage. Theoretical and empirical backgrounds were to be published afterwards, in successive Volumes of the Series, thereby substantiating my ideas as intended.

At first, I was hesitant to present a new theory without the necessary theoretical and empirical foundations, as I feared losing support from the academic community in the unconventional approach I was to follow.

A major event in my personal life, however, made me decide to proceed along this proposed course. I was led to believe there was a sense of urgency in disclosing unexpected elements of this new 'Model of Motivation', as referred to in the Prologue and Epilogue of this Volume.

So, here I present this first 'introductory Volume' in the 'Series on Motivation'. There are a number of important implications to the approach chosen.

The first, and most important, is that in this introductory presentation no empirical evidence is provided, where the forementioned dissertation already contains a summarized overview of empirical findings directly available to the reader (with reference to p. 4 and p. 14). Instead, I chose for this introduction to relate the Model presented here to major theories from literature and to research findings obtained from associated fields of study. I felt compelled to make a liaison in this manner to the long tradition of existing studies on motivation in the field of applied psychology.

A second implication is that this introductory Volume, by its nature, restricts the theoretical inferences I made in defining this new Model to the prime essentials, postponing a comprehensive and in-depth analysis to subsequent Volumes that are to appear in the Series (with reference to p. 5 and p. 411).

I am aware of the unconventional approach chosen, and call upon the reader to abide with me on this journey. Those wishing to contact me are kindly referred to my university or institute addresses mentioned in a brief description of the author, p. 467.

# Summaries of its Content...

For those in search of a quick introduction, reference is made to following general overviews:

- For a brief introduction to the Model of Motivation, see pp. 397 - 400.
- For a visualized 1-page introduction, see Fig. 13.9., p. 393.
- For a comprehensive overview, see pp. 376 - 389.
- For a more technical overview, see pp. 390 - 392.

*... of the Content of this Book*

## ... and Some Guidelines to Accompany it by

*This introductory Volume aims at an intended audience ranging from the casual reader, to those seeking detailed information or a liaison to existing literature from an academic perspective. A structure has been used in each Chapter to accommodate each reader and increase ease of access...*

Those seeking a general introduction to the Model of Motivation introduced in this Volume only need to read the main text in each Chapter, without proceeding to the different Sections contained in the gray areas provided at the end of each Chapter.

If you prefer to go into details, continue reading Section 1 on *Definitions* in those gray areas of the Chapter.

If your aim is to find connections between the Model of Motivation and main theories that have been presented in literature, read Section 2 on *Theories* in the gray areas of the Chapter.

If you want to know which major findings were obtained from research in literature, advance to Section 3 on *Research* in each Chapter.

*Dat ik het goede heb verstaan*
*in wat U in Christian aan mij geeft*

*May the grace of his gentle presence*
*transcend the sorrow*
*of his loss*

*Forever*

# Prologue

In nearly all activities one sets about, a purpose, an intention or an act of will can be seen. And all these intentional acts appear to have a common origin in the will of the individual to intervene in his or her destiny and surroundings, both mentally and physically.

Over the last hundred years an astonishing library of ideas, thoughts, insights, theories, research findings and 'best practices' has been produced on the subject, detailing almost every aspect of 'human motivation', as it has been conceptualized in literature.

Surprisingly, this vast body of knowledge on human motivation could not prevent conflicts, discrimination, genocide, poverty or injustice from occurring, all of which are a direct result of our will 'to intervene in our destiny'.

Despite our present knowledge, no substantial insights appear to have been generated to prevent us from almost identical expressions of these atrocities to reoccur over the course of our time. The crucial elements that could lead us to these precious insights are grounded in our knowledge and understanding of the intricate mechanisms that constitute the process of motivation, which is at the core of these frightful expressions. No one wants this. And it seems that strong and compelling forces beyond our measure are at work within this mighty process. It seems to lead us astray, despite a deep sense of urgency felt by most, if not all, involved in the noble pursuit to have the human condition strive and prosper in a better world.

This study, most ambitiously, finds its origin in these fearful considerations, made long years ago.

The study has expanded over a period of almost thirty years, and aims at initiating further thought and understanding in the field of human motivation. At its core is a fundamental departure from common practice in generating knowledge and insights. The approach has led to a new theoretical 'Model of Motivation' and to the formulation of determinants that are essential in adequately addressing its intricate mechanisms.

If these findings hold true, they appear to lead to a number of profound implications.

This Volume, marking the first of a series of ten, provides a general introduction to this theoretical Model, that is to be further described in detail in subsequent Volumes.

# Table of Contents

*This "Tree of Life" - Sangre de Christo, Crestone, CO., USA*

# Introduction

## *Motivation*

### *Outlines for a Model on Mechanisms of the Mind and their Quest for Expression*

Imagine yourself sitting in a room with a view...

Contemplating your life as time goes by, sitting, as it were, under this 'tree of life', and wondering, in the early morning hours or in the twilight of your day, what it is that made you do the things you did. Or didn't do...

There is no story more exciting than the one that tells the tale of who we are and why we do the things we do, or (even more exciting) didn't do. And most of all: the convincing reasons we use (in hindsight) for our actions and achievements, or for our failures and postponements.

What is it that makes us dream and wonder? That drives us and inspires us? That made us achieve things we are proud of, or took us on ventures we would rather forget? What is it that makes us fulfill the things we aspire, or that prevents us from doing the things we set out to do and makes us postpone these essentials, sometimes even until it is too late?

What is it that drives us to unprecedented heights, and what is it that paralyzes us, or re-ignites our spirit, full of hope, after failures or months of despair?

These processes that characterize every one of us, that seem to be at the center of our being, that determine who we are and define the 'human condition', these processes are captured in a concept we defined, barely a hundred years ago, as 'human motivation'.

The approaches that have been taken in searching for the roots of human motivation have been manifold. And over the years, a wide range of theories on motivation have appeared in scientific literature.

This book, which is to be the first in a series covering several parts, or 'Volumes', presents a theoretical 'Model of Motivation' that has been developed in the course of many years of research. It provides an introduction to this new Model, following its first presentation in a dissertation published in 2016.

The approach that has been taken in developing this theoretical Model has been different from the usual approaches in the study of human motivation. Following its first appearance, arrangements have been made to provide background information on the theoretical inferences it contains, and on the implications it entails.

This Volume is a first introduction to a new theoretical Model of Motivation, which first appeared as a dissertation in 2016.

The dissertation can be found on line in open access, at Scholarly Publications Leiden University: https://scholarlypublications.universiteitleiden.nl/handle/1887/39174

A series of publications are to appear, in a 'Series on Motivation' consisting of ten Volumes, to be published by Amsterdam University Press, the Netherlands.

This first Volume from the Series is to present a general introduction to the Model of Motivation, and to the 'Mechanisms of the Mind' that are contained in its underlying processes.

## The Series and its Background

The approach to motivation that was followed in the dissertation proved to be a radical departure from the approaches that had been taken until then in the formulation of theories. A brief overview is presented of its background.

The approach taken in the dissertation proved to be a radical departure from approaches to motivation practiced until then in the formulation of theories.

A combination was made of both inductive and deductive approaches, leading to a unique Model of Motivation that is presented in this Volume.

More information on the 'Series on Motivation' can be obtained online at the Amsterdam University Press site: aup.nl/en/

More 'traditional' approaches to motivation have been using a method commonly known as a 'deductive approach'. From a theoretical construct, a hypothesis is formulated and verified through empirical research. A conclusion either confirms or rejects the hypothesis, which, in turn, reflects on the theory. The approach has the advantage of being robust: it gradually progresses on verified and validated knowledge that is often being replicated, adding further to the strength of its findings.

But there is a danger in the approach...

The alternative, which is seldom seen in current literature, is referred to as an 'inductive approach'. These theories are inferred from simple but repetitive, often personal observations. From these observations, patterns are detected, leading to tentative hypotheses that are empirically tested and verified. The approach lacks the supremacy of a repeated empirical validation and depends heavily on the premises and argumentations used to substantiate the theoretical construct it infers. But the inductive approach has a characteristic that is missing in deductive reasoning: *by its nature it provides complete coverage and a creative uniqueness that almost adds a personal touch to these theories...*

In the dissertation an integration was made of both approaches leading to the Model of Motivation that is presented here...

## Introduction to Motivation

Theories on motivation all seek to provide a fundamental knowledge of the intricate processes involved in activities we undertake, or intend to initiate. As motivation determines not only why we do the things we do, but also what we do to ourselves and to others, it also affects the course of events in our daily lives. Why situations persist which we all agree shouldn't, or why they make us fall back in passive resilience, despite our good intentions.

As a consequence, theories on motivation can provide us with essential leads to insights and implications that offer a better understanding, not only of ourselves, but also of people and the occurrence of events surrounding us. And perhaps even, in due course, a better understanding of how to address others in these events by motivating them as best as we can. And this applies to all settings of our lives. In our relations with our loved ones, our children, in our work, in education, and in welfare, to name but a few...

So, we have a noble cause in pursuing knowledge about this process of motivation; in how it progresses, and how it affects (and obscures) the many aspects of our lives and those of others, and in how it affects in general what we might call the 'human condition'.

How are we to proceed in providing insights into this process?

> Motivation provides essential information not only on 'why we do the things we do', but also on how it affects many aspects of our lives, the occurrence of events, and, more in general, on what we might call the 'human condition'...

At first, one might think of motivation as 'a flow of collective energies' where everybody plays a part, and where the outcome, somehow, leads to action, behavior, performance, achievement.

But this doesn't do justice to the intricacy of the processes involved and obscures our understanding even further...

Let us start by making a number of assumptions to help us in the approach. This is the procedure we usually follow both in scientific research and in designing scientific theories: we assume, a priori, a number of things that can help as first steps in simplifying a complex problem or phenomenon that we are trying to verify through research or to capture in a theory.

Now, in defining our theory on motivation, an important assumption we make is that there is a distinction between how motivation works, or how the process unfolds within the individual, and how motivation can be addressed, can be made to work, can be managed. *In short, we make a distinction between the content of the process that internally drives people to do the things they do, and the methods we may use externally to influence this process.*

This distinction will prove to be essential in the approach we will take in describing motivation in this first Volume of the 'Series on Motivation'. And this distinction will define the entire outline of the study, that will be covered subsequently in the Series.

So, let us briefly clarify why this distinction has been made, and why it is imperative in the approach taken in this study.

And, as we intend to do throughout this Volume, for this, we refer to a separate exhibit which is to provide further background information, as follows[1]:

*see the exhibit next page* ➔

[1] For more on these exhibits that are used throughout the text, see pp. 16-17.

## Why a 'Process of Motivation' and a 'Process of Interference'?

So, why this distinction? Let us try to visualize our case... Our aim is to provide insights into the intricate and complex 'thing', which is defined as 'motivation'. Where to start in capturing this construct?...
Let us illustrate, first, what we are aiming at:

Here it is: lots of people, with thoughts of their own. The one influencing the other; the other being told what to do. The next person having thoughts of his or her own and trying to start 'whatever-it-is', and communicating about it with others; and this, in turn, inspiring someone else to pursue further dreams... It is a 'cacophony' of thoughts, ideas, voices that are all somehow related to motivation:

This 'cacophony' of motivation needs simplification. So, we will observe only two of these people, *in the assumption that if we look at all the processes involved between these two people, we assume they will be the same for all others.* So why bother observing them also?
Now, observing these two, which are now representatives of the entire group, we can assume both to have thoughts of their own, and to influence and affect one another:

This mutual interaction could be further simplified. We can assume that 'having thoughts of their own' unfolds in a similar manner in both individuals. And, in addition, we can assume that 'influencing and affecting' each other, proceeds also in identical steps for both:

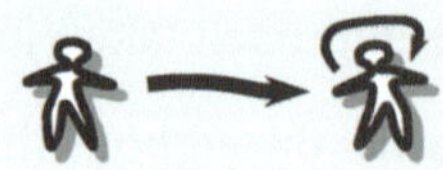

So, we assume that all processes involved in motivation occurring in this large group of people can be reduced to two fundamental states that can be used to explain and capture all these processes: the one is defined as a 'Process of Motivation'...

... and the other as a 'Process of Interference':

So it is assumed that if we are to observe motivation, we need to make a distinction between how motivation works and how motivation can be addressed. Between the process that emerges and progresses 'in our heads', and the steps an outsider needs to make in order to influence us in this process. This distinction between what occurs 'internally' in the 'privacy of our minds', and what needs to be done 'externally' by others in order to affect our motivation, appears to be clear and self-evident at first sight. But, most remarkably, this distinction has not been made in current literature (or is at best implicitly made), causing profound confusion both in theory and in the interpretation of findings from research.

*As a fundamental assumption underlying our approach, then, let us make a clear distinction, and define the constructs and mechanisms involved in how motivation works as being part of a 'Process of Motivation', and methods and procedures involved in addressing and managing motivation as being part of a 'Process of Interference'.*

*We will use capital letters to indicate both Processes and the assumptions made in referring to this distinction.* So, if we are to refer to elements of the Process of Motivation, we will use capital letters, (as in 'Goal', or in 'Phase'), to clearly differentiate these constructs from those used in literature and in other settings, both in theories and in findings from empirical research.

This first Volume, then, in the 'Series on Motivation', is to provide an introduction to the *Process of Motivation.* And thus, is to exclude coverage of all aspects involved in addressing or managing Motivation, as referred to in a *Process of Interference.*

A distinctive feature in the Model of Motivation presented here, is that it differentiates between a 'Process of Motivation', and a 'Process of Interference' which is meant to address or manage Motivation.

Assumptions, then, are essential in defining theoretical models. In addition to the important distinction between the Process of Motivation and the methods used to externally influence Motivation in the Process of Interference, a number of further assumptions are briefly mentioned, that follow from the observations made previously in the exhibit[1].

And a second assumption, based on these observations, is that the proposed Model aims at the individual and that this Process of Motivation occurring in the individual progresses in similar patterns in all individuals[2].

In addition, and as a further refinement of this second assumption, it is assumed that these patterns in which the Process of Motivation manifests itself, occur irrespective of one's gender, personality, age or background, amongst others[3].

So, these underlying assumptions help us in defining the Process of Motivation and to capture its essentials in the proposed theoretical Model[4].

[1] A complete overview and background rationale of assumptions made in the study is provided in a separate Volume, Volume II of the 'Series on Motivation'.

[2] Otherwise, if each Process of Motivation would be different in each individual no generalized observations would be possible. And as a consequence, no general Model of Motivation capturing the Process of Motivation in essential constructs that reoccur in most, if not all individuals, would be possible!

[3] Which, in turn, touches on the issue of generalizability. The less affected by gender, personality, age and background, the more a model becomes applicable in a variety of settings. This, however, comes at a price, which is mentioned in the next observation: the proposed Model thus becomes highly abstract in conceptualizing the Process of Motivation.

[4] From these series of important assumptions underlying the Model, a concluding observation can be made *that the Model is to describe the Process of Motivation at a high level of abstraction.* This important observation is briefly elaborated on p. 41.

## Introduction to Volume I

In this first introductory Volume, then, of the 'Series on Motivation', we will restrict ourselves to the Process of Motivation as it occurs in an individual, and we will leave the Process of Interference and the addressing, or management, of Motivation to be covered separately in other Volumes of the Series.

How are we to proceed?

In successive steps, we will reveal every aspect of the Process of Motivation. We will come to realize Motivation is a sequential Process in which each step, defined as a 'Phase', builds in succession on a previous step. The Process starts in fantasy, in a so-called 'Phase of Expectancies', covered extensively in Chapter 1. We will observe that a Process of Motivation evolves around an objective. Where many objectives in our daily lives coexist, there are many Processes of Motivation evolving next to each other, and influencing their different outcomes.

> The Model of Motivation presented here consists of eight distinct sequential steps, or 'Phases', through which the Process of Motivation progresses towards achieving an objective.
>
> The Process evolves back to its origin several times, and thus manifests itself as a stepwise, cyclical Process.

The Process gradually manifests itself towards actual behavior in a second Phase, a 'Phase of Effort', as covered in Chapter 2. Followed by a 'Phase of Internally Evoked Self-Assessment', Chapter 3, where evaluations bring us to deploy clever strategies and mechanisms to help us 'protect and preserve' the objectives we have reached, either partly or in full, as we have set ourselves to do.

Despite these protective measures, this 'cocoon' in which our Efforts are regulated and maintained according to our standards and wishes, is sooner or later likely to be disrupted by actions, or events, or influences, obstructing this carefully orchestrated balance. Chapter 4 covers these interfering actions or events, in a 'Phase of Reality'.

In presenting the Model, Chapters 1 to 8 are to cover each a separate Phase in the Process of Motivation.

As the Process evolves back and becomes cyclical, Chapter 9 is to cover this subsequent cycle of the Process, and Chapter 10 the intricate mechanisms involved.

And these, in turn, will lead to profound implications in Chapter 11 and Chapter 12.

Finally, a last Chapter is to conclude and summarize the main findings.

The repercussions of a Phase of Reality are manifold, and are covered in Chapter 5 in a 'Phase of Impact'. And this Phase is followed by a sequence of evaluative steps in the Process of Motivation that are covered in successive Chapters: a 'Phase of Externally Evoked Self-Assessment' in Chapter 6, a 'Phase of Anticipated Change' in Chapter 7, and a 'Phase of Dedication' in Chapter 8: the last Phase which will lead us back to reconsider our initial settings in a Phase of Expectancies, thereby turning the Process of Motivation into a cyclical, recurring Process.

This cyclical Process of Motivation will be visualized in successive steps throughout the different Chapters, covering each of these eight distinct Phases, as depicted in Fig. 0.1.:

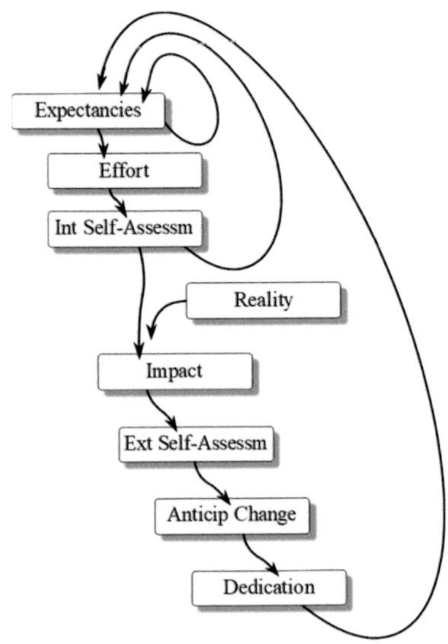


*Fig. 0.1.*
*A visualized overview of the Model of Motivation*

So, each step in the Model is covered in a different Chapter, one for each Phase. As we reach Chapter 8, then, we can observe the Process of Motivation in its final form. Chapter 9 will subsequently uncover the intricacies occurring when this Process evolves back to the first Phase, thus covering a second cycle in the Process of Motivation. Chapter 10 will cover regular patterns that occur as the Process further unfolds. Chapter 11 and Chapter 12 reveal far-reaching implications as we observe these successive cycles. In both Chapters, these implications are briefly commented on with examples, anticipating on a more extensive coverage in later Volumes of the Series. Finally, in a concluding Chapter, a summary is provided of the proposed Model of Motivation.

In addition, however, to this detailed presentation and overview of the Model of Motivation, the introduction of the Model in Volume I of the 'Series on Motivation' also provides a linkage, or connection, to important theories on the subject that have appeared in literature over the past seventy years, since the early 1950s. In progressing through successive Phases of the Model, each Phase is to be observed in connection to those theories, or important elements thereof, thus elaborating on the Model, or adding further, or differing perspectives, thereby providing a context and liaison with existing views on Motivation.

An integral part of those theories that have appeared in literature are the outcomes from research that have been generated in their respective fields of study. Where findings from research on the Model of Motivation have been presented in Mennes (2016), and can be found in open access (as referred to on p. 4), and where a comprehensive overview of all research findings associated to the Model is to appear in a separate Volume, Volume VII of the Series, we will restrict our coverage of research findings to those associated with the various theories from literature that are covered in each Chapter as they relate to the Model.

*In this first introductory Volume of the 'Series on Motivation', then, each Chapter is to cover a separate Phase in the Process of Motivation, as proposed in the Model.*

*And each Chapter in this Volume is to provide a connection to important theories and research as they have appeared in literature, whereby it seeks to relate the Model of Motivation to findings obtained from a long tradition of existing studies on the subject in the field of applied psychology.*

## Introduction to the Content

*In this Volume, then, within each Chapter, a recurring structure will guide us through the description of the eight successive Phases and their connections to existing theories and research.*

*Each Chapter starts with a general description with examples that illustrate the basics aimed at those who seek a general understanding of the various Phases of the Model of Motivation.*

*This general description is separated from a next partition in the text, where the general description is further elaborated on in more detail. In a separate part, or 'Section', definitions and refinements are provided of each Phase covered in the preceding description. In addition, in a second Section reference is made to associated theories as they have appeared in literature, complemented in a third Section by research findings, thus providing an overview and summary of current thinking on Motivation, as related to each Phase of the Model.*

*This second partition, then, following the general description of each Phase in each Chapter, is subdivided into three Sections:*

1. Definitions
2. Theories
3. Research

*To clearly differentiate this partition with its three Sections from the main text, the partition has been given a different background color (in gray) and a smaller font.*

Throughout these three Sections, additional information, background implications and examples are provided to add and clarify the topics that are covered.

To demarcate these informative additions from the rest of the text in the three Sections, they are presented in the form of separate 'exhibits', as briefly referred to earlier when covering the distinction between a Process of Motivation and a Process of Interference. Each exhibit has its specific headings and references. A color scheme is used in these informative exhibits, depending on their content as commented on in more detail on the next page.

*Color indications are used in the various exhibits,*
*see next page* ➔

Although the informative value of these Sections and exhibits is evident, there is an additional reason to provide these overviews, clarifications and commentaries.

As stated at the start, there is no story more exciting than the one that tells the tale of who we are and why we do the things we do. In essence, we are all experts in defining our own Motivation. Perhaps not fully conscious of all the details, but in retrospect we often are aware of our experiences to be able to compare those with the ones suggested in the Model, and in theories and research that are presented in literature. Not only do these findings contribute in explaining our thoughts, feelings and actions. The reverse is also true... If these findings provide explanations in a way that confirms our own impressions (or better still, reveals our true intentions to ourselves), then those experiences by themselves also provide a form of confirmation, both for the Model of Motivation we are to present and for the findings obtained in theories and research from literature.

In following pages of this 'Introduction to the Content', an overview is provided in more detail of these three Sections and of the information and features they are to contain to supplement the information in each Chapter.

## Chapter Contents and Structure used

In the following Chapters, each Chapter is to present a general description of a separate Phase in the Model of Motivation. Each Phase is introduced in the main text by a general description, with examples and explanations.

For those seeking more in-depth information, additional details are provided in subsequent 'Sections', following the general description. To clearly separate these Sections, they feature a different background color (gray), and a smaller font. Throughout the text, additional information is provided in separate exhibits. Depending on their content, each exhibit is displayed in a specific color:

In each Chapter, a general introduction on a separate Phase of the Process of Motivation is provided.

In distinct 'Sections', Definitions, Theories and Research are covered.

Additional information is provided in separate exhibits, where different colors are used depending on their content:

- Clarifications of selected topics
- Examples
- Implications of findings, related topics
- Topics beyond the scope of study
- Summaries

## 1 Definitions

For those seeking more detailed information, a first Section on 'Definitions' is provided, describing in more detail each Phase covered in each Chapter, and especially the Stages that it consists of as proposed in the Model of Motivation.

Section 1 in each Chapter is dedicated to an in-depth description of each Phase covered from the Model of Motivation.

For more detailed information, overviews and assumptions especially on the various Stages these Phases consist of, reference is made to Volume III in the 'Series on Motivation'.

However detailed these descriptions are, reference is made to a more in-depth description of the Model of Motivation, which is to appear in a separate Volume, Volume III of the 'Series on Motivation'.

Although the main text in each Chapter, with its storyline and examples, is meant to provide the reader with materials and context to position and compare the ideas with one's own frame of reference and experiences, the Section on Definitions is also meant to extend on these personal experiences.

Having a theoretical Model of Motivation is one thing, providing enough information to have these theoretical constructs add meaning and provide insights into one's own personal experiences is yet another. As stated, if the Model proves to be adequate in explaining our thoughts, feelings and actions in ways that confirm our own impressions, then these, in turn, also provide support for the Model we are to present.

So, the Section on Definitions with its more in-depth descriptions is meant to provide, not only insights into the Model of Motivation, but also a means of personalized verification to the accuracy and relevance of our findings. In the approach we will use, reference will be made to further descriptions and clarifications in exhibits provided throughout the text.

## 2 Theories

For those wishing background information on related theories, a separate Section is provided, with references to important theories of motivation in current literature.

The Model of Motivation is to be related in Section 2 to theories that have appeared in literature.

Those theories are clustered according to six major categories. Only prominent theories are observed. For a (schematic) overview of 120+ theories of motivation, reference is made to Volume III of the Series.

As stated, relating the Model to prominent theories of motivation provides a liaison to thoughts and findings obtained from a long tradition of existing studies on the subject.

Many great ideas and theories on motivation have been proposed since the 1950s, the most important of which will be described throughout the text. Insights are provided on how these findings from theories relate to the Model, and we will observe how theories, over the years, have covered different Phases proposed in the Model. As such, these theories will be presented over various Chapters covering these Phases. Throughout the text, references are provided to these theories as they are progressively covered.

As we proceed through the Phases, we will find that although these major theories have been developed from different perspectives and different scientific disciplines, they all seem to be related in their common origin to provide insights in motivation. And although the aim is to find relations and congruencies between the Model and these various theories, it appears the reverse is also true: the Model of Motivation seems to provide insights into how these theories are mutually related in this common cause.

There are many theories covering the subject. We will restrict ourselves to six major clusters in capturing those prominent theories covered in literature. As a basis for clustering, relevant literature has been used, where various classifications used in literature have been combined and (occasionally) extended[1]. Within each cluster, a selection has been made of the most important theory, or theories, including references.

As we progress in covering the Phases of the Model, we will refer to those major clusters in different Sections throughout the text. In order to keep an overview as we proceed through our coverage, color codes are used as a reference.

*Theories are covered in colored exhibits, see next page* ➔

It is to be noted that only theories related to the Process of Motivation are observed, thereby excluding theories aimed at addressing motivation, as those are assumed to be related to a Process of Interference.

An overview of theories related to a Process of Interference, will appear in later Volumes of the Series.

So, progressing on the thoughts of others, and comparing those theories with the Model of Motivation, provides a means to relate to those theories and to verify the assumptions and propositions made in the Model. Where the Model assumes a complete coverage of the Process of Motivation as it manifests itself, all these (major) theories from literature are assumed to display a clear relation with one or more of the proposed Phases in the Model.

A final and most important observation is to be made on the coverage of theories in Section 2. In the selection made, no theories related to a Process of Interference have been included, as previously elaborated on in the 'Introduction to Motivation' [2].

[1] Amongst others, reference is made to: Elliot, Dweck & Yeager, 2017; Kanfer, Chen & Pritchard, 2008; Latham, 2012; Reeve, 2005; Renninger & Hidi, 2019a; Ryan, 2012; Ryan & Deci 2018; Sansone & Harackiewicz, 2000a; Shah & Gardner, 2008; Weiner 1980b, 1992.

[2] Those theories include, among others: Equity theory (Adams, 1965); Hackman and Oldham's job characteristics model (Hackman & Oldham, 1975, 1976, 1980); Herzberg's dual-factor theory (Herzberg, 1966, 1968); Locke and Latham's high performance cycle (Latham, 2007; Latham, Locke & Fassina, 2002; Locke & Latham 1990); Porter and Lawler's model of motivation (Porter & Lawler, 1968); and McGregor's 'theory X - theory Y' (McGregor, 1960).

## Colored Clusters of Current Theories of Motivation

The Model of Motivation is to be compared to current theories of motivation. These theories are clustered according to six major categories.

In different exhibits throughout the text, background information is provided on these prominent clusters of theories. For convenience, color codes are used in referring to these major clusters.

The six clusters of theories are as follows, together with the color codes used for reference:

The Model of Motivation is related to the most prominent theories from literature, clustered according to the following six major categories.

Throughout the text, color codes are used to refer to each of these clusters:

1. Expectancy-value theories
2. Goal-setting theories
3. Goal-orientation theories
4. Self-determination theory
5. Social cognitive theories
6. Attribution theories

## 3 Research

Given the embedment in and connection with present theories from literature, Section 3 on research extends on these findings by providing an overview of empirical evidence that has been advanced by researchers in the respective fields of study[1].

In Section 3, these findings are observed and referenced as they relate to the Model of Motivation. Where connections can be made between theories and the Model of Motivation, findings obtained from research in those fields of study confirming the plausibility of those theories may also reflect on assumptions made in (related areas of) the Model.

Findings from research, as they relate to the theories observed in literature, are mentioned in Section 3.

As such, it is to be noted that no findings directly related to research on the Model are reported.

These overviews are to appear in Volume VII of the Series.

Finally, as stated earlier in the 'Introduction to Volume I', it is noted that no references are provided to research conducted over the years directly related to the Model of Motivation. These findings are to be reported on extensively in Volume VII of the Series. For a summarized overview of these results, reference is made to the dissertation mentioned earlier (Mennes, 2016, refer to p. 4).

[1] A brief observation for those less familiar with the various forms of scientific enquiry and analysis. Verifying the assumptions made by means of empirical research is often perceived as a way of providing some sort of 'proof'. But the truth of the matter is that in scientific research we cannot really prove that 'things are as they are'. We can only prove with certainty that processes are either not happening as we had expected (and in doing so we subsequently disregard such a theory), or we can establish that processes are indeed progressing as expected and not occurring by chance, in which case we assume such empirical findings provide an indication of the plausibility of our assumptions. So, the approach is not meant to obtain 'proof'. Rather, in providing an overview of findings from research and their analyses, only a confirmation (or rejection) as to the plausibility of these assumptions can be made.

## Summary

In a 'Series on Motivation', covering the outcomes of almost thirty years of research, the present Volume is to provide a general introduction to a new Model of Motivation, and, as the title implies, to the 'Mechanisms of the Mind' that are involved in the underlying processes it contains.

In describing the eight Phases the Model of Motivation consists of, each Chapter will cover a separate Phase.

Every Chapter starts with a general, easily accessible overview that is meant to provide a rough understanding of these Phases, with examples to illustrate the basics.

This general description is physically separated from a next partition, where the general description is further elaborated on in more detail. To clearly differentiate this partition, it has been given a different background color (in gray) and a smaller font. This separate partition is subdivided in three recurring Sections that are to provide further information on each Phase:

**1 Definitions**

For those seeking in-depth information (for more details, refer to p. 18).

**2 Theories**

For those wishing information on related theories (for details, see pp. 19-21).

**3 Research**

For those interested in related research findings (for details, refer to p. 22).

For research directly related to the Model, see: Mennes, 2016 (refer to p. 4). An extensive overview is to be provided in Volume VII of the Series.

*A Room with a View - Sintra, Portugal*

# Chapter 1
## *A Room with a View*
## *Phase 1 - A Phase of Expectancies*

Imagine, if you will, that you are sitting at a window overlooking the scenery: in front, a vast tree capturing the sunlight in early summer, casting shadows of greenish light; a small village nearby, and more at a distance, a landscape with trees and rolling hills...

This is where motivation starts: a view through a window on the world, as it unfolds before our eyes.

Let us elaborate a bit more to see what occurs as the Process of Motivation begins, and how it evolves through time.

You are sitting in a room. It is a room with a view. On a vacation in Portugal, at Sintra in the southern part of the country. And you are contemplating this scenery, this world as it unfolds. The huge tree in front must be centuries old, its shadow spreading over a small reclusive garden, and next to it: people in a street, doing their business, talking. Further out, the sounds of people playing a game. And in the distance, rolling hills, like stairways full of lavish green with some junipers and cedar trees. Distant hills, and glorious clouds emerging from the sea that must be farther behind.

This room with a view, looking on to the world, initializes a train of thoughts, ideas, desires that will evolve gradually into aspirations that are to materialize into different objectives. And these objectives, in turn, will set in motion a sequence of events, a journey, which in the end will lead you to decide to go on a trip to the end of the world, and even to leave your current job to pursue your ideals elsewhere...

So we have quite a journey ahead. Let us start by marking its beginning!

Initially, at the very start of this Process of Motivation, not much seems to happen. There are no actions. Our thoughts seem to wander from one observation to the other. But in a few moments, we will come to realize that our room with a view has initiated six distinct objectives... The one small and, at first, insignificant; the other with dramatic impact on the rest of our life...

Awareness of a wish, an aspiration that we want something, occurs in small steps, or rather in cycles of sequential steps. First it is a vague notion, barely discernable. But gradually it intensifies. Or then again it disappears, leaving room for new thoughts and associations.

Let us proceed through these sequential steps, observing the occurrences that will gradually grow into the first of these six objectives.

As I watch these people walking through the streets of their village, everyone with their specific destinations, I realize I too have a 'destination of my own', here in Sintra, Portugal. Nothing spectacular, really: it is a visit I'm considering to a place that captures my imagination. It is known as the 'Palace and Gardens of Monserrate'. I have this vague, romantic notion of the place, a country house acquired by a wealthy English family in the mid-nineteenth century. It wouldn't cost that much energy to visit, but somehow something prevents me from going there... Is it a fear of being disappointed if I were to visit the place? The many tourists, which I fear will affect or even break the charm of this famous place with its marvelous gardens. Gardens landscaped and fashioned at the time with plants imported from exotic locations following their discoveries in the mid-nineteenth century, making it indeed an exquisite location to visit.

*The Palace and Gardens of Monserrate*
*Sintra, Portugal*

As I follow these thoughts and reflections, I come to realize that this visit also marks an important personal occasion, and needs to fulfill my expectations even more than I had initially realized. So, what about going there *twice?* It is near where I'm staying, and a first visit could be a tryout for the next. A bit foolish, rather... But it helps in making my decision. I experience it takes away some of the nasty little fears I have about visiting this appealing place. Finally, I decide to go there on these terms. And now that I think of it, why not go there *now?*

Let us stop these thoughts and deliberations here for a moment, as they fully illustrate the first steps of the Process that will, in due course, *motivate* me to go and visit a place I clearly hold dearly, but have never visited before. The first thing that occurs is a 'vague notion', a knowledge that gradually turns into properties of a desire, an aspiration that provides direction. The aspiration becomes an objective, a wish. A vague, romantic notion of a place turns into contemplating a visit. And once I visualize visiting Monserrate, the sense of direction enables an assessment of what needs to be done, in terms of investment, in order to get there. And this does not imply a simple arithmetic of a stepwise action plan. It is an assessment, of which I am barely conscious, of pros and cons, and especially of fears and pleasures involved. And if fears seem to dominate, despite anticipated pleasures, alternatives appear for the investments needed. And in this subtle awareness, circularity emerges. Investment is assessed in both positive and negative consequences, with repercussions in more subjective terms, with anticipated fears or failures versus pleasures and obtained satisfactions. And these, in turn, re-ignite the idea of visiting the place and seeing its long-awaited 'Palace and Gardens'. As we will see, this propelling Process consists of five steps, and results either in action, as in our case, or in dismissal of the idea, which will then end and fade away, to be substituted by new aspirations causing new Processes of Motivation to emerge.

Splitting up the idea, the objective, of going to Monserrate on two occasions is a clever mechanism that anticipates on things to come. Later, in Chapter 10, we will come back to these mechanisms that seem to play an important role in the Process of Motivation...

These first hesitant steps are to initiate what we, in the Introduction, defined as a 'Phase'. And these steps are to mark a first Phase in the Process of Motivation.

To further illustrate this initial Phase, let us use a second example. This time, less sophisticated. No romantics involved; straightforward. I hear these folks playing a game. They seem to be playing tennis. Great! It captures my attention: it awakens, inspires, focuses. And gradually 'visualizes' into awareness of an intent, an objective of my own: to play tennis. It wouldn't cost too much energy. It has been ages since I played, but I know the game, I know how to play. And it's great fun!

Let us, again, step back for a moment and, this time, notice we went through five distinct steps, and sharpened these steps in a cyclical manner. First the awareness, then the focus, then the appraisal of the action needed. Instantly followed by assessments of potential success, and resulting fun. Which, in turn, steers-up a renewed cycle: intent, objective, energy appraisal that is fed by assessments of success (and potential failure), and satisfaction (or frustration). And this cyclical Process feeds-back to further focus on intent and refines the objective, gradually steering our way to subsequent action. Or, alternatively, to dismissal of the idea, which will then end and fade away: no more tennis, in that case.

So, prior to the physical action, there are successive cycles of steps that occur in this first Phase of the Process of Motivation, consisting of growing awareness and further evaluative appraisal, which eventually leads to action, or to rejection or dismissal.

There is a third option, however, which is to be our third example...

These people walking in the streets remind me of another necessity that painfully materializes into awareness: today it is my turn for grocery shopping. Now, I have *no* affection for grocery shopping. But I feel obliged, simply because we took turns, my beloved and I, and I'm the one who happens to be 'on duty' this day... Now, this is about a 'moral-and-decent-thing-to-do'. So, in this third example, there is awareness, there is a need (or objective), there is anticipated investment, but this time there are no revenues, no gains. Only a subjective appraisal urging me to proceed into doing those wretched groceries. I am not proceeding into action, nor can I dismiss my duties. And I will remain in this cyclical Process, placidly enduring the pain of postponement (or guilt) for the remainder of the day...

So, the idea, the intent, or objective can remain in this cyclical Process as an unaddressed objective.

A Process of Motivation, then, starts with a number of initiating, successive cycles of steps that could eventually lead to an objective (that is to be pursued in a next Phase of the Process), or it could lead to rejection and dismissal, whereby the Process ends. Alternatively, as in this third example, the idea can remain in this cyclical Process, as an unaddressed objective. One of many, it is assumed, that can remain unattended for hours, days or even years. The unaddressed

The Botanic Gardens - Singapore

objective can take many forms, which can have great impact at later stages of the Process. Let us view three last examples illustrating the options that may occur.

The examples are initiated by this great tree in front of my view, and the thoughts I have of sumptuous gardens. They remind me of visits I made to the Botanic Gardens in Singapore, where my mother used to take me as a young child. Huge trees that are still there after all these years. And my thoughts wander further to my last visits there, and, much later, to an identical place I visited while staying in Hong Kong. This cyclical Process of awareness and emerging thoughts that we have now uncovered, brings me gradually to a fourth example, then, of an unaddressed objective that I have treasured for more than a year now: an intended return to Hong Kong, which is a place dear to me. So, my thoughts lead me to focus and reconsider an objective dating back many months. Sitting here in Sintra, Portugal, and enjoying being abroad and away from daily work, makes me reconsider this intended trip. Where, again, I decide to postpone: awareness is apparent, the objective is evident, but the investment needed leads to a pragmatic decision where an objective assessment exceeds subjective feelings that would have brought me there much earlier. The objective is left unattended, but on different grounds than my postponement of duties in the previous example. Yet, the succession of steps remains the same: awareness, objective, intended investment, appraisal of pros and cons, and resulting satisfaction or frustration. Much later, as the Process of Motivation is to progress further, as it is to be covered in next Chapters, the odds will appear more favorable, and unforeseen events will eventually take me there, quite unexpectedly...

Our fifth example. Let us add complexity and see if these steps remain the same...

Instigated by this view with its impressive tree, and by my recollections of the Botanic Gardens of Singapore, I am reminded of visits I made, long years ago, to those in Leiden, the Netherlands. At their entrance, it had this magnificent tree, which dated back to the end of the seventeenth century. Its charm and its reclusive atmosphere made me return many times, on special occasions. And so, these visits became, in a sense, pilgrimages to memories that accumulated as years went by. I still have the impression it somehow played a role in accepting a job offer at Leiden University, marking the end of years of research and travel... So far in this example, the train of thoughts, meandering through time, is not associated to a Process of Motivation. There is no awareness of a desire, of a need, an intent, an objective; and as such, there is no 'Motivation'. We will come to realize that it is the formulation, the awareness of such an intent, or objective, that is to mark the start of a Process of Motivation. If there is no objective, then there is no Motivation. Now, let us assume that from this moment on, my train of thoughts is changing. While thinking of my work at Leiden University, this paper comes to mind that I need to finish. It is an unaddressed objective. I started it, but then urgent business elsewhere prevented me from finalizing a first draft, which has now remained unattended for years. Urgent business? I am not aware of having any pressing matters at hand, recently... Which brings me to reconsider those priorities. And in this emerging train of thoughts, this time, a desire, an intent, surfaces after many years. And with this awareness reappearing, a sequence of steps emerges that is similar to the one previously observed: emerging awareness, an unattended objective with an investment that at the time seemed impossible to meet, but now, in this newly emerging cycle, appears obsolete. I am forced to reconsider. And in a new cycle of this stepwise Process, I come to realize, not only that time investment is not an obstacle anymore, but that I have to admit something else prevents me from embarking on this project. In the two previous examples, it was either a subjective assessment of hardly any satisfaction that would be obtained, or an objective assessment of exceedingly high costs involved that prevented me at this stage from further pursuing activities to reach these objectives. But this time, it is the reverse: an assessment in an opposite direction. It is *fear of failure*. The steps involved are not aimed at costs, or at success or satisfaction, but rather at frustration, and at failure, and fear. The fourth and fifth steps of the Process are formed by assessments that are mutually opposed: it is an objective step consisting of assessments of both achievement and failure levels, followed by a subjective step consisting of appraisal of effects in terms of satisfaction and frustration. And this time, in our example, these failure and frustration levels prevent me from proceeding into action. What if I fail in writing this paper? The alternative, of doing nothing and only fantasizing about 'whatever-great-paper' is to be written one day, by far exceeds the *danger* to be faced with the embarrassment, the *catastrophe* of failure. Many, many initiatives that could have been creative, brilliant 'contributions-to-mankind' have thus found their premature end in the obscure mechanisms associated with fears of failure.

These recollections of the Botanic Gardens at Leiden bring me to the sixth and last of the examples. And it is the most complex and intricate of all...

My ambition at the time, as a young boy, as I visited these premises of an illustrious university, was to someday be part of this world where knowledge, insights, and vigorous pursuit of truth were accompanied, in this august assembly of scholars, by an atmosphere of tolerance and wisdom, where personal autonomy in pursuit of knowledge was held in highest regard, together with the implicit expressions of prestige, intellect and reputation.

Romantic thoughts of a young boy at a tender age. But these were my motives. At least in my imagination. Why do you pursue a certain job? What is it that attracts us in being a manager, a CEO, a diplomat, a psychologist, or, in my case, a university lecturer? Why talk and stand in front of 100+ students, telling them how the world is (or at least appears to be, according to you)? It is the hidden objective, the implicit motive. And in a sense, it is unattended, often cleverly disguised by tokens of expressed success: nice titles, beautiful houses, cars, extravagant outfits... Let us focus on one of these unattended, hidden objectives, instigated by a youthful dream, which is to engage in finding knowledge and truth and experiencing autonomy (and a bit of prestige and reputation alongside these noble pursuits). It is an implicit objective, not explicitly aimed at. In that sense, it is unattended, but in a different manner than in the previous examples, where subjective or objective assessments played a role that prevented me from pursuing these objectives. Here, in this example, the unattended objective is implicitly adhered to, or fulfilled: being part of such an institution means one has autonomy in the pursuit of knowledge and truth. As such, these (seemingly) unattended goals define the way we express ourselves, where we stand for, the things we want to be associated with. They represent a different class of objectives that are generated in comparable, successive, cyclical steps but remain hidden, or 'latent', while creating many objectives that are 'derivates' of these profound and 'archetypical' goals. They seem to define, not only our deepest desires and aspirations, but also the way we would like our surrounding world to be. Examples of these profound and hidden, or 'latent', goals are those that implicitly adhere to the notion of honesty, integrity, fairness, truthfulness, in a world that can be controlled and where justice prevails...

These intricate goals capturing an aspired notion of how things 'ought to be' will exemplify at a later stage, in Chapter 11, the single most intriguing mechanism occurring in the Process of Motivation: a mechanism to be referred to as a 'Stratagem of Coping'. The implications of these Stratagems, used in specific cases, are indeed far-reaching. In my example, it will lead me from my room with a view to a trip to the end of the world, marking a final decision to leave my current job and to pursue my devoted ideals elsewhere...

So here, in summary, are our six examples, or objectives, that are to illustrate the successive steps and Phases in which the Process of Motivation unfolds towards its denouement, to be commented on in the next Chapters:

- A visit to the Palace and Gardens at Monserrate;
- A match exposing my tennis abilities;
- The wretched business of grocery shopping;
- A long-awaited return to Hong Kong;
- A manuscript, left unattended for years;
- And an implicit objective to be part of an institution where autonomy prevails in the noble pursuit of knowledge and truth.

Before proceeding to a next Phase of the Process, let us first, in Section 1, provide a more formal description of this first Phase in the Process of Motivation, defined as a *'Phase of Expectancies'*.

Motivation is assumed to be a stepwise, cyclical Process that evolves around an objective that has been set. Each step in this Process is defined as a 'Phase'.

The first Phase in the Process of Motivation is a Phase of Expectancies.

This is the Phase where the Goal is defined in a circular assessment of investment needed and revenues obtained.
No overt activities yet occur within this Phase, which makes it a largely evaluative, mental Phase, highly reflecting one's personal preferences within the Process of Motivation.

*Phase 1 in the Model of Motivation is covered in detail on pp. 35-38. A summary is provided on p. 49.*

## 1 Definitions

Awareness that we want something through gradual cycles ends with the formulation of an objective, or goal. It is the first gradual sequence initiating this intricate Process we came to define as a 'Process of Motivation'. And it starts in fantasies and expectations, in a Phase defined as a 'Phase of Expectancies'.

A first Phase in the Process of Motivation centers around an emerging objective. An awareness, a vague notion gradually materializes into a distinct objective. As such, the objective, represented in the concept of a 'Goal', is at the center of the Process of Motivation. If there is no Goal, there is no Motivation. Thus, in a Phase of Expectancies the Goal is gradually shaped in a cyclical Process consisting of five distinct steps, defined as so-called 'Stages'. The first, a *Stage of Attitude*, is characterized by an inclination, a mindset, a thought or idea represented as a 'cognition'. Initially, in a first cycle of this cyclical Process, these cognitions are vague, undetermined. These undirected cognitions come and go, and either 'evaporate' or become more oriented towards a notion. A vague notion at first, that could sharpen into a more distinct manifestation as contours of a *Goal* emerge, the second Stage in this progressively emerging Process. As soon as the notion of a Goal materializes, a *Stage of Energy* occurs, where the assessment is made of the necessary investments, in terms of effort, action, behavior needed in order to reach this particular Goal. A Stage of Energy, in turn, initiates a twofold assessment of outcomes, one characterized by an objective valuation of chances of success, or risks of loss, in a *Stage of Achievement and Failure*, and the other by a subjective appraisal in a parallel *Stage of Satisfaction and Frustration.* And these outcomes re-define the initial mindset of a Stage of Attitude that had initially set this Process in motion, whereby it becomes cyclical.

In a Phase of Expectancies, then, the objective of the emerging Process of Motivation is gradually shaped and intensified, and is to progress in a next Phase towards concrete action. If in this stepwise cyclical Process of awareness and appraisal, its viability is questioned, and doubts on the outcomes progressively occur, the steps gradually fade away and disappear, and the Goal is discarded whereby the Process ends. Or, alternatively, and somewhat surprisingly, it could stay within these realms of fantasy and remain there temporarily, or, in some cases, for years to come...

Let us visualize and capture these sequential steps in arrows representing the dynamic nature of the Process, centered around the Goal.

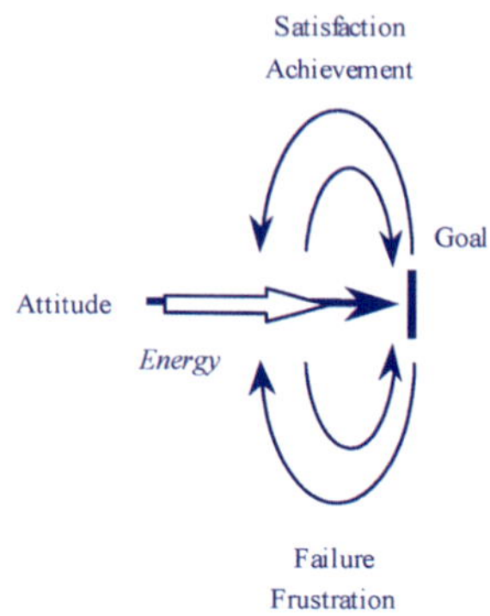


*Fig. 1.1.*
*A visualized overview of Phase 1,*
*a Phase of Expectancies*
*in the theoretical Model of Motivation,*
*consisting of:*

1. A Stage of Attitude
2. A Goal
3. A Stage of Energy
4. A Stage of Achievement and Failure
5. A Stage of Satisfaction and Frustration

The Phase of Expectancies is the first of many Phases that are to come, and that will constitute the Process of Motivation as it cycles and progresses around a particular Goal. In Fig. 1.1., then, this first Phase of Expectancies is visualized, marking the start of the Process of Motivation as it gradually expands in subsequent Phases towards completion, in either reaching the Goal or progressing, through alternative venues, towards a state where balance and stability is reached. These Phases are to be covered in detail in the next Chapters.

For convenience in introducing these next Phases in the Process of Motivation, the five Stages of a Phase of Expectancies can be further summarized, and reduced into a single diagram, as presented in Fig. 1.2., with one arrow depicting its cyclical nature, and one arrow pointing towards a next Phase in this dynamical Process of Motivation aimed at reaching the Goal that has been set.

With the Goal being at the center of a Phase of Expectancies, there are a number of characteristics, or properties, to be mentioned in 'Goal design'.

The Goal can be defined as 'easy' or 'difficult' to reach, in a property defined as *'Attainability'*. When Attainability is high, one perceives the Goal as easy to reach, given the Energy one is willing to invest. If Attainability is low, the investment is expected to be more demanding in obtaining results.

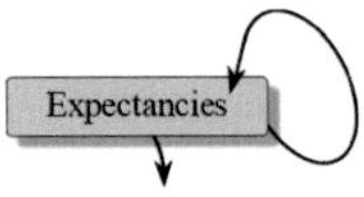


*Fig. 1.2.*
*A Phase of Expectancies*
*Visualized as the first of successive*
*Phases in the description of the*
*Model of Motivation*

A second property is defined as *'Clarity'*. As the name implies, high Clarity makes a Goal precise, well-defined, while low Clarity makes it vague and indistinct.

These properties will prove to have remarkable assets to help us in achieving them. A brief example: if I design my Goal as having low Clarity, it would most probably not lead to much Satisfaction; but it comes with a great advantage: it is very easy to reach, as I can always assume, due to its unprecise features, that I successfully reached it, at least to some extent. So, although Satisfaction is likely to be less pronounced, success, however limited, is always assured.

Because of these properties, and the effects they have on the Process of Motivation, there is more to come on Attainability and Clarity, first in Chapter 2, and more extensively in Chapter 10.

A third property of the Goal is arguably the most important. It is its importance, or *'Significance'*. *'Significance of the Goal'* is what defines the investment in terms of Energy we are willing to invest. But it also defines the intensity of Satisfaction once the Goal is reached. And, most importantly, the level of Frustration it provides in case the Goal has not been attained according to the levels of Achievement we have set. Significance of the Goal is what will appear to be the primary determinant of many mechanisms aimed at preserving the Process of Motivation. More on these so-called 'Mechanisms of Anticipation' in Chapter 10. We will refer to the Significance of the Goal on many occasions throughout the text, especially in Chapters 4 and 5 as well as Chapters 9 and 10.

There are a number of implications emerging from these ideas on how the Process of Motivation is initiated. Two implications are prominent and will be covered more substantially as we progress in describing how Motivation further unfolds... *In a first exhibit, these two implications are introduced, to be covered later in further detail* ➔

In addition, these implications refer to an important underlying assumption made in the Model.
*See exhibit underneath* ↓

### An Assumption in the Model

In the nature of these steps, in how we progress through Motivation, inevitably our personality plays a role.

However, in the observations made so far, our personality has been left out of our considerations in the assumption that although personality plays a role (such as ambition or perseverance), it does not affect the 'mechanics' of the Process of Motivation: the sequence of steps that are involved and that we are trying to uncover is assumed to remain the same.

As indicated in the Introduction, assumptions help us to simplify complexities. And this is one of them, made in the Model to assist in capturing Motivation. Assumptions in the Model are covered in detail in Volume II of the 'Series on Motivation'.

### First Implications

There are a number of implications emerging from these first findings marking the start of the Process of Motivation.

Two implications are worth mentioning at this stage.

In following these successive steps, can we learn to be proficient and smart in the strategies we choose? If so, we will be able to become better at steering up a Process of Motivation, and thus become more proficient in motivating ourselves... This would be a first implication: the better we are at 'playing' and fantasizing, the more agile and adept we become in making assessments when to engage and when to withdraw.

We will observe these ideas on how to optimize one's Motivation as an important and recurrent theme in literature, where it has been addressed from various angles, including what makes us marvel and wonder...

*More on 'curiosity' ➔p. 48, 77, 179.*

... and what strategies, or 'types of Goals', are best in steering and maintaining one's Motivation:

*More on 'mastery' ➔pp. 75-78, 130-133.*

... and how causal thinking and one's perspective may dramatically affect our performance and well-being:

*More on these ➔p. 246, 247.*

# 2 Theories

The conceptualization of a Phase of Expectancies and its five distinct Stages centered around an objective has emerged in different forms and expressions in the literature on motivation.

The concept of a goal and goal formation in motivation was introduced in the second half of the twentieth century. Until then, motivation research had been influenced by behaviorism that had dominated during the early 1920s and 1930s, extending into the 1960s and 1970s (Latham, 2007; Weiner, 2019). In his 1951 publication, Hull was one of the first to recognize specific goal-related properties as motivators of behavior. At first, the concept was largely unexamined in the literature (Nolen, 2019), until gradually the concept gave rise to further insights in many areas in the psychology of motivation, leading to various theoretical approaches that are summarized in the clusters we referred to in the Introduction. A brief historical overview precedes descriptions of these theories that are to extend further over the next Chapters. Findings that have emerged from empirical research in these early studies on motivation provide valuable input for the assumptions made in this first Phase of Expectancies.

What brings people to do the things they do? In the early years of motivation research, experimental psychologists like Watson, Hull and Skinner focused on needs and drives, and reinforcement contingencies which dominated behaviorism (Watson, 1925; Hull, 1943, 1951, 1952; Skinner, 1938, 1953, 1974; for overviews refer to: Mills, 1998; O'Donohue & Kitchener, 1999). After the Second World War, there was a strong tendency aimed at 'improving humanity', by dramatically changing the concept and nature of those studies. Maslow, one of the most prominent post-war psychologists at the time[1], eloquently referred to these years: "It was the beautiful program of Watson that brought me into psychology. But its fatal flaw is that it's good for the lab and in the lab, but you put it on and take it off like a lab coat (...). It does not generate an image of man, a philosophy of life, a conception of human nature. (...) If you treat your children at home in the same way you treat your animals in the lab, your wife will scratch your eyes out. My wife ferociously warned me against experimenting on her babies" (A. Maslow, quoted in Lowry, 1979, Volume II, p. 1059). Maslow was in search of the actualization of a person's potentialities. In the preface to the second edition of his work on "motivation and personality" (1970), he further introduces this concept of self-actualization and his theory of human motivation: "Growth toward self-

[1] See: Haggbloom et al. (2001); Kenrick, Griskevicius, Neuberg & Schaller, 2010. Latham (2007) referred to Maslow's need hierarchy theory as a "seismic event" (p. 117).

actualization and full-humanness is made possible by a complex hierarchy of 'good preconditions'. These physical, chemical, biological, interpersonal, cultural conditions matter for the individual finally to the extent that they do or do not supply him with the basic human necessities and 'rights' which permit him to become strong enough, and person enough, to take over his own fate" (Maslow, 1954, in second edition 1970, Preface, p. xxx).

*See exhibit* ➔

This driving force at the center of human motivation was further elaborated on in various fields of psychology and the social sciences.

David McClelland extended Maslow's thoughts to the field of what is now called 'work motivation'. McClelland, much like Maslow, added precision to addressing this driving force, which was conceptualized at the time as a 'need for achievement', that could promote active entrepreneurship in people and serve as a moving force behind rapid economic growth (McClelland, 1961). "(...) in the 1960s we set grandiose goals for ourselves to transform society in a hurry, applied massive doses of inappropriate behavioral technology, and by and large failed to reach these goals. But we can be more successful if we diagnose problems precisely, set more moderate goals, and apply appropriate behavioral technology to achieve them" (McClelland, 1978, p. 201).

Self-actualization:
Maslow's inspired views

In his approach, Maslow was one of the first to realize that people have a natural tendency towards growth and fulfillment. And the means to reach growth was assumed to progress through a 'hierarchy of needs'.

However, the concept of a 'hierarchy of needs' has often led to an over-simplification of his views, in the assumption it refers to a sequentially orchestrated road towards achieving a state of motivation. In fact, Maslow proposed a different view. Referring to the five needs contained in his model, he states: "(...) our theoretical discussion may have given the impression that these five sets of needs are somehow in a step-wise, all-or-none relationship to each other (...). In actual fact, most members of our society (...), are partially satisfied in all their basic needs and partially unsatisfied in all their basic needs at the same time. A more realistic description of the hierarchy would be in terms of decreasing percentages of satisfaction as we go up the hierarchy of prepotency" (Maslow, 1943, p. 388).

The core of his views is eloquently captured when Maslow summarizes, in his magnum opus *The Farther Reaches of Human Nature,* self-actualization as: "(...) the becoming fully human, the development of the fullest height that the human species can stand up to or that the particular individual can come to" (Maslow, 1971, p. 169.

Unfortunately, despite the transformative impact that was envisioned, very few of these efforts have been sustained (Conroy, 2017) or have become the conceptual foundation they deserved to be for a new field of study.

Addressing this driving force was one thing, theoretically capturing the parameters that enable and steer this force was another. John Atkinson, a student of McClelland and a remarkable theoretician, provided such a theoretical framework[1]. His theory of achievement motivation introduced the perspective of anticipation and expectancies and their effects on subsequent performance. Initially, together with McClelland and his colleagues, Atkinson differentiated between a motive to approach success and a motive to avoid failure (Atkinson, 1957; McClelland, Atkinson, Clark & Lowell, 1953).

*See exhibit next page* ➔

The motive to approach success became known as a 'need for achievement'; the motive to avoid failure as a 'fear of failure'. Both concepts are reflected in the anticipatory nature of the distinct Stages of Achievement and Failure, and especially of Satisfaction and Frustration.

[1] What is a good theory? What are essential attributes that define whether a theory is robust and precise in its definition? In later Volumes of the 'Series on Motivation', the subject is to be covered more extensively. A number of observations are made, which are meant as a brief introduction.

A theory, or rather: a theoretical model, seeks to make a simplified version, an approximation, of a more complex phenomenon or environment (e.g. Weiner, 1986). One of the essential criteria lies in whether the description occurs at a correct 'level of abstraction' (also referred to as 'abstraction ladder', see: Hayakawa, 1941; or 'structural differential', see: Korzybski, 1933). Instead of looking at the 'content' of a concept ('what' an objective is aiming at, such as obtaining a certain job, reaching the 'highest score', wanting 'this particular car', 'that particular phone', 'these specific shoes', or 'that particular brand' of 'whatever-kind-of-gadget'), one observes a 'level higher', and only the abstract properties of a concept (these refer to a particular construct, namely a 'Goal'), without confounding these properties with those at other levels of abstraction. An example: an apple, fruit and 'a nice taste' are descriptions of an object at various levels of abstraction, fruit being the highest and most abstract; an apple being an expression at a lower level and specifying aspects, or elements, or a category of fruit in more detail; with 'a nice taste', specific properties of the previous level are further elaborated on, where the taste, or color, or size of the apple is further described and detailed. In theorization, defining concepts within a theoretical model while confusing these hierarchical levels of abstraction creates imperfect descriptions and weakens the representation of reality a model seeks to capture (for further reference on the original Hayakawa, 1941 publication, see expanded reprints: Hayakawa, Berger & Chandler, 1978; Hayakawa & Hayakawa, 1990).

In the Model of Motivation an attempt is made at describing the Process of Motivation at a high level of abstraction, in the assumption that the various possible expressions of a Goal (i.e. their 'content', as previously described as a 'particular car', or 'phone', or 'shoes', or 'gadget') evolve and progress along similar lines. The higher the level of abstraction, the easier it is to extrapolate any expression of a Goal, and obtain a similar explanation for other Goals in the way the Process of Motivation evolves towards its attainment.

## *Related Topics: a Need for Achievement*

The thought that people have an inherent striving or yearning towards what Maslow referred to as 'self-actualization' came to be known (in a slightly different construct) as a 'need for achievement'. Following McClelland in his search to provide cues to enhance economic growth by addressing this 'need for achievement', Atkinson focused on the constructs involved in their relations and in the patterns occurring within these relations. And in doing so, he conceptualized many of the regulatory processes that are contained in the Model of Motivation.

<u>*Risks of success and fear of failure*</u>

*In applying the mathematical equations, Atkinson obtained two intriguing implications (that appeared to be supported by research):*

*(a) We are at our best "(...) when there is greatest uncertainty about the outcome, i.e., when subjective probability of success is .50 (...)";*

*(b) Those aiming at success should prefer intermediate risks, while those aiming at avoiding failure, "(...) should avoid intermediate risk, preferring instead either very easy and safe undertakings or extremely difficult and speculative undertakings" (Atkinson, 1957, p. 371).*

So, the strength of Atkinson's theory was that it provided insights into the mechanics, the processes surrounding an objective (although the objective was not yet at the core of motivation, as it would eventually emerge).

To give a flavor of his mathematical precision in defining motivation (thus labeled at a high and consistent 'level of abstraction'), here are two of the formulas he worked with:

$$T_S = M_S \times P_s \times I_s$$

$$T_{AF} = M_{AF} \times P_f \times (-I_f)$$

The tendency to either approach or avoid an achievement-oriented activity $(T_A)$ is a function of the strength of the tendency to approach $(T_S)$ minus the strength of the tendency to avoid the task $(T_{AF})$, or: $T_A = T_S - T_{AF}$

The tendency to approach $T_S$ is a product of the 'motive of success' $(M_S)$ which is *the need for achievement*, the perceived probability of success $(P_S)$, and the incentive value of success $(I_S)$, or pride in accomplishment.
The tendency to avoid, or *the fear of failure*, $T_{AF}$ is a product of 'the motive to avoid failure' $(M_{AF})$, the perceived probability of failure $(P_f)$, and the incentive value of failure $(-I_f)$, or shame given non-attainment of the goal.

Atkinson's theory of achievement motivation set in motion a new era of theorizing on human motivation (Conroy, 2017).

The anticipatory, estimating properties suggested in his theory led to a new paradigm in theorizing that eventually clustered into theories referred to as *'expectancy-value theories of motivation'* (Atkinson, 1957; Eccles-Parsons, Adler, Futterman, Goff, Kaczala, Meece & Midgley, 1983; Wigfield, 1994; Wigfield & Eccles, 1992, 2000). As summarized by Weiner in 1985: "Motivation is believed to be determined by what one can get (incentive) as well as the likelihood of getting it (expectancy). This is the essence of the position of Expectancy x Value theorists" (p. 559).

*See exhibit* ➔

*The effects of the past and their ways of expression...*

*If, in the early years of your life, you have had bad luck and experienced a series of setbacks or failures, chances are these could have affected the way you appraise situations to this day...*

*We will come to realize that over-challenging young children could have unintended adverse effects, as expressed in fear of failure or other forms of affective reactions.*

*More on these effects ➔ p. 77, 215.*

## 1.1. Expectancy-value theories

According to expectancy-value theories, one's behavior is a function of the expectancies one has of attaining an objective, and the value of the objective towards which one is working.

Within this interplay, two stable motives play an important role affecting the outcome to achieve in a particular situation: a 'motive of success' and a 'motive to avoid failure'. The 'motive of success' is a remnant of the 'need for achievement', which Atkinson defined as a central construct in his theory of achievement motivation.

Modern expectancy-value theories differ from earlier work where in current theories "(...) both the expectancy and value components are defined in richer ways, and are linked to a broader array of psychological, social, and cultural determinants" (Wigfield & Cambria, 2010a, p. 36).

Most prominent in these contemporary versions is the *Eccles et al. expectancy-value theory of achievement motivation.* In this theory two components are thought to determine whether one is to pursue and engage in an activity (called a 'task') and how well one is to perform: *task value* and *expectancies for success.*

*(Continued)*

Most prominent in these expectancy-value theories is the so-called *'Eccles et al. expectancy-value theory of achievement motivation'*, where determinants are suggested of one's achievement-related choices in the pursuit of activities, or *tasks.*

*See exhibit* ➔

Various elements in the expectancy-value construct and its anticipatory nature, prior to the actual Effort (conceptualized as 'behavior'), show resemblance to a Phase of Expectancies. Expectancies for success have been defined in conceptualizations that are comparable to the Model of Motivation, where a refinement is observed in Stages of Achievement (following Atkinson, 1957) and Satisfaction (following Eccles-Parsons, Adler, Futterman, Goff, Kaczala, Meece & Midgley, 1983; Eccles & Wigfield, 2002; Wigfield & Eccles, 1992, 2000). Moreover, task

Elements that occur in a Phase of Expectancies are also referred to in expectancy-value theories.

Background information on these theories is provided in the first of a number of exhibits on theories of motivation, as elaborated on in the Introduction.

### 1.1. Expectancy-value theories

In expectancy-value theory, then, two components are assumed to determine task choice and performance (such as a student's motivation for learning):

- *task value,* or the extent to which one wants to pursue a task, where importance (attainment value), attractiveness (intrinsic value), usefulness (utility value), and cost play a distinctive role;
- *expectancies for success,* or the subjectively estimated probability of success on a given task.

It goes without saying that both components (especially the expectancies for success) are heavily related to the way we assess 'how smart we are'...

*More on 'competence'* ➔*p. 202.*

... and to prior experiences and outcomes...

*More on 'self-efficacy'* ➔*p. 198, 203.*

... affecting, in turn, the way we perceive and value ourselves...

*More on 'self-concept'* ➔*p. 287.*

For further reading, reference is made to: Eccles-Parsons, Adler, Futterman, Goff, Kaczala, Meece & Midgley, 1983; Eccles & Wigfield, 2002; Wigfield, 1994; Wigfield & Eccles, 1992, 2000.

*Next related thread 1.2.* ➔*p. 206.*

value has overlapping properties with Stages of Attitude and Significance of the Goal, where task value, in its diversification is primarily associated to correspond with the second Stage of Goal-setting in a Phase of Expectancies.

As such, findings obtained from the vast terrain of empirical research on the Eccles et al. expectancy-value theory of achievement motivation can provide us with an indication on the accuracy of the Model of Motivation and the assumptions made about a Phase of Expectancies.

# 3 Research

Beliefs and values, as assumed to exist according to *expectancy-value theories,* relate to performance and activity choice, indicating the functional connection to a subsequent Phase of Effort, which is covered next in Chapter 2. In other words, these anticipatory mechanisms do seem to lead to subsequent action: reporting on longitudinal studies conducted over successive years with children, it appears that these anticipatory, regulatory processes are the best predictors of how well one is to perform on subsequent tasks. One's belief about one's ability in fact appears to be an even better predictor than previous grades that were obtained on a subject. To quote Wigfield and Eccles (2000), in summarizing main findings on these longitudinal studies: "(...) children's beliefs about their ability and experiences for success are the strongest predictors of subsequent grades in math, predicting those outcomes more strongly than either previous grades or achievement values". In addition, "(...) children's subjective task values are the strongest predictors of children's intentions to keep taking math (...)" (p. 77; see also: Durik, Vida & Eccles, 2006; Eccles & Wigfield, 2002; Hulleman & Harackiewicz, 2009; Musu-Gillette, Wigfield, Harring & Eccles, 2015; Rosenzweig & Wigfield, 2017; Wigfield & Cambria, 2010b).

So, once these cognitive, regulatory processes have come into effect, as proposed in the Model of Motivation, the road towards completing these intentions appears to be evident. The question remains where this knowledge on personal abilities and competencies comes from. It is to be expected that it builds on experience that has been gradually obtained in a long succession of attempts at reaching various objectives in the past, and on successful completion of these attempts. In other words, this gradual accumulation and development of insights in one's personal abilities is likely the result of completing a large array of previous Processes of Motivation from which this personal expertise is gradually acquired.

We will cover this personal quest into one's potential at a later stage, as we gradually progress through the various Phases of the Process of Motivation, notably in Chapter 5 and more extensively in Chapter 6.[1]

[1] Evidence for this gradual buildup of one's personal potential has been obtained from these studies in expectancy-value theories, although the outcomes have been somewhat disturbing: it appears that younger children have more positive achievement-related beliefs, in other words: the older you get, the less confident you become (Eccles, Wigfield, Harold & Blumenfeld, 1993; Eccles, Wigfield & Schiefele, 1998; Stipek & Mac Iver, 1989; Watt, 2004; Wigfield, Eccles, Yoon, Harold, Arbreton, Freedman-Doan & Blumenfeld, 1997; Wigfield, Eccles, Schiefele, Roeser & Davis-Kean, 2006).

Finally, and in more general terms, research in the field of expectancy-value theories has provided indications that expectancies and values relate positively to one another, providing further evidence for the assumed circularity and reciprocity in the Model of Motivation between associated Stages of Achievement and Failure, Satisfaction and Frustration on the one hand, and Goal-setting on the other (Eccles & Wigfield, 1995, 2002; Jacobs, Lanza, Osgood, Eccles & Wigfield, 2002; Meece, Wigfield & Eccles, 1990; Wigfield, Eccles, Yoon, Harold, Arbreton, Freedman-Doan & Blumenfeld, 1997).

Although empirical studies published during the 1960s and 1970s were generally supportive of expectancy-value theories (Mitchell & Nebeker, 1973), a number of concerns gradually arose, notably on the assumed rationality in the decision-making process, and on a number of methodological issues (Heneman & Schwab, 1972; Mitchell, 1974; Van Eerde & Thierry, 1996), which led to the development of new models in the field of motivational psychology. In work motivation, to be covered in Chapter 2, the role of the goal concept became more prominent, initiated by an article that had appeared earlier in 1968. And in the field of educational research, where goal-orientation theories gradually became prominent, following an emphasis on essentials initiating motivation, to be covered more extensively in Chapter 3. Important areas of research in those emerging fields included curiosity, interest and information-seeking, as briefly commented on in the exhibit.

*See exhibit next page* ➔

## *Related Topics: Curiosity, Interest and Information-seeking*

Related to the findings obtained from expectancy-value theories is the topic of information-seeking, which has been extensively researched in the field of educational psychology.

What makes us focus?
What are cues that grab our attention?

Curiosity and interest have been frequently used interchangeably (Grossnickle, 2016; Renninger & Hidi, 2016). However, a distinction can be made between both concepts.

Curiosity refers to "(...) a desire to seek and learn new information by exploring novel and uncertain environments, (...) interest is the motivation to seek and learn new information that is linked to some form of existing knowledge, which then continues to develop" (Renninger & Hidi, 2019b, p. 277). Interest is 'domain-specific' (Bong, 2001b; Eccles, Wigfield, Harold & Blumenfeld, 1993), which means you are attracted to certain things and not to others, and this tends to increase with age (Denissen, Zarrett & Eccles, 2007).

So, in a sense, the older you get, the less curious you become about the new and the unexpected...

*Open-minded in the midst of increased complexity ...*

*If interest appears to become more 'domain-specific' as we grow older, a number of pressing questions come to mind:*

*Do we tend to seek more confirmation in things that capture our attention as we grow older ("Oh, I know all there is to know about this, remember")? Or is it instead a 'joy-of-recognition' we seek ("Oh, I know what that is, I remember having seen it before")? Or is it because we become more demanding, or rather because we become more cautious and vigilant for the new?*

*In any case, we seem to be drawn with age to a world we 'already know'... Which then leads to the question: how can we stay open-minded in a world that is becoming increasingly complex?*
*And are we up for the task?*

*More to come on these topics...*

Research warns us:
the older you get, the less curious you become for novelty things...

## *Summary*

The Model of Motivation that seeks to describe the Process as it unfolds consists of eight steps, or 'Phases', the first of which is a 'Phase of Expectancies'.

This Phase of Expectancies is a mental, evaluative Process centered around an objective, or 'Goal', and aimed at assessing the properties that are needed in order to obtain success, achievement and gratification. It is a cyclical, regulatory Process in which no overt activities yet occur, and as such it seeks a preparatory balance to assess the necessities of proceeding into subsequent action.

In a Phase of Expectancies, the Goal is gradually shaped in a cyclical Process consisting of five distinct so-called 'Stages'. The first, a *Stage of Attitude*, is characterized by an inclination, a mindset, a thought or idea. Initially, these thoughts come and go, and either 'evaporate' or become more oriented towards a notion. Progressively, this notion can sharpen into a more distinct manifestation as contours of a *Goal* emerge, the second Stage in this progressively emerging Process. As soon as the notion of a Goal materializes, a *Stage of Energy* occurs, where the assessment is made of the investments, in terms of action or behavior, needed in order to reach this particular Goal. This Stage of Energy, in turn, initiates a twofold assessment of outcomes: one characterized by an objective valuation of chances of success, or risk of loss, in a *Stage of Achievement and Failure*, and the other by a subjective appraisal in a parallel *Stage of Satisfaction and Frustration*; and these outcomes re-define the initial mindset of a Stage of Attitude that initially set this Process in motion, making it cyclical.

Elements from this first Phase of Expectancies also appear in so-called 'expectancy-value theories', which provide further insights into associated regulatory processes.

And from research in this field evidence has been obtained for the 'anticipatory regulating mechanisms' prior to the initiation of Effort, or behavior, which is to occur in a next Phase of the Process of Motivation.

# Chapter 2
## *An Act of Will...*
## *Phase 2 - A Phase of Effort*

Our room with a view has set the stage for elaborate and associative thinking. Few of the things that pass our mind materialize into concrete action. Think of the 'archetypical' objectives that reside in our mind to have a world where honesty, integrity, fairness, truthfulness, and justice prevail. They represent 'latent' objectives that do not lead to action, although they determine adjacent Processes of Motivation which, in turn, profoundly affect the way we perceive our surrounding world and environment.

In an intricate Process that started with vague notions, gradually six objectives emerged that we now use as examples to observe the Process of Motivation as it further unfolds. And as these examples emerged in different settings, a number of the objectives did not materialize into action. As we saw, sometimes the benefits simply do not outweigh the disadvantages, either objectively or subjectively, to invest Energy in obtaining these objectives. Either the outcomes are not appealing (as in our grocery shopping) or they call for a disproportionate investment (as in our anticipated Hong Kong adventure). In addition, on some occasions the thought of things that may occur generates a fear of failure that is to postpone any action (as with the manuscript that was left unattended), leading in turn to unforeseen repercussions affecting other Processes of Motivation, as we will uncover shortly in the next few Chapters...

But with some objectives, apparently, it is different.

These objectives do indeed materialize into action. But the moment they do, they are to lead to subsequent effects on the Process of Motivation. Given the action, it is now plain to see, not only for ourselves *but also for others or for other circumstances,* the extent of our action. Whether we have been successful or not, the degree in which we have been successful in reaching the objective, in which we achieved. Or failed.

In a first example, the objective was to visit the Palace and Gardens of Monserrate, Portugal. The next step in the Process of Motivation consists of the act of going there. This Phase, defined as a *'Phase of Effort'* is the actual manifestation of the intention (in terms of Energy) that I had to invest in order to achieve the Goal that was set. So, a Phase of Effort is directly associated to a Stage of Energy, in the properties or expressions that were anticipated on. Effort is materialized Energy. If, in a Phase of Expectancies, I thought of Energy in terms of driving there, or parking my car, or entering the premises, a Phase of Effort consists of the actual realization of these plans.

The same applies to my tennis adventure. A Phase of Effort, here, forms the expression of my intent: without too much fuss, to simply start playing again. And the act in a Phase of Effort reflects this, in 'whatever' expression I had envisioned to play tennis again: hitting a ball against the wall (or rather: trying to hit a ball in my first attempt), or doing a perfect serve, or even the act of buying a new tennis racket could be an example of these intended expressions.

Now the fact is that the remainder of our examples are left unattended in this second Phase of Effort. The groceries were postponed, and so was my intention to go to Hong Kong or to attend to my manuscript. Even this objective of writing a paper, which remained hidden because of my fear of failure (although it appeared indispensable for my academic activities), had no follow-up in concrete activities. And these objectives that appeared to be concealed behind the unobservable façade of a Phase of Expectancies, are examples of the average state in which the Process of Motivation manifests itself. To engage into concrete activities, by itself, exposes the attempt and makes it, in a sense, irreversible. For ourselves *and* for others. So, the measures that are active in the concealed environment of a Phase of Expectancies serve to protect against these influences that occur once concrete and observable activities appear in a Phase of Effort.

Fortunately, we seem to have quite a few tricks to help us out when things turn differently than anticipated, even when the act to engage is successful and we achieve the Goal we had set...

For now, however, the Phase of Effort simply consists of the act to engage in the behavior we intended.

The second Phase in the Process of Motivation is a Phase of Effort.

Here is where the action occurs, or may occur, as an outcome of the previous Phase, the Phase of Expectancies.

The Phase of Effort consists of all activities aimed at reaching the Goal that was previously defined.

*Phase 2 in the Model of Motivation is covered in detail on pp. 53-55. A summary is provided on p. 63.*

## 1 Definitions

A Phase of Effort is the second Phase in the Process of Motivation. It consists of a single Stage: a Stage of Effort.

The principal aim of a Phase of Expectancies was to gradually define and rephrase the Goal. In these first Stages of the Process of Motivation one only anticipated on things to come. A Goal had been set and analyzed on what it would be worth investing in terms of Energy, on chances of success of the investment, and on the benefits in terms of Satisfaction. But nothing had been physically undertaken to reach what one had set in mind. It was a mental exercise, a Phase of Expectancies; and the analysis either led to a cyclical re-adjustment, a gradual fading away of intentions, or to a sustained status quo.

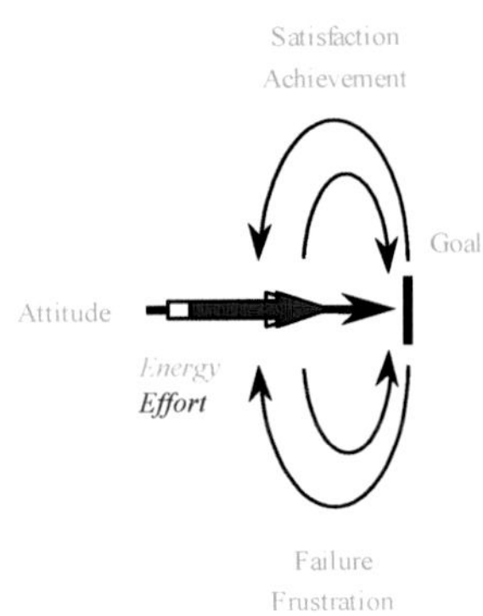


*Fig. 2.1.*
*A visualized overview of Phase 2,*
*a Phase of Effort*
*in the theoretical Model of Motivation,*
*consisting of a single Stage:*

6. A Stage of Effort

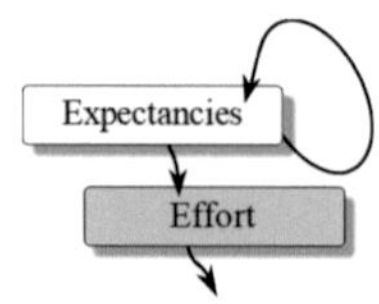


*Fig. 2.2.*
*A Phase of Effort*
*Visualized as part of successive Phases*
*in the description of the*
*Model of Motivation*

Now, following these cyclical and gradual adjustments in a Phase of Expectancies, the Process can eventually lead to a next Phase, where concrete activities are deployed in order to achieve what has been set in mind, as visualized in Fig. 2.1.

Not all Goals lead to action, but when they do, the Process of Motivation takes on a new dimension: concrete overt action ('behavior') is displayed, which, in turn, can lead to a succession of subsequent intricate Processes. As such, this subsequent Stage following those from a Phase of Expectancies warrants the designation of a separate Phase in the Process of Motivation: a Phase of Effort. This Phase follows as an outcome of a Phase of Expectancies, as depicted in Fig. 2.2.

Whereas in a previous Stage of Energy only an assessment was made, in a Phase of Effort the action occurs, and the nature of the activity is such that it is evident and perceptible. So, in short, a Phase of Effort consists of a single Stage in which a tangible, overt, externally oriented activity occurs[1].

Now, it is to be expected that there is a relation between properties of the Goal that have been set and this subsequent Phase of Effort. Three properties were mentioned earlier, in Chapter 1: Clarity, Attainability, and Significance of the Goal.

The higher the Clarity in which the Goal has been set, the more precise we

[1] There is a small, but significant problem, however, which is almost philosophical: when is an action 'an action'? If I decide to play tennis, things are obvious whether I engage in the act or not. But if I decide *not* to do so, am I then still acting? The answer lies not in a philosophical perspective, but for a Process of Motivation in the formulation of the Goal that has been set. If I am confronted with a dilemma, either to act or not to act, the activity in a Phase of Effort may very well consist of 'not doing something', thereby acting in accordance with the Goal that has been set. To illustrate: a student once wrote in an essay that she had been confronted with a dilemma either to 'pinch a bike' as she put it, and get safely home, or not to get caught in the act. In the end, she did not take the bicycle, and in doing so, she thought she *did not* proceed to a Phase of Effort, although the fact was that she *did*. Her Goal was to 'make an educated decision', and not to either 'pinch a bike' or not. In taking the appropriate decision, the Process of Motivation *did* proceed to a next Phase of the Process, and, as it so happened, to subsequent steps in the Process that gave her a gratifying sense of 'having done the right thing'...

formulated the objective, the more daring the attempt to reach the objective. The more precise, the better we know when the Goal has been reached, and the higher the precision in which we will be able to assess the extent to which we were successful, and consequently, the higher the resulting pleasure of obtaining what we set ourselves to accomplish. However, if we fail, we fail miserably; as the consequence of precision is that we will be well aware of the fact. There is no way to compensate as the result is apparent and plain to see. *So high Clarity can lead to increased pleasure, but it comes at a price when we fail. It is therefore more than likely we use high Clarity for defining those Goals we are fairly certain we will eventually reach. And consequently, for those Goals with high Clarity, we are likely to display high levels of Effort.* Once we dare to set ourselves Goals with high Clarity, the same mechanism propels us to invest high Effort.

The opposite applies to Goals that are low in Clarity. It serves a great purpose for the Goals we are not certain we can successfully achieve, to define them with *less* precision. Not only do we often feel less qualified to define precision for those Goals, it also serves a purpose to define them with less Clarity. The less precise, the better we are able to find cues to convince ourselves we *did* reach our Goal, or at least to some extent. For the less precise we have been in defining our Goal, the more easily we can state (or pretend) that we have reached what we want. But such vague objectives also come at a price, as the pleasure we experience in obtaining such Goals is likely to be much lower than for the ones we defined with great precision. *So less Clarity in defining a Goal makes us less vulnerable for potential mishaps and can protect us against disappointments, but it also comes at a price. And it is more likely we use these Goals when we are hesitant or more fearful for the outcomes. And consequently, for those Goals with low Clarity, we are likely to display lower levels of Effort.*

So, there appear to occur regularities and recurrent patterns in the Process of Motivation as it progresses towards an objective. The same mechanisms appear to apply to Attainability in the Goal we set. Once we are more confident, Attainability can be set high and with great precision or Clarity. Or, conversely, we can decide to set Attainability low in order to protect ourselves against the risks to fail in the attempt: "This really seems to be beyond reach, but, you know, at least I will give it a try."

These recurrent patterns that occur in the Process will be covered in more detail once we have progressed through the entire Process of Motivation. We will come to realize that the concept of Significance of the Goal, or its perceived importance, further regulates these mechanisms: the more Significant the Goal, the more measures we take to safeguard ourselves against misfortunes, resulting in remarkable (and disturbing) consequences...

# 2 Theories

The conceptualization of a Phase of Effort has emerged most prominently in studies in the field of goal-setting, where *goal-setting theory* has been most prominent.

*See exhibit* ➔

In 1968, an influential article appeared where Edwin Locke proposed that conscious goals and intentions are determinants of motivation and performance. His article stimulated intense research interest in the goal construct and its potential effects on motivation and performance, especially within a work environment (Kanfer & Chen, 2016).

<u>Work motivation and its field of study</u>

There are a number of distinct fields of study within psychology. In the psychology of motivation, one of the prominent fields of study is work motivation. A main focus has been how to inspire or steer people towards productivity.

Within work motivation, Goal-setting theory "is quite easily the single most dominant theory in the field, with over a thousand articles and reviews published on the topic in a little over 30 years" (Mitchell & Daniels, 2003, p. 231; see also: Kanfer, Frese & Johnson, 2017).

## 2.1. Goal-setting theories

Goal-setting theory "(...) states that there is a positive linear relationship between a specific high goal and task performance" (Latham & Locke, 2007, p. 291).

In summary:

- The 'higher' (or more difficult) the goal, and the more specific it is formulated, the better the outcome, in terms of Effort, or performance.
- In addition, commitment is a 'moderator' in these outcomes: the more committed, the higher the outcome, the Effort, or performance.

These findings apply to so-called 'self-set goals', the ones you define for yourself; as well as to so-called 'assigned goals', the ones that are defined by others and given to provide direction in addressing motivation.

Both approaches do show high results. *However, the processes involved producing these results are highly different.* More on the background of these findings, p. 59.

For general overviews on goal-setting theory, see: Locke & Latham, 1990. 2013, 2019.

For more overviews on goal-setting theory, see p. 136.

*Next related thread 2.2.* ➔ *p. 135.*

## 3 Research

The Locke article gave a boost to research on goal-setting in the field of work motivation, but also, surprisingly, set the concept of a Goal, as defined in a Phase of Expectancies, at the center of attention. As observed by Pervin (1989), this orientation towards the concept of a goal as a central motivational construct enabled conceptual thinking on motivation to change its sole focus on needs or reinforcers, as we have previously seen in Chapter 1. Since then, the overriding common theme in almost all psychological approaches to motivation has been the construct of a goal (Austin & Vancouver, 1996; Mitchell & Daniels, 2003).

Does an intention to attain a goal, given that its chances of success are acceptable and given the satisfaction that will occur once it is reached, does this process eventually lead to action? Yes, it does, as numerous studies showed once goal-setting theory had focused the attention on the subject. However, the results that were obtained used constructs that were slightly different than the ones used in the Model of Motivation, so that we need to re-phrase these findings, according to the context in which they were found.

Most prominent in the numerous studies and field experiments was the positive relation that could be established between performance, or Effort, and what was called 'specific goal-formulation' or 'goal difficulty'. The more specific a goal was formulated (in terms of what we called Clarity), the better the performance, as a result. In addition, if such a goal was more difficult (in terms of what we called Attainability), the higher the performance, or Effort (Locke & Latham, 1990, 2013, 2019; Latham, 2012; Mento, Steel & Karren, 1987; Mitchell & Daniels, 2003)[1]. Moreover, so-called 'goal commitment' (or the Energy one is willing to invest) was found to be essential to produce this motivational effect (Locke & Latham, 1990; Locke, Shaw, Saari & Latham, 1981). In a subsequent meta-evaluative overview Klein, Wesson, Hollenbeck and Alge (1999) were able to demonstrate that goal commitment moderated the relationship between goal difficulty and performance: "(...) high performance comes about only when goal difficulty and goal commitment are both high. Difficult goals do not lead to high performance when commitment is low and high levels of commitment to easy goals also fail to generate high performance" (Klein, Wesson, Hollenbeck & Alge,

[1] However, and these observations are often omitted in the various overviews, these 'high' and 'specific' goals need to be (literally) attainable and not beyond reach, as they often appear to be in targets or so-called 'key performance indicators', or 'KPIs', used in a work environment. As stated by Locke: "Goals that are set too high can be demoralizing; there is a fine line between stretching people and discouraging them" (Locke, 1996, p. 123).

1999, p. 886). These findings on the relation between (what is often called) 'high', specific goals, goal commitment and performance provide support for the assumptions made in the Model on Goal-setting, Clarity, Attainability and the regulating mechanisms involved in defining Energy, leading to subsequent action in a Phase of Effort.

However, there is a second observation to be made on those findings.

Research on goal-setting began with one specific question: "Does goal setting affect one's performance on a task (...). With the discovery that the answer is yes, research was conducted to answer further questions but this was not done in any particular order" (Latham & Locke, 2007, p. 290). The result was that an important issue, according to the Model of Motivation, was addressed differently: in research on goal-setting, no clear distinction was made between a Process of Motivation and a Process of Interference. As a result, some reservations must be made before applying the results obtained to the assumptions made in the Model.

Does it make any difference if someone else defines a goal for you or if you are the one who regulates the action and defines the goal on your own terms? According to our initial statements made in the Introduction, it does...

'Self-set goals', as they are referred to in literature, are the outcome of a Process of Motivation. They follow specific steps, as we have already seen in Chapter 1 when covering the first five steps from a Phase of Expectancies. As we will come to realize, there are twenty-four steps in total. And these steps, or Stages, produce distinct effects as the Process of Motivation progresses.

'Assigned goals', which are defined by others, follow different rules than the one's we observe in the Process of Motivation. Simply because someone else has a perspective that does not necessarily coincide with our own. In fact, once we come to cover the Process of Interference, we will find that the difference in perspectives is *by far* the main source of demotivation in numerous settings: the 'rules of engagement', which are set by an outsider (often with the best of intentions), are seldom perceived by the addressee in the manner intended. We will cover these issues elsewhere in subsequent Volumes of the Series. For now, we will only observe that although findings obtained from studies in goal-setting theory produce the same outcomes, *the mechanisms involved in generating these outcomes are distinctly different for self-set goals in a Process of Motivation than they appear to be for assigned goals in a Process of Interference* [1].

*For more details, see the exhibit next page* ➔

[1] These observations could provide an explanation for a number of inconsistencies that Locke and Latham have observed in critical reviews of their work, e.g. Latham, Erez & Locke, 1988; Locke & Latham, 2002). More on these in Chapter 5.

Goals: self-set or assigned?

The higher (or more difficult) and specific the goal, the higher the performance.

However, depending on the setting, the processes involved are different...

There is a difference between someone else being clear about the things (the objective) they want you to do, or *you* defining goals entirely for yourself without someone else interfering. The effects are the same, as we have seen in research findings obtained in studies on goal-setting theory; but the mechanisms involved in assigned as opposed to self-set goals are different, according to the Model of Motivation.

Where someone else sets a clear goal that is challenging (difficult) yet achievable, as in *assigned goals*, this provides guidance on what is expected from you. But it also conveys trust and confidence in the abilities you have: it acknowledges your expertise, or your worth. This approach is highly motivating as we shall observe when we cover the Process of Interference in subsequent Volumes in this 'Series on Motivation'.

In *self-set goals*, however, the outcome is also highly motivating, but the mechanisms involved are different. Once you engage in your quest to reach an objective, it starts with uncertainties. Uncertainties about your abilities, your expertise, your perseverance, your competence, your intellect. And if you decide to engage in a first attempt and you succeed, a second round will make you more confident of these outcomes. Now, in defining a Goal, we have already seen a number of ingenious strategies at work: at first (as we saw in our example in the text), you go to Sintra deciding 'just to have a quick look around'. The Goal is vague and unclear. But as you gather evidence on your achievements and successes, on your knowledge and on your worth, you gradually gain momentum and define your Goals in a more precise manner: "I am not just playing tennis for fun (which is always successful), but now I am playing to *win*".

So, Clarity in Goal-setting does not come by itself. It grows as you gradually become more confident that you will get there in the end. And, as we observed previously, the more precise the Goal in terms of Clarity, the greater the Satisfaction you will obtain in Achievement. So, Clarity and precision are the outcome of your growing confidence, commitment and motivation.

In short, then, these self-set Goals do not drive Motivation, *they are the outcome of the Process;* according to the Model of Motivation, they are the result, the gauge of a successful fine-tuning of other essential parameters in a previous Phase of Expectancies in the Process of Motivation.

## *Related Topics: the Issue of Goal Difficulty*

Following research in the field of goal-setting, the question comes up which properties in defining a Goal are most successful?

Unfortunately, there are a number of issues emerging that need to be addressed before an adequate answer can be given...

*Goal difficulty is related to many concepts and constructs in studies on motivation.*

*We will cover the issue of goal difficulty further (either directly or indirectly) on different occasions throughout the analysis, notably when we come to assess our abilities and successes, where external input appears to play an important role...*

*More on 'competence' ➔p. 202.*

*... or determine how well we performed, through processes of self-awareness where we reflect on personal efficacy...*

*More on 'self-efficacy' ➔p. 198, 203.*

*... and evaluate ourselves as a consequence...*

*More on 'self-concept' ➔p. 287.*

What are successful properties of a goal? Which properties generate success most of the time?

Research in the field of goal-setting theory shows: "(...) the most effective goals for increasing performance are those that are specific and difficult" (Locke & Latham, 2019, p. 97).

However, there is a problem with this statement and its definition of 'difficulty'. How do you know if a goal is difficult? Where do you obtain knowledge of being (potentially) successful, or risking failure? Is it from previous experience? But what if there is none? And if there is, who at the time determined that you were successful? Was it you or someone else who played a role in determining that you were?

The conceptualization of goal-difficulty has raised some debate...

Goal difficulty refers to and depends not only on the properties of the goal, but also on one's capabilities, one's confidence and ambition, one's observations and personal assessments, and those of others in the contextual setting.

We will cover these issues as they occur in the Chapters to come...

The findings obtained, then, from the vast amount of studies that have been produced by research on goal-setting theory, especially on self-set goals, provide an indication that elements that are defined in a Phase of Expectancies according to the Model of Motivation appear to lead, as expected, to performance and action in a Phase of Effort, once one is determined to do so.

The findings, however, from research in goal-setting theory do not produce further insights into the specific mechanisms involved. In the extensive and elaborate research findings obtained over the years, emphasis has been on providing insights into the effects of goal-setting on performance, persistence and (academic) achievement, and much less on the intricate interplay of cognitive, affective, self-regulatory processes leading to these outcomes[1] [2].

[1] As the emphasis on performance prevailed, already in 1987, a meta-analytic study on goal-setting and performance concluded that the emphasis of research had to change towards identifying underlying mechanisms which contribute to these relationships (Mento, Steel & Karren, 1987).

[2] An attempt at filling the gap was made later with the introduction of the so-called 'high performance cycle' (see: Latham, Locke & Fassina, 2002). Outcomes of research findings will be covered when observing a Process of Interference, notably in Volume V of the 'Series on Motivation'.

## *Related Topics: Information-seeking*

What are the cues that make us invest Effort? Apart from research on regulatory mechanisms leading to Effort, the concept of information-seeking has also been a topic in the field of educational psychology and, more recently, in the field of neuroscience...

*If reliability plays a role in seeking and selecting information, it appears that to some extent risks are involved in seeking new ventures. Risks that are minimized when those novelties come from a reliable source.*

*What is the role of risk-taking, and what are the threats involved?*

*More on these topics in the next Chapter, notably p. 77.*

What is it that makes us seek new ventures and invest Effort in what is called 'information-seeking'?
It is not *only* novelty...
It appears to be novelty *and reliability* of new cues that trigger us...

What makes us actively seek new ventures? What is it that attracts us to invest Effort in finding out about new things, without knowing beforehand what the outcomes will be?

Although the concept of information-seeking has remained one of the most intensively studied topics in the field of educational psychology, its origins are still unclear. More recently, findings have been obtained from the field of neuroscience (for recent overviews, see: Dey & Gottlieb, 2019; Gottlieb, Oudeyer, Lopes & Baranes, 2013), revealing that attention can be perceived of as a mechanism aimed at seeking and selecting information in order to make decisions, where gradually knowledge accumulates and helps in organizing sampling strategies. In these attempts, most remarkably, *reliability of cues* appears to play a most prominent role.

It is not the mere presence of novelty and new information that triggers us, it appears that provenance also plays a role: our interest is drawn first and foremost when we are confident it comes from a reliable source...

## *Summary*

A second Phase in the Model of Motivation, is a 'Phase of Effort', in which activities are deployed to reach the Goal that has been set, as defined in a previous Phase of Expectancies.

Not all Goals lead to action, but when they do, the Process of Motivation takes on a new dimension: concrete overt action ('behavior') is displayed, which, in turn, is to lead to subsequent steps in this intricate Process.

Whereas in a previous Stage of Energy within a Phase of Expectancies, only an assessment was made, in a Phase of Effort the anticipated action occurs. A Phase of Effort consists of a single Stage in which a tangible, overt, externally oriented activity becomes evident and perceptible.

The conceptualization of a Phase of Effort has emerged most prominently in studies in the field of goal-setting and goal-setting theories.

Despite a number of issues and observations, research related to goal-setting theory has produced considerable evidence that the Process of refining the properties of one's Goal in a cyclical Phase of Expectancies, in terms of assessments of difficulty or refinements in Clarity or Attainability, *does* lead to subsequent action in a Phase of Effort. And the better we are at progressing through a cyclical Phase of Expectancies, the greater the chances we proceed into action in this Phase of Effort. Whether we are successful in the act, depends on mechanisms emerging in a next Phase of the Process of Motivation.

*The Palace and Gardens - Monserrate, Portugal*

# Chapter 3
## *In Pursuit of Success...*
## *Phase 3 - A Phase of Internally Evoked Self-Assessment*

The Palace and Gardens of Monserrate, Portugal!

It is what the name implies... The place offers a combination that is seldom seen: it combines glamorous extravagance with the restraint subtilities of nature. But before getting carried away by the romanticism of the place, let us proceed from where we stood after moving into action in a Phase of Effort...

From all the objectives that went through my mind in my room with a view, only two materialized into action: going to Monserrate and starting my sports exercises...

First, then, Monserrate. From the mindset I had, which gradually evolved in a Phase of Expectancies, I finally ventured into taking the risk to visit the place. So, now I'm here; and I dare say that I am rather successful. Have there been any setbacks, obstructions, were there any frustrations or disappointments? Perhaps that it took a while to get here, and we had some preparations to make beforehand. But these were marginal. So, assessing the experience in a detached manner, the outcomes have been favorable: the pros exceed the cons. In an objective balancing of success and failure the one outnumbers the other.

But now for the *subjective* experience. At first, one might say: "I am delighted, overjoyed by the experience", so a subjective assessment appears to be fine also. But this is not what actually happens. And we will come to realize in a next Phase, Chapter 4, that being too casual in our current observations will have detrimental effects on our analysis of upcoming events... For what is happening is that in the overwhelming experience, we did not realize that *we changed our objective.* Let us recall, that our objective was (ingeniously formulated) to simply 'go there'. And we had a clever afterthought to go there twice if things would turn out favorably. So, in this first assessment, we only assessed in subjective terms *the decision to go*, which turned out to be most satisfactory. Now, almost instantly, we subsequently decide to make amendments to our Goal. We now have the courage to sharpen our initial Goal, and as our visit progresses, so does the Effort we invest and the revenues we obtain, both objectively and subjectively.

These *instant* actions, are what makes the Process of Motivation difficult to disentangle. For in this split second, a new manifestation of the Process has emerged: *it becomes cyclical again.* After this third evaluative Phase, the Process of Motivation evolves back to the first Phase, where the Goal is re-assessed within its constraints, its 'parameters'. And these are now much more favorable than we thought at first. With this new experience, we dare to sharpen our Goal from a mere 'going-there' to 'going-there-to-have-a-great-and-romantic-experience-of-amazement-and-wonder'. In this cyclical Process, which gradually progresses with time well-spent, a 'status quo' emerges, in which the Effort invested is attuned, harmonized, to the revenues obtained. The Process becomes a 'cocoon'. And as we leave late in the afternoon, we are overconfident a next visit would be as memorable as the one we have had today.

And from this cocooned experience, we make plans for this renewed visit; and we decide it is to be arranged 'first thing' the next day...

But audacity comes at a price, as our next visit to Monserrate will be slightly different, as the arrangements for a visit will prove to be beyond our control...

The cocoon, in which we erroneously thought no outside interference would occur, will be dramatically disrupted in a next

Phase (which is most appropriately called a 'Phase of Reality'). Had we kept our initial Goal to simply go there, we would have been much more successful in the upcoming events. But let us not diverge on things to come...

Let us rather observe our next example, before attempting to define the various Stages which appear in this present Phase.

Fortunately, with my tennis exercises, things appear to be more easy... Recall that I had set myself to simply 'play tennis'. And after having started the action, in this new Phase, I will now decide on whether it is as 'fun' as I had anticipated. As in the previous example, two distinct steps occur; the first assessing in objective terms the revenues and return on investment, the second evaluating the subjective outcomes. In that sense, it is a reoccurrence of steps, or Stages, that emerged earlier in anticipating on investments in a Phase of Expectancies.

After having invested in a Phase of Effort, then, the Process of Motivation progresses into this next Phase, where assessments are made of these activities, in two successive Stages that resemble the previous Stages of Achievement and Failure, and Satisfaction and Frustration which occurred in a Phase of Expectancies. The difference between both is that these two previous assessments were mental exercises preceding the actual Effort, whereas now, both assessments are aimed at the 'real thing', following after the actual Effort has occurred.

The Process subsequently becomes cyclical again. Given the outcomes of both assessments, preparations are made to fine-tune the Goal and its parameters once more in a Phase of Expectancies. Not always, but in most cases, in most Processes of Motivation, this cyclical feedback leads to amendments, where one becomes more prudent or, as the case may be, more daring...

Let us once again return to the example we set in playing tennis.

I anticipated in a Phase of Expectancies that the experiment would be rather 'fun'...

And so it was! After having had the experience again, and the thrill of playing with satisfaction, I kept on going in my exercise. Which is another way of saying *that I continuously cycled through these first three Phases.* And as I kept on going, I 'cyclically' assessed the revenues and satisfaction I got out of the experience. But then, while still having 'great fun', my slightly deteriorated overall condition (which I managed to conceal until then) gradually took over in terms of fatigue, occasional failure and, finally, frustration. Satisfaction *and* Frustration. Both are, as previously observed, two separate entities. By this time, having cycled through a number of consecutive cycles in these first three Phases of the Process, I now decide to stop.

And in this final observation, an essential new detail emerges. For I could *maintain* my initial Goal, and thus end my series of successive Efforts in Failure and Frustration. But I didn't. Again, cycling through these Phases I gradually *changed* my Goal from 'playing-tennis' (which is quite safe) to 'playing-tennis-and-having-fun' (which is a bit more risky) to 'playing-tennis-and-having-fun-for-15-minutes-a-day-to-improve-my-condition' (which is a real winner). Ingeniously changing our Goal continuously is what we usually do. In doing so, we preserve the integrity of the Process. And we maintain our Motivation. And thus, we create a 'status quo', a cocoon, where continuous, subtle amendments are made to the Goal we set and to the Process of Motivation that leads us there.

So, contrary to what is yet to follow in the Process of Motivation, in this third Phase we *exclusively define ourselves* the outcomes we experience from the Effort we invested: this third Phase in the Process is a *'Phase of Internally Evoked Self-Assessment'*.

In this Phase, three properties of the Goal mentioned earlier now become prominent, and will provide a basis for ingenious mechanisms to occur in the Process of Motivation, to which we will refer more in detail later, in Chapter 9 and Chapter 10.

Let us briefly elaborate, using the example to illustrate.

The next day, as everything went so smoothly with my tennis exercises (and my physical condition), I decide to make amendments on these sequentially changing Goals. In a moment of audacity, I decide to take up the challenge and apply for a match that is to take place later in the week. And I decide to rearrange my Goal accordingly.

At first, the Goal was simply to 'play tennis'. Now, after I gained confidence that I could play well and that the Goals I would set were within reach, I now re-define them to become more achievable (this is what we defined as 'Attainability' in Definitions, Chapter 1 and Chapter 2). In addition, to obtain more impact, more 'fun' from the experience, I make the Goals more precise, so that in achieving them I would obtain even more fun: "Look how I did! I told you so! Great fun!" (this was referred to earlier as 'Clarity' in defining the Goal, mentioned in Definitions, Chapter 1 and Chapter 2).

Furthermore, in re-defining my objective, a new property emerges: the property of 'importance', referred to earlier as 'Significance of the Goal' (as mentioned in Definitions, Chapter 1). As I re-define my Goal, this property of Significance becomes more evident. As I grow more confident, so it becomes more important to me, not only to reach the Goal of 'playing-tennis', but to 'play-tennis-having-fun-and-improving-my-condition'. With this increase in prominence of the Goal, the necessity of reaching it to 'full standards' also increases. And this is to make me more vulnerable to Achievement and Satisfaction, but also to Failure and Frustration. And to unforeseen interference...

And here also, as things turn for the best, audacity is to play a role in a next Phase of the Process...

Let us first summarize our findings, and compare the ideas to those of others and to research findings that have been obtained in literature.

The third Phase in the Process of Motivation is a Phase of Internally Evoked Self-Assessment.

Every action leads to a reaction...

Phase 3 is the *personal assessment* of the attempt made in the previous Phase of Effort to reach the Goal that has been set, in terms of Achievement and Failure, Satisfaction and Frustration.

The Phase provides input for renewed amendments in Phase 1, and therefore adds circularity to the first three Phases of the Process of Motivation.

*Phase 3 in the Model of Motivation is covered in detail on pp. 71-74. A summary is on pp. 85-86.*

## 1 Definitions

What happens once we set ourselves to engage in a Phase of Effort? Did we reach the objective, whereby the Process stops, or, conversely, do we persevere until we achieve what we have set ourselves to accomplish?

The assessments of the effects that occur following a Phase of Effort are made in a subsequent Phase, defined as a 'Phase of Internally Evoked Self-Assessment'.

The assessments made in a Phase of Internally Evoked Self-Assessment appear to be more complicated than one might expect at first sight.

What are the terms for the assessment? Obviously, those that have been defined previously in a Phase of Expectancies: the Goal has been set in Clarity and Attainability, which reflect the anticipated levels of Achievement or Failure, and their subsequent assessments of Satisfaction and Frustration, given the Energy we were expected to invest. Now, given the Effort, did we actually reach those levels of success and pleasure as anticipated?

A Phase of Internally Evoked Self-Assessment consists of two distinct Stages: a Stage of Realization and a Stage of Actualization, which both reflect the previous Stages of Achievement versus Failure, and Satisfaction versus Frustration.

We seldom fully reach our Goals, that is for 100%. It is often a mixed experience. In addition, the 'pros' do not necessarily match the 'cons'. In a *Stage of Realization,* an objective assessment is made of the levels of both success and failure, and these levels are not necessarily symmetrical: they are not extremes on a single continuum. Having reached the Goal for 80% does not inevitably imply that the attempt failed for 20%. We could assess our achievement at 80%, but at the same time experience that the price of having achieved at that level has been too high, and therefore that we were ineffective and failed for, say, 50%. You can be successful and at the same time experience failure, where both measures do not necessarily relate to each other[1].

[1] This assumed asymmetry in assessing Achievement and Failure in a Stage of Realization, and in subjective terms in a Stage of Actualization, has seldom been applied in literature. Asymmetry has been mentioned by Herzberg, but was received with reservation (Herzberg, 1966, 1968).

In a subsequent *Stage of Actualization,* the assessment is made in subjective terms: appraisals of 'pleasure and pain' are made of the outcomes following a Phase of Effort. As in a Stage of Realization, it is assumed that reaching the Goal is practically never completely satisfactory within a single attempt. Rather, the objective is reached to a certain extent, but often the attempt also fails, or fails to a certain degree. A Stage of Actualization is the outcome of both assessments, in terms of enjoyment *and* disappointment.

So, after a Phase of Effort, results are assessed in both objective and subjective terms. And these assessments are, in a sense, replications of the ones that were made previously in a Phase of Expectancies, except that they are now aimed at the actual outcomes obtained in a Phase of Effort.

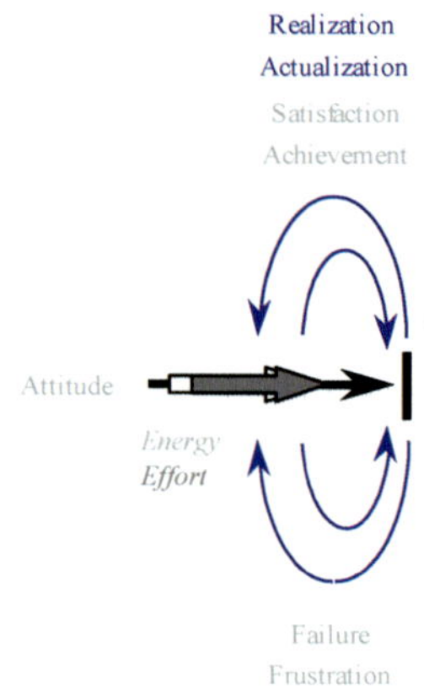


*Fig. 3.1.*
*A visualized overview of Phase 3,*
*a Phase of Internally Evoked Self-Assessment*
*in the theoretical Model of Motivation,*
*consisting of:*

7. A Stage of Realization
8. A Stage of Actualization

In Fig. 3.1., these reversed assessments of the outcomes of Effort are again visualized and captured in arrows representing the dynamic nature of the Process of Motivation.

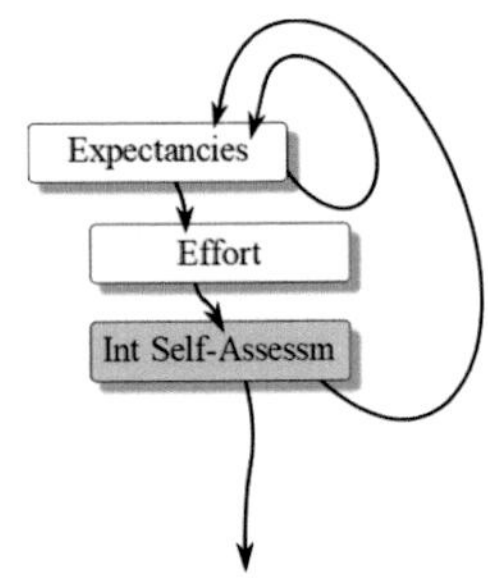


*Fig. 3.2.*
*A Phase of Internally Evoked Self-Assessment*
*Visualized as part of successive Phases in the description of the Model of Motivation*

Both these assessments, in turn, can lead to renewed amendments to the Goal, and associated parameters, whereby the Process of Motivation is brought back to its initial Stages, and therefore becomes cyclical again. Given the outcomes observed, a mental re-assessment is made in a newly cycled Phase of Expectancies, re-defining suitable Energy levels as compared to possible outcomes in terms of objective, 'economic' standards in Stages of Achievement and Failure, or in terms of subjective experiences in Stages of Satisfaction and Frustration. And these re-attunements can lead to renewed investments in a Phase of Effort, which, in turn, are then re-assessed in this third Phase of Internally Evoked Self-Assessment.

*In all these successive Phases, within this cyclical Process of Motivation, there is no external interference, and the assessments are based uniquely on the observations and perceptions of the individual.*

These successive Phases and their cyclical nature can be summarized, and reduced into a simplified diagram, as presented in Fig, 3.2., where arrows in succession reach this Phase of Internally Evoked Self-Assessment after the Effort has been invested. These outcomes lead to probable amendments that are made in a Phase of Expectancies, as visualized by one arrow cycling back, depicting the cyclical nature of these first three Phases. One arrow points towards a next Phase in the dynamical Process of Motivation aimed at reaching the Goal that has been set.

Now what are the repercussions of these assessments of achievements we intended to do: how well we did, how successful we were. Obviously, these assessments have repercussions on the way we perceive ourselves, on our abilities and competencies. As such, constructs used in literature, such as competence, ability, self-efficacy and self-concept, are all related to the Process of Motivation. They are, in a sense, consequential 'derivatives' of the Process. *However, there appears to be an important distinction between the assessments made in a Phase of Internally Evoked Self-Assessment and appraisals that are made following external input (such as influences on the Process from others, or from external occurrences, incidents or circumstances); and between those assessments and the subjective effects on perceptions of ourselves.*

Although the distinction between these various assessments and constructs appears to be less explicit in literature, we are to cover theories and findings from associated research, using these distinctions that are made in the Model. Thus, as we cover successive Phases, those constructs are observed according to the Phase they refer to[1].

With the third Phase of Internally Evoked Self-Assessment, then, the Process of Motivation evolves into a cyclical Process, which gradually reaches a balance, carefully matching intended Energy and actual Effort to the outcomes in reaching the Goal in terms of Achievement and Satisfaction.

But within this cocooned balance, chances are that interference emerges that has not been previously foreseen... These and other effects are to be covered more extensively in the next Chapter.

Preceding these forthcoming events is an overview of related theories and findings obtained from research in literature.

[1] Thus, following constructs from literature are covered, among others:

- In Phase 6, external input will affect appraisals in constructs such as 'competence' and 'self-efficacy';
- In Phase 7, external input will affect appraisals in constructs referred to as 'attributions';
- In Phase 8, external input will be observed in cognitive and affective reactions and on perceptions of the self.

## 2 Theories

What are successful goals, or successful goal strategies, that provide the best outcomes in this third Phase of the Process?

There has been a long tradition of research aimed at finding which kind of goals would lead to which kind of outcomes, in terms of Achievement, Satisfaction and performance in general. Central to these studies was the achievement goal construct, where first empirical research appeared in the 1980s, gaining momentum in the 1990s, and becoming most prominent in the new millennium (Elliot & Hulleman, 2017). Theories of motivation in this field have become commonly known as *goal-orientation theories* of motivation.

*See exhibit* ➔

As in much of the findings obtained in the field of motivational psychology, the results were surprising and mostly counter-intuitive: *If one is to strive for results aimed at demonstrating one's competence, results tend to be poor. However, if one seeks to develop one's ability to master or improve a task, the outcomes are much more positive!*

Demonstrating competence, revealing how 'good we are', means risk-taking, according to the Model of Motivation. One sets a standard, and in order to be successful, one has to meet that standard. In this Phase of

### 3.1. Goal-orientation theories

Once the goal concept was recognized as the central concept in motivation, researchers became interested in its various manifestations. Following up on the leads provided by the achievement concept and the cognitive processes involved in the expectancies towards these goals, the attention focused on the content and expression of these goals.

Especially researchers from the field of educational psychology became interested in what types of goals would produce what kind of results, particularly in the field of learning.

These theories are usually referred to as 'goal-orientation theories'.

Initially, goal-orientation theories of motivation made a distinction between two types of (achievement) goals:

- *Performance-oriented goals* (also referred to as 'ego goals', 'ego involvement' and 'ability goals') focus on the demonstration of competence relative to others;
- *Mastery-oriented goals* (also labeled as 'task goals', 'task-involvement' and 'learning goals') focus on the development of competence and task mastery.

(Ames, 1992a; Dweck, 1986, 1989; Elliott & Dweck, 1988; Nicholls, 1984, 1989).

*(Continued)*

Internally Evoked Self-Assessment, we define those standards ourselves: we are either successful or we are not. And *'Performance-oriented goals'*, as they are referred to in literature, therefore tend to produce a duality in their outcomes. And often, this duality tends to produce poor outcomes.

The other type of goals one could set, according to goal-orientation theories, are goals aimed at developing one's abilities to master a task. Here, the dichotomy between being successful or not becomes less prominent. We are not attempting to demonstrate competence or proficiencies; on the contrary, we are attempting to learn and improve. From this perspective, failure has a different connotation. Failure is 'part of the game' when one's intention is to develop and master one's abilities. In this sense, there is no risk-taking, as the outcomes can never be detrimental to these intentions. As a result, these *'mastery-oriented goals'*, as they are referred to, are regularly found in literature to be associated with an extensive range of positive outcomes.

*See exhibit* ➔

In short, then, seeking mastery and growth appears to be a much better strategy in goal-orientation than seeking competition.

These findings, in turn, have had pronounced effects in what we referred to earlier in Chapter 1 and Chapter 2 as the field of 'curiosity, interest and information-seeking'.

*See exhibit next page* ➔.

### 3.1. Goal-orientation theories

The initial goal-orientation theories made a remarkable assumption underlying their theory. The outcomes of both these goal-orientations (in terms of affect, cognition and behavior, referred to as 'nomological networks') were assumed to be distinctly different. Mastery-oriented goals were thought to lead to a *positive, adaptive* set of processes and outcomes, whereas performance-oriented goals were assumed to produce *rather negative, maladaptive* processes and outcomes (Dweck, 1986; Nicholls, 1984).

At first, research on the dichotomous model provided support for these assumptions, with profound implications (Ames, 1992a; Dweck & Leggett, 1988; Kaplan, Middleton, Urdan & Midgley, 2002; Midgley, 2002; Pintrich, 2000a; Pintrich & Schunk, 1996; Urdan, 1997; Utman, 1997).

Subsequent analyses, however, led to further refinements, to be covered subsequently in Chapter 5 and Chapter 6.

For further reading on these earlier goal-orientation theories, see: Elliot, 2005; Elliot & Dweck, 2005; Elliot, Dweck & Yeager, 2017; for a summarizing article, see: Elliot & Hulleman, 2017.

*Next related thread 3.2.* ➔ *p. 131.*

## *Related Topics: Curiosity and Interest*

Findings from goal-orientation theories have had profound effects, especially in the field of curiosity, interest and information-seeking...

Those effects emerge when we observe Failure in performance-oriented or mastery-oriented contexts.

The moment I consider myself as 'having failed', my interest stops and I wouldn't bother getting further involved. And curiosity vanishes: "Oh dear, this is not the way it ought to go! I'll stop and go no further!..."

But if I would have a different mindset, where Failure is less prominent and becomes 'part-of-the-game-of-finding-out-things', then the Process of Motivation becomes less disturbed by Failure or Frustration: "Oh dear, what is happening now? Fear not, and let me retry! As it still is great fun, now isn't it?!"

If in embarking on a new venture, we find ourselves amidst experiences of Failure, we will become hesitant to renew those activities. More to come on this topic in Chapter 6.

*Going for a ride…*

*Here is the best illustration of how this mighty skill works in children at the start of their lives…*

*I took my youngest son on a drive to grandma. So, I put him in his little seat in the back of the car, and already there was great excitement: curiosity and interest come by themselves at that age…*

*So, I took my seat and off we went.*

*Within seconds I heard great laughter from the back: we were moving!! To the child, this was a new thing. And by nature, everything new is exciting. And as it happens, a child is drawn towards the unknown. Towards mastery.*

*As we shall see, our only business is to be with them and* not *to interfere in this journey: by nature, they have all the necessities at hand.*

*Accompanying my child on his journey, just being there, was the greatest ride of my life…*

Curiosity and interest are driven by a mindset where mastery should prevail, instead of performance, winning or competition...
In essence, one is to explore without worrying about 'giving the wrong answers'.

As commented on more recently by Niemivirta and his colleagues: "(...) children endorsing learning goals [or mastery-oriented goals] seemed to consider errors and setbacks as part of the learning process and tools for improvement, whereas (...) children endorsing performance goals seemed to perceive errors as indications of failure and, subsequently, lack of competence" (Niemivirta, Pulkka, Tapola & Tuominen, 2019, p. 571).

This inclination to be curious and interested in our surroundings, which comes to us almost naturally at the earliest age, needs protection at all cost, as it contains the ingredients to enjoy the Process of Motivation to its 'full potential', by adequately addressing perceptions of failure. The strategy of aiming at learning and mastery, instead of demonstrating competence, appears to be the best strategy according to goal-orientation theories.

These theories, then, not only underscore the importance of adequate strategies in addressing the goals we set, but also the prominent effects occurring in those strategies, originating from perceived success and perceived failure. These central concepts used in goal-orientation theories are reflected in a Phase of Internally Evoked Self-Assessment, where these opposed forces correspond with the duality occurring within a Stage of Realization and a Stage of Actualization. And where these Stages, in turn, provide essential input for subsequent adjustments and improvements in the Goals we set in a Phase of Expectancies.

Years before these insights were obtained from goal-orientation theories, a doctoral student in psychology at Carnegie-Mellon became fascinated by this inherent inclination in young children to ceaselessly explore and investigate objects and situations they encounter. As he reflected on later, Edward Deci commented: "They challenge themselves to become competent, apparently just for the enjoyment of doing it. Children are not passively waiting to be drawn into learning by the offer of rewards but rather are actively engaged in the process of learning, Indeed, they are *intrinsically motivated* to learn" (Deci & Flaste, 1995, p. 20). He had borrowed the concept from Harlow, a pioneering psychologist who had used the term in his research on rhesus monkeys (Harlow, Harlow & Meyer, 1950, as referred to in Deci, 1971). While observing his monkeys, Harlow had noticed how the animals spent hours working on a kind of puzzle apparatus, and had used the concept to explain why they spent so much energy where the only possible reward seemed to be the fun and enjoyment of the activity itself. And Deci subsequently used the concept: "Clearly, something in them is alive and vital; something in them wants to master the challenges of their lives. The term intrinsic motivation seems to apply just as well to these children as it did to Harlow's monkeys" (Deci & Flaste, 1995, pp. 18-19).

Now, a most disturbing observation had prompted Deci to study motivation in the early 1960s: "(...) One of the most troubling problems we face (...) is that as children grow older they suffer a profound loss. In schools for example, they seem to display so little of the natural curiosity and excitement about learning that was patently evident in those very same children when they were three or four years old" (Deci & Flaste, 1995, p. 19). What had caused this sharp decline, then, in this wonderful disposition?

At the time, in the mid-sixties, Skinner's behaviorism prevailed, where reinforcement contingencies were used to explain the elementary processes involved in motivation (see Chapter 1). Motivation was thought to be induced by reinforcements, or 'rewards': no stimulus, no response.

Deci came up with a rather daring explanation of the sharp decline in interest: "(...) I had the fleeting - and surely blasphemous - thought that maybe all the rewards, rules, and regimentation that were so widely used to motivate schoolchildren were themselves the villains, promoting not an excited state of learning but a sad state of apathy" (Deci & Flaste, 1995, p. 22).

He developed a research design to explore how rewards affect this form of intrinsic motivation. In subsequent experiments, he found that once subjects were paid for doing a particular task, they lost interest in the activity (Exp I & II, Deci, 1971).

These experiments marked the beginning of a new, visionary theory on motivation, now referred to as *'self-determination theory'*.

*See exhibit* ➔

## 4.1. Self-determination theory

Self-determination theory, developed by Deci & Ryan (1985; Ryan & Deci, 2000, 2018, 2020), represents a broad framework encompassing several theories on human motivation (for detailed overviews of these so-called 'mini-theories', see Ryan & Deci, 2018, Part III).

Self-determination theory assumes that the individual is an active organism with tendencies towards growth, mastering and development of a coherent sense of self.

Self-determination theory posits that there are "(...) three basic psychological needs that must be satisfied for psychological interest, development, and wellness to be sustained" (Ryan & Deci, 2018, p. 10). These basic needs are: *autonomy, relatedness* and *competence:*

*More on 'autonomy'* ➔ *p. 80.*

*More on 'relatedness'* ➔ *p. 134.*

*More on 'competence'* ➔ *p. 208.*

Self-determination theory is different from other approaches to motivation "(...) in its emphasis on the different types and sources of motivation that impact the quality and dynamics of behavior" (Ryan & Deci, 2018, p. 14), where five distinct sources or *styles* are observed:

*More on 'regulatory styles'* ➔ *pp. 290-291.*

*(Continued)*

Providing rewards, then, appeared to have led to these sharp declines in interest. But what had caused those effects to be so detrimental?

In 1968, Richard de Charms had introduced a concept defined as 'personal causation'. It referred to the assumption that one has a deeply felt desire to be the instigator or the 'personal causation' of one's actions (the 'origin' as he defined it), rather than to be the subject of control from the outside (to be a 'pawn'). These insights led Deci to assume that in the experiments, rewards had undermined these feelings of 'personal causation': "Perhaps there is an innate or *intrinsic* need to feel a sense of personal autonomy or self-determination - to feel a sense of what de Charms had called personal causation. That would imply that people need to feel that their behavior is truly chosen by them rather than imposed by some external source (...)" (Deci & Flaste, 1995, p. 30).

These insights provided a first indication for what is now referred to as a '*need for autonomy*', which is one of three basic needs proposed in self-determination theory. And failure to satisfy and fulfil those needs is believed to lead to decreased well-being and a variety of maladaptive consequences.

*See exhibit* ➔

### 4.1. Self-determination theory

In self-determination theory, three basic psychological needs must be satisfied for psychological interest, development, and wellness to be sustained: *autonomy, relatedness* and *competence* (Deci & Ryan, 1985; Ryan & Deci, 2000, 2018, 2020).

*Autonomy* literally refers to regulation by the self (Ryan & Deci, 2006). Thereby the concept has several important implications.

"The hallmark of autonomy is (...) that one's behaviors are self-endorsed, or congruent with one's authentic interests and values (...). When acting with autonomy, behaviors are engaged wholeheartedly (...)" (Ryan & Deci, 2018, p. 10). Therefore: "Autonomy concerns a sense of initiative and ownership in one's actions. It is supported by experiences of interest and value and undermined by experiences of being externally controlled, whether by rewards or punishments" (Ryan & Deci, 2020, p. 2).

As a consequence, when addressing Motivation from the perspective of a Process of Interference, preserving this need for autonomy is expressed in attempts to appreciate and respect the internal frame of reference of the individual (Ryan & Deci, 2020).

More on the construct of autonomy: Ryan & Deci, 2006, 2018 (Chapter 3).

*Next related thread 4.2.* ➔ *p. 134.*

A need for autonomy has since become a central concept in self-determination theory (Ryan & Deci, 2018)[1]. Autonomy can be understood as both phenomenological and functional. Phenomenologically, it concerns "(...) the extent to which people experience their behavior as volitional or as fully self-endorsed" (Ryan & Deci, 2018, p. 97), originating from one's own accord, genuine, authentic. And functional, in that it brings into the action the whole of one's resources, interests, and capacities: "Autonomous actions more fully engage individuals' talents, abilities, and energies" (*ibid.,* p. 98).

However, the concept of autonomy has also been the most controversial construct in self-determination theory (Ryan & Deci, 2018). Partly, this controversy appears to originate from confusion about the concept of autonomy. Autonomy is *not* equivalent with independence from external influence, or implying separateness and individualism (*ibid.,* Chapters 3 and 4; Ryan & Deci, 2000).

*See exhibit* ➔

[1] The concept of a need in self-determination theory is distinctly different than the one used in drive theories (see Chapter 1). As commented on by Deci & Ryan (2000), in drive theory "(...) needs are understood as physiological deficits that disturb the organism's quiescence (...). By contrast, (...) rather than viewing people as passively waiting for a disequilibrium, we view them as naturally inclined to act on their inner and outer environments, engage activities that interest them, and move toward personal and interpersonal coherence" (p. 230).

On Autonomy and confusing interpretations...

The difficulties that arise in using concepts in theories on motivation that are also used colloquially, in 'everyday language', have led to serious problems, not only affecting clarity in constructs used in theories on motivation, but also affecting research, obscuring the outcomes of empirical findings.

Referring to self-determination theory, Patall & Hooper (2019), describe confusing empirical results produced on the concept of autonomy that appears to have been frequently interpreted as 'independence'. In reviewing the relationship between concepts of choice and autonomy, they observe: "Part of this confusion comes from the fact that 'autonomy' is an umbrella term that has been used for a wide variety of constructs, though most frequently it is conceptualized in two ways: as independence and as volitional functioning (...). According to many developmental and social-cultural theories of psychology, autonomy is the extent to which an individual engages in behaviors and makes decisions without relying on others (e.g. Bandura 1989; Markus & Kitayama, 1991; Smetana et al., 2004; Van Petegem et al., 2012). In contrast to this conceptualization of autonomy as independence, self-determination theory defines autonomy as self-endorsed or volitional functioning (...) (Ryan & Deci, 2000)" (Patall & Hooper, 2019, p. 247).

In defining a need for autonomy, self-determination theory provides a compelling case for the assumptions underlying the initial Phases as proposed in the Model of Motivation. Where a need for autonomy is reflected in the personal, coherent and autonomous sequence of the three initial Phases as proposed in the Model, the insights provided in self-determination theory appear not only to suggest the importance of addressing the goals we set according to our own standards, it defines those Phases, in particular a Phase of Internally Evoked Self-Assessment, as essential to preserve and maintain an optimized use of personal resources and well-being as part of the Process of Motivation.

In short, then, both goal-orientation theories and self-determination theory provide, from different perspectives, insights into motivation that appear to correspond with the notion of a sequential Process as suggested in the initial Phases proposed in the Model of Motivation. Both theories extend the (more abstract) sequential steps from the Model into a wide array of outcomes and effects that appear to provide an indication not only of the importance of these initial Phases, but also of the necessity to maintain the integrity of these Phases intact. Both from the perspective of the individual and from the perspective of an outsider, an actor, with the intent to address or manage these Processes.

Both categories, or clusters of theories, have provided many research findings that stress these effects and outcomes from their respective perspectives. However, as stated earlier, in these findings the distinction between both perspectives, between a Process of Motivation and a Process of Interference, appears to be less explicit. Nonetheless, the outcomes are rather unambiguous, and thus provide a broader view and further diversification of the propositions made in the Model of Motivation, as to be covered next.

## 3 Research

Research outcomes have substantiated these ideas proposed by *goal-orientation theories* and *self-determination theory*.

Findings from research on the *dichotomous goal-orientation concept* provided strong support for the positive implications of mastery-oriented goals, and mastery-oriented motivation (Elliot, 2005; Nicholls & Burton, 1982; Pintrich & Schunk, 1996; Senko, Hulleman & Harackiewicz, 2011). Errors and setbacks appeared to be considered as part of the learning process. In addition, effects could be observed that are indicative of a Phase of Internally Evoked Self-Assessment, in terms of an assessment of Achievement and Failure, Satisfaction and Frustration, where mastery-oriented goals appeared to be related to higher levels of motivation (Meece & Holt, 1993; Niemivirta, 1998; Tuominen-Soini, Salmela-Aro & Niemivirta, 2008, 2012; Valle, Cabanach, Nunez, Gonzalez-Pienda, Rodriguez & Pineiro, 2003) and well-being (Daniels, Haynes, Stupnisky, Perry, Newall & Pekrun, 2008; Tapola & Niemivirta, 2008; Turner, Thorpe & Meyer, 1998).

In contrast, performance-oriented goals appeared to be associated with lower levels of motivation (Conley, 2012; Gonçalves, Niemivirta & Lemos, 2017; Luo, Paris, Hogan & Luo, 2011; Pastor, Barron, Miller & Davis, 2007; Tuominen-Soini, Salmela-Aro & Niemivirta, 2008; Tapola & Niemivirta, 2008; Valle, Cabanach, Nunez, Gonzalez-Pienda, Rodriguez & Pineiro, 2003) and less positive emotional outcomes (Elliot, Murayama & Pekrun, 2011; Flanagan, Putwain & Caltabiano, 2015; Luo, Paris, Hogan & Luo, 2011; Pintrich, 2000a; Tapola & Niemivirta, 2008)[1].

However, as commented on earlier, findings on performance-oriented goals also produced results that were less articulate and that gave rise to a mixed picture (Harackiewicz, Barron & Elliot, 1998; Niemivirta, Pulkka, Tapola & Tuominen, 2019; Urdan, 1997). This, in turn, led to a further refinement in conceptualization of the performance-oriented goal construct into performance-approach and performance-avoidance goal-orientation. Performance-avoidance could be linked to a wide array of negative processes although performance-approach goal

[1] Research on learning and educational psychology has produced a large body of knowledge on various goal-orientations and their effects on learning and motivation, and related areas affecting educational outcomes. These findings will be covered more extensively in Chapter 5 and Chapter 6. For recent overviews, see: Lazowski & Hulleman, 2016; Lin-Siegler, Dweck & Cohen, 2016; Niemivirta, Pulkka, Tapola & Tuominen, 2019; Senko, 2016. For a more general overview on goal-orientation theories and research: Elliot & Dweck, 2005; Elliot, Dweck & Yeager, 2017; Karabenick & Urdan, 2014.

orientation (i.e. seeking the challenge of high performance) in a few instances produced positive outcomes, such as persistence and high performance (for overviews, see: Midgley, Kaplan & Middleton, 2001; Smith, Duda, Allen & Hall, 2002). These findings, diversifying the performance-oriented goal construct are covered more extensively in Chapter 5.

In the field of *self-determination theory*, a core hypothesis has been that more autonomous forms of motivation lead to enhancement of engagement, learning and wellness (Ryan & Deci, 2020). A large empirically-based literature has demonstrated a positive relation of interventions aimed at preserving or maintaining autonomy and various academic outcomes (Cerasoli, Nicklin & Ford, 2014; Deci, Koestner & Ryan, 1999; Howard, Gagné & Bureau, 2017; Lepper & Henderlong, 2000).

However, it must be underlined that this general conclusion is intended to point to the importance and propelling properties of autonomously induced motivational processes, and *not* to the instrumental and environmental conditions and circumstances initiating motivation. As we will cover extensively in Chapter 5, there has been a heated debate on the effects of rewards in various expressions on motivation in general and performance in particular [1] [2] [3]. As we will see in Chapter 5, we are only to observe the Process of Motivation, and not the effects of various rewards, incentives or contingencies aimed at influencing this Process, in what we referred to as a 'Process of Interference' in the Introduction to this Volume.

[1] For a brief historical overview on these debates, see: Sansone & Harackiewicz, 2000b.

[2] Where a need for autonomy is prevalent in what self-determination theory defines as intrinsic motivation, research in the field has been dominated for several decades (notably between 1970 and 2000) by the question whether extrinsic rewards in various expressions (inducing extrinsic forms of motivation according to self-determination theory) affect intrinsic motivation. More on these findings in Chapter 5.

[3] Two areas of research have extended on this intrinsic–extrinsic debate. And, although indirectly obtained, findings from both areas have provided a further confirmation for the concluding observation made on effects of autonomy, as related to an assumed prevalence of Phases 1, 2 and 3, in general, and a Phase of Internally Evoked Self-Assessment in particular, as proposed in the Model of Motivation:

- Research on effects of various forms of autonomous versus controlled settings on motivation (for overviews: Deci, Koestner & Ryan, 1999; Lepper & Henderlong, 2000) and performance (for overviews: Cerasoli, Nicklin & Ford, 2014; Cerasoli, Nicklin & Nassrelgrgawi, 2016);
- Research on effects of various forms of so-called choice provisions, extending from fully self-endorsed (autonomous) to externally regulated (for overviews: Patall, 2012; Patall, Cooper & Robinson, 2008; Patall & Hooper, 2019).

## *Summary*

In a third Phase in the Model of Motivation, a twofold assessment is made of the outcomes from a preceding Phase of Effort. Was the Goal reached that we set ourselves to attain? And if so, to what extent were we successful?

The assessments of effects following a Phase of Effort are made in a subsequent Phase, defined as a 'Phase of Internally Evoked Self-Assessment'. The Phase often calls for re-amendments to be made to the Goal and its parameters, as defined in a first Phase of Expectancies, whereby the Process of Motivation is brought back to its initial Stages and therefore becomes cyclical again.

In these three successive, cyclical Phases, initiated by a Phase of Internally Evoked Self-Assessment, no external interference occurs and the assessments are based uniquely on the observations and perceptions of the individual.

A Phase of Internally Evoked Self-Assessment consists of two distinct Stages: a Stage of Realization and a Stage of Actualization, which both reflect the previous Stages of Achievement versus Failure, and Satisfaction versus Frustration. In a *Stage of Realization,* an objective assessment is made of the levels of both success and failure. In a subsequent *Stage of Actualization,* the assessment is made in subjective terms: appraisals of 'pleasure and pain' are made of the outcomes of a Phase of Effort.

Two clusters of theories are associated with this third Phase of the Process: goal-orientation theories and self-determination theory. Both provide, from different perspectives, insights into motivation that appear to correspond with the notion of a sequential Process as suggested in the initial Phases proposed in the Model of Motivation. Both theories extend the (more abstract) sequential steps from the Model into a wide array of outcomes and effects that appear to provide an indication not only of the importance of these initial Phases, but also of the necessity to keep the integrity of these Phases intact. Two conceptualizations in particular refer to this notion: in goal-orientation theories as proposed in strategies defined as mastery-oriented, and in self-determination theory in the concept of autonomy, which appears prominent in the theory.

These findings are substantiated by extensive research in both fields.

And from those studies an additional finding appears to emerge that points at a further important observation: the evaluative Process occurring in a Phase of Internally Evoked Self-Assessment not only aims at Realization (Achievement) and associated Actualization (Satisfaction), but also seems to induce fear, especially fear of failure. In observing next Phases of the Model of Motivation and substantially supported by findings from research, these effects seem capable of producing mechanisms that may profoundly influence the Process of Motivation as it further unfolds.

# Chapter 4
## *Reality and its Discontents*
## *Phase 4 - A Phase of Reality*

'All's well that ends well'...

The various objectives I have set are either reached or carefully re-attuned the way I want them to be; or set aside and postponed, awaiting a better opportunity to be fulfilled according to my standards.

Let us observe what is to happen to my initial mindset, as I progressed through the Process of Motivation and cycled through the various Goals I had set.

And of course, as we have seen, there can also be Failure and Frustration, and the more adaptable we are, the better we appear to be at avoiding or re-attuning our objectives. But in most of the Goals we tend to set, a cyclical re-attuning ends up in Satisfaction, or at least in a desirable state of affairs we can live with.

Now, in the examples observed that had progressed into action, or Effort, I had been successful and satisfied to the extent that I, without really noticing, sharpened-up my Goal, carefully attuning its features and properties to the successful outcomes I expected to obtain.

Such was the case in my visit to Monserrate. And, as planned, I am now returning: Monserrate revisited. The mindset I have, which is prompted by the various assessments I made in cycling through Phases 1, 2 and 3, is that I will relive the same experience. Recall that the Goal I had set in the end was to have a 'great-and-romantic-experience-of-amazement-and-wonder'. But this time, things will be different, and they will take me by surprise. Already upon entering the parking area a sense of bewilderment overwhelms me and the illustrious intentions I had. The place seems overcrowded. Three buses are trying to take full control of the small car park, and a huge gathering of tourists, apparently visiting the southern parts of Portugal, seem to have made Monserrate part of their itinerary. Gone are my feelings of 'what-ever-experience' I was trying to revisit. And gone are my cheerful thoughts of Palaces and Gardens.

Without going into detail on the subsequent comments and statements I make about people who, incidentally, are as much entitled to having a great visit as I am (and which is, by all means, to their credit...), it *does* illustrate not only the effect of the disruption of the unfolding Process of Motivation, but also of the multitude of subsequent steps that occur as a result of the unforeseen event. *All these steps, as we will come to realize, are aimed at one single thing: preserving the Goal and the initial Process of Motivation as much as possible.*

Let us progress through these steps separately.

And the first of these, obviously, is the occurrence of the event that creates this confusion: the appearance of what we might refer to as 'Reality'. It defines a next, so-called *'Phase of Reality'*, which is characterized by its intrusion, or interference, in the Process of Motivation.

Earlier, in the Introduction, we made a distinction between the Process of Motivation and the Process of Interference. And this is where this Process of Interference 'taps into' the Process of Motivation. At present, we will only observe its effects on Motivation and discard how this Process of Interference could be successful in its intervention, as referred to in the Introduction.

This first step, then, defined as a Phase of Reality, starts with awareness, the realization that an actor, an action or an event intrudes in our carefully attuned attempts at reaching an objective. And this intruding Reality has two essential properties: its perceived importance and its 'disruptive properties' on the Process. *The first, its importance, is referred to as the 'Significance of Reality'. The second is defined as its 'Impact'. The Impact of Reality will be covered later in Chapter 5. In the present Chapter, where we observe a Phase of Reality, we concentrate on Significance.*

*In short, a Phase of Reality consists of an event, which could be an occurrence, or a person, or an incident, which has not been anticipated on in the Process of reaching our Goal.*

Let us return to Monserrate to illustrate...

Successful attempts at reaching the Goal I had set are now disrupted by Reality, by an occurrence I did not anticipate on. Clearly, the event is highly important to me. So, Reality in this case is perceived as 'highly Significant'. The more I have set my mind to having this 'experience-of-amazement-and-wonder', the more Significant the unforeseen intrusion by my fellow-tourists becomes.

This is where Significance of the Goal, as we defined earlier, re-emerges in our attempts to capture this Process of Motivation as it unfolds. The more I was looking forward to having this great experience again, the more Significant the Goal was perceived to be, and the more intense the intrusion I now feel on the parking lot. The higher the perceived Significance of a Goal, the more likely it becomes that any disrupting event (or any person associated with it) is perceived to be Significant. It is a first pattern occurring in observing the Process of Motivation: the more we perceive our Goal to be Significant, the more likely it becomes that an intrusion from an interfering Reality is also perceived as Significant.

In a Phase of Reality, then, the intrusion that occurs becomes more Significant, the higher the perceived Significance of the Goal. And these effects occur not only in case of a negative interference, but also with a positive intrusion in the Process of Motivation.

Let us use our second example of the upcoming tennis match to illustrate the various expressions that may occur...

I had planned this famous match in my previous coverage of events, and I had observed that Significance of my Goal had increased, cycling through the first three Phases of the Process of Motivation. Therefore, the stakes are now high in winning this match. As stated, we will not at this point observe the effects. They will be elaborated on in upcoming Chapters. Here, we only observe the event that will have influence on the unfolding Process, and the Significance it has.

So, I am fully confident of winning, and that I will obtain full Satisfaction from my Efforts.

Now, suppose I *do* win! Satisfaction is complete, and the more Significance assigned to the Goal, the more Significance is assigned to my triumph, *my victory.* Again, the way I will proceed in savoring my success is to follow later. The point to note is the relation between both the Goal and Reality in terms of Significance. If things had turned out differently, and I would have lost, the expression of Significance in the *disaster* that occurred would have been likewise. Note that if Significance of the Goal had been low, the confrontation with Reality would have been less profound... Which will have repercussions (to be observed later) in carefully attuned mechanisms that we will come to observe in-depth: mechanisms of 'pretending' not to care or to be 'indifferent', so as to neutralize these effects in the things that affect us most...

So, the intrusion from Reality and its Significance are affected (and sometimes even regulated) by the Significance of the Goal from which it protrudes.

This intricate interplay can take numerous forms. Sometimes the challenge of the unknown (like a tennis match) is exactly what we seek, as we are venturing into 'uncharted land'. We are challenging ourselves by *seeking* this confrontation with Reality, thereby demonstrating the boundaries of our strength, competence, experience, in challenging a Reality that is perceived to be Significant. But in most cases, Reality intrudes in a Process of Motivation that has been attuned to our desires and needs in previous Phases, and which now disrupts this balance, in either a negative or (on happy occasions) a positive way. And a Phase of Reality is the moment at which we perceive and realize the unexpected interference occurring in our Process, as expressed in the assessment of Significance, which is central in this Phase of Reality. These various expressions in which Reality is manifested are the subject of a more extensive study in the coming Chapter, as we make an attempt at discerning patterns in these various forms of interference, which will help us in observing its effects in subsequent Phases of the Process of Motivation.

Now, at first sight, all this seems pretty straightforward. But unfortunately, it is not...

There are two confusing issues, especially in observing the Process of Motivation as it further unfolds after this event.

The first issue lies in the nature of Reality itself. The phrasing 'Reality comes in...' appears to be clear to us all: it is the unexpected, intruding experience we are all familiar with. We did so well, and now 'Reality comes bashing in...' But we have to be more precise, for what is the difference between the Monserrate in Phases 1, 2 and 3, and the Monserrate as it appears to us now? It is clearly the same Reality... Although it now manifests itself as interfering with our expectations. *And this is our first and crucial issue: in Phases 1, 2 and 3 there was no Reality, there was no clear intrusion.* Everything went according to our own plans in a Phase of Expectancies, and our own investments in a Phase of Effort, and we could make assessments in a Phase of Internally Evoked Self-Assessment entirely according to our own standards. *In that sense there was no 'Reality coming in...'*. But now our perception becomes affected. We are driven to reconsider the entire situation. We are forced to see our

Process of Motivation being interfered with and disrupted. And we did not foresee this happening in our carefully defined Phase of Expectancies. So, at first glance it might seem the same 'scenery', the same Reality we operate in, but now it manifests itself to its full extent and becomes the issue of 'Reality coming in...', where it now interferes with the carefully orchestrated Process of reaching my objective. The first issue, then, that arises by the introduction of Reality, lies in its nature: *it is now both an intrusion and it is unforeseen. It may have been there already, but now it becomes apparent; it manifests itself.*

Which brings us to the second issue that could lead to confusion, especially as we progress further through the Process of Motivation: it is *our* perception of Reality. It is the way *we* see things happening. Much in the same way as we were observing, according to our own standards, the chances of reaching our Goal in a Phase of Expectancies, and to our own standards the investments in Effort, and to our own standards our evaluation of the state of affairs in a Phase of Internally Evoked Self-Assessment, we are now observing Reality according to our standards. So, Monserrate need not be that awful to an outsider; or this tennis match could be quite successful for an enthusiastic observer who gives us praise for our achievements and our great form. Instead, it is *you* setting the standards and defining the level of intrusion, as it is *you* who is experiencing the intrusion in all its unforeseen aspects.

So, at first, in Phases 1, 2 and 3, in a sense, Reality was absent. It was absent in that there was no intrusion. And it was absent in that nothing unforeseen occurred within this setting. Perhaps all the ingredients were there physically. But from our perspective, there was no interference occurring.

A Phase of Reality changes all these perceptions and turns our surroundings, the setting in which we act, into an eventful interference. It is as if a concealed, hitherto seemingly 'non-existent' Reality, suddenly comes to life...

To illustrate this, here is our third example.

The groceries! I had completely forgotten about them, conveniently. And now my beloved suddenly complains... Reality has come to life and intrudes unexpectedly! The way I respond is familiar to us all: I am annoyed for having made the postponement. And I am disturbed for being exposed. However, at this Phase in the Process, I only perceive the interference and acknowledge its importance. Recall that I had the intention to do this grocery shopping, but had postponed the thing because, at the time, I could not perceive enough return on my investment in a Phase of Expectancies. So, I conveniently laid it to rest, as a 'good intention'. In the next Chapters, as we cover the Process of Motivation further, this seemingly uneventful occurrence will lead to a complexity of further reactions from my side...

Reality, this time, confronts me with a postponed, inconvenient Goal and thus intrudes unexpectedly with the Process of Motivation. Let us add further complexity in our fourth example.

Recall I had the intention to go to Hong Kong. But I had left the idea for pragmatic reasons as the investment needed came at an inconvenient moment in time. Now this postponed objective will enter the stage once again with our next and fifth example, as it will make me reconsider the investment. Let us, for now, only observe Hong Kong and add the prospect of going there once again as a renewed opportunity, *instigated by an upcoming, unforeseen intrusion that is to appear next.*

Now, recall that in our fifth example, the intention or Goal was to proceed working on a paper. Fear of Failure had prevented me from further pursuing any activities. But now, 'Reality comes in...' It is not the paper itself that provides the interference. It is my boss, who emails me to ask whether I anticipate to write an article in the coming six months. *Note that he is not even referring to my paper, and emails me without any negative intentions.* But for me, given the negative associations which led me to postpone my writings, the email is perceived as an intrusive, unexpected event of high Significance, disrupting a Process of Motivation that had carefully reached a status quo of permanent inactivity. This postponed or 'dormant' Goal has now been triggered by Reality. And it will set in motion a train of reactions, and assumptions, and statements that will affect other hitherto unaddressed objectives. And these, in turn, will dramatically change the Process of Motivation as it is to further progress in time... The intrusion in this fifth example not only awakens the negative frightful prospect of resuming writing my paper, *but also awakens the previous unattended, yet attractive, idea to flee the intrusion and escape to Hong Kong.*

But more on these effects later...

Earlier, we saw that unaddressed objectives tend to proliferate, and thus can interfere in all kinds of circumstances or events, without us being consciously aware of the effects that they may cause. Normally, they tend to remain hidden, and unaffected, often for many years. But in some instances, they cause great disturbances. A final example to illustrate this is my ambition and 'latent' objective to be part of a university, as a 'vestige in the pursuit of truth', a 'sanctuary of integrity and devotion', where autonomy prevails. This is where 'things are done as they ought to be'. And within this frame of mind, I receive this disturbing email interfering with my plans. Observe that the upcoming (unverified) assumptions do not occur at this Phase yet. But the Significance of Reality intrudes and ignites, or 'taps into' this 'latent' Goal, which has been defined in a Phase of Expectancies, and is now determining the Significance of the event. In a next Phase, we will assess its Impact on this carefully attuned Process of Motivation.

So 'all's well that ends well' is seldom where the story ends, despite our intentions. A Process of Motivation is most likely to be disrupted at some point, as my vacation has now been. With unaddressed, 'dormant' and 'latent' objectives from the past being disturbed by unforeseen intrusions...

Fortunately, however, we have mechanisms to address these intrusions from Reality, both positive and negative.

But first, let us summarize our findings of this fourth Phase of Reality, and observe findings from literature that substantiate the observations.

The fourth Phase in the Process of Motivation is a Phase of Reality.

The 'cocooned' balance obtained in reaching the Goal, is frequently disrupted by an unforeseen event or sequence of events.
A Phase of Reality is the moment in the Process of Motivation in which awareness occurs for the outside intrusion affecting the Process of reaching the Goal.

This awareness manifests itself first in perceived importance, or 'Significance', assigned to the intrusion. Thus, perceived 'Significance of Reality' is an important characteristic of this Phase of the Process.

*Phase 4 in the Model of Motivation is covered in detail on pp. 96-98. A summary is provided on p. 101.*

# 1 Definitions

In the gradual, cyclical balance that was reached within a Process of Motivation, sooner or later a disruption is likely to occur, affecting the integrity of the Process of reaching the Goal, either in a negative or in a positive sense.

In a number of subsequent steps, the disruption in the unfolding Process of Motivation is addressed, aiming at preserving the initial Process of Motivation as much as possible. And a first step, or Stage, in this subsequent, sequential Process obviously consists of a detection and appraisal of the intruding event or sequence of events.

A Phase of Reality consists of this single Stage, and is characterized by the intrusion, or interference, in the Process of Motivation[1]. It is a 'Phase of Reality' that will stir a series of reactions that are aimed at preserving the initial settings as much as possible. And a first step in this series is the awareness of the necessity to act. In this Phase of Reality, we assign meaning, importance or 'Significance' to the event.

So, in the Process of Motivation, where a Goal was carefully defined and where a balance was reached between Effort and obtained Satisfaction, suddenly something unexpected happens. *Reality is an event or a group of events that is perceived by the individual as an interference in the Process of Motivation, disrupting the cyclical state where previously a balance was found*[2 3]. *The external interference can be caused by an actor or group of actors, or by an occurrence or a perception, cognition or affect associated with an occurrence. In a Phase of*

[1] The concept 'Reality' can take on many forms. In defining the concept, we observe Reality as it manifests itself, in subjective terms, to the individual. Hence, it is to be frequently referred to as 'perceived Reality'. The subject will be covered more extensively in Volume II of the 'Series on Motivation'.

[2] The interference through Reality does not necessarily have a negative connotation and could be positive in that it enhances and strengthens the Process of Motivation. Nonetheless, when Reality is perceived as interfering, either in a negative or in a positive way, with one's intentions, the Process of Motivation is perceived by the individual as being interrupted.

[3] Referring to a Process of Interference (aimed at addressing and managing Motivation, as defined in the Introduction), it is assumed in the Model that a Phase of Reality is the single Phase through which this Process of Interference can affect the Process of Motivation.

*Reality an assessment is made of the interference, in terms of importance or Significance.*

The influence of a Phase of Reality seems to affect every Stage of the Process we have observed so far. But obviously the chain of events starts at the very heart of the Process of Motivation: with the Goal. Reality in the Process seems to be contrasted with the Goal one sets.

In visualizing a Phase of Reality, the single Stage is therefore positioned in parallel with the Goal. *Without actually assessing its impact or the way it affects the Goal at this Stage, we first attach meaning, or 'Significance', to Reality.* The more we value the importance, or Significance of Reality, the larger we can represent Reality, as visualized in Fig. 4.1.

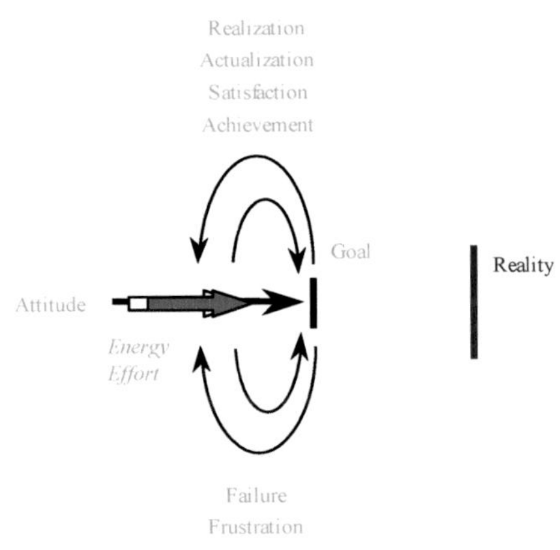


*Fig. 4.1.*
*A visualized overview of Phase 4,*
*a Phase of Reality*
*in the theoretical Model of Motivation,*
*consisting of a single Stage:*

9. A Stage of Reality

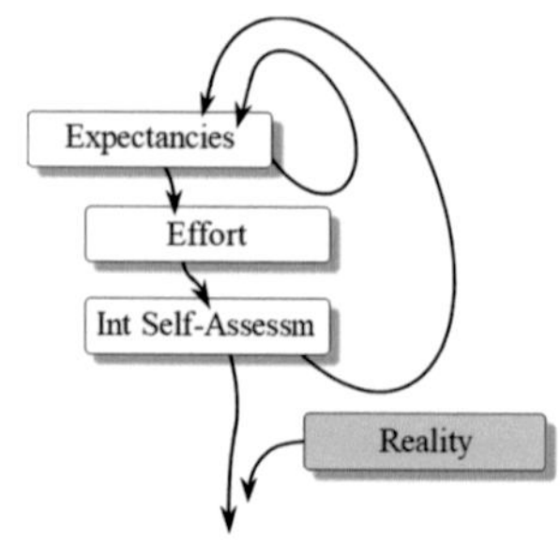


*Fig. 4.2.*
*A Phase of Reality*
*Visualized as part of successive Phases*
*in the description of the*
*Model of Motivation*

In summarizing the subsequent Phases in the Process of Motivation, then, a Phase of Reality follows on the first cyclical Phases that generated assessments of the Effort that had been invested in order to achieve the Goal that had been set in a Phase of Expectancies.

As summarized in Fig. 4.2., this next Phase in the Process is given a different position in contrast to these first Phases. The interference that occurs with the dynamics of the first three Phases leads to subsequent regulations and adaptations, as will be observed in the next Chapters, covering the subsequent preemptive measures. So, the 'collective input' obtained from the first three Phases is joined by the confrontation from Reality and, in turn, is to lead to a next Phase of the Process, as visualized by both arrows situated in parallel.

Some patterns were detected between Reality and the Significance of the event, or interference, as contrasted to the Goal that had been set:

- Goals that are perceived as highly Significant often coincide with an interference from Reality that is perceived as highly Significant;
- Goals that are perceived to have low Significance often coincide with interference from Reality perceived to be low in Significance.

Finally, a Phase of Reality, by its nature, has a distinctive property: its introduction can cause dramatic effects, as a result of reviving what were called *'dormant' Goals,* which are Goals that have been set, often long ago, in a Phase of Expectancies and that have remained there in a state of inactivity. In addition, Reality can have a similar effect on Goals that were referred to as *'latent' Goals*, or Goals that are more implicit and aimed at how we wish our surrounding world to be, associated with virtues such as honesty, integrity, morality and respectability. The effects of addressing these dormant and latent Goals can lead to mechanisms with profound impact, to be covered more extensively in Chapter 9, Chapter 10 and Chapter 11.

## 2 Theories

Although environmental influences have always been a distinctive feature in literature on the psychology of motivation, the various gradations of importance in the influence of these environmental factors have not yet taken prominence in current theories. As we shall see in Chapter 5, in observing the effects on motivation, the influence of situational factors appears to have been defined implicitly, with no distinction between gradations.

This marginal attention in theories from literature for gradations in perceived Significance of Reality has important implications, as we shall observe in the next Chapter [1].

[1] In addition, as a Phase of Reality is the 'primal portal' for addressing the Process of Motivation, these implications also extend to a Process of Interference. In later Volumes, when the subject is covered extensively, we will come to realize that using gradations of Significance in interference is a profoundly important technique in management of Motivation.

# 3 Research

Research on the effects of external influences on motivation emerged in the mid-twentieth century, following studies by Adorno on aggression and aggressive behavior (Adorno, Frenkel-Brunswick, Levinson & Sanford, 1950). The Adorno studies marked a change in focus towards environmental factors, which had been mainly oriented at internal needs and drives. Where in the Adorno studies intra-psychic influences were believed to be predominant, the general conclusion from a growing body of research was that intra-psychic influences did not appear to be the only mechanisms to instigate aggression, with situational factors playing an essential, regulating role (Berkowitz & Geen, 1966; Berkowitz & LePage, 1967; Berkowitz, 1970, 1974; Milgram, 1963, 1964, 1965, 1974; Zimbardo, 1969), although it remained unclear whether Reality was instigating aggression or aggressive behavior was enhanced by situational factors originating from Reality.

Subsequently, the effects of Reality have been researched in various fields of psychology, especially in educational psychology and work motivation.

The effects of parents on the development of expectancy-related beliefs and values, as researched within expectancy-value theory, were demonstrated in the varieties of feedback children received from their parents and the way they interpreted and came to understand these reactions on their performance (Dweck, 2002; Wigfield, Tonks & Klauda, 2009). And these, in turn, appeared to influence children's values in the activities they engaged in (Wigfield, Eccles, Schiefele, Roeser & Davis-Kean, 2006). As previously seen, researchers became increasingly interested in how different educational settings affect motivation, not only in tasks and activities, but especially in how teachers organize and structure these activities in the classroom environment, which provided further evidence for situational effects occurring on student motivation (Ames, 1992b; Maehr & Midgley, 1996; Nolen & Ward, 2008; Perry, Turner & Meyer, 2006; Stipek, 1996; Urdan, 1997).

Although all these studies implicitly acknowledged and underlined the importance of outside actors or events and the effects they yield on the Process of Motivation, there appear to have been very few studies on the regulatory influence of perceived *Significance* of these actors or events on the Process.

## Summary

The fourth Phase in the Model of Motivation is a 'Phase of Reality', where an event, or series of events, intrudes into the Process of Motivation. The interference can have both positive and negative outcomes on the Process. But in this Phase of Reality, only the importance or perceived 'Significance' of the event, or series of events, is observed.

A Phase of Reality consists of a single Stage, marked by this intrusion, or interference, in the Process of Motivation. The disruptive interference can be caused by an actor or group of actors, or by an occurrence or a perception, cognition or affect associated with an occurrence.

Although environmental influences have been a distinctive feature in literature on the psychology of motivation since the mid-twentieth century, the various gradations of importance in those external influences and their perceived Significance, have had only marginal attention in theories from literature, which is reflected in research outcomes.

# Chapter 5
## *Repercussions*
## *Phase 5 - A Phase of Impact*

The Process of achieving my Goals went so well...

Sitting at my window, my fantasies brought me from visiting romantic places to destinations and travel arrangements at the other side of the world. And I was the master of these fantasies, and carefully orchestrated which of these were to lead to action and which were to remain dormant.

And then this well-orchestrated picture was disrupted by the introduction of Reality...

At first, the interruption was weighed in a Phase of Reality. And now is the time to assess its effects on the Process of Motivation, in which I featured as the only actor on stage, designing my own Goal, investing my Effort, and assessing Achievement and Satisfaction according to my standards.

So, let us again observe the examples we used. But this time, the approach asks some discipline, as we tend to proceed into opinions or beliefs, assumptions and conclusions about this intrusion from Reality, which could easily lead us astray. Because these expressions are *preceded by a number of successive steps and Phases that have profound implications for the Process of Motivation as it further unfolds.* And by jumping directly to these, often passionate, conclusions we would miss the essentials that are at the basis of these sentiments.

One step at a time, then, in the approach to be taken...

Following the debacle at the parking lot (which we will now define as a confrontation with Reality), the subsequent assessment I make is the extent to which it affects the Process of reaching the Goal I had set. And it does... Recall that Monserrate was supposed to be this 'great-and-romantic-experience-of-amazement-and-wonder'. Its Significance grew by the hour... And now that I reach the busloads and the crowds of tourists, not only the Significance of its intrusion, but also its impact becomes painfully clear. It is opposed to my intentions; it couldn't be farther away. There is a wide gap, a pronounced discrepancy between my objective and this intrusion; between the Goal in its Process of Motivation and Reality in its impact. And following its impact are those feelings emerging as a consequence: bewilderment, confusion, annoyance and indignation.

Preceding these feelings of outrage, then, there is an initial step, or Stage, in which I first assess the *repercussions* of Reality on my doings. This first assessment of repercussions is essential for the Process of Motivation, as it is to unfold further. *It is a 'Phase of Impact', where the assessment is expressed in terms of a gap, or 'Discrepancy', between the Goal I had set myself to achieve and Reality disrupting this Process.* The feelings of outrage in degrading the place are to follow much later, and are initiated by this single step, or Stage of assessment, in a Phase of Impact. In the series of Phases that are to follow, we will see that this Phase will largely determine whether I feel outrage or simply decide to turn to the 'sensible' conclusion of returning to the place just before closure, when the crowds are off to their next destination...

The first example, then, is one of a negative disruption, causing high Impact and pronounced Discrepancy. But disruption can also turn out to be positive. Our second example was a successful tennis match. In the first three Phases of the Process, as evidence of my successful attempts accumulated, I gradually became more confident and steadily increased the Clarity of my Goal by cycling through these first three Phases, from 'playing-tennis' and 'playing-tennis-and-having-fun' to 'playing-tennis-and-having-fun-for-15-minutes-a-day-to-improve-my-condition', which was an ingenious approach not only to maintain my Motivation, but also to obtain a higher level of Satisfaction by gradually increasing the edge, as my confidence of success grew in the Process. This 'cocooned success', in the end, gave me enough confidence to venture into my 'uncharted talents' and actively seek and challenge a confrontation with Reality in applying for a match to demonstrate my abilities. "And I *did* win, didn't I?" Resulting expressions of increased confidence and extended superlatives for the noble sport of tennis in general, and my adversaries in particular, will be dealt with later. In this Phase of the Process, *it is the Impact I observe,* and, this time, the event accentuates the outcomes from the previous Phases, and the Discrepancy between Reality and my Goal (*to win*) is therefore small.

So, clearly, Reality interrupts and affects the course of the Process of Motivation as it unfolds. And its Impact is addressed by the Process of Motivation in subsequent Phases and Stages as it progresses. We do not proceed directly into action, or draw our conclusions from the shortcomings of the intervention or its merits. These conclusions are preceded by a number of intermittent steps. And we will observe these Phases briefly, in a moment, before proceeding to a more in-depth analysis in subsequent Chapters, especially Chapters 6, 7 and 8.

Now, this interruption in the Process of Motivation can manifest itself in different ways, and could even appear at first glance to initiate Motivation by itself, instigating action on its own accord. My third example illustrates the apparent potential in a positive way, with the fourth example demonstrating a negative outcome.

The groceries. This recurrent annoyance is now catching up with me and will finally bring me to action. Supposedly. At first sight, the complaints made by my beloved seem to instigate a Process of Motivation on its own. Reality seems to induce Motivation. *In fact, however, the Impact from Reality addresses a Goal already present, which I had conveniently postponed.* And we will encounter an unexpected reaction: my annoyance and my subsequent lighthearted behavior. Although my initial intentions were forthcoming and the agreements were clear from the start, we will come to realize that these subsequent reactions are meant to conceal feelings of guilt for postponing the deal, and will set in motion a series of mechanisms that will add further intricacy to the Process. More to come, then, on this issue of grocery shopping...

The fourth example illustrates the addressing of a dormant objective by the Impact from Reality, with an apparent positive reaction. The prospect of a trip to Hong Kong appears to instigate Motivation, but instead it awakens a dormant Goal, an objective that had been constantly postponed (as in our previous example), which is to be the prelude to an adventurous year, which, incidentally, will be based on misleading assumptions that I am to make about these perceptions of Reality. More to come also on these so-called 'Representations' I am to make of Reality and its Impact...

Note that in both examples affecting the Process of Motivation, the Goal is not addressed *directly*, and Impact is to be followed by a number of intermittent Phases, as just mentioned.

In both examples, then, Reality appears to initiate a Process of Motivation (getting those groceries done, or embarking on a journey to Hong Kong), whereas in fact it 'taps into' an existing Process of Motivation, which remained postponed, or dormant, until its Impact brings this Process back to life.

In both our last examples, a comparable effect occurs.

We had, in our fifth example, my superior emailing me on my prospects of submitting an article in the coming few months. And I was on high alert. I even overreacted (although, *in fact*, he didn't even refer to my postponed paper). Here, again, Reality appears to set in motion a Process of Motivation. But it doesn't. And the steps, this time, are even more subtle than the ones we observed before. I perceive Reality as a warning: "You'd better get started..." Why? Because Reality, as before, *'taps into' an existing objective.* I had already set my mind to writing this paper, but fear of failure prevented me from doing so. A dormant Goal was being addressed. Hence the annoyance.

But there is more, as our last example will show...

Those reactions where we overreact to Reality tend to proliferate. We often become prejudiced with preconceived ideas, jumping to conclusions about Reality and our surroundings, *based on Processes that are related to latent Goals.* And these interpretations can lead us astray, as in the course I am bound to follow in my sixth example. My latent objective was to be part of a university with highest principles and moral values; and autonomy. And this email which featured as Reality in the Process of Motivation from the previous example *now becomes part, in all its complexity, of this Process as well.* The perception of Reality (and the subsequent steps that are to follow) now reflects on this latent Goal in the example. It 'opens my eyes' to a Reality that not only intrudes in this carefully preserved Goal, but also appears to be highly Discrepant as well! *It affects me because of this latent Goal.*

*So Reality, in these few examples, appears to initiate a Process of Motivation, but in effect 'revives' Processes that have been lingering on as dormant Goals, and Goals we defined earlier as 'latent'.*

Let us summarize our findings, before proceeding to a next level in observing the Impact from Reality.

After having progressed through successive Phases, once the Goal had been set and Effort invested, we assessed the extent of our success in reaching what we wanted in this sequential Process of Motivation. Either we reached our Goal substantially or we persisted in renewed attempts, making amendments to the Goal or the investments we made. And gradually, in this cyclical Process covering the first three Phases of the Process of Motivation, a form of stability emerged, a 'cocoon', where Goal attainment appeared to be balanced with the investment in Effort we made. *According to our terms…*

In this cyclical balance, however, a disruption occurred induced externally in a Phase of Reality. In a subsequent Phase of Impact, the repercussions are assessed of the interference within this 'balanced cocoon'.

The Impact from Reality in the Process of Motivation is considerable. Not only when effects are perceived as negative, but also when these effects seem to be positive. There is an interference in a Process that so far evolved and progressed entirely to our own standards.

The fifth Phase in the Process of Motivation is a Phase of Impact.

Following awareness of Reality in a previous Phase of the Process, in a Phase of Impact an assessment is made of the extent to which Reality differs from the Goal that has been set. This divergence is defined in terms of Discrepancy.

Discrepancy is perceived to be small when the Impact is thought to affect the Process of reaching the Goal in a positive direction.

Discrepancy is large when the Impact is thought to affect the Process of Motivation in a negative way.

Thus, Impact from Reality is defined in terms of Discrepancy, indicating a positive or negative effect on the Process of Motivation.

*Phase 5 in the Model of Motivation is covered in detail on pp. 119-128. A summary is provided on p. 180.*

The appearance of Reality in the Process of Motivation is a 'seismic' event...

And considering these effects of Impact and Significance on the Process, it would assist us in our further observations when two important questions are to be answered at this point, before we proceed to the next Phases in this unfolding Process.

The first question: Does the Process of Motivation progress along similar lines, through similar Stages and Phases, regardless of the expression and manifestation of its Goals? In other words, are 'well-defined' Goals, as the ones we saw in the first two examples, affected differently than the 'postponed', 'dormant', or even 'latent' Goals we saw in the last examples? Is the sequence of successive steps in those affected Goals always the same, in all circumstances, in each Process of Motivation? In other words: *Is the Process of Motivation following Impact from Reality identical in all manifestations of a Goal?*

A second question, in a sense related to the previous one: Does Reality have the capability, or potential, to start and steer a Process of Motivation on its own accord? Does it always need a corresponding Goal in order to effectively initiate Motivation? And although these questions are reminiscent of a Process of Interference (which we decided in the Introduction to ignore), we have to address the issue as it reflects on the essential question just mentioned: *Does the Process of Motivation, in those instances, remain the same in its progress as we have observed so far? Do we have a Process of Motivation that remains identical, irrespective of interference that may affect its course as it progresses?*

To help us clarify, we shall briefly define at this point these next, successive Phases before proceeding to a more in-depth analysis of these Phases in subsequent Chapters.

Let us, again, use examples, but different from the ones we have been using so far, to mark this brief departure from our storyline.

To determine those Phases, then, we will first start with a clear Goal, combined with a Reality that is as unpredictable as it can be in the effects it causes. So the outcome of Impact could go either way, with a positive or negative effect in reaching our Goal. In addition, for ease of reference in determining those Phases, the result must be clear and the Impact must provide a precise and unambiguous result. So that we may observe patterns and regularities in those Phases at a later stage, when we examine those Phases in more detail in next Chapters.

So let us address our first question: is the Process of Motivation in its sequence of subsequent Phases following Impact identical in all manifestations of the Goal?

Here, then, is the example: a little girl wants to catch a great fish! A simple, and lighthearted example after the complex events we just encountered...

And here are the details, together with her portrait, for convenience, to be used again later as reference (when we are going to observe patterns in those subsequent Phases).

*See exhibit next page* ➔

Now, the story reveals there is a sequence of steps that occur prior to the conclusion of success. The conclusion appears to be instantly made, but it is not...

Let us summarize this sequence of steps:

- The *criteria* that provide a reference have been defined in the initial Phases of the Process, especially Phase 1 (they are comparable to the settings, or the scale of a measuring device, a gauge, or a meter);
- Then, there is a *measurement* based upon those criteria: given the interference from Reality, a Phase of Impact determines if Reality matches, exceeds or fails those criteria (are they equal to, below or above the 'red line' in the 'settings' of the meter?).

On Catching a Fish...

So, here is the story of this little girl who wants to catch a great fish... The Goal is clear, and has been set in Phase 1. She goes to the river, Phase 2, and sits there, waiting for things to come. Notice that Phase 3 has low profile, as the end result is obtained only when Reality becomes apparent.

And we start the example with a positive Impact.

The little girl sits for an hour, patiently cycling through Phases 1, 2 and 3 and maintaining hope on having this great catch any minute now...
Suddenly, Reality pops in... and here comes her great prize! The best fish ever, with the highest Significance!

The Impact is obvious, Discrepancy between Goal and Reality is as small as can be, with Reality almost coinciding with the objective set... And note how the girl cleverly exaggerates the size of her great prize as soon as she gets hold of her catch. *And it is here that the successive steps are revealed following the Impact. For she doesn't jump to this conclusion at once: it follows a reasoning, a stepwise sequence...*

It is an almost instant succession of clever assessments, but they do occur in order to reach the uplifting conclusion that "the fish exceeds our highest expectations":

- First, one has to assess the new situation as compared to the initial settings made in the Phases prior to the catch, especially Phase 1, where the Goal was defined: what were the criteria against which the Impact from Reality is to be observed?
- ... And did we meet those criteria? We might conclude that in our case Reality surpassed those criteria by far!
- Now, are those criteria adequate, given the new situation?
- ... Or do they need amendments?
- And, given these outcomes, *only then the conclusion can be made* that the little girl made a GREAT catch, in fact the best she has ever made. And note how these superlatives help to further acknowledge the joyful outcome of this great event!

Which then brings us to three subsequent steps that eventually lead us to our final reaction:

- An assessment of the *adequacy* of those criteria, given the preceding experience of the Impact from Reality;
- And given the assessment of adequacy, should *amendments* be made to counteract, enhance or stabilize the situation?
- Leading, eventually, to a *conclusion,* following the Impact from Reality, that is either positive or negative.

So, after Impact, there appears to be a threefold sequence of effects.

We seldom reach full success as the girl did in her attempt at catching a fish. As we will observe later, in Chapter 8, following the Impact from Reality, the Process of Motivation is re-initiated to encompass these new outcomes obtained from Reality. And these amendments are initiated by the preliminary threefold assessments just mentioned that follow the Impact from Reality.

We thus obtain three subsequent steps, or Phases, that are likely to follow a Phase of Impact.

Now, let us observe the other option, of a negative outcome, to find if this sequence remains the same.

Here, again, is the story, but this time featuring a little boy ...

*See exhibit next page* ➔

From the story, the sequence of subsequent assessments appears to remain the same following a negative Impact. Initial Phases define the criteria against which the interference from Reality is assessed in terms of Impact. And from there, the progressive assessment in subsequent Phases appears identical:

- An assessment of *adequacy* of initial criteria, defined in initial Phases;
- Followed by assessments of possible *amendments*;
- Which then leads to a *conclusion* following Impact.

## ... Or Not!?

For this occasion, we change the scenery, this time having a little boy trying to catch this great fish...

The little boy is sitting patiently for an hour, cycling through Phases 1, 2 and 3 and maintaining hope on having his catch. It is a personal evaluation to 'keep up the good work' which has nothing to do with the unfortunate fact of a Reality where no fish is willing to bite...

So, there he sits. And at a certain moment, after having cycled through Phases 1, 2 and 3, at least a *hundred* times, he comes to realize that time is running out on the adventure...

Note that in this example, Reality emerges in 'shades of awareness'. It is in no way comparable to the 'all-or- nothing' 'catch-of-a-lifetime' from the previous example. This time, the introduction comes in gradations (we will come to realize later that in fact, Reality appears in subsequent cycles as the Process of Motivation progresses towards awareness). At first, in 'the blink of an eye', there is the idea: "What am I to do if no fish appears?" As this first awareness of a negative Impact occurs, it also appears to follow a sequence of steps *before* the poor boy concludes that his Effort is in vain and "no fish will EVER show up!" By the way, the whole thing becomes "a shame", now that he thinks of it: "What an awful way of killing animals! No more fishing for me!"

And here again, we can observe that not only a sequence of events leads to a conclusion, but also *that this sequence has a distinct purpose to neutralize the Impact that has been so disappointing.*

So, the succession of assessments that emerges not only serves to lead to a conclusion ("no fish will EVER show up"), *but also to provide the cues to neutralize the discouraging effects on the Process of Motivation ("all things considered, I think fishing is a shame, really!").*

This radical conclusion is reached in a same sequence of assessments:

- First, one compares the situation with the initial settings made in Phase 1: the Goal materializing in a great catch.
- Those criteria form the basis against which the Impact from Reality is observed; and those criteria appear not to have been met...
- Thereby doubting the adequacy of criteria,
- ... in turn necessitating a course of action...
- ... which then leads to the conclusion that failure is imminent. And again, superlatives are used, but this time to neutralize negative effects of Impact.

Now having observed those subsequent Phases, let us proceed to the next question, and determine if the Process of Motivation remains unchanged in these successive steps even if it appears to be entirely initiated by Reality.

Sometimes, our surroundings seem to propel us into action, without any discernable Goal from where the action could have originated. Does Reality have the inherent potential to initiate a course of action that could evolve into a Process of Motivation without any Goals from ourselves being present? And if it does, would that lead to the same set of subsequent steps that have just been proposed? Or will the Process of Motivation follow a different route, depending on specific attributes in the source of interference from Reality? And thus, would different forms of Reality result in different expressions in the Process of Motivation?

*If it does, there would be more than one manifestation of the Process of Motivation, depending on the interference from Reality. And consequently, these successive steps following Impact could differ from the ones we just observed.*

To help us out in this vital issue, let us observe a simple yet appealing expression of Reality in the form of a next example.

This time, I use a (related) fairy tale as a metaphor of an 'enchanting' Reality, which is to tempt us to engage in a world all of us would fancy living in: an unexpected encounter with *magic and wizardry!* Who wouldn't fancy meeting a wizard, bringing us fame and fortune? And, on top of things, having the looks of the kindest of creatures, in the form of a non-intrusive *magical fish*?

We reintroduce the boy in this fairy tale. The question now is if such an 'epitomc' of an unexpected and unforeseen Significant Reality can, by itself, initiate action and evolve into a Process of Motivation in much the same way as we observed until now?

*See exhibit next page* ➔

About a Fish and a Fairy Tale...

Many years ago, there lived a little boy whose name was Matteo Motivation. He was the son of a village chief who had married the daughter of a fisherman. The child was exceptional in his kindness and his friendliness and was loved by everyone.

His life had been an easy one, for the village had prospered ever since a mysterious event had occurred shortly after his parents had married. The villagers told the tale of a wizard fish in the waters nearby, which allegedly had impressive magical powers to foretell one's future. Matteo had heard lots of stories in his young days about the wondrous predictions this great fish had made, changing the lives of many into one of prosperity and good fortune...

One day, Matteo went for a walk and, as it happened, came across the river where this magical fish was supposed to dwell along its shores.

So, off he went to the water and full of gentle curiosity bent over to see if he could catch a glimpse of this mysterious creature...

Suddenly, the fish appeared:
"Hello, I am Proximo Providence, the fish with the gift to foretell thy destiny in wisdom and prosperity..."
"Well hello to you too! I am Matteo and I happened to walk by..."
"I know thee, and I know thy mother well... Long years ago she saved my life from being caught at fishing, and ever since I've offered to her and her beloved my gift as a token of my gratitude. Because thou art thy mother's son, I will grant thee an audience. Shall I foretell thee how to retain thy place in a world devoted to thee, in attention, admiration, respect and sympathy?"

Anxious to retain his place in a friendly world filled with those kind virtues, Matteo was eager to hear the words of the wizard...

And the magical fish responded:
"If thou art to seek glory and fame,
thy eyes will remain without luster
and will become hollow in their sight...
But if thou art to seek kindness, in respect,
dignity and trust to everyone, thy eyes will
shine upon wisdom and prosperity and
will be filled with the luster they deserve."

And off he went, leaving Matteo behind...

So, what are we to make of the steps that follow this encounter of a child with Providence? Let us observe the options in possible reactions Matteo might give.

Let us start with the option used so far, in which Matteo would have had a Goal of going to the river and talking to the wizard. It would probably have been less explicit and unarticulated. In reply to his offer, he would react: “Yes, please do, that’s what I’m here for”. In which case, the Process would evolve the way it has done so far: there is an initial Goal that has been set, and following the Impact from Reality, there is a threefold assessment based on the standards defined by this Goal. So, this example in essence provides no change or amendments to the three steps we just proposed.

A second option would be that the offer by the wizard appeals, not to a specific Goal, but to ‘things-everybody-wants-in-life’, to an objective we referred to earlier as a *‘latent’* Goal. The prospect of ‘wisdom and prosperity’ brings to life this desire. Now, in this case, although the objective is not as clear as the previous one, there is a similar threefold stepwise Process following Impact. The criteria just mentioned are there: “This brings to mind an implicit wish I have had for many years: to have people relish in my presence”. So, the first step would be to ascertain the adequacy of this latent Goal: “I did well to treasure this wish the way I did!” And next the course of action: “How do I do this, please tell me”. Eventually leading to a third step in which the wizard fish (in conclusion) is covered with gratitude for his *benevolence* in sharing his *wisdom* and *magical* recommendations. So, here in this second example of a latent Goal, we seem to follow the same sequence of steps following Impact.

The third and last option, then, and the focus of our second question, would consist of a Reality without any apparent Goal: we had no clue. Never thought that such a wizard was in existence. “But now that you’re here, could we discuss some further issues?” The Impact from Reality, this time, takes us by surprise, and seems to instantly lead to action. But here also, at closer examination, the same sequence of evaluative steps occurs as the one we have seen before. Let us observe. The wizard comes 'out of the blue'. *But the Impact such a confrontation evokes does have an origin.* Otherwise there would have been no 'wonder in awe', no awareness, no interest. The source of this awareness must come from previous experiences, either with Goals that have been set in the past as part of 'old', or 'adjacent' Processes of Motivation that are providing those cues. Or it must stem from previous experiences with a comparable Reality. In the event that there would have been *no* such previous experiences, either from similar Goals or from similar versions of Reality, there would be no Impact, and Reality would not have captured Matteo's attention. So, we have two options: recollections from past Goals or previous experiences with Reality. *In both cases, a Discrepancy is observed in Impact with a Goal that is inherently present, based on past experiences.* From these experiences, the encounter would progress along these lines: "Now, I recall having heard about this wizard, and I should pay attention to what he's telling me". In the observation, there is first awareness of a Discrepancy, as there is no adequate corresponding Goal to attend to, and it should be defined, because meeting such a wizard is indeed a major event. The alternative, experience from past encounters with Reality, follows a comparable strategy: "Now, this is the opportunity of a lifetime, and I should pay attention to what this prodigious fish is telling me".

So, even in the event of an intruding Reality without a contrasting Goal, there appear to be equal successive steps that follow the Impact from Reality:

- Although there are no criteria, Reality *does* produce Impact, relating to a frame of reference; leading to the observation that this frame of reference lacks more pronounced criteria;
- The observation of inadequacy leads to a decision on a course of action to subsequently implement those criteria;
- Which, in turn, leads to the conclusion that Reality necessitates, is important, or Significant, enough to do so...

*In other words, the Process of Motivation remains unchanged in its successive steps, even if it appears to be entirely initiated by Reality and external circumstances.*

*As a consequence, then, of the observations made, we conclude that any form of control, influence or regulation from Reality (and, consequently, any form in which interference occurs) is expected to encounter a Process of Motivation in the distinctive manifestation of a series of three successive Phases.*

Now, admittedly this story hasn't been very realistic (let alone scientific) in determining the sequence of steps following Impact in the Process of Motivation. But at closer examination the case becomes more compelling when we follow a rationale based on logical reasoning.

First, we can follow the rational argument that a reaction on *any* intervention must first raise awareness (which occurs in Phase 4) and the realization of its intrusive nature on the ongoing Process (Phase 5, a Phase of Impact), *before a reaction can occur.* And in order for this reaction to occur, one must have a 'reason', or criteria (as obtained from the first three Phases, and especially the Goal, as defined in Phase 1). And given the awareness and realization of interference in a Phase of Impact, inevitably the adequacy of those criteria emerges (step 1, as will occur in a subsequent Phase, which is then to be Phase 6), followed by a decision on a 'course of action', either positive or negative, in necessary amendments (step 2, to occur in a subsequent Phase 7), before the outcomes in terms of conclusions and sentiments towards the interfering Reality can occur, which are 'derivatives' of these preceding assessments (step 3, or Phase 8). These effects in terms of sentiments experienced from and experienced towards Reality and its Impact are the subjective outcomes from these assessments.

*So, the stepwise sequence of successive Phases that are assumed to follow a Phase of Impact are most likely to occur in any form the Process of Motivation appears to manifest itself.*

A reaction following a Phase of Impact, then, is to lead to a sequence of three subsequent Phases, which are to follow directly after the event.

Now that we know that the Process of Motivation following Impact progresses along the same sequence of Phases, irrespective of its effects on the Process or the extent of external interference, we will observe these distinct Phases in more detail in the next three Chapters.

First, however, let us summarize by reformulating our observations in a series of further definitions in Section 1, observe what various theories have to say in Section 2, and explore findings obtained from research in Section 3.

We will come to realize, however, that literature related to a Phase of Impact needs an introduction, to be provided as a 'Prelude' to Section 2 and Section 3.

After the Impact from Reality, the Process of Motivation progresses further in three successive Phases.

Each Phase is covered in detail in subsequent Chapters 6, 7 and 8.

A first Phase, referred to as a 'Phase of Externally Evoked Self-Assessment', is covered more extensively in Chapter 6.

A second Phase, referred to as a 'Phase of Anticipated Change', is covered in Chapter 7.

A third Phase, referred to as a 'Phase of Dedication', is covered in Chapter 8.

*Phase 6 in the Model of Motivation, a 'Phase of Externally Evoked Self-Assessment', is covered in Chapter 6 and in detail on pp. 188-192.*

*Phase 7 in the Model, a 'Phase of Anticipated Change', is covered in Chapter 7, in detail pp. 229-233.*

*Phase 8, a 'Phase of Dedication', is covered in Chapter 8, in detail on pp. 264-273.*

## 1 Definitions

Disruption occurred in the cyclical balance that was reached within a Process of Motivation, which affected the Process of reaching the Goal, either in a negative or positive sense.

A first step addressing the interference consisted of awareness of the intrusion in terms of Significance. The next step, then, in a Phase of Impact, is to assess the extent of the intrusion.

In assigning Significance to Reality, the contrast between Reality and the Goal becomes evident. By assigning Significance, you subsequently come to experience the Impact of Reality, given the course intended to reach the objective through the Process of Motivation. The Impact can be positive or negative, and scales on a continuum between both extremes. When the Impact of Reality is positive it enhances the Process of Motivation, in the sense that it facilitates the Process of reaching the Goal, or sustaining the Goal that had previously been reached. The Impact of Reality is negative when it harms the Process of reaching the objective or when it necessitates a re-appraisal of an objective already reached

The contrast between Reality and a Goal can be considerable (and therefore disruptive), or again, it can be small (and therefore supportive), with all intermediate options. *The Impact of Reality is the Discrepancy experienced by the individual between the subjective Reality observed and the Goal that has been set*[1]. *A Phase of Impact consists of a single Stage, in which this assessment is made.*

Impact and Discrepancy are large when they impair the Process of reaching my objective, as was the case in visiting Monserrate where unexpected intrusion occurred. But the Impact could also take a different form, when a course of action followed in the Process of Motivation is jeopardized, as in my grocery shopping adventures and in the postponement of a paper or delay in an intended trip.

[1] The concept of 'Impact' could be misleading, as it is often used colloquially in another connotation. An 'enormous impact' can be either positive or negative. In our case however, the concept is solely used to indicate *Discrepancy*. With 'enormous impact' we refer to a 'considerable Discrepancy', which will always be perceived as negative to the Process of Motivation. In our terminology an 'enormous impact in a positive sense' would rather be a combination of a highly Significant Reality with a small perceived Discrepancy. In spoken language the concept of 'Impact' includes both Significance and Discrepancy. However, to provide clarity in the succession of Stages and Phases that comprise the Process of Motivation, a distinction between both entities has been made.

But the Impact from Reality can also be positive (although the phrasing suggests otherwise), where perceived Discrepancy is small. Following the cyclical Process in the first three Phases, the interference from Reality can provide support or confirmation in my pursuit to reach my objective. Winning a tennis match, the admission to a program of great standing, reaching a long-awaited position, or procuring a desirable item, such as a piece of art or a fashionable new outfit. All expressions of an interference from Reality that is highly supportive of the Goals that have been set, or that can even be the materialization of these ambitions.

The Impact of Reality, then, is expressed in terms of a perceived Discrepancy between Reality and the Goal that has been set. *Its focus, therefore, is on distance and as such the concept can be visualized by a gap, or '$\delta$'.*

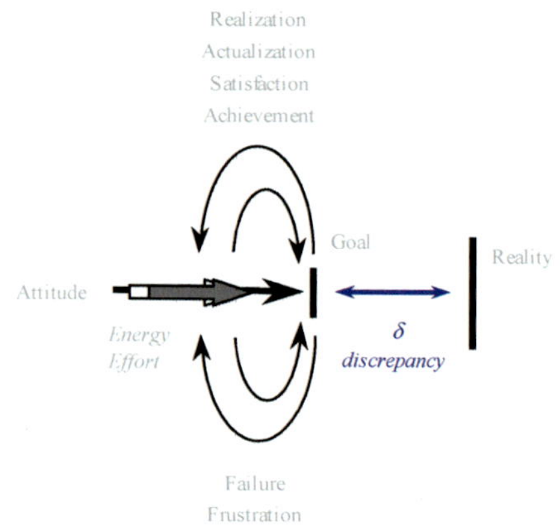


*Fig. 5.1.*
*A visualized overview of Phase 5,*
*a Phase of Impact*
*in the theoretical Model of Motivation,*
*consisting of a single Stage:*

10. A Stage of Impact

Fig. 5.1. provides a visualized overview of this fifth Phase in the Process of Motivation. The Impact or Discrepancy is depicted as a gap between the subjective Reality observed and the Goal that has been set. The gap can be either small or large, depending on a perceived positive or negative interference in the Process of reaching the Goal.

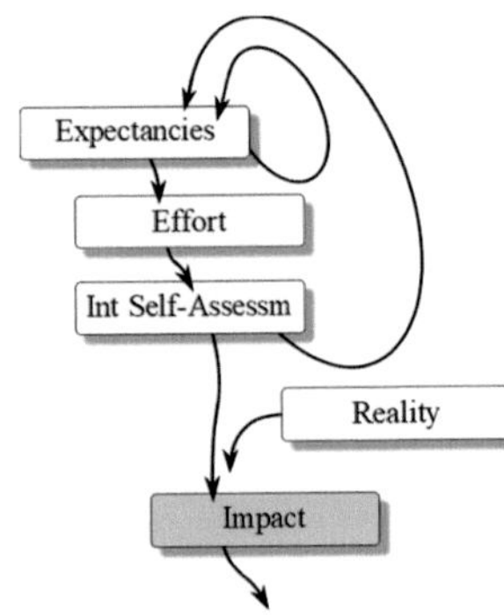


*Fig. 5.2.*
*A Phase of Impact*
*Visualized as part of successive Phases in the description of the Model of Motivation*

In summarizing this next Phase within the context of the previous Phases in the Process of Motivation, Fig. 5.2. depicts the Phase of Impact as it combines the 'collective input' obtained from the first three Phases associated with attainment of the Goal, with the confrontation from Reality, to produce the perception of Discrepancy distinctive of a Phase of Impact.

What are the effects of interference from Reality on the Process as it further unfolds?

To analyze these effects, one has to observe the various manifestations in which the Process of Motivation could proceed following Impact. At first sight, it appears that a huge number of options may occur. However, when considering the essential constructs that emerge in the Process and their respective properties, these options can be considerably reduced to facilitate the analysis.

The Model of Motivation assumes that two concepts are essential and can serve to reduce the available options in observing these effects of interference:

- Reality: where the Model of Motivation assumes Reality has two dimensions: its *Significance,* or importance, as defined in a Phase of Reality, and its *Discrepancy*, as defined in a Phase of Impact;
- Goal: as central concept and 'raison d'être' of the Process of Motivation in the Model, the Goal has a number of properties, covered in Chapter 1; among these, *Significance of the Goal* appears as an essential property.

These concepts, then, can be observed on their specific dimensions and properties as they occur in combination, thereby facilitating the analysis.

*See exhibits next pages* ➔

*<u>The options emerging in the Impact from Reality</u>*

In a Phase of Reality, the source of interference is determined in terms of Significance. In a Phase of Impact, the intensity of the intrusion on the Process of Motivation is defined in terms of Discrepancy.

Obviously, the effects of the interference can be manifold, but it would help to somehow classify all these variations in interference if we intend to observe its effects on the Process of Motivation: in some cases, the effects are only marginal, but in others the effects can be dramatic.

So how are we to classify the vast amount of options in which the interference manifests itself?

First, let us use only the extremes that may occur, assuming that the 'intermediate expressions' more or less follow the extremes toward which they tend to incline. That leaves us with two continua, each with two extremes we observe:

- For a Phase of Reality: either a low perceived Significance of Reality or a high perceived Significance of Reality;
- For a Phase of Impact: either a negative Impact with high Discrepancy or a positive Impact with low Discrepancy.

This would lead to four combinations in which a Phase of Reality and its Impact on the Process of Motivation would be manifested:

- A low perceived Significance in a Phase of Reality and high Discrepancy (with negative effects) in a Phase of Impact;
- A high perceived Significance in a Phase of Reality and high Discrepancy (with negative effects) in a Phase of Impact;
- A low perceived Significance in a Phase of Reality and low Discrepancy (with positive effects) in a Phase of Impact;
- A high perceived Significance in a Phase of Reality and low Discrepancy (with positive effects) in a Phase of Impact.

Now, we could further diversify these options if we observe the Goal that is being interfered with: in assuming a continuum, we could differentiate the Goal into a Goal with high perceived Significance and a Goal with low perceived Significance.

And this, in turn, would then lead to eight combinations: each of these four, combined with a Goal that has either a high perceived Significance or a low perceived Significance.

*Fortunately, only two of these eight combinations tend to have substantial effects on the Process of Motivation, which makes them more prominent subjects for further study.*

<u>*Effects of Interference*</u>

Let us observe the various combinations to determine in which of the eight options effects are likely to occur, and are to be used in our further study of the Process of Motivation. In visualizing Significance, we can scale the size of both the Goal and Reality, and define Impact by assigning distance:

*1. High Significance of Goal, low Significance of Reality, negative Impact*

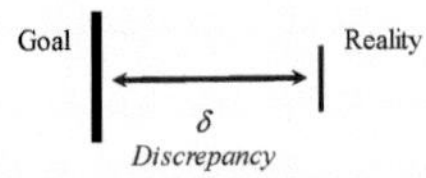


A first combination: a Goal with high Significance where Reality is perceived as insignificant. Although Discrepancy is large, it appears highly unlikely that such a Reality would obstruct attempts at reaching such a priced Goal. Therefore, the effects of interference on the Process of Motivation are expected to be minimal.

*2. High Significance of Goal, high Significance of Reality, negative Impact*

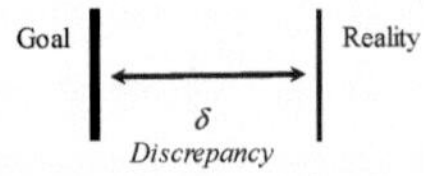


In contrast, the combination of high Discrepancy, high Significance of the Goal and high Significance of Reality appears to be much more likely to produce effects, as the obstructive manifestation of Reality profoundly appears to affect my attempts at reaching a Significant Goal.

*3. High Significance of Goal, low Significance of Reality, positive Impact*

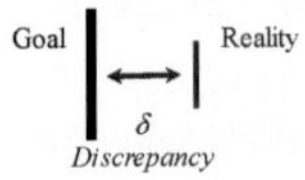


In parallel, when Reality appears to be highly supportive of the Goal I seek to achieve, and Discrepancy is therefore small, positive effects could occur. However, these effects are marginal, producing only modest interference in this case, as Reality is perceived as non-Significant.

*4. High Significance of Goal, high Significance of Reality, positive Impact*

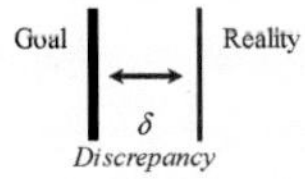


When, however, Reality is perceived as Significant, these effects dramatically increase as a consequence of its supportive manifestation in my attempt to reach my Significant Goal.

*(Continued)*

So, from the available combinations, two options emerge that are likely to produce substantial effects in interference from Reality: a highly Significant Goal in combination with a Reality that is perceived as Significant, where Impact is either negative with high Discrepancy or positive with small Discrepancy.
Let us observe the options occurring with low Significance of the Goal:

*5. Low Significance of Goal, low Significance of Reality, negative Impact*

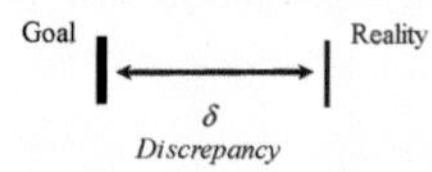


A Goal with little Significance is confronted with a Reality that is perceived as also having little Significance. The effects are marginal: neither the Goal nor Reality has enough 'standing' to produce dramatic effects on the Process of Motivation. As a result, although Discrepancy appears to be large, it will hardly affect the Process of Motivation.

*6. Low Significance of Goal, high Significance of Reality, negative Impact*

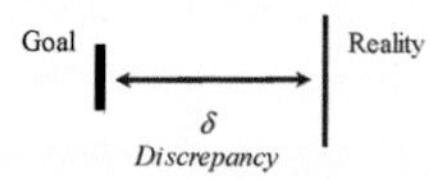


A highly Significant Reality has much more 'power' to affect the Process of Motivation, with (in this option) negative Impact and high Discrepancy. Now, although this option is more likely to occur than the previous one, the Goal has insufficient Significance to produce such a (negative) effect on the Process of Motivation. Its limited Significance does not justify such a profound effect.

*7. Low Significance of Goal, low Significance of Reality, positive Impact*

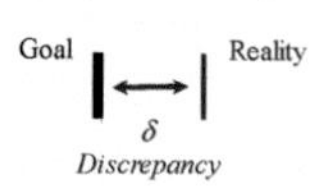


As in option 6., both Significance of the Goal and Significance of Reality are insufficient to instigate substantial effects on the Process of Motivation. Despite a positive Impact, interference is likely to be minimal.

*8. Low Significance of Goal, high Significance of Reality, positive Impact*

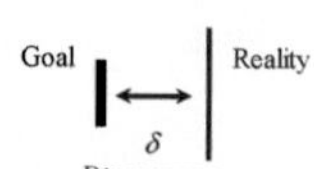


Despite the high Significance of Reality and the positive Impact on the Process, the effects are also expected to be modest as the Goal has only limited Significance and doesn't warrant profound subsequent actions.

To analyze the effects of interference, then, the essential constructs and their respective properties can assist to considerably reduce the available options, thereby facilitating the analysis of those effects on the Process of Motivations.

As observed, the Process in all its manifestations can be captured in eight principal variations using its most important concepts in their expressions on extremes of respective continua. *The effects of interference on the Process of Motivation appear to be substantial and of great consequence in only two of these distinct manifestations: when Significance of both the Goal and Reality is high, with Discrepancy perceived to be either large (with negative Impact, option 2, p. 123), or small (with positive Impact, option 4, p. 123).*

So, from the vast array of available options, on only two occasions substantial effects are likely to occur. And we will use these observations simplifying the effects of Impact when we will subsequently observe theories from literature and associated research findings.

Preceding those observations on findings from literature, however, and to conclude our overview of a Phase of Impact, let us briefly reintroduce the three subsequent Phases that we found are to follow Impact, and comment on those Phases from this perspective on effects on the Process of Motivation. We can finalize our overview by using the constructs we applied in observing effects of interference to clarify those subsequent Phases further, and define their specific role within the Process of Motivation.

Again, we will use the central concept of the Goal, as contrasted to an interfering Reality, with Impact expressed as a perceived Discrepancy between both, as depicted in Fig. 5.3.:

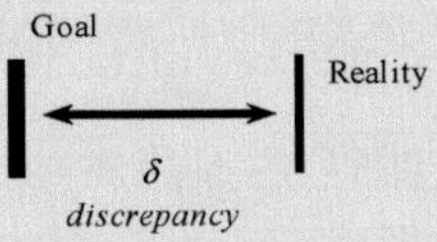


*Fig. 5.3.*
*Visualized Model of the interplay between Goal, Reality and Impact, as occurring in the Process of Motivation*

As we saw, the Phase of Impact initiates a re-orientation of the Goal versus Reality. And within this framework, this re-orientation proceeds in three steps, or three consecutive Phases. From this perspective, each Phase has a distinctive characteristic:

- *Goal;* In a first step of these consecutive Phases, as a direct response to the confrontation with Reality, a re-appraisal is made of the manner in which the *Goal* and associated parameters were set; it is an evaluation of adequacy.
- *Goal versus Discrepancy;* Given this re-evaluation of the Goal and its parameters, an appraisal is made of the potential readiness to decrease *Discrepancy* and to close the gap that has been observed; it is an assessment of amendments to be made.
- *Goal versus Reality;* And given this outcome, in a final step, a re-evaluation is made of *Reality* in terms of perceived 'support', or 'non-support'; and as such, it is a concluding assessment of Reality following its Impact.

So we could add and refine our previous observations, from a threefold perspective that emerges when a Goal is confronted with an interfering Reality, and three consecutive Phases are used to re-assess the consequences of Impact.

Preceding an actual re-adjustment, then, of the Goal and its associated parameters, as a reaction to the unexpected confrontation with Reality, a threefold assessment occurs of the Impact of Reality, given its Significance. This threefold assessment is passive in nature: no actual changes are to take place at this point in the Process of Motivation. It is a passive re-appraisal of the three distinct consequences the confrontation with Reality has led to.

In each of these three distinct Phases we are to observe the effects of interference, especially in the two cases, just found, where these effects of interference appear to be substantial, where Significance of both the Goal and Reality is high, and perceived Discrepancy is either small, or large.

In following Chapters 6, 7 and 8 we are to cover these respective Phases, in more detail, leading to a first overview of the Model of Motivation.

Let us first proceed, however, with observing theories and research from literature associated with a Phase of Impact. Assisting in our overview are a number of examples to clarify the intricate and at times confusing interaction between Reality and the Goals we set, especially when both are perceived to be Significant, as it is regulated by perceived Discrepancy in a Phase of Impact. We will use these examples at the end of this Chapter to help us clarify observations to be made when covering the literature in Section 1 and Section 2.

*See exhibits next pages* ➔

In addition, however, we will address a critical issue in a Prelude to both Sections that has led to profound controversies over research findings produced from the various fields of study.

## *Main Effects of Impact: Some Examples*

So, two options are likely to have substantial effects following Impact in the Process of Motivation: when Significance of both the Goal and Reality is high, and when Discrepancy is either perceived to be high (option 2, p. 123), or low (option 4, p. 123).

Now, at first sight, these options appear to be straight forward. But let us have some examples, to illustrate some surprising variations that will prevent us from making generalizations, especially when different Goals emerge in different situations. And, as it happens, at different stages in our lives...

*These examples will prove to serve an important role, as we subsequently proceed into covering related theories from literature. To assist us in referring to these examples at a later stage, we provide numbers to each of these as a reference.*

Consider the case, then, of a young family...

*Example 1: A young girl at the age of 1...*
We have a baby girl that just started walking around on her tiny little feet. We are all fascinated by the enchantment these young children provide us, when we have the privilege to share their first steps in our world. *Everything* is appealing to them; everything is exciting and explored with great attention. And we are compelled not to interfere, for fear of disrupting the enchantment the occasion brings us. And when we do, or rather have to, to prevent our young baby girl from hazardous situations, we are almost hesitant to intervene, as she will be inconsolable for having interfered in her Great Adventure.

Here we have a Significant Goal (*everything* is worth exploring) and we have a Reality that almost always matches up, or even coincides with the Goal that has been set. It is as if Failure at this stage of our lives is non-existent. It is an integral part of exploring the world around us. And when Reality, in the form of a concerned parent, causes Discrepancy, it so happens that disappointment, anger, sadness are well-articulated...

*Example 2: Her sister at school, at the age of 8...*
Now, her sister goes to school, and the scenery changes. Let us consider in two subsequent examples the succession of events.

At first, this natural tendency to discover and explore without fear can be maintained. And within this setting, Reality tends to be perceived as less intruding for it sustains her Goals to reach out and seek novelty.

*Example 3: Her sister as she gradually progresses...*
Now suppose, at a certain moment, her teacher comes with feedback (and let us agree that this is what teachers are for). And let us assume the teacher's feedback is precise and to the point. The input from Reality now takes on a new form. The young girl, within this setting, perceives her teacher to be Significant. Two options now occur within this new situation:

a) The input coincides with the Goal (or Goals) that she has set for herself. From here, she will try to retain the approval provided from her teacher as it sustains these Goals. But now, with this explicit input acknowledging her Goals, she is likely to seek out this external recognition; and most likely, her Goals will thus become more 'externally oriented': seeking approval, recognition, and praise...
b) Or the input now appears Discrepant with the Goal (or Goals) she has set.

In either case, Reality induces different reactions than she previously displayed.

*Example 4: Her mother in her new job, at the age of 30...*
Now, while her daughter is not too happy with the new regime at school, her mother rather enjoys the clarity that is provided in her new job. So, having a set of clear and precise details about what is to be expected from her helps her to perform according to her wishes, where the Goal she has set is to outperform expectations of her immediate manager. So, in mom's case, a set of clear and precise targets reduces Discrepancy in the attempts at reaching her Goal (or Goals).

*Example 5: A mother's change in perspective...*
However, these circumstances change when an announcement is made:

a) The company decides to define targets for each employee. And this is to affect the way she perceives this Reality, in terms of Discrepancy with her Goal;
b) Suppose she is asked to define those targets herself; she is likely to define this 'imposed Reality' in such a way that it minimizes Discrepancy;
c) But suppose management decides to increase those targets... Surprisingly, it works well in her case, as she perceives the change as a (further) acknowledgement of her expertise ("Well, given those targets, I say these folks *do* believe I have what it takes to get there!"), thus decreasing Discrepancy. But things appear to turn out differently with her colleague, who outraged by this "act of ultimate disrespect" decides to leave the company "right away"...

*Example 6: And, finally, her grandma, in her prime at 50...*
But grandma thrives in her job, where no such clarity is provided *at all.* When initially asked, she suggested to have her "make her own rules". In this, she feels acknowledged that her boss leaves her with such freedom to define the content (and thus the quality) of her job. She perceives this lack of precise targets as a token of appreciation, which ignites her performance and feelings of responsibility. She is not only in control; she is the *acknowledged expert* in what she does. At this point in life, she has gained experience, ability, competence in her view, and thus allowing her to set those vague and unprecise targets is perceived as acknowledging her qualities, leading to perceptions of a minimal Discrepancy with the Goal (or Goals) she has set.

## A Prelude to Section 2 and Section 3

In the next two Sections, we are to embark on a somewhat perilous journey...

We are to cover theories that are associated with a Phase of Impact. A Phase in which Reality, or an unexpected outside event or actor, emerges and influences the Process of Motivation. In covering those theories, we will approach limitations that we initially imposed on the analysis in the Introduction, where we defined that only a Process of Motivation was to be observed and where outside interventions were to be excluded, as these were considered to be part of a Process of Interference.

In remaining as close as we can to this initial restriction, we are to venture nonetheless at times close to the 'realms' of a Process of Interference, as these occasional digressions are necessary for an adequate analysis of the literature.

But the journey becomes perilous also for another reason.

We will observe theories that have been the source of heated debate and controversies that appear to be 'without precedent'. And the approach we are to follow in an analysis on the causes of these controversies calls for an in-depth coverage in order to do justice to the various perspectives used by those theories.

The result is an extensive coverage in Section 2 and Section 3. To keep track of the progress we make in the analysis, here is an overview of the approach we will follow:

- First, we cover relevant theories from literature, pp. 130-137;
- From there, we will observe those controversies in more detail, p. 137, with a summary, p. 138;
- This will lead to an analysis based on the Model of Motivation, with a number of propositions, pp. 139-146;
- We will proceed to observe research findings in Section 3, pp. 148-150;
- The propositions from Section 2 are then to be used as a reference when observing these findings from research more closely, pp. 150-164;
- We will analyze our findings and come to three important observations, pp. 165-174;
- We come to final conclusions on these observations, pp. 175-176;
- Which then leads to a final summary, p. 177.

*To skip this elaborate coverage,*

- *Proceed to a summary of controversies in theories, p. 138;*
- *Proceed to a concluding overview, as based on the Model, p. 177.*

# 2 Theories

What are the effects of Impact, and which theories to be found in literature describe these effects? And, more importantly (and to be covered in the next Section), are there research findings based on these theories that provide an indication supporting the assumptions that have been made in the Model of Motivation, especially on this Phase of Impact?

There are three important theories that appear to provide support as well as important additional insights into the effects of Impact: further extensions to the dichotomous model in *goal-orientation theories* and elaborations in both *goal-setting theory* and *self-determination theory*.

Recall that in the dichotomous achievement goal model in *goal-orientation theories*, a distinction was made in mastery-oriented goals, and performance-oriented goals (see Chapter 3). Mastery-oriented goals were assumed to produce a positive, adaptive set of processes and outcomes, whereas performance-oriented goals were thought to lead to negative, maladaptive outcomes (Dweck, 1986; Nicholls, 1984).

So, according to the Model and the assumptions made, what happens when you aim for mastery, and what happens when you aim to perform?

The Model of Motivation assumes there is a distinct difference between both goals, or strategies, when Reality enters and affects the Process of Motivation in a Phase of Impact.

According to the Model, aiming at mastery of a competence dramatically reduces the effects of Impact. In defining mastery-oriented goals, one becomes less vulnerable to unforeseen events: "It didn't turn out the way I thought it would, but that doesn't really matter as I had no clear objective in mind; I simply wanted to learn and get acquainted with the subject, and I was certainly not appraising how well I was doing." So, in a sense, one is protected from interference in one's Process of Motivation when using mastery-oriented goals.

When aiming at performance, however, the Model assumes that effects of Impact increase dramatically. In defining performance-oriented goals, the intent is to demonstrate one's competence as related to others. And in this approach, it is either 'win' or 'lose', either reaching what one intends to obtain or failing in this attempt.

As we saw earlier in Chapter 3, it gradually became clear that findings from research on the dichotomous model provided relatively strong support for the positive outcomes of mastery-oriented goals, but that outcomes of performance-oriented goals produced mixed results on those early studies, with either positive or negative or even no clear patterns emerging.

According to the Model of Motivation, these findings can be explained from the dichotomous effects occurring in a Phase of Impact, similar to those previously observed in a Phase of Internally Evoked Self-Assessment. The effects from Impact are less pronounced and intruding when aiming at mastery, but are much more distinct when aiming at performance: one either attains what was intended or not, and perceived Impact from Reality thus either provides support for one's performance or not (resulting in mixed results and a diffuse picture in research findings, producing either positive or negative patterns in the outcomes).

These diverse findings, then, gave rise to an addition to the dichotomous model, presented at the end of the nineties by Andrew Elliot and Judith Harackiewicz (1996). In their so-called '*trichotomous model of achievement goals*', the dichotomous model was extended with a distinction between approach and avoidance in performance-oriented goals.

*See exhibit* ➔

### 3.2. Goal-orientation theories

Initially, in the dichotomous achievement goal model, the mastery- and performance-oriented goals were defined with a positive connotation: they both assumed a striving focusing on success: successful mastery of a competence or successful performance of a competence in relation to others.

These goals where therefore construed as so-called 'approach goals', focusing on success (Ames, 1992a; Nicholls, Patashnick, Cheung, Thorkildsen & Lauer, 1989).

In the trichotomous model of achievement motivation, proposed by Elliot and Harackiewicz (1996), this interpretation was to be further extended with associated tendencies aimed not only at approach, but also at avoidance strategies.

The approach-avoidance motivation concept distinguishes two types of goal pursuit:

- An *approach strategy*, in which one strives to approach (and thus attain) success;
- An *avoidance strategy*, in which one strives to avoid failure.

At first, in the trichotomous model, the distinction between approach and avoidance was only made in performance-oriented goals, leaving mastery-oriented goals unchanged from the dichotomous model.

*(Continued)*

Commenting on this extension, in the trichotomous achievement goal model of the approach and avoidance concepts, years later Elliot stated that they had overlooked this distinction, "(...) with a long and rich history in the achievement motivation literature (...)" (Elliot & Hulleman, 2017, p. 45).

The idea of approach and avoidance appears to be in accord with the Impact and Reality constructs used in the Model of Motivation. It implies an interference occurring, affecting outcomes and resulting effects that can have positive and negative Impact on the Process of Motivation. More prominently than in the dichotomous model, the outcome in terms of success and failure have been incorporated in the trichotomous model; and the resulting effects in terms of approach versus avoidance are articulated. In further extensions to the trichotomous model, the constructs of Reality and Impact will appear even more prominently, as we will observe in Chapter 6.

These further diversifications, in line with the constructs of Reality and its Impact proposed in the Model of Motivation, open an array of refinements and insights as to where Impact leads to. The construct of performance-approach diversifies the notion of a positive Impact from Reality and low perceived Discrepancies; and the construct of performance-avoidance expands on the notion of a negative Impact and high Discrepancy. In addition, and as we shall find in outcomes from

### 3.2. Goal-orientation theories

Thus, in the trichotomous achievement goal model, a distinction is made in:

- *Performance-approach goals,* aimed at demonstrating competence relative to others. These goals are assumed to be positive predictors of some outcomes, but negative predictors of others, depending on the nature of these outcomes;
- *Performance-avoidance goals,* aimed at avoiding demonstrating incompetence relative to others. These goals are expected to give rise to a negative, maladaptive pattern in processes and outcomes;
- *Mastery-oriented goals,* aimed at developing competence and task mastery, as conceptualized in the dichotomous model. And these goals are assumed to produce a positive, adaptive pattern in processes and outcomes.

(Elliot, 1997; Elliot & Church, 1997; Elliot & Harackiewicz, 1996).

Later, the trichotomous model was to be further extended, as covered in Chapter 6.

For further reading on the trichotomous achievement goal model in goal-orientation theories, see: Elliot, 1997, 1999; Elliot & Covington, 2001; Elliot & Harackiewicz, 1996.

*Next related thread 3.3. ➔ p. 194.*

research, these effects from Impact can even change over time, where a performance-approach strategy can lead to unexpected Discrepancy, turning the initial approach strategy into one of avoidance[1].

So according to goal-orientation theories, performance-oriented strategies in some cases are expected to produce positive effects, in turn, further instigating performance-approach strategies in accord with the Model of Motivation. And in other situations, or different moments in time, those strategies are assumed to yield adverse effects when interference produces negative effects which, according to the Model, would lead to performance-avoidance strategies. In contrast, following a mastery-oriented strategy in goal-orientation, the effects from Reality are assumed to be less pronounced, as the intrusion from Reality is perceived to be part of one's objective or attempt at mastering a task or experience, whereas a performance-oriented strategy turns an intruding Reality into a clear-cut experience: one either attains what was intended or not. Where Reality, affecting the outcome, thus provides either support for one's performance or not.

So findings obtained from theorizing along those lines of a trichotomous model produce outcomes that are in accordance with effects proposed in the Model of Motivation, especially occurring in a Phase of Impact. And these findings thus allow for a verification, using results obtained from empirical research in the field of goal-orientation theory, in the next Section.

But there appears to be some tension between those ideas, notably on positive effects of performance-oriented strategies in goal-orientation and observations made in a theory covered earlier, which highlighted the positive effects of self-endorsed motivational processes. Recall from Chapter 3 that in the field of *self-determination theory*, a central hypothesis was that more autonomous forms of motivation were to lead to enhancement of engagement, learning and wellness (Ryan & Deci, 2020). External interventions could impede this need for autonomy and thereby affect motivation, conceptualized as 'intrinsic motivation'. We will explicitly address these differences when observing research findings, where these conflicting views and findings have been prominently covered in literature.

In addition, however, and underlining the importance of a supportive Reality, is a construct introduced in self-determination theory as *'relatedness'*.

[1] It is to be noted that in observing and relating goal-orientation theories to the Model of Motivation, a difference is made between the construct of a *Goal*, and the construct of *goal-orientation*. The Goal construct refers to an isolated occurrence, object, event or state, whereas goal-orientation reflects a preferred pattern, a general tendency, or strategy the individual tends to follow. Most unfortunately, much of the empirical research has not made this differentiation explicit, or even considered it to be relevant (Niemivirta, Pulkka, Tapola & Tuominen, 2019). To clearly differentiate between both constructs, when making comparisons with the Model of Motivation we are to refer to the construct of goal-orientation as *goal-orientation strategies*.

The people surrounding us, are highly important in providing the necessary conditions for growth and well-being.

In self-determination theory, the construct of relatedness refers to an essential need to feel connected to others, which extends not only to individuals but also to one's community. It concerns the need to form a secure connection or unity with those we are close with.

*See exhibit* ➔

So, the need for relatedness is not instrumental. As stated by Ryan and Deci, it is "(...) not concerned with the attainment of a certain outcome (e.g., sex) or a formal status (e.g., becoming a spouse, or a group member), but instead concerns the psychological sense of being with others in secure communion or unity" (Ryan & Deci, 2002, p. 7).

But relatedness has two sides. If we have a basic need to feel cared for by others, we are most likely to have a need to provide care to those others in return. This reciprocity is an essential element in defining relatedness[1].

[1] There has been confusion on the construct of relatedness, suggesting it is implicitly contradictory to the need for autonomy. The confusion, however, stems from misinterpreting autonomy with independence (see exhibit Chapter 3).

### 4.2. Self-determination theory

In self-determination theory, three basic psychological needs must be satisfied for psychological interest, development, and wellness to be sustained: *autonomy, relatedness* and *competence* (Deci & Ryan, 1985; Ryan & Deci, 2000, 2018, 2020).

*Relatedness* is defined as the need to experience a sense of belongingness with others.

And as such: "Relatedness (...) concerns feeling socially connected. People feel relatedness most typically when they feel cared for by others. Yet relatedness is also about belonging and feeling significant among others. Thus equally important to relatedness is experiencing oneself as giving or contributing to others (...)" (Ryan & Deci, 2018, p. 11).

"(...) Relatedness concerns a sense of belonging and connection. It is facilitated by conveyance of respect and caring" (Ryan & Deci, 2020, p. 2).

More on the construct of relatedness: Ryan & Deci, 2018 (notably Chapter 7 and Chapter 12).

*Next related thread 4.3.* ➔ *p. 208.*

A third theory from literature that relates to a Phase of Impact is *goal-setting theory*, that has been a prominent and leading theory in work motivation, as commented on previously in Chapter 2 (Kanfer, Frese & Johnson, 2017; Mitchell & Daniels, 2003).

Recall that goal-setting theory states that there is a positive relationship between a specific 'high' goal and task performance: the 'higher', or more difficult the goal, and the more specific in its formulation, the better the outcome, in terms of task performance. And this applies, as we observed, to self-set goals, to assigned goals, and goals that are set participatively. In Chapter 2, we covered self-set goals; now, with the introduction of Reality and its Impact on the Process of Motivation, we will address assigned goals, while participative goals are to be covered elsewhere[1].

*See exhibit* ➔

Locke had written his doctoral dissertation on effects of intentions (Locke, 1964), which led to the first propositions that were to lead to the development of goal-setting theory in 1990. Latham had been doing research

[1] The issue of participative goals has been addressed in a remarkable collaboration following divergent findings obtained by Erez and her colleagues. The article (Latham, Erez & Locke, 1988) was given an award from the Academy of Management as it was the first published paper based on a joint collaboration of antagonists (Latham, 2007). It will be covered later in the 'Series on Motivation' when addressing a Process of Interference.

### 2.2. Goal-setting theories

Referring to Chapter 2, in assigned or participative goals, "the focus of goal-setting theory is on the core properties of an effective goal" (Locke & Latham, 2002, p. 714).

In summary, main findings are:

- The 'higher' (or more difficult) the goal,
- ... and the more specific (or precise) it is formulated,
- ... the better the task performance.

A number of *moderators* (or boundary conditions) regulate this outcome:

- *Ability:* the individual must have ability (knowledge, skills) to attain a goal; ability moderates the strength of the positive relation between goal difficulty and performance: the more one feels confident about one's abilities, the higher the performance;
- *Commitment:* commitment refers to the importance or centrality that the individual places on obtaining a goal; the more committed, the higher the outcome;
- *Feedback:* feedback enables the individual to track progress towards a goal;
- *Complexity:* the more straightforward the task, the higher the performance;
- *Situational variables:* the presence of needed resources, or unfavorable constraints regulate attainment of an assigned goal.

*(Continued)*

for his thesis to identify behaviors that differentiate effective from ineffective teams, when in 1969 he came to read a first article from Locke. Locke and Latham independently discovered the importance of what they defined as 'goal-setting' for significantly improving performance of both individuals and teams within a work setting. The two first met in 1974 at the annual meeting of the American Psychological Association (See: Latham, 2007; Locke & Latham, 2019). As organizational psychologists, they focused on productivity, hence on the essential determinants between goal-setting and performance. And the first issue they addressed was the relationship of goal difficulty to performance.

They gradually extended their findings to include goal specificity and a range of related so-called 'moderators' and 'mediators'. As they recently commented: "We did not begin our research with theory building in mind. (...) We were acutely aware of the dangers of premature theorizing (...)" (Locke & Latham, 2019, p. 97)[1].

*See exhibit* ➔

[1] Based on goal-setting theory, Latham and Locke developed a model providing a framework for understanding motivation in the workplace, referred to as the 'high performance cycle', or HPC (Latham, 2007; Latham, Locke & Fassina, 2002; Locke & Latham 1990). As the HPC is meant to provide a basis for interventions in the workplace, it will be covered later in the 'Series on Motivation', when observing a Process of Interference.

## 2.2. Goal-setting theories

Thus, ability, commitment, feedback, complexity and situational variables moderate the strength of the positive linear relationship between goal difficulty and performance.

In addition, *mediators* (or causal mechanisms) explain the relationship between goal specificity, goal difficulty and performance:

- *Choice* or *direction:* a specific goal affects choice and focuses one's attention; goal clarity increases intensity and attainment;
- *Effort:* goal difficulty affects effort; the more difficult a goal, the more effort is invested;
- *Persistence:* goal difficulty affects persistence;
- *Strategies:* a difficult goal cues the recall of certain strategies.

Thus, a goal may affect choice, effort, persistence and strategies, but one will not be able to attain the goal unless ability and commitment are present and adequate provisions are made for feedback and addressing complexity and situational variables.

For further reading: Latham, 2012; Latham & Locke, 1991, 2007; Locke, 1968, 1991; Locke & Latham, 1990, 2002, 2013, 2019. For overviews of goal-setting literature: Locke, 2000; Locke & Latham, 1990, 2005; Locke, Shaw, Saari & Latham, 1981. For an historical overview: Latham, 2007; Locke & Latham, 2019.

So, to summarize these theories that appear to have a relation with a Phase of Impact as proposed in the Model of Motivation, *goal-orientation theories* diversify in various strategies where external input from Reality can have various effects depending on Impact according to the Model. *Self-determination theory* posits that these external influences have detrimental effects on (intrinsic) motivation as they are perceived to be mostly controlling, and appear to only have positive effects when aimed at support of a basic need of autonomy. Whereas *goal-setting theory* claims that the more precise and challenging (assigned) goals are defined, the higher the effects in terms of performance and productivity.

Now these conclusions are in contradiction with each other, at least in part. And in our exposé of theories, we appear to have uncovered a serious controversy, which has led to what has been referred to as one of the most heated debates in the applied psychology literature (Cerasoli, Nicklin & Ford, 2014; See also Latham, 2007, notably Chapter 5; Sansone & Harackiewicz, 2000a, 2000b).

In summary, here are the essentials:

- If, according to *self-determination theory,*
  - (intrinsic) motivation is to boost performance,
  - ... and external incentives and rewards are claimed to have a deteriorating effect on (intrinsic) motivation,
- ... how can *goal-orientation theories* claim that performance-oriented approach strategies appear to have positive effects on performance,
- ... and (most importantly), how can *goal-setting theory* claim that the more precise and challenging we provide an (external) goal, or target, the higher these positive effects on performance appear to be?

And to add to the confusion, we will come to find that an overwhelming amount of research studies in all three areas claim to confirm these seemingly contradictory statements.

So, let us analyze these differing ideas on effects of external influences, and observe if the Model of Motivation can provide an indication of where these differences originate from (and, as such, seek an indirect theoretical validation for the assumptions made in the Model on the Process of Motivation).

To assist us in our attempts at clarifying these divergent theories we will use a number of essential distinctions made so far in observing the Process of Motivation:

1. We will observe the distinction between a Process of Motivation and a Process of Interference.

In one of the most controversial issues in literature on motivation, three major theories appear to have divergent views on the effects of external interference:

- Where, according to *self-determination theory,*
  - (intrinsic) motivation is to boost performance,
  - and external rewards and incentives are claimed to have a deteriorating effect on (intrinsic) motivation,
- *Goal-orientation theories* claim that performance-oriented approach strategies appear to have positive effects on performance,
- and (most importantly), *goal-setting theory* claims that the more precise and challenging an (external) goal, or target, the higher these positive effects on performance appear to be.

*A conclusion on outcomes of these divergent views is provided on pp. 175-176.*
*A summary is provided p. 177.*

2. In doing so, we will observe differing effects of self-set versus assigned goals, following previous observations made in Chapter 2. In observing effects of Impact, emphasis will be laid on assigned goals.
3. In doing so, we will observe the differing effects of Significance in both the Goals and perceived Reality, versus Impact.
4. Finally, in doing so, and to simplify the analysis, we will use options 2 and 4 from the various possible combinations we observed earlier, pp. 123-124, where effects are most likely to happen when interference occurs in the Process of Motivation. To further clarify, we will make use of the examples provided pp. 127-128, at the end of our analysis.

In the analysis, we will start by observing goal-setting theory and further differentiate in goal-orientation theory and self-determination theory.

To enable a verification of the various propositions suggested as based on the Model of Motivation, a summary is provided in the form of annotated propositions that will be used as a reference when observing findings from research in literature in Section 3. Where self-set goals have been covered previously in Chapter 2, numbering is restricted to cover assigned goals only.

An overview of the analysis, then, is provided in following pages.

*See exhibits next pages* ➔

*Controversies between theories*

## Self-set Goals

*1. Self-set goals in goal-setting theory*

As observed in Chapter 2, self-set Goals that are clear, well-defined and challenging have a long history in their making. They 'survived' the cyclical Process in Phases 1, 2 and 3 with such success that one has gained confidence and courage to have those Goals adjusted and attuned to precision, and made to reflect the cyclical experience one has previously obtained. We have seen the threats in defining Goals with such precision. Recall from Chapter 2 that Goals that are precise have the advantage to further emphasize one's Satisfaction in cases of Achievement, but when one fails, one fails miserably. According to the Model of Motivation, self-set Goals that are clear and precise and challenging do not in themselves provide the necessary impetus that leads to behavior, or performance, or productivity. They do not appear to have such 'inherent propellant' properties. They rather reflect those previously successful strategies and outcomes. And maintaining those Goals in accuracy can serve as a beacon to acknowledge and confirm these outcomes through subsequent action.

*2. Self-set goals in goal-orientation theories*

Likewise, performance-oriented strategies reflect experience and successful outcomes in goals that are self-set. As such, and according to the Model, they are not assumed to have 'inherent propellant' properties, but rather to reflect a history of successful previous experiences in goal attainment within a particular setting, pertaining to a particular subject.

*3. Self-set goals in self-determination theory*

From the perspective of self-determination theory, self-set goals by their nature have the potential to serve a basic need for autonomy as covered in Chapter 3. Likewise, when these self-set goals appear to be well-defined, they reflect a history of previous successful outcomes which, in turn, are likely to produce Effort in order to sustain and have the gratifying output that is expected to result from these investments. Conversely, when less clear, they are likely to be associated with less pronounced Effort, and thus yield less performance and less productive outcomes.

*In short, then, well-defined self-set goals do not instigate Effort or performance, or productivity. According to the Model of Motivation, they are rather the resultant of adjustments and strategies that favor such precision to consolidate and confirm previous experiences that have led to these results. As such, these precision-driven self-set goals appear to be a resultant, rather than a cause.*

*Controversies between theories*

## Assigned Goals

*1. Assigned goals in goal-setting theory*

The story becomes more complex when goals are assigned externally. As stated, we are to cover the essentials of externally induced Processes of Interference later in this 'Series on Motivation'. Rather, let us analyze effects that occur from external interference on the Process of Motivation, by elaborating on the observations made so far in the Model as we progressed through its Phases. From this perspective, the perception of Reality and its Impact *always* reflect on the Goals one has set. Within the context of work motivation, which has been the main focus in goal-setting theory, these assigned goals (by definition) are *not* goals defined by the individual, but rather serve as indicators in attaining those personal goals. When one's objective is to be successful in one's job, or to retain one's position or obtain promotion, gratuities, bonuses or dividends, they provide indication of the extent to which these objectives are within reach or have been obtained. *Assigned goals, according to the Model of Motivation, are not defined as Goals but represent Reality in various forms*. And the better and more precise Reality is defined, the better it serves as a guide to reach the Goal or Goals one has set in relation to one's work environment. The better those cues provided through Reality serve in guiding towards these objectives, the higher the Effort invested, the higher one's productivity, and the better one's performance.

So, from this perspective, goals that are specific and challenging are likely to relate to high performance and productivity as suggested in goal-setting theory. But the goal construct in goal-setting theory is different from the construct used in the Model: those are the goals of the company's manager or management. Those (externally defined) assigned goals serve as targets, as indicators, to guide the personal Goal or Goals as defined by the individual or employee. So within a work setting, these 'assigned goals' from management are likely to assist and improve those work-related personal Goals, resulting in increased Effort, better performance and higher productivity.

Now suppose, alternatively, that these personal Goals and Reality diverge, and these guiding properties appear as Discrepant. Then two options emerge.

The first option is the most obvious. The imposed Reality is Discrepant with the personal Goal of being successful, or retaining one's position, or obtaining rewards in various forms. If Discrepancy persists or increases with those personal Goals, in such a work-related setting, one is likely to leave.

*(Continued)*

And by doing so, a remaining 'pool of employees' is likely to reflect, through this self-selective process, a population of employees with personal Goals that tend to be more or less aligned to those of the company or institution. (Which, in turn, to a certain degree may reflect positively on data obtained from research within these settings.)

A second option is that an apparent Discrepancy is perceived as an indication of perceived potential, thus leading to a reformulation of one's Goals: "These folks with their targets seem convinced of my potential and abilities to reach those targets, and I'll show them in due course."

In sum, then, within particular settings such as a work environment, a perceived Reality that is 'specific' and 'challenging' (conceptualized as a 'goal' in goal-setting theory), is likely to create an optimal opportunity to perform according to one's personal objectives. In case of Discrepancy, one either leaves, or re-defines a perceived Reality to coincide and align with those personal objectives.

*So, according to the Model of Motivation a first proposition would summarize the effects of goal-setting theory as follows: Assigned goals, expressed as Reality according to the Model, do provide, when clearly defined, an important indication against which an assessment of personal Goal attainment can be made, especially within a work setting, thus serving as an important incentive for sustaining or increasing Effort, that is likely to be reflected in concepts of 'increased motivation', 'productivity', 'performance', as referred to in literature.*

*2. Assigned goals in goal-orientation theories*

Recall that in goal-orientation theories, at first, performance-oriented goals (which are often externally induced and oriented in their aim at displaying ability and competence relative to others), appeared to produce a mixed picture in effects on performance. However, when later a distinction between constructs of approach and avoidance was made, the findings for approach-oriented strategies in performance-oriented goals, appeared to confirm the assumptions made in goal-setting theory. If we are to follow a performance-approach strategy, which reflects as we saw, a history that shaped our confidence to have personal Goals well-defined and delineated, these clearly defined externally oriented Goals serve a purpose: when confronted with an acknowledging Reality that suits our performance-oriented ambitions, these 'assigned goals' serve as a beacon against which we gradually shape our personal Goals. And when both are perceived to be Significant, those effects, according to the Model of

*(Continued)*

Motivation, are likely to intensify.

The story changes, however, when these external sources appear Discrepant to our ambitions, which leaves us to either change or adapt our Goals to align with this Reality, or develop mechanisms to deal with this intrusion. The repercussions of which are far-reaching as we shall see in coming Chapters, notably, Chapter 10 and Chapter 11.

*So, following the Model of Motivation, two subsequent propositions are to be made: Assigned goals, defined as Reality according to the Model, are assumed to produce mixed effects in performance-oriented strategies:*

- *When perceived Discrepancy* 2 *is low, Reality is assumed to acknowledge performance-oriented ambitions, serving as a beacon against which these personal Goals are shaped and leading to approach-oriented strategies. However, these strategies are susceptible to change depending on experiences with an interfering Reality.*
- *High perceived Discrepancy* 3 *is assumed to have important detrimental effects leading to avoidance-oriented strategies. These effects are further increased when situational circumstances such as educational settings prevent withdrawal.*

So, performance-oriented strategies in goal-orientation theories can have positive effects as expressed in approach-oriented strategies, but may diverge from assumptions made in goal-setting theory, when avoidance-oriented strategies are chosen.

In addition to the effects occurring in performance-oriented strategies, other assumptions made in goal-orientation theories also appear to deviate from those made in goal-setting theory. According to goal-orientation theories, it is assumed that mastery-oriented strategies lead to high results in achievement and performance, where external influences only play a marginal role. We already covered the positive effects of mastery-oriented strategies. Aiming at mastery, one becomes less vulnerable to unforeseen or Discrepant effects from Reality, as the intrusion from Reality is perceived to be part of one's objective to master a task or experience. And even when Discrepancy is perceived to be high, the effects of Impact are assumed to remain limited on the same grounds.

*(Continued)*

But there is a problem, however. Which appears to have important implications within a learning environment, or when we are to arouse curiosity and interest to explore our surroundings...

As we saw, the external Reality (which provides the criteria against which we assess our actions) may become important, thus Significant in the Process of reaching our Goal. For once we obtain a confirmation from this external source, it reaffirms the Goal we have set. And as such, *it also becomes a source of acknowledgment we gradually and persistently tend to seek.* These goal-oriented strategies can therefore generate a gradual 'external standardization' of criteria, whereby we assess the success of our Goal attainment. And thus, by seeking this (Significant) approval, we gradually turn towards an external Reality.

The unintended effect, then, especially when goal-oriented strategies are predominantly mastery-oriented, is that we tend to gradually 'externalize' our standards. When Discrepancy is small, the effects of this 'external standardization' are marginal, and, as observed, serve to acknowledge the strategy that is followed. However, the external input can become distracting and can divert us from an inquisitive course of action (aimed at mastery), to an approval-seeking (thus performance-oriented) strategy. The effects are not as pronounced as in performance-oriented strategies. But they are there, nonetheless...

*In short, externally assigned goals can become detrimental for the wonderful inherent properties associated with curiosity, interest and information seeking. Now, these effects are usually less prominent when limited within the settings of one's work. But the repercussions are different within a learning environment, or when the intentions are to develop curiosity and explore our surroundings.*

*In summarizing, then, two additional propositions can be made pertaining to goal-orientation theories. Assigned goals, defined as Reality according to the Model, are assumed to provide limited effects in mastery-oriented strategies:*

- *Where perceived Discrepancy* 4 *plays only a limited role, as Impact from Reality is perceived to be part of one's objective to master a task or experience.*
- *However, especially in cases* 5 *where perceived Discrepancy is low, there appears to be a potential risk to actively seek an acknowledging external*

*(Continued)*

*Reality, whereby a shift can occur towards a gradual 'external standardization' of criteria, thereby decreasing mastery-oriented strategies, which can subsequently erode curiosity to seek other challenges in other areas of performance, and interest for novelty situations.*

*3. Assigned goals in self-determination theory*
According to the Model of Motivation, assigned goals represent Reality, and as such, *always* interfere with the initial Phases that have led to the design and fine-tuning of a Goal one tries to reach. And the Impact can be perceived as having high, or low Discrepancy with the Process aimed at reaching one's objective. Where self-determination theory defines autonomy as a most important need, which was seen to prevail within the first Phases of the Model (as commented on in Chapter 3), it follows that interference from Reality in the form of externally assigned goals is always expected to obstruct to a certain extent this need for autonomy. And we will come to observe mechanisms that will anticipate on this intrusion in next Chapters.

These effects of interference, however, cover a wide range which coincides largely with observations made in the Model.

When Discrepancy is perceived to be small, effects are expected to be positive, as the Impact from Reality is perceived to be supportive. And when Discrepancy is perceived to be large, effects of Impact increase to become detrimental.

However, as we observed in goal-orientation theories, the Impact from Reality can change those effects in an unexpected direction, which has been profoundly researched in self-determination theory: *when the Impact from Reality takes on the form of an incentive (promised prior to a task or action) or reward (given after the task or action has occurred).*

As we observed, Reality in the form of assigned goals is commonly experienced as interfering to a certain degree with one's personal Goal. According to self-determination theory, the external interference is captured in the concept of external regulation and control. As such, when interference through external regulation occurs, *the acceptance of an external incentive or reward also implies that one accepts to engage in an interaction and in its implications for attaining one's personal Goal. According to the Model, by accepting an interfering Reality in the form of an incentive or reward, its effects or its Impact thus become part of the Process of Motivation in attaining or maintaining one's Goal. As such, it is most likely to become important, or Significant.*

*(Continued)*

When such a Significant Reality is perceived to have low Discrepancy, it is found to acknowledge one's attempts at reaching the Goal that has been set. As a result, and in accordance with the observations made on 'external standardization' in goal-orientation, this positive Impact is most likely to affect the Process of Motivation in such a way that one seeks to maintain its positive effects on the Process. This implies, then, that incentives or rewards, by their nature, are most likely to generate profound effects, *as amendments need to be made, in order to maintain the positive Impact one has sought by engaging and accepting those incentives or rewards. And in doing so, one gradually aligns with and incorporates those external standards.*

Effects largely coincide, then, with those observed in goal-orientation and the assumed effects of an 'external standardization'. However, as the effects of incentives and rewards, by their nature, are assumed to inflate Impact, these effects are to be referred to as an 'external adaptation', to reflect the difference, although subtle, between both expressions of Impact.

So, when Reality takes on the form of an incentive or reward, its effects on the Process of Motivation are assumed to inflate and to further increase Impact.

*To summarize, then, three final propositions emerge that are assumed to occur in the Process of Motivation according to the Model, and that appear to confirm assumptions made in self-determination theory. Assigned goals, defined as Reality according to the Model, that take on the form of external incentives or rewards, are likely to affect the Process of Motivation aimed at attaining or maintaining a personal Goal:*

6

- *When perceived Discrepancy is low, Reality is assumed to be supportive, and thus to lead to positive effects on Motivation.*

7

- *When perceived Discrepancy is high, these effects of Reality are perceived to be negative, and Impact can become detrimental.*

8

- *However, especially when perceived Discrepancy is low, there appears to be a potential risk in using incentives and rewards, as they tend to lead, by their nature, to an 'external adaptation' towards Reality, thereby affecting the integrity of a personal Goal.*

So, within each theory that has been observed, a clarification can be made for the seemingly divergent or even conflicting assumptions that have been made. An assigned goal works fine within the settings proposed in goal-setting theory. And these findings do not contradict assumptions made in goal-orientation, which focuses on different underlying constructs as proposed in the Model of Motivation. And although self-determination theory appears to contradict parts of the assumptions made, especially in goal-setting theory, the propositions based on the Model of Motivation provide a first insight into a potential clarification of divergent views.

Based on a number of essential restrictive assumptions, then, the Model of Motivation provides an alternative view which appears to reconcile the divergent ideas between the three observed theories.

Essential in the analysis has been the distinction between a Process of Motivation and a Process of Interference, leading to a different perspective on the goal construct between self-set and assigned goals, and the differing effects they produce. Furthermore, the distinction provides an understanding of the differences in perspectives between the individual and an external actor or group of actors, or circumstances, and the contrast in perceptions of effects they might cause. In addition, it appears that making a distinction in a Phase of Impact between Goal and Reality, regulated by their respective perceived Significances and affected by perceived Discrepancy between both constructs, enables, at least to some degree, a reconciliation between the differing views observed between goal-setting theory at one end of the spectrum and goal-orientation theories adjacent to self-determination theory at the other.

It now remains to be seen what outcomes of research have generated to further add to these insights.

We will first observe general outcomes as they have appeared in literature in these three areas of study, before proceeding to verifying the propositions that have been put forward in our analysis using the Model of Motivation.

Preceding an overview of research findings in Section 3, are some thoughts articulated as further observations to be included in due course to the conclusions we will make at the end of the Section.

*See exhibit next page* ➔

## *Afterthoughts on Controversies in a Phase of Impact*

We have made attempts to reconcile differences in theories that have a relation to a Phase of Impact, where there appears, at best, to be only limited consensus on how to motivate people and have them thrive in what they do.

In various comments, allusion was made to the distinct difference between defining a course, or *strategy*, on how to proceed as an individual in a Process of Motivation aiming at a Goal one seeks to achieve, and managing, as an external actor, the instrumental *techniques* to direct or persuade an individual to follow a course of action, through what was called a Process of Interference.

In addition to this essential distinction, there is also a diversity in Goals set that are perceived to be Significant, and in perceptions that are made of an intruding Reality. From this perspective it appears to be 'too easy' to suggest that context or situational factors make the difference. It doesn't do justice to the subject of our studies, which we may refer to as 'the human condition': how people act in the diversity of circumstances they are confronted with, and the complexities involved in the act of will to intervene within these settings.

To help us clarify our point, let us quote the memorable and eloquent description by Allen Shawn of 'the human condition', and what is needed to sustain its sense of purpose: "A species in which everyone was General Patton would not succeed, any more than would a race in which everyone was Vincent van Gogh. I prefer to think that the planet needs athletes, philosophers, sex symbols, painters, scientists, it needs the warmhearted, the hardhearted, the coldhearted, and the weakhearted. (...) It needs those who can capture the passing impression of cherry blossoms in a fourteen-syllable poem or devote twenty-five pages to the dissection of a small boy's feelings as he lies in bed in the dark waiting for his mother to kiss him goodnight. It needs people who can design air conditioners, and it needs people who can inspire joy" (Allen Shawn, 2007, from: *Wish I Could Be There - Notes from a Phobic Life,* pp. 249-250).

What is needed, then, to have people thrive within these settings, and seen from these differing perspectives?

If these verses capture the essence of the human condition, one could refer to the complexities involved in researching motivation by stating that the subject of our study is not simply to motivate by using a standardized approach or an algorithm. In due course, when we are to observe a Process of Interference, we will have to include and define techniques whereby *distinct personal* objectives (as expressed in designing the best air conditioners, or at inspiring joy), are adequately addressed to their full potential...

# 3 Research

We are to observe, then, the three main areas of research that were associated with a Phase of Impact: *goal-orientation theories*, *goal-setting theory* and *self-determination theory*.

First, in *goal-orientation theories,* we observed a number of assumptions that could be related to observations made according to the Model of Motivation.

One either attains what was intended or not. Consequently, as suggested from the Model, the Impact from Reality is assumed to be much more pronounced in performance-oriented, than in mastery-oriented goal pursuits. One either 'wins' (where Reality provides support for one's performance, with a positive Impact) or 'loses' (where outcomes provide non-support or less support, resulting in negative Impact) or, alternatively, 'avoids' effects of Impact by defining less-conspicuous mastery-oriented goals. A resulting tendency confirming these assumptions, would suggest negative outcomes following performance-avoidance goals, as related to negative Impact, and positive outcomes following performance-approach goals, as related to positive Impact.

Findings that have appeared in literature from research on the *trichotomous model of achievement goals* according to goal-orientation theory have affirmed these assumptions. As we shall see when covering findings in more detail shortly, the effects of Impact provided a distinctly different pattern in both sets of data. Research confirmed the earlier findings that performance-approach strategies tend to have a positive effect on effort and graded performance (for overviews, see: Elliot, 1999; Elliot & Hulleman, 2017; Kaplan & Maehr, 2007; Linnenbrink, 2005; Midgley Kaplan & Middleton, 2001), but appeared to be negatively related to well-being (Kaplan & Maehr, 1999), anxiety, emotional exhaustion and stress (Tuominen-Soini, Salmela-Aro & Niemivirta, 2008, 2011, 2012). Performance-avoidance could be linked to a wide array of negative processes and maladaptive adjustments (Elliot & Hulleman, 2017), extending from anxiety and stress (Tuominen-Soini, Salmela-Aro & Niemivirta, 2008, 2011) to depression (Sideridis, 2005). In contrast, mastery-oriented strategies, especially in expressions of approach strategies, could be positively associated with a range of indices related to well-being in general (Kaplan & Maehr, 1999), effort, persistence and interest in particular (Linnenbrink, 2005)[1].

[1] More recently, as we shall observe in more detail when covering findings from research in Chapter 6, research has focused on a further diversification of mastery-oriented strategies, and has further progressed in observing combinations of these different strategies.

However, as indicated, these findings appeared to be at least partly contradicted by the large body of research produced in the field of *goal-setting theory*. Let us first have an overview of principal findings, and from there proceed to observe the validity of the propositions made based on the Model of Motivation.

As we saw, research on goal-setting theory has dominated the field of work motivation (Kanfer, Frese & Johnson, 2017; Miner, 2003; Mitchell & Daniels, 2003; Pinder, 1998). In 1990, findings from over 400 studies indicated that "(...) the most effective goals for increasing performance are those that are specific and difficult" (Locke & Latham, 2019, p. 97), and set within attainable boundaries[1]. It generated a further avalanche of subsequent studies, which brought Latham to summarize their achievements in 2007: "By the close of the $20^{th}$ century, research had shown that setting specific difficult goals increases performance on over 100 different tasks, involving more than 40.000 participants in at least eight countries (Locke & Latham, 1990, 2002)" (Latham, 2007, p. 63).

And these findings obtained from research on goal-setting theory, in turn, appear to further deviate from findings previously observed in *self-determination theory*. The controversies arose mainly around findings obtained from research on effects that are captured in self-determination theory in constructs of intrinsic and extrinsic motivation, and will be addressed in more detail when we are to observe the divergent findings between the three major theories.

First, however, let us summarize findings obtained from research on the construct of relatedness, one of three needs that are essential to self-determination theory.

The need for relatedness has been less studied in research than needs of competence and especially autonomy in self-determination theory (Vallerand, Pelletier & Koestner, 2008). In summarizing the effects of interpersonal context, Ryan and Deci stated: "Illustrative field studies in education, parenting, and management showed that the quality of the interpersonal climate or ambience can be related directly to the intrinsic motivation of people within it" (Ryan & Deci, 2018, p. 165). In addition, a set of studies on personal relationships by Patrick, Knee, Canevello and Lonsbary (2007) revealed that satisfaction of the need for relatedness tended to be the strongest predictor of well-being and commitment to the relationship and to effective resolution of relationship conflicts. However, and most essential to self-determination theory, it is in the combination with an

[1] As stated earlier in Chapter 2, these 'high' and 'specific' goals need to be attainable and not beyond reach. To quote Locke and Latham, as they refer to appendices in their 1990 article: "Often overlooked by subsequent researchers are our Appendixes C and D (...), which present guidelines for conducting laboratory and field experiments. (...) In field settings, impossible-to-attain goals can lead to demoralization and punishment. In organizations, goals should be challenging yet attainable" (Locke & Latham, 2019, pp. 97-98).

environment that is perceived as being autonomy supportive that these effects appear to take their full potential. Where parents provided autonomy support and interpersonal involvement (together with optimal structure), children displayed more intrinsic motivation, enhanced performance and well-being (Ryan, Deci & Grolnick, 1995) and more exploratory behavior (Frodi, Bridges & Grolnick, 1985). As stated by Ryan and Deci: "When the climate is informational or autonomy-supportive, people's intrinsic motivation tends to be higher; when the interpersonal climate is controlling, intrinsic motivation tends to be lower" (Ryan & Deci, 2018, p. 165).

So, Reality appears to be essential, but once it interferes and perceptions of autonomy are thwarted its effects on motivation deteriorate. And these findings from research in self-determination theory appear to be in disagreement with findings obtained in goal-orientation theories, notably in effects related to performance-approach strategies, and seem to even contradict those obtained from research on goal-setting theory.

Previously, in Section 2, a number of assumptions were made that were based on the Model of Motivation, to reconcile these diverse outcomes from research in the three areas of study. In Section 2, a summarizing overview of these differences was presented, accompanied by an explanatory overview to provide an indication of where these differences came from. The overview led to a series of propositions made according to the Model. And these propositions were intended to help us find, in due course, whether outcomes obtained from research were to confirm these assumptions, thus adding to the reliability of our attempts at clarifying these opposed views.

So, now is the time to verify and compare those propositions more in detail to findings obtained from literature.

In the overview, the comparison is preceded by a brief summary of each proposition in a separate exhibit, as it has previously been formulated in Section 2. To structure the overview, the numbering used in Section 2 for each proposition, is used as a reference.

A reminder that a number of important prior observations were made.

As referred to earlier, it must be noted that in the overview of findings, the emphasis lies on the perspective of a Process of Motivation, whereas a vast majority of research has been focusing on what was defined as a Process of Interference. Therefore, in the interpretation of results, a cautionary reserve must be made. Moreover, in observing findings, the context and constructs used in the various research approaches may differ slightly from those used in the Model of Motivation. In addition, the propositions are considered for the three theories, within the context of *assigned goals*. As stated, we already observed effects from self-set goals, as they relate to the Model of Motivation, in Chapter 2. Finally, the observations are made on differing effects of high perceived Significance in both the Goals and perceived Reality, versus Impact.

First, then, propositions 1 is observed, related to *goal-setting theory.*

1

*Assigned goals in goal-setting theory*
Assigned goals, expressed as Reality according to the Model, do provide, when clearly defined, an important indication against which an assessment of personal Goal attainment can be made, especially within a work setting, thus serving as an important incentive for sustaining or increasing Effort that is likely to be reflected in concepts of increased motivation, productivity and performance.

Referring to proposition 1, it has already been observed that an overwhelming amount of studies provided support for the assumption that assigned goals, when clearly defined and challenging, provide an important indication against which an assessment of personal Goal attainment can be made, that may serve as an incentive for sustaining or increasing Effort.

As mentioned, goal-setting theory focuses primarily on motivation in work settings (Locke & Latham, 2002)[1]. If one's personal Goal is to become successful in one's work (which is highly likely within a work environment), all cues that are provided on how to enable reaching such a Goal become essential and Significant. Those cues have been conceptualized as Reality, according to the Model of Motivation. If these cues are well articulated as clear and exciting indicators, then, according to the Model, it is highly likely to assume that the more precise and challenging those indicators are, the more informative and appealing Reality becomes, serving as a benchmark and reference in attaining those personal Goals.

In research on goal-setting theory, findings have repeatedly demonstrated a positive relation between clearly defined and challenging (assigned) goals (or

[1] Although goal-setting theory has focused primarily on work motivation, it has not been limited to work settings, and research has expanded recently in areas ranging from sports and physical activity (Jeong, Healy & McEwan, 2021; Swann, Rosenbaum, Lawrence, Vella, McEwan & Ekkekakis, 2021), to leadership development (Kaufman, Israel & Rudd, 2008), to name but a few...

'specific high goals', as they have been referred to in goal-setting theory) and increased motivation (for an overview: Locke, Shaw, Saari & Latham, 1981), productivity (for an overview: Locke & Latham, 1984), or performance on a task (for overviews: Latham, 2007; Latham & Locke, 1975; Locke, 1968; Locke & Latham, 1990, 2002). Simply urging to 'do one's best' provides insufficient cues, and consequently leads to lower performance in comparison to these 'specific, high goals' (Locke & Latham, 1990, for an overview: Locke & Latham, 2002). In line with these findings, is that progress towards these 'specific, high goals' needs to be adequately communicated: the combination of goals and summary feedback is more effective than setting goals alone (Bandura & Cervone, 1983; Erez, 1977; Strang, Lawrence & Fowler, 1978).

A range of associated findings have been reported[1]:

- *Satisfaction:* the more precise the cues, the more likely it becomes to successfully reach one's personal Goals; and when those Goals are challenging, those cues also increase to reach those Goals, leading to greater satisfaction. The Effort pays off and results in satisfaction[2]. Hence, the more precise and challenging those cues, or 'goals', as they have been defined in goal-setting theory, the higher one's satisfaction when those are attained (Judge, Thoresen, Bono & Patton, 2001; Mento, Locke & Klein, 1992; Wiese & Freund, 2005), which in turn leads to higher commitment (Cooper-Hakim & Viswesvaran, 2005; Latham & Locke, 2007; Mathieu & Hamel, 1989; Mathieu & Zajac, 1990).
- *Commitment:* the more successful one becomes in reaching one's personal Goal, the more important the cues become that enable this success, and consequently the more dedicated one becomes towards reaching those targets. Hence, the more precise and challenging those 'goals', as defined in goal-setting theory, the more committed one becomes (Locke, 1968; Klein, Wesson, Hollenbeck & Alge, 1999), which in turn leads to higher performance (Allscheid & Cellar, 1996; Cooper-Hakim & Viswesvaran, 2005; Seijts & Latham, 2001).

[1] It is to be noted that a majority of references used have only reported (or performed) meta-analyses based on correlates, which do not provide causal direction. The inferences that are made on assumed causal directions are therefore to be observed with caution and are meant to be hypothetical.

[2] As commented on by Locke and Latham: "(...) high satisfaction is the result, not the cause, of high performance when rewards are commensurate with performance" (2002, p. 712). Which incidentally addresses an important issue in work motivation where no direct connection has been found between job satisfaction and subsequent productivity. The observations reconfirm earlier findings made in the 1960s by Lawler & Porter (1967) that job performance affects (job) satisfaction, not the reverse.

- *Ability:* in reaching those personal Goals successfully using cues that are clearly defined and challenging, one also gains confidence in one's abilities to reach those personal Goals in due course. Hence, the more precise and challenging those 'goals', as defined in goal-setting theory, and the more successful one becomes, the more one's perceptions of one's ability improve (Selden & Brewer, 2000), which in turn leads to higher perceived self-efficacy as to be further covered in Chapter 6.

Proceeding next, on observing outcomes from research on *goal-orientation theories,* a number of findings confirm these effects, although some outcomes also provide contrasting views that need further elaboration.

We observe the first of two propositions that were made.

2

*Assigned goals in goal-orientation theories*
Assigned goals, defined as Reality according to the Model, are assumed to provide mixed effects in performance-oriented strategies:

- When perceived Discrepancy is low, Reality is assumed to acknowledge performance-oriented ambitions, serving as a beacon against which these personal Goals are shaped and leading to approach-oriented strategies. However, these strategies are susceptible to change depending on experiences with an interfering Reality.

Referring to proposition 2, it has already been mentioned that in earlier research in the field of goal-orientation theory, performance-oriented strategies produced results that appeared to be less articulate, giving rise to a mixed picture (Harackiewicz, Barron & Elliot, 1998; Niemivirta, Pulkka, Tapola & Tuominen, 2019; Urdan, 1997). Later, when the performance-oriented goal construct was further refined into performance-approach and performance-avoidance goal-orientation, findings appeared to lead to a number of positive outcomes, such as persistence and high performance (for overviews, see: Midgley, Kaplan & Middleton, 2001; Smith, Duda, Allen & Hall, 2002).

In sum, performance-approach strategies tend to have a positive effect on effort, persistence and graded performance (Bong, 2009; Elliot & Harackiewicz, 1996; Harackiewicz, Barron, Carter, Lehto & Elliot, 1997; Harackiewicz, Barron, Tauer, Carter & Elliot, 2000; Harackiewicz, Barron, Tauer & Elliot, 2002; Middleton & Midgley, 1997; see for general reviews: Kaplan & Maehr, 2007; Linnenbrink, 2005; Midgley Kaplan & Middleton, 2001).

But performance-approach strategies come at a price. Findings from literature consistently found associations that are negatively related to well-being (Kaplan & Maehr, 1999), to anxiety, emotional exhaustion and stress (Daniels, Haynes, Stupnisky, Perry, Newall & Pekrun, 2008; Kaplan & Maehr, 2007; Midgley, Kaplan & Middleton, 2001; Roeser, Strobel & Quihuis, 2002; Smith, Sinclair & Chapman, 2002; Tuominen-Soini, Salmela-Aro & Niemivirta, 2008, 2011 notably Study 1, 2012), where even associations with forms of depression emerged (for an overview on the subject: Sideridis, 2005).

Performance-oriented goal strategies, even when approach-oriented, have an inherent disquieting property of being dependent on interference, or Impact, from Reality in order to attain the intended objective to demonstrate competence. One seeks external confirmation, or, as stated by Ryan and Deci while observing corresponding insights between goal-orientation theories and self-determination: "Performance goals, even when approach-oriented, are commonly experienced as controlling pressures, whereas mastery goals tend to be both implemented and experienced as informational" (Ryan & Deci, 2020, p. 12).

Despite a performance-approach orientation, task involvement appeared to be inferior with relatively low expectations of success: "(...) the pronounced emphasis on relative ability elicited distracting thoughts about a possible failure, which in turn lead to self-doubt and discomfort" (Niemivirta, 2002, p. 265). Tuominen-Soini and her colleagues estimated that over one third of students belonged to this category. Commenting on their profile they observed: "It is likely that, in the long run, constant concerns about outperforming others and succeeding in school pose a threat to success-oriented students' well-being, which, in turn, might induce negative affect and cognition in the face of difficulty (...)" (Tuominen-Soini, Salmela-Aro & Niemivirta, 2012, p. 301).

The second of the two propositions defined in Section 2 was as follows:

3

*Assigned goals in goal-orientation theories*
Assigned goals, defined as Reality according to the Model, are assumed to provide mixed effects in performance-oriented strategies:

- High perceived Discrepancy is assumed to have important detrimental effects leading to avoidance-oriented strategies. These effects are further increased when situational circumstances such as educational settings prevent withdrawal.

Referring to this third proposition, it was found that expectations of being graded made students more likely to adopt performance-avoidance goals (Pulfrey, Buchs & Butera, 2011; Yu, Levesque-Bristol and Maeda, 2018; see also: Hout & Elliott, 2011; Nichols & Berliner, 2007). Research has repeatedly demonstrated a positive relationship between performance-avoidance strategies and test anxiety (Elliot & McGregor, 1999; Middleton & Midgley, 1997), which can even give rise to strategic forms of self-handicapping defending against threats to self-esteem (for reviews, see: Higgins, Snyder & Berglas, 1990; Urdan & Midgley, 2001)[1] [2]. In a recent study, this group appears to comprise a quarter of students as they progress across the transition from elementary to secondary school (Tuominen, Niemivirta, Lonka & Salmela-Aro, 2020).

Performance-avoidance could be linked to a wide array of negative processes and maladaptive adjustments, such as anxiety, hopelessness, and lower performance, interest and enjoyment (Elliot & Hulleman, 2017; Elliot & McGregor, 2001; Elliot, McGregor & Gable, 1999; Grant & Dweck, 2003; Harackiewicz, Barron, Carter, Lehto & Elliot, 1997; Harackiewicz, Barron, Tauer, Carter & Elliot, 2000; McGregor & Elliot, 2002; Middleton & Midgley, 1997; Niemivirta, 2002; Pekrun, Elliot & Maier, 2009; Pintrich, 2000a; Sideridis, 2005; Skaalvik, 1997; Smith, Sinclair & Chapman, 2002; Tapola & Niemivirta, 2008; Urdan, 2004; however, for additional comments, see: Tuominen-Soini, Salmela-Aro & Niemivirta, 2012)[3].

So, failure to meet demands appears to have considerable Impact and undermine persistence and performance in performance-oriented strategies. But these effects of failure appear to be less pronounced in mastery-oriented strategies (Dweck & Leggett, 1988). Earlier, in Chapter 3, we already referred to findings that indicated that errors and setbacks appeared to be considered part of the learning process when pursuing mastery-oriented goals.

Two additional propositions, 4 and 5, were formulated, addressing mastery-oriented strategies in goal-orientation theory:

[1] If we are to assume that younger children have not yet been exposed to the experience of being graded on their performance, an effect observed earlier could give reasons for concern. Recall from observations made in Chapter 1 that research findings suggested that younger children appear to have more positive achievement-related beliefs; extending those observed effects with the effects obtained from grading, would possibly imply that the older you get, the less confident you become...

[2] More on learned helplessness and self-handicapping in Chapter 7.

[3] A number of discrepant findings have been found, however, in emerging research within different cultural settings. Notably, reference is made to: Liu, Wang, Tan, Ee & Koh, 2009; Wang, Biddle & Elliot, 2007.

4

*Assigned goals in goal-orientation theories*
Assigned goals are likely to provide limited effects in mastery-oriented strategies:

- Where perceived Discrepancy plays a limited role, as Impact from Reality is perceived to be part of one's objective to master a task or experience.

Unlike findings for performance-oriented strategies, those for mastery-oriented goals have been found to be more consistent across studies. Referring to proposition 4, it was found that pursuit of mastery-oriented goals was positively associated with a range of indices related to well-being in general (Kaplan & Maehr, 1999), and more specifically to effort and persistence, interest and positive emotions, effective learning strategies and depth of information processing (Archer, 1994; Daniels, Haynes, Stupnisky, Perry, Newall & Pekrun, 2008; Elliot & Harackiewicz, 1996; Harackiewicz, Barron, Tauer, Carter & Elliot, 2000; Linnenbrink, 2005; McGregor & Elliot, 2002; Niemivirta, 2002; Nolen, 1988; Pajares, Britner & Valiante, 2000; Pekrun, Elliot & Maier, 2006; Senko, Hulleman & Harackiewicz, 2011; Tanaka, 2007; Tapola & Niemivirta, 2008; Tuominen-Soini, Salmela-Aro & Niemivirta, 2008, 2011, 2012; Van Yperen, 2006; Wolters, 2004), leading to higher levels of academic achievement (Duchesne & Larose, 2018; Gonçalves, Niemivirta & Lemos, 2017; Roeser, Strobel & Quihuis, 2002; Schwinger & Wild, 2012; Tuominen-Soini, Salmela-Aro & Niemivirta, 2008)[1] [2].

As far back as the early 1960s, the important effects of what are now referred to as 'mastery-oriented strategies' in goal-orientation had already been observed, where successes and failures were considered to be purely informational rather than as rewards or punishments (Bruner, 1962), leading a number of early psychologists to caution against their use within educational settings (Holt, 1964; Montessori, 1967; Rogers, 1969). In a broad assessment of research findings, Nicholls later hypothesized that in goal-oriented strategies, "(...) provided difficulty levels (normative or objective) are not extreme, all or most individuals will expect to be able to gain in mastery. As this is an end in itself, they should

[1] To further diversify the mastery-oriented construct, Niemivirta distinguished between mastery-intrinsic and mastery-extrinsic goal-orientations. In gaining competence and mastery, some students use intrinsic criteria, such as the feeling or experience of knowing and understanding for evaluating whether mastery has been achieved, whereas others use extrinsic criteria, such as grades (Niemivirta, 2002). In conclusions, the mastery-intrinsic goal orientation construct has been followed, as it represents the traditional conceptualization of mastery orientation (Pulkka & Niemivirta, 2013).

[2] Interestingly, in a further development in the goal-orientation framework, research has gradually focused on multiple goal-orientation, to be covered more extensively in Chapter 6.

apply high effort to maximize their mastery and perceived ability. Consequently, they should perform effectively" (Nicholls, 1984, p. 340).

Those findings favoring the effects of mastery-oriented strategies in goal-orientation theory have since led to frequent appeals aimed at reconsidering current, more traditional approaches to educational programs[1].

5

*Assigned goals in goal-orientation theories*
Assigned goals are likely to provide limited effects in mastery-oriented strategies:

- However, especially when perceived Discrepancy is low, there appears to be a potential risk to actively seek an acknowledging external Reality, whereby a shift can occur towards a gradual 'external standardization' of criteria, thereby eroding curiosity and interest.

Despite these positive effects in mastery-oriented strategies, we earlier assumed that a potential detrimental effect could occur, associated with perceived low Discrepancy in a Phase of Impact. Referring to proposition 5, and the assumption of what was described as a gradual progression towards 'external standardization' potentially eroding curiosity and interest, it has been found that over a period covering more than 25 years, student motivation appears to decline, beginning in elementary school (Hornstra, van der Veen, Peetsma & Volman, 2013; Lazowski & Hulleman, 2016), proceeding as children progress through grade-school and middle-school years (Anderman & Maehr, 1994; Eccles & Midgley, 1990; Gillet, Vallerand & Lafreniere, 2012; Lepper, Corpus & Iyengar, 2005) and extending to higher levels of education (Hidi & Harackiewicz, 2000). Eccles and colleagues discussed the decline in motivation in terms of a progressively greater mismatch between one's personal needs (especially related

[1] Since then, theorists have argued for implementation of programs aimed at promoting the adoption of mastery goals and discouraging adoption of performance goals. Among others, reference is made to: Ames, 1992a, 1992b; Anderman, 1998; Kaplan & Maehr, 1999; Maehr & Midgley, 1991; Roeser, Midgley & Urdan, 1996; Wolters, 2004. However, see also: Anderman, 2020).

In addressing the issue, Tuominen-Soini and her colleagues more recently concluded: "(...) it would seem that classroom environments that promote ability concerns and rely on social comparison and competition are likely to promote ill-being, especially among those whose focus is on validating their competence (...). In contrast, an emphasis on personal progress and self-improvement (...), might prove to be more successful in terms of enhancing task commitment, efficacy beliefs, and intrinsic motivation, even among the more avoidance-focused students (...)" (Tuominen-Soini, Salmela-Aro & Niemivirta, 2008, p. 263.

to those associated with autonomy) and the demands of the classroom environment (Eccles & Midgley, 1989; Eccles, Midgley, Wigfield, Buchanan Reuman, Flanagan & MacIver, 1993; see also: Lepper & Henderlong, 2000). And with those demands gradually increasing as students progress through educational transitions, the effects have been associated with negative outcomes, such as a decrease in mastery-oriented strategies (Anderman & Anderman, 1999; Anderman & Midgley, 1997; Shim, Ryan & Anderson, 2008) and a decrease in interest and academic achievement, combined with increased stress (Anderman & Anderman, 1999; Bong, 2009; Isakson & Jarvis, 1999; Roeser, Eccles & Freedman-Doan, 1999; Wang, Chow, Hofkens & Salmela-Aro, 2015; Wigfield, Eccles, Schiefele, Roeser & Davis-Kean, 2006; however, see also: Gonçalves, Niemivirta & Lemos, 2017; Tuominen-Soini, Salmela-Aro & Niemivirta, 2012).

Together, these findings not only provide a first confirmation of the ideas related to the Model, they also disclose a disquieting observation. Not only do the strategies we choose to reach our Goals regulate perceptions of perceived Discrepancy and the way in which Reality affects our Motivation, *they also point to the conclusion that those effects in a Phase of Impact, to a large extent determine our well-being.*

*And these findings appear to cascade further to the inevitable conclusion that effects of Discrepancy and Impact in a Process of Motivation appear to have profound consequences. Much more than initially anticipated.*

Achievement goal orientations are seen to represent not only a motivational mindset that frames ambitions, strivings and expectations; these Goal-related strategies, when confronted with the Impact from Reality, appear also to deeply affect perceptions of adequacy, of competence and worth. And findings, notably from research in the field of education, lead us to conclude that a majority of young students appear to be affected by those effects occurring in a Phase of Impact in the Process of Motivation[1].

[1] Observations point to an estimate of more than half of young students being affected. As stated earlier, research indicates that over one third of students appear to follow a performance-approach oriented strategy aimed at outperforming others, giving rise to concerns about their well-being (Tuominen-Soini, Salmela-Aro & Niemivirta, 2012). In addition, a more recent study appears to indicate that the group of students that adopts a performance-avoidance strategy currently comprises a quarter of students as they progress across the transition from elementary to secondary school (Tuominen, Niemivirta, Lonka & Salmela-Aro, 2020). It must be noted, however, that these studies were conducted within a Western-European setting (i.e. Finland). And, as stated earlier, in more recent research emerging within other cultural settings, differing findings have been obtained (Liu, Wang, Tan, Ee & Koh, 2009; Wang, Biddle & Elliot, 2007).

Let us finalize our analysis of the propositions made on the diverse findings from theories that are associated with a Phase of Impact and effects of perceived Discrepancy, by observing outcomes from research in *self-determination theory.*

As stated, the assumption was that the more Reality is experienced to be supportive of one's Goal, hence the smaller the Discrepancy, the better the effects on the Process of Motivation. In self-determination theory these effects are captured in constructs of intrinsic and extrinsic motivation[1]. Where the construct of extrinsic motivation partly refers to a Process of Interference, which is not to be addressed presently as indicated in the Introduction, our focus will be on the construct of intrinsic motivation that has generated a large amount of research findings and can provide further indications for the assumptions that were made[2].

In considering these findings related to intrinsic motivation, we have seen in Section 2 that those research outcomes have given rise to considerable debates, especially on the assumed effects of external forms of intervention on intrinsic motivation (Ryan & Deci, 2000)[3]. As observed, however, the observations are restricted to the effects of Impact as they are assumed to occur within a Process of Motivation[4].

Three propositions were previously formulated, the first of which was referred to as 'proposition 6', in Section 2:

[1] For more on intrinsic and extrinsic forms of motivation in self-determination theory, see Chapter 8.

[2] In considering the forces that move a person to act, self-determination theory distinguishes so-called 'regulatory styles', that range from being externally to being internally regulated, from being externally controlled to being self-endorsed, autonomous, or *self-determined.* Along this continuum, the construct of extrinsic motivation refers in various degrees to external regulation. And thereby it is assumed to capture the effects of Reality and its perceived Discrepancy and reflect its various expressions, ranging from low to high perceived Discrepancy and Impact. The concepts of internal and external regulation, and the construct of extrinsic motivation are therefore to be covered extensively when observing the Process of Interference in subsequent Volumes of the 'Series on Motivation'.

[3] Most of the research on the effects of environmental factors and events on intrinsic motivation have focused on the issue of autonomy versus control (Ryan & Deci, 2000). Notably, its emphasis has been on observing the effects of a range of external incentives and rewards on the construct of intrinsic motivation, commonly referred to as the undermining of intrinsic motivation by extrinsic rewards (Deci, Koestner & Ryan, 1999).

[4] Extending on the previous observations, much of research in the field of self-determination, has focused on these autonomy-supportive techniques, which are considered to be part of a Process of Interference falling beyond the scope of our study. For overviews, following references are made:

- Pertaining to the field of education: Reeve, 2002; Reeve, Bolt & Cai, 1999; Ryan & Deci, 2020;
- Pertaining to parenting: Grolnick, 2009; Ryan & Deci, 2018, Chapter 13;
- Pertaining to the field of work motivation: Ryan & Deci, 2018, Chapter 21.

6

*Assigned goals in self-determination theory*

Assigned goals, defined as Reality according to the Model, that take on the form of external incentives or rewards, are likely to affect the Process of Motivation:

- When perceived Discrepancy is low, Reality is assumed to be supportive, and thus to lead to positive effects on Motivation.

Referring to proposition 6, it was found from research in the field of self-determination theory that, although no specific reference was made to an assigned goal, a perceived low Discrepancy with Reality, in the form of acknowledgement of feelings, opportunities for self-direction and providing opportunities for independent work, appeared to increase motivation (Deci & Ryan, 1985; Koestner, Ryan, Bernieri & Holt, 1984; Ryan & Deci, 2000; Reeve, 2002)[1].

Findings obtained from research in the field also provided further confirmation of the complex interaction between external forms of intervention and motivation, as conceptualized as intrinsic motivation in self-determination theory. Amidst the debate on effects of external intervention on intrinsic motivation, new insights in literature gradually emerged that these forms of external intervention and intrinsic motivation interact and affect each other in ways that are consistent with the assumptions made in the Model of Motivation.

Within this interaction, defined in the Model as the Impact from Reality on the Process of attaining or maintaining one's Goal, there appears to be agreement on two tendencies that are relevant for the assumptions made:

- When external interference, in the form of assigned goals, incentives, rewards, is *related* to a specific task or activity, it will be more likely to produce detrimental effects and less likely to produce beneficial effects on motivation, conceptualized as intrinsic motivation.
- When external interference, in the form of assigned goals, incentives, rewards, is *non-related* to a specific task or activity, it will be less likely to produce detrimental effects and more likely to produce beneficial effects on motivation, conceptualized as intrinsic motivation.

[1] Reference is made to effects on intrinsic motivation, and (occasionally) on self-rated perceptions of self-determination.

In these two summarizing tendencies, however, derived from a broadest possible range of currently available data[1] [2] [3], it is to be noted that reference is made to a number of observations that extend partially outside the area of our present study[4] [5] [6].

[1] In literature, research findings refer to the various degrees of external regulation (as captured in the construct of extrinsic motivation) and its effects on motivation (captured in the construct of intrinsic motivation). As referred to earlier, controversies concentrated notably on the undermining of intrinsic motivation by external rewards.

[2] The observations have been based on principal findings obtained through meta-analyses performed by, among others: Cerasoli, Nicklin & Ford, 2014; Deci, Koestner & Ryan, 1999; extended with reviews from: Lepper & Henderlong, 2000 and Ryan & Deci, 2000, 2018, notably Chapter 6.

To avoid unintended confusion in the use of constructs, a general phrasing has been used with a distinction between related versus non-related assigned goals, incentives or rewards.

[3] Commenting on their meta-evaluative overview, extending over 40 years of research in the field, Cerasoli, Nicklin & Ford, eloquently stated: "Our intrinsic-extrinsic dichotomy oversimplifies motivation. However, it enables us to demonstrate that not only do both intrinsic and extrinsic motives matter, they interact with one another" (2014, pp. 999-1000). Where they conclude: "counter to claims otherwise, our research demonstrates the joint impact of incentives and intrinsic motivation is critical to performance" (*ibid.*, p. 1001).

[4] As referred to earlier, various degrees of external regulation are captured in the construct of extrinsic motivation, which is to be addressed when covering a Process of Interference.

[5] The controversies on the undermining of intrinsic motivation by external rewards have at least in part been the result of interpretations of so-called 'meta-evaluations' or 'meta-analyses'. At least ten meta-analyses have extensively covered the issue (for details: Cerasoli, Nicklin & Ford, 2014), some covering 128 studies spanning three decades (Deci, Koestner & Ryan, 1999), extending more recently to an overview which included 154 sources covering four decades (Cerasoli, Nicklin & Ford, 2014).

There are substantial statistical and theoretical limitations when testing significance on data obtained from meta-analyses (Hunter & Schmidt, 2000, 2004; National Research Council, 1992; for a critical review: Lepper & Henderlong, 2000). More explicitly, however, an essential element has remained circumstantial and at least underrated in these critical reviews. Statistical procedures that have been used in a vast majority of the studies involving these meta-analyses, can only produce insights into *general* tendencies, as they relate in most cases to data-sets that are based on (derivatives of) correlates, accounting for only (very) limited amounts of explained variance. For a general overview on meta-analysis: Lipsey & Wilson, 2001.

[6] In the various meta-analyses, external influences in the form of assigned goals, incentives or rewards related to a specific task or activity are usually referred to as being *'contingent'*; and assigned goals, incentives, or rewards that are not related, as being *'non-contingent'*. Further differentiations have been made, notably in *'performance-contingent incentives'*, that are incentives promised for attaining a specific level in a task or activity. For more on these categories: Cerasoli, Nicklin & Ford, 2014; Deci, Koestner & Ryan, 1999, 2001; Ryan & Deci, 2018, Chapter 6.

In short, then, and positioned within the context of the Model, findings suggest and confirm that the more an external Reality relates to the Goal one has set, the more likely it appears to interfere with the Process of attaining or maintaining this Goal, and the more likely it is to impair its integrity. And conversely, the more remote (or 'non-related') a perceived Reality appears to be from those Goals, the less profound its interference. Stated differently: in these cases, there is no substantial intrusion in the Process of Motivation, and therefore, by definition, Impact is minimal[1].

So, when Reality appears to be related to one's Goal, it is likely to produce detrimental effects, and thus to be perceived as interfering with the Process of Motivation, with high Discrepancy; and when Reality appears to be non-related, it becomes more likely to produce beneficial effects on the Process, with low Discrepancy.

Finally, then, and elaborating on these effects, when Impact is perceived to be Discrepant with one's Goal in a Process of Motivation, findings obtained from research in self-determination theory provide a confirmation of the detrimental effects assumed to occur according to the Model.

[1] In the various studies that have been analyzed, reference is made to incentives, or rewards as being *non-related* to a specific task or activity. In a strictest sense, when Reality is perceived to be entirely non-related to the Process of reaching one's Goal, there is no perceived confrontation or interference with the Process of Motivation, and therefore (by definition) no Impact. However, in those studies the effects are also referred to as being less likely to produce detrimental effects and more likely to produce beneficial effects on the Process of Motivation. Therefore, it is assumed that these incentives or rewards bear an association, however distant, to a Goal that has been set. And as such, are associated with a Process of Motivation aimed at attaining such a Goal. Its Impact is less likely to produce detrimental effects and more likely to produce beneficial effects on the Process. Therefore, its Impact on the Process of Motivation is minimal and perceived Discrepancy is low.

According to the Model of Motivation, it is essential to explicitly distinguish a non-related, and thus non-interfering Reality from a Reality with minimal Impact and low perceived Discrepancy, as these perceived expressions of Reality are highly important in the support they yield on the Process of Motivation, especially when perceived Significance of Reality is high.

As we will come to realize when observing a Process of Interference, it marks the difference between non-interference from an outside actor based on disinterest (thus unrelated to one's Process of Motivation), or because of dedicated trust in one's capacities (and thus highly related to one's Process of Motivation).

7

*Assigned goals in self-determination theory*
Assigned goals, defined as Reality according to the Model, that take on the form of external incentives or rewards, are likely to affect the Process of Motivation:

- When perceived Discrepancy is high, these effects of Reality are perceived to be negative, and Impact can become detrimental.

Referring to proposition 7, it was found that a perceived high Discrepancy with Reality, in the form of directives and threats were to diminish motivation (Deci & Cascio, 1972; Ryan & Deci, 2000, 2018, Chapter 6), as were effects of deadlines (Amabile, DeJong & Lepper, 1976), and negative feedback (Deci & Cascio, 1972; Vallerand & Reid, 1984)[1]. In addition, when a competitive element was introduced, it was found that effects were highly detrimental to motivation for those who performed poorly. As commented on by Ryan and Deci, in summarizing reward effects: "(...) the type of reward that was the most detrimental of any reward category was the one (...) in which people's rewards are a direct function of their performance, such that those who perform best get the largest rewards and those who perform less well get smaller rewards" (Ryan & Deci, 2018, p. 140).

These findings from research in self-determination theory, have also provided unexpected insights and a further, though indirect, confirmation of the assumption made on a gradual 'external adaptation', as defined in proposition 8:

8

*Assigned goals in self-determination theory*
Assigned goals, defined as Reality according to the Model, that take on the form of external incentives or rewards, are likely to affect the Process of Motivation:

- When perceived Discrepancy is low, there appears to be a potential risk in using incentives and rewards, as they tend to lead, by their nature, to an 'external adaptation' towards Reality, thereby affecting the integrity of a personal Goal.

[1] These studies and reports of outcomes reflect high perceived Discrepancies. It must be noted, however, that these findings do not imply negative effects to occur per se, especially for deadlines and negative feedback, as various alternative expressions can be effective and can lead to less pronounced Discrepancies (Burgers, Eden, Van Engelenburg & Buningh, 2015; Carpentier & Mageau, 2013; Koka & Hein, 2003). These are to be addressed when covering Processes of Interference.

Referring to proposition 8, these effects have been confirmed in the form of a decline in engagement, conceptualized as intrinsic motivation in self-determination theory, following external intervention. In many studies, the effects have been observed of so-called autonomy-supportive practices and teacher styles on motivation, conceptualized as intrinsic motivation[1]. Within these settings, the effects of outside interference in the form of grading and evaluations have been registered, and findings appear to provide an indication for the assumed tendency of external adaptation. Research findings indicate that students focusing on grades, were less interested and had lower conceptual understanding (Benware & Deci, 1984; Grolnick & Ryan, 1987), as well as lower long-term achievement outcomes (Klapp, 2015)[2].

Grading, then, seems to divert one's focus. And these decrements in performance quality have been observed in more general terms with children when working for an expected reward (Garbarino, 1975; Greene & Lepper, 1974; Kruglanski, Friedman & Zeevi, 1971; Lepper, Greene & Nisbett, 1973; Loveland & Olley, 1979; McGraw & McCullers, 1979), while these rewards have been consistently found to decrease creativity (Amabile, 1983, 1996; Hennessey & Amabile, 1998)[3] [4], and to erode curiosity and interest (Greene & Lepper, 1974; Lepper, Greene & Nisbett, 1973), as we previously observed in findings from goal-orientation theory.

[1] Where autonomy-supportive environments will be found to match low Impact and perceived Discrepancy when observing effects in Processes of Interference, the outcomes of studies reveal the positive effects mentioned earlier, notably on performance, achievement, engagement, conceptual understanding and well-being (for overviews, see: Reeve, Ryan, Deci & Jang, 2008; Ryan & Deci, 2018, notably Chapter 14).

[2] In addition, self-determination theory suggests it is largely the controlling aspect that leads to these results, thwarting a need for autonomy: "(...) especially because grading is often more comparative than effectance-relevant in its functional significance". (Ryan & Deci, 2018, p. 381). As we shall observe when covering a Process of Interference, the alternative view as proposed by self-determination theory does not contradict the propositions made according to the Model of Motivation.

[3] There have also been divergent findings, but these appear to originate from differences in the definitions of creativity and in the nature of experimental tasks that were employed. For details and a general overview, see: Hennessey, 2000.

[4] An interesting study, in which children were "immunized" and trained in helping to distance themselves from socially imposed extrinsic constraints (and thus to decrease perceptions of Significance in Reality, thereby reducing the effects of Impact as proposed in the Model), revealed that creativity was maintained and even increased, in accordance with assumptions made in the Model (Hennessey, Amabile & Martinage, 1989; Hennessey & Zbikowski, 1993).

Where do we stand in the observations we have made?

A number of propositions have been formulated and observed on findings from research. These propositions were outcomes of an explanatory overview, where we made an attempt at providing an alternative view for differences that had emerged between the three leading theories associated with a Phase of Impact. As stated initially, if these propositions were to be confirmed by findings from research, it would reflect on the explanatory attempts we made at clarifying these divergent theories from which these findings originated.

As we saw in observing those theories, goal-setting suggested to have us define 'specific high goals', and in goal-orientation performance-approach produced results that partly confirmed those ideas, although mastery-oriented strategies appeared to yield more successful results. And, at the other end of the spectrum, self-determination theory stated that any form of controlled intervention would thwart a need for autonomy, and would thus be detrimental to motivation, conceptualized as intrinsic motivation.

Now that we found confirmation for most, if not all, of the propositions made, we are in a position to make a number of summarizing observations, and present an alternative view to these findings, before finalizing our conclusions.

In this alternative view, we propose three important observations that appear to have led to diversity. To structure the analysis that is to lead to these main observations, we will refer to each of these in separate headings:

- *Differing perceptions in elementary constructs;*
- *Selective effects of Goal-intent;*
- *Differential emphasis on the Process of Motivation.*

At the start of our analysis based on the Model of Motivation, we defined a clear demarcation between a Process of Motivation, in the various expressions through which an individual makes an attempt at reaching a Goal, and a Process of Interference, aimed at addressing this intricate Process by external means. We explicitly focused only on the Process of Motivation; postponing analyses of the profoundly different Processes related to Interference to subsequent Volumes in the present 'Series on Motivation'. Moreover, we made a distinction in a progressive expression of perceived Significance, both in the Goal and in Reality, leading to two states or conditions where the Process of Motivation was most likely to be affected in its course: when Significance of one's Goal and perceived Significance of Reality affecting its attainment were both experienced to be high.

These various distinctions and characteristics proposed by the Model of Motivation, enabled us to make various observations on findings obtained from research in the three observed theories.

In the observed theories, there appears to be no clear and unambiguous demarcation between a Process of Motivation as manifested in an individual, and a Process of Interference aimed at addressing this Motivation, as proposed in the Model. This, in turn, leads to potential differences in perspective between an individual in his or her attempt at reaching a Goal, and an external actor (or situation or condition), in attempts at influencing this Goal. Moreover, no explicit differentiation appears to have been made between elementary constructs that are referred to in the Model of Motivation as a 'Goal', and its interfering 'Reality', where both constructs appear to have been perceived as identical, or interchangeable. In addition, it was found that in research findings, differentiations in (levels of) perceived Significance in both constructs have rarely been made.

These observations appear to have led to a number of divergent findings from research in the three areas of study. These differences, then, are probably caused by what is referred to as *'differing perceptions in elementary constructs'*.

Let us refer to examples provided earlier in this Chapter, and elaborate briefly on previous comments that have been made to clarify these observations.

*See exhibit next page* ➔

But there appears to be more.

A number of outcomes from research at first led us to believe that the observed differences were the resultant of situational or contextual differences. At first sight, a number of findings would justify such a conclusion. We observed that what works within a business environment, doesn't necessarily apply to a classroom setting. Perceived Reality takes on a different form when a Goal is to reach certain standards in order to outperform expectations of one's superior; but such an objective is likely to affect a personal Goal that is aiming at mastery and understanding, in the examples just observed in a young boy or girl, where Impact from Reality is perceived differently, and where other standards are pursued.

So, context plays a role, and even an important one, but there appears to be more than situational circumstances to account for the differences in findings observed. According to the Model, a personal Goal is what steers the Process of Motivation. It is through the Goal that has been set that the Process of Motivation is 'set in motion' to attain that objective. And specific circumstances could be favorable in reaching a specific Goal, whereas others can be obstructive. Some situations are favorable for Goals that are in need of precise cues to be attained, whereas others assist by instigating clever strategies to successfully reach them, and yet other situations that appear to avoid any form of interference may favor Goals that aim to fulfill these specific ambitions.

## *Differing Perceptions in Constructs: Some Examples*

Differences in findings from research caused by *differing perceptions in elementary constructs* have been observed on a number of occasions. Earlier, in demonstrating the effects of Impact, we considered the case of a young family, and we can apply the examples we used then to illustrate our case...

*No distinction between a Process of Motivation and a Process of Interference: effects on perspective*

Recall in Example 1, p. 127, the little baby girl that had just started to walk around in this new and wondrous world. From her perspective, an optimal approach with highest effects would be to have her thrive in mastery and maintain her autonomy. But every parent will acknowledge that from *their* perspective, the approach and its effects can appear rather different... The same applies to Example 2, p. 127, her sister aged 8, who first attends school. We have seen the optimal approach of mastery-oriented goal-strategies, as seen from her perspective. But we have also made allusion in our observations to the different perspective from a teacher, who has, in his or her role, a 'society-induced' responsibility to attain certain levels of competence or proficiency, which necessitates her to emphasize performance-oriented goal-strategies in the child with consequences referred to in Example 3, p. 128. In both cases, approach and effects differ dramatically. Finally, in observing her mom in Example 4, p. 128, the perspective of the company (aimed at productivity), happens to coincide with her ambitions (to excel in her job), which this time leads to convergent outcomes.

So, effects of an approach can be different when perceived from the perspective of a Process of Motivation or a Process of Interference induced by an external actor.

*Concept confusion: the difference between self-set and assigned goals*

We have made allusion to the essential differences in mechanisms associated with self-set and assigned goals. Recall in the exhibit provided in Chapter 2, p. 59, and in the distinction made at the start of the overview, p. 139, that properties of self-set goals are a resultant, rather than a cause in observing effects. As stated in the present Chapter, in observing effects of Impact, we only considered assigned goals *as an expression of Reality*. Confusing both constructs inevitably leads to differences occurring in findings obtained.

*Significance: differences occurring caused by differing perceptions of Significance*

Differences in effects have occurred as a result of disregarding the effects caused by differences in perceived Significance, in constructs of the Goal and Reality, as covered in the exhibit pp. 122-124.

In the intricate interplay of forces affecting the Process of Motivation, circumstances could be such that they provide an optimal environment for certain Goals, and in that sense not only appear to be favorable to, but also to attract certain Goals, working as a catalyzer. Work situations are likely to favor precision-driven targeting, in a classroom setting mastery-oriented strategies could be made to prevail, and where circumstances favor personal growth and well-being, it is likely to attract autonomous striving. It is not the situation creating a Process of Motivation, it is a Process of Motivation with its specific personal Goal finding ground to flourish in one situation and to decline or even deteriorate in another.

To have us conclude, then, that the observed differences are to be attributed to situational or contextual differences, fails to do justice to the complexities of the Process of Motivation, where the Goal determines the outcomes. It is not the context, or situation, or external factor that is leading, it is the personal Goal that one sets. According to the Model, the Process of Motivation is centered and evolves around a personal Goal. Circumstances can be made to affect this Process, to enable, facilitate or catalyze attainment of a Goal, *but it is never the cause, the origin leading to action.*

In addressing those Goals, the three theories appear to demonstrate divergent preferential emphasis on the types of Goals they tend to address. This second major observation is referred to as *'selective effects of Goal-intent'*.

As such, these selective effects that caused divergent findings appear to have affected outcomes of research in two different ways:

- *'Typical' selective effects:* as referred to, certain environments appear to have an optimal effect on certain types of Goals, and thus become attractive for those seeking the attainment of those Goals;
- *'Atypical' selective effects:* but we also observed on many occasions that these environments can have different effects than intended, and appear counterproductive to those for which these incentives were intended.

We are thus to conclude that some environments can be made to optimize certain Goals under certain circumstances, but can never be made to optimize *all* Goals under *all* circumstances. And this accounts for divergence in findings.

To clarify these second observations, let us refer to the eloquent description by Shawn that was used earlier, to capture the human condition and to sustain its sense of purpose. Where the human condition in its 'strivings' is characterized by a multitude of Goals, we could use its most elementary expression to 'design air conditioners' and 'to inspire joy' as a metaphor...

*See exhibit next page* ➔

## Selective Effects of Goal-Intent: An Elaborate Example

In addition, differences in findings from research are likely to be caused by *selective effects of Goal-intent.* Earlier, on p. 147, we referred to a quote from Shawn to capture the human condition. A metaphor used to capture its 'elementaries' could serve to illustrate this second observation...

Referring to his extensive description, ranging from Japanese haiku to Proust, we feel compelled to simplify his eloquent description, to people that aim 'to design air conditioners' and those that aim 'to inspire joy'... Let us use both to illustrate how circumstances are dependent on one's Goal to become effective in a Process of Motivation.

At first, circumstances could appear to define an optimal setting for Motivation to thrive: precisely defined technical specifications by an R&D department calling for precise, hands-on standards that can act as 'specific high goals'. And if the engineer's striving would have been to exceed expectations from his boss, meeting those standards in the shortest possible time would certainly serve the purpose. But if the engineer's objective would rather have been to be creative, to become a genius, or produce a breakthrough in mechanical engineering, those targets become restrictive constraints. How to manage a creative mind and inspire to venture into those unchartered grounds? If it is by defining specific targets (such as strict specifications, or other specific targets), one need not point to where those incentives would lead...

The same applies to inspiring joy. One could assume that the optimal ambiance of a famous theater or concert hall, calling for restraint, non-intrusive and 'autonomy-oriented' support, would create the optimal setting for a highly motivated performance. But suppose, after years of practice, a musician has gained enough confidence to seek out the highest form of competition in order to obtain fame and fortune, then winning a prestigious concours, in an extremely competitive environment, with the highest possible targets, rewards, incentives, would become a most gratifying experience and an optimal setting for this specific and highly ambitious Goal.

In Motivation, there is no such thing as a 'one-size-fits-all' approach...

It is not Reality, the external factor, actor, situation that determines a Process of Motivation, it is in the Goal, and the particular properties we set. And it is in the optimal alignment to the Goal that a Process of Interference will yield the results it seeks to obtain. More to come on the Process of Interference...

We come to our third, final and most important observation.

Recall the comment made in Section 1 that for effects to occur in a Process of Motivation the Model proposes that two constructs are essential: the Goal and Reality. In a Phase of Impact, when observing the various combinations between both constructs, it was found that Impact, or Discrepancy, largely regulated the effects produced in the interaction. Thus, for effects to occur in a Process of Motivation, the constructs of the Goal and Reality, produce effects determined by Impact, or Discrepancy.

We can use these three constructs to demonstrate what we referred to as a *'differential emphasis on the Process of Motivation'* that may have contributed to the differences observed in research findings obtained for the three theories.

If we observe the three theories, each appears to emphasize in their approach one of these essential constructs:

- *Goal-setting theory* appears to emphasize optimal attributes for the construct defined as 'Reality' in the Model in order to improve a Process of Motivation;
- *Goal-orientation theories* appear to emphasize optimal attributes associated with the construct of a Goal, especially by providing insights into the effects of Goal-related strategies on the Process of Motivation;
- *Self-determination theory* appears to emphasize optimal properties of Impact, especially by providing insights into the effects of reducing Discrepancy on the Process of Motivation.

Let us elaborate on these observations for each of those theories, summarized as a 'differential emphasis on the Process of Motivation', and illustrate each with the examples provided earlier to clarify those differences in research findings.

As we observed in Chapter 2 and in the present Chapter on a number of occasions, in observing goal-setting theory, assigned goals (by definition) are *not* goals defined by the individual, but rather serve as indicators in attaining those personal goals. When one's objective is to be successful in one's job, or to retain one's position, or to obtain promotion, gratuities, bonuses or dividends, they provide an indication of the extent to which these objectives are within reach or have been obtained. Assigned goals, according to the Model of Motivation, are not defined as Goals, but represent Reality in various forms. And if one's Goal is to excel within a particular setting defined as Reality (e.g. one's work), the better and more precise Reality is defined, the better it serves as a benchmark or reference in reaching those Goals. And in this Phase of Impact, we mainly focused on these assigned Goals, as contrasted from self-set Goals, where different mechanisms were at work, with differing expressions in the Process of Motivation, as covered previously in Chapter 2.

So, from this perspective in assigned goals, those that are specific and challenging are likely to relate to high performance and productivity as suggested in goal-setting theory. To illustrate, let us refer to the previously mentioned examples provided earlier in this Chapter.

*See exhibit next page* ➔

Divergence occurs when other constructs essential to the Process of Motivation are emphasized, as in goal-orientation theory.

At first, there appeared to be similarities in findings, when defining a Goal-oriented strategy aimed at demonstrating one's performance relative to others, which when successful was likely to initiate subsequent further action, referred to as 'approach-oriented'.

However, goal-orientation theory, in observing the effects from a different angle, in emphasizing the effects of defining a Goal according to such strategies, detected side-effects in the Process of Motivation that appeared to *also* produce detrimental effects. If one is to follow a performance-approach strategy, the Model of Motivation assumes that a gradual buildup of experience has produced enough confidence to justify a risk of Failure following confrontation with Reality in a Phase of Impact. When effects are successful the performance-approach strategy in reaching the Goal is intensified. When effects appear unsuccessful, the effects on Motivation deteriorate. Performance-approach calls for a daring strategy. The approach in Goal-orientation works fine as a strategy, as long as chances of perceived success are assessed to be high, but the price one pays is an inconvenient dependency on external appreciation, approval or acknowledgment. Defining one's Goal based on such strategies appears highly dependent or even induced on external gratification. And this, in turn, leads to consistent findings associating performance-approach strategies with anxiety, emotional exhaustion and stress, and more in general, affecting one's well-being.

And conversely, if one is to follow a performance-avoidance strategy in the Goals that are set, the Model of Motivation assumes that a gradual buildup of experience leads us to prevent a serious risk of Failure following confrontation with Reality in a Phase of Impact that even justifies all negative consequences associated with withdrawal. This strategy seeks 'to avoid at all cost', leading to the consistent negative findings on Motivation and well-being found in research.

So performance-oriented goal-orientation at first appeared to provide comparable results in research findings as goal-setting theory, in terms of positive effects on effort, persistence and graded performance. But defining one's Goal according to such strategies also produced adverse effects and led to findings that clearly differentiated both theories from each other.

## *Differential Emphasis on the Process: Some Examples*

Finally, differences in findings from research appear to have been caused by *differential emphasis on the Process of Motivation.* Again, we refer to the examples used earlier when we considered the case of a young family, and apply the examples we used to this third observation...

*Goal-setting theory*
Proceeding where we left in Example 4, p. 128, we had a mother enjoying the clarity provided by her superiors in her new job, where her main objective was to outperform expectations, and thus (in a parallel Process of Motivation) secure her future at the company.

In observing the Model that attempts at capturing the Process of Motivation, the emphasis of goal-setting theory lies on optimizing attributes associated with the construct of Reality to further optimize a Process of Motivation. Especially, as observed, from the perspective of an external actor, or actors. When Reality matches or coincides with the Goal set by the individual (which is most likely in a work environment), positive effects emerge; if not, productivity declines (and departure is likely to be imminent, thereby affecting remaining populations and potentially causing bias in research findings).

Focusing on optimizing attributes of Reality, making it precise and challenging thus improves Motivation when objectives are aimed at Reality to fulfill their needs. As seen previously, it thereby attracts those Goals that are aimed at performance, according to standards and criteria that tend to be external. But the Process of Motivation remains centered on the Goals that are set by the individual. And it is through those Goals that these expressions of Reality exercise their influence and control.

Optimizing attributes of Reality thus serves an important role in steering Processes of Motivation that evolve around those types of Goals. But as we also observed, those Goals within these settings can also diverge, as in our technician aiming at a technological breakthrough, or our musician, seeking an optimal ambiance instead of highest forms of competition in performing arts.

It appears there are more aspects to addressing Motivation, as we shall observe when covering a Process of Interference...

*(Continued)*

*Goal-orientation theories*
In using Example 5, p. 128, we can observe how the Goals we set appear to be heavily dependent on the strategies we use to attain them. Recall that an announcement was made by the company, where we observed three variations.

In the first option (Example 5a), the company decided to define specific targets for each employee. As observed from the perspective of goal-orientation theories, this would assist the individual in defining strategies that are thus 'tailored' to the Goals the employee seeks to achieve. In this approach, goal-orientation theories appeared to have found positive effects on Motivation (or rather 'performance') in findings from research, which appeared to correspond to those obtained in goal-setting theory. But goal-orientation theories also produced evidence that in those (performance-oriented) strategies, goal attainment was heavily dependent on Reality and thus appeared to be linked to a wide array of negative processes and maladaptive adjustments.

In goal-orientation strategies where 'mastery' prevails, this dependency on Reality for appreciation, or approval, or acknowledgement, practically disappears. In performance-oriented strategies this dependency dominates. As with the young mother in the example, when she is asked to define targets herself (Example 5b), where she can minimize Discrepancy, the dependency on Reality remains. Even when an external Reality closely relates to the Goal one has set, it interferes with the Process of attaining or maintaining this Goal, and is therefore likely to impair its integrity. In a sense, 'the threat remains'...

And this interference and its effects appear clearly in the third option (Example 5c), where Reality (management) decides to increase the target she had set. Depending on her Goal, this increase leads to either a small Discrepancy, or a (dramatic) increase, as witnessed in the departure of her friend...

Goal-orientation theories thus appear to focus on the Goal and the optimization of strategies that lead to successful goal attainment.

*Self-determination theory*
Finally, self-determination theory focuses on yet another aspect, or characteristic of the Process of Motivation. It concentrates on attributes that are associated with the construct of Impact, seeking to minimize Discrepancy and reducing effects from (external) interference from Reality. Interference which always seem to have an effect on the Process of Motivation. But again, depending on the Goals that are set, this interference can be dramatic and intruding, or can be perceived as part of a specific Goal that has been set. Consider Example 6, p. 128, where grandma appears to 'thrive' in her job. And an external Reality, despite its prominent presence appears to optimally affect a Process of Motivation by explicitly providing her with the necessary means to feel acknowledged in the Goals she has set.

And these differences in findings were further accentuated when observing strategies in goal-orientation aimed at mastery. As suggested in the Model, a Process of Motivation appears to benefit from a 'mastery-inclined' strategy where we have no intention to demonstrate competence or proficiencies relative to others, but rather attempt to learn, improve, develop. And from this perspective, there is no risk of Failure as outcomes can hardly be detrimental to such Goals. As a result, interference of Reality becomes much less pronounced, and thus leads to an extensive range of positive outcomes as we found in outcomes from research.

So goal-orientation does not exclude the findings and ideas proposed in goal-setting theory. It emphasizes different aspects in the Process of Motivation. What are 'the best Goals' in achievement-related contexts? What properties do we need to assign to those Goals in order to obtain optimal outcomes? In observing goal-orientation theories we referred to 'goal-orientation strategies' in tracing those properties, and studies from this perspective produced a wealth of data that can be illustrated using the examples we used earlier.

🡐 *See exhibit previous page*

A difference in emphasis on these Goal-related properties produced outcomes from a different perspective than those from goal-setting theory, where emphasis was put on optimizing effects of a perceived Reality. In this, goal-orientation theories in a sense bridged a gap halfway between goal-setting at one side of the spectrum and self-determination theory at the other.

Self-determination lays emphasis on decreasing Discrepancy between Goal and Reality in a Phase of Impact, as proposed in the Model of Motivation. From this perspective, findings confirmed the alternative view proposed by the Model, that the more an external Reality relates to the Goal one has set, the more likely it becomes that it is to interfere with the Process of attaining or maintaining this Goal, and the more likely it is to impair its integrity, especially when Significance in both constructs is perceived to be high. And the more remote a perceived Reality (defined as 'non-related' in evaluations of numerous meta-evaluations), the less profound its interference with those Goals. Thus, according to the Model, self-determination aims at reducing interference and effects of Impact on the Process of Motivation.

In this respect, and in a final comment, instead of expressing its relation ('related' versus 'non-related') to the Goal (or 'task' or 'activity'), the Model of Motivation proposes the construct of 'perceived Discrepancy', as interference per se, appears to be expressed in the extent of 'divergence', rather than 'affiliation'.

And we can use a final example, referred to at the start of our analysis, to illustrate our case.

🡐 *See exhibit previous page*

Let us, then, finally come to conclusions on this long road that has been filled with controversies and debates.

A first conclusion is that all findings from research obtained from the three fields of study do justice to a common purpose to have people thrive in what they do. It has been a central theme in all studies observed.

A second conclusion is that the propositions made according to the Model of Motivation do not appear to contradict the vast body of findings produced from research in those three areas of study. As such, the Model of Motivation and the constructs that have been used so far to capture the Process of Motivation in its elementary form appear to provide a framework that could serve as a basis to integrate the diverse research findings that have been observed so far.

And from this second conclusion follows a third, which has been summarized in three important observations. Let us use, in this third conclusion, these three observations to structure our analysis of the divergence in findings obtained in the three most important theories associated with a Phase of Impact in the Process of Motivation.

*Thus, differences in theories and findings from research are believed to originate from:*

- *Differing perceptions in elementary constructs;*
- *Selective effects of Goal-intent;*
- *Differential emphasis on the Process of Motivation.*

There appears to be a diffuse picture, in current theories, of constructs that are considered to be essential for a Process of Motivation according to the Model. *These differing perceptions in elementary constructs appear to be the result of omitting an elementary distinction made in our analysis between a Process of Motivation and a Process of Interference. In addition, constructs of the Goal and Reality appear to have been used interchangeably; diversification in effects of perceived Significance in both constructs have rarely been the subject of study.* These differing perceptions of constructs that are deemed essential for adequately capturing the intricate Process of Motivation have most likely been a source of divergent findings, both in theoretical conceptualization and in associated research findings.

Although we have been tempted to believe that situational factors would have played an important role in obtaining a diverse picture between the various theories, an alternative view is proposed by the Model, where selective effects of Goal-intent appear to be the source of considerable variation in outcomes in the three fields of study.

*According to the Model, a Process of Motivation is not steered by situational factors but by a Goal that has been set, and on which situational factors can exert influence. Situational factors manifest their influence in the extent to which they facilitate the individual in reaching those Goals. Differences observed between findings occur where these theories exert preferential effects in their approach, thereby appealing to certain Goals, producing a positive effect on the Process of Motivation, whereas the outcomes differ when conditions and circumstances change. Thus, circumstances exercise a selective influence on specific Goals.* And where these Goals tend to dominate, the effects become substantial. But in circumstances where other aspects of personal Goals tend to prevail, or reactions to those circumstances are atypical, the effects are less pronounced or even detrimental to the Process of Motivation. In examples we referred to differences in circumstances occurring in work-related versus educational settings. *These selective effects of Goal-intent that deeply influence a Process of Motivation according to the Model appear to have been an additional source of divergent findings between the three theories we observed.*

In a Process of Motivation, then, according to the Model, a personal Goal is leading and situational factors can be made to optimize this Process of Goal attainment. These insights lead to a third and final observation.

If we are to assume that the Model of Motivation provides us with a framework of the stepwise Process that leads to Goal attainment, we can observe that each of these theories emphasizes in its approach a specific aspect, or attribute, within this sequential Process. As we progressed in analyzing the Process of Motivation, we observed that for effects to occur the constructs of the Goal and Reality, regulated by Impact, or Discrepancy, were essential. *These central constructs enabled us to identify a third principal source of differences occurring in findings obtained by the three theories in their fields of study:*

- *Goal-setting theory* appears to concentrate on essential attributes associated with the construct of *Reality,* as proposed in the Model, in order to optimize a Process of Motivation;
- *Goal-orientation theories* appear to concentrate on attributes that are associated with the construct of the *Goal,* as proposed in the Model, and especially the Goal-related strategies that appear to be successful within the constraints of Reality and its interfering Impact;
- *Self-determination theory* appears to concentrate on the construct of *Impact,* as proposed in the Model, and especially at minimizing Discrepancy and reducing effects from outside interference.

*Thus, in a third observation, an emphasis on differing central constructs in the Process of Motivation appears to have been a third and most important cause for divergent findings amongst the three observed theories.*

In one of the most controversial issues in literature in the field of motivation, the Model of Motivation proposes an alternative view to reconcile divergent findings from research on three major theories, as observed on p. 138.

It is suggested that differences between these three major theories associated with a Phase of Impact in the Process of Motivation appear to occur, as a resultant of:

- *Differing perceptions in elementary constructs:* Conceptual differences have occurred between the theories, as a resultant of omitting an elementary distinction made in the Model between a Process of Motivation and a Process of Interference. Moreover, constructs of Goal and Reality appear to have been used interchangeably, where diversification in effects of perceived Significance have rarely been the subject of study.
- *Selective effects of Goal-intent:* A Process of Motivation is not steered by situational factors but by a Goal that has been set. Situational factors manifest their influence in the extent to which they facilitate the individual in reaching those Goals. Where the three theories exert preferential effects on certain Goals, differences in findings have occurred.
- *Differential emphasis on the Process of Motivation*: Each theory appears to emphasize a specific construct within the Process of Motivation, as proposed by the Model:
    - *Goal-setting theory* concentrates on essential attributes associated with the construct of Reality to optimize a Process of Motivation;
    - *Goal-orientation theories* concentrate on attributes associated with the construct of the Goal, especially on Goal-related strategies that are successful within the constraints set by Reality to optimize a Process of Motivation;
    - *Self-determination theory,* concentrates on attributes that are associated with the construct of Impact, seeking to minimize Discrepancy and reducing effects from external interference from Reality to optimize a Process of Motivation.

*These three observations are assumed to have made the three theories to diverge in their findings.*

*In this final conclusion, then, an alternative view is proposed where differences in findings amongst major theories associated with a Phase of Impact are likely to have originated from differences in perceptions of constructs, from circumstances exercising a selective influence on specific Goals, and from differential emphasis on constructs that are considered to be essential in a Process of Motivation according to the Model proposed.*

These observations, in turn, appear to lead to an important implication. With the Model of Motivation gradually progressing, we can make a preliminary observation on its exposure to interference. If the Model so far appears to have provided an adequate structure to capture the Process of Motivation as it appears to manifest itself, it gradually becomes clear from its inherent structure that external influences, in order to become effective, need to match or at least align with a personal Goal that has been set. Depending on the situation, the content of a personal Goal can be anticipated on between reasonable margins, but when situations become more complex, addressing these personal Goals becomes increasingly difficult. In our attempts to uncover the Process, a preliminary conclusion can be made, which is to anticipate on our analysis of a Process of Interference: *There appears to be no such thing as a 'one-size-fits-all' approach to managing Motivation.* Addressing a Process of Motivation is most likely to be a tailor-made affair, and the more it centers or attunes to a personal Goal that has been set, the better the outcomes of this Process of Interference are likely to be[1].

From this perspective, an optimal role for an external actor is likely to be much more diverse than we might have assumed until now. In recent research, gradually new perspectives appear, and an example can be found in the intriguing results obtained from studies that are aimed at ways to instigate curiosity and interest in young children.

*See the exhibit next page* ➔

[1] It follows from the observations that in a Process of Interference, not just one *but at least all three constructs* need to be addressed within a tailor-made setting to have an optimal effect on the Process of Motivation. An aspect that will prove to be essential in the multitude of variations that we will come to observe when analyzing a Process of Interference in subsequent Volumes of the Series.

## *Related Topics: Curiosity and Interest*

An example of a tailor-made approach to Motivation comes from the field of 'curiosity and interest'.

*A grandmother and her grandson...*

*My grandmother (I called her 'Oom') was a remarkable person. She could reassure a child within minutes. Here is what she did...*

*When the child would come to her, full of fears by the novelty of a new experience, she would simply respond by 'voicing' the feelings of the child: "Oh Oom," she would say, mirroring those feelings, "I am too scared to move, but I am brave and bold! So, let me see what we have here, and start an adventure!" Voicing those feelings thus reassured the child, made him open up, and take on the challenge inherent to unchartered and novel situations...*

*The child, I'm afraid to say, was me... And her approach gave me courage and confidence to embark on new adventures until this day...*

How to instigate curiosity and interest? It appears that it is not so much by challenging a child, but rather *by 'voicing' a child's feelings and setting the example...*

Referring to our previous findings on curiosity and interest, an essential question in a Phase of Impact would be: how could we address and ignite feelings of curiosity and interest, especially in a child?

Although the subject falls beyond our scope (as it refers to a Process of Interference), we will briefly cover it here, as it relates to Impact...

We saw earlier that fear of failure is an important ingredient in frustrating curiosity and interest. Rather, a mastery-oriented mindset, where failure is almost 'part-of-the-game-of-finding-out-things', sparkles the initiative to embark on new ventures.

And how do we facilitate these initiatives? By encouragement? Perhaps. Although they could inadvertently pressurize a child... We will come to realize that an essential ingredient is by decreasing Discrepancy. How? By having the child express his or her feelings, expectations, fears, and by affirming these in response. Better still (and adding to this powerful reassuring confirmation), it is by showing the child we share these same feelings and fears (see: Gordon, 1975, 1991).

How to instigate curiosity and interest? It appears it is not by challenging a child, but rather by *'voicing' those feelings and setting the example...*

## *Summary*

The fifth Phase in the Model of Motivation is a 'Phase of Impact'. The Impact of Reality is the Discrepancy experienced by the individual between the Goal that has been set and the subjective experience of an interfering Reality.

Impact and Discrepancy are large when Reality impairs the Process of reaching the Goal. Impact is positive and Discrepancy is small when Reality provides support to the Process of Motivation.

A Phase of Impact consists of a single Stage in which this assessment is made.

We next observed theories from literature and came to realize that the different assumptions that had been put forward by three theories had led to a serious controversy, referred to as being one of the most heated debates in the applied psychology literature. A summary of these opposed views is provided on p. 138.

It appeared the Model of Motivation was able to reconcile these differences using a number of propositions that had been formulated. The distinction between a personal Goal and the Impact with an interfering Reality provided a number of insights that produced an alternative view in which each theory appeared to contribute to a different aspect within this complex and intricate Process of Motivation. And when findings from research were observed that were obtained from these differing areas of studies, these propositions reconciling the different perspectives were found to be confirmed, substantiating the ideas suggested in the Model. An overview of these principal conclusions is provided on p. 177.

But there was a further realization when observing the vast number of studies that had been done in these differing areas. Not only do the kinds of goals we set and the strategies we choose to reach them regulate perceptions of perceived Discrepancy in the Impact from Reality that affects the Process of Motivation, they also to a large extent determine our well-being. The Impact from Reality, appears to affect perceptions of adequacy and worth, of being acknowledged and recognized, which is likely to lead to a range of subsequent reactions.

These findings from research lead to the inevitable conclusion that effects of Impact have profound consequences. Much more than we had first anticipated.

# Chapter 6
## *Truth and Contemplation*
### *Phase 6 - A Phase of Externally Evoked Self-Assessment*

So, the Process of Motivation was interrupted by an unforeseen event defined as 'Reality'. Significance of the intrusion has been observed in a Phase of Reality, and the Impact on the Process, in terms of Discrepancy with the Goal that had been set, in a Phase of Impact as covered in Chapter 5.

As we observed, the Impact is most likely to lead to a plethora of emotions, especially when the Goal we had set is perceived to be important, Significant. But let us refrain for a moment from those emotions, from feelings of annoyance and distress, or delight and victory, of anger and indignation, as we observed in the many examples we used. We'll return to these, and their implications, in Chapter 8. As we observed earlier, this Phase of Impact does not lead *directly* to those effects. A series of steps precedes those feelings, and we will observe these steps in the present and in the next two Chapters.

Why those feelings as a reaction to an intruding Reality? There is a cue that triggers those feelings. And this cue lays in the ambitions I had originally set. The intruding Reality is either opposed to or in accord with those ambitions: the things I initially had in mind in the Goal I defined in a Phase of Expectancies. Following an assessment of Significance, the extent of Impact of the intrusion in the Process of Motivation, the effects are primarily defined by the Goal. It is the Goal that defines the criteria upon which I am to react, in emotions, in cognitions, and in due course in actions and behavior... The more important the Goal, the more explicit those criteria, and the more prominent those reactions.

A Phase of Impact does not imply a simple observation whether there is a perfect match, or an incompatible Discrepancy. In a Phase of Impact, we observe Discrepancy as related to the Goal we had set. And a Phase of Impact leads to an important next Phase in the Process of Motivation where we observe the *adequacy* of those criteria set in a Phase of Expectancies.

This next Phase, then, is a *'Phase of Externally Evoked Self-Assessment'.* In this Phase, we re-assess the aspirations and intentions we had as defined in the Goal and the parameters we had set in a Phase of Expectancies, given the new perspective provided through the Impact from Reality on the Process of Motivation. "Did we do well to define our Goal the way we did, was our assessment adequate of investments needed, or have we been too confident (or too uncertain) in assessing our Achievements, given the encounter we had with this unforeseen Reality?" Note that this re-assessment of adequacy at this point in the Process of Motivation is made without actually changing those criteria, as this will happen at a later step in the Process, when it has progressed through all evaluative stadia in reaction to the Impact from Reality, as was briefly mentioned in the previous Chapter.

So let us observe how this re-assessment of criteria, of aspirations and intentions occurs in the various examples we used so far.

First, the example of Monserrate. Where we anticipated on an experience of 'inspiration-and-awe'. Before getting annoyed, I assess the experience in comparison to the source of what I intended to achieve, namely the Goal I had set. And as I am obviously not very successful, given my recent experience: "Did I do well in defining the Goal the way I did?" Was it wise to have this 'all-inclusive-experience-of-inspiration-and-awe' in visiting Monserrate, or would these criteria need further amendments, and would I be well-advised even to contemplate alternatives instead of visiting these premises (whereby, incidentally, the current Process of Motivation would cease)?

My second example, which happily turned out to be more successful... And here, contemplating the adequacy of initial criteria as defined in the first three Phases, especially a Phase of Expectancies, I could foresee a more daring approach to further increase my investment, as the Impact from Reality provides me now with a perspective of further success. Although increasing intended investment would also increase the risks in case of Failure, I am confident, given these encouraging results obtained through the positive outcomes from Reality in the form of this match, that a renewed confrontation would be as successful as this one, and would thus further propel my level of confidence... Observe, as stated, that at this Phase in the Process, I am only anticipating. These intentions pave the way to further successive steps that will gradually influence my perception of Reality, prior to the actual Effort I will invest when the time is ready.

The groceries... How I wish things would have been different. My postponement was perfect. And then Reality set in and disrupted my carefully orchestrated Process of Motivation. Although the example is deceivingly simple, the effects of Impact are surprisingly complex. My initial frame of reference was to postpone. Reality challenges this state of affairs in its Impact: it is against the deal I made. So, I *have* to make amendments; I feel obliged to do so. And these feelings of, in a sense, being pressurized, will emerge later in the Process as I contemplate these feelings in Phase 8. The assessment of adequacy in the present Phase, Phase 6, of my initial intent to postpone (together with an intended course of action to be defined in Phase 7), will determine my mindset, leading to those feelings towards this antagonizing Reality in Phase 8...

In my fourth example, Reality had a comparable effect to revive a Process of Motivation that until then had remained inactive. It 'tapped into' this Process of what we called a 'dormant' Goal, a Goal that was consciously set aside and remained inactive for a considerable time: in my case the prospect of a trip to Hong Kong that I had postponed for years. And at this Phase in its Process, it is triggered by the provocative Impact of an adjacent Process in my next example. In this Phase of Externally Evoked Self-Assessment the adequacy of the postponement of the trip (or rather: the decision made in Phase 1, and further refined in Phases 2 and 3, to cease investing further Effort to pursue the Goal of going to Hong Kong), this decision is put into question; which, in a next Phase, will bring me to reconsider this strategy of postponement.

In my fifth example, I had my superior emailing me on my prospects of submitting an article. I had set my mind on writing a paper, but fear of failure prevented me from doing so. And here something unexpected happened. The intrusion from Reality affected the postponement of this dormant Goal. But the Process appeared to be affected also by the exposure occurring in the subsequent example. Recall that my frame of reference was determined by what we initially called a 'latent' Goal, to be part of a university with highest principles and uncontested moral values on autonomy. And now, Reality in the form of this email is affected by this latent Goal, which now determines my frame of reference. In re-assessing the adequacy of my Goal in the present Process of Motivation, *this latent Goal from this parallel Process, now also defines the outcomes of my judgment.* My perception of Reality further deteriorates. And because fear of failure was prominent in the decision to postpone this paper, it is highly unlikely that I am prepared to reconsider the line of reasoning that led me to this outcome, following the input from Reality. And this evaluative conclusion in this Phase of the Process of Motivation to maintain my original Goal, in turn, will determine my mindset in the emotional reaction I will have in a subsequent Phase when assessing Reality, and assessing the email of my superior. The frame of reference of my initial latent Goal, then, together with the present assessment of adequacy to maintain postponing my paper, makes it highly unlikely that this final upcoming assessment is going to be positive...

As we will come to realize later, the outcomes of this evaluation, and the effects of this latent Goal, will also affect the course of events in other examples. But more on these later, when we will cover the next steps following our present Phase of Externally Evoked Self-Assessment.

Why did this event tap into this particular latent Goal? It could have evoked a similar reaction in many other latent Goals, but given my personality, my history, my previous experiences, given this what we might call 'constellation of past and present Processes of Motivation', it happened to address this particular Goal. Now, our personality and these previous experiences have been left out of the analysis, and considered as 'given' (as briefly commented on, in an exhibit, in Chapter 1), so as not to confuse our analysis of the elementary steps in the Process of Motivation. The assumption we made at the time was that although personality, previous experience, competence do affect the various choices we make, the outcome, in terms of successive steps that determine the Process of Motivation (which was our primal objective), remains the same. But we are reminded in the example that these constructs *do* play a role in the experience and perception we have of the Impact Reality has on a particular Goal and its associated Process of Motivation.

Back to our final observations on this sixth Phase of the Process.

In our sixth and final example there was a latent Goal that had been interfered with through the Impact from Reality, which now instigates a series of evaluative reactions in this Phase of Externally Evoked Self-Assessment. Recall the email from our previous example which prompted a reaction in our present Process. Reality brought to life, as it were, this latent Goal, where I found a university was to be a sanctuary, a stronghold of integrity and devotion, where autonomy prevailed. In this last example, we could re-phrase these observations slightly. Where so far, in the examples we used, the

Goal was used as a reference that triggered, through the Impact from Reality, to re-assess its adequacy, in this example we now observe an *opposite phenomenon* where Reality, through its Impact, happens to trigger a specific latent Goal. Earlier in Chapter 5, we found there is a multitude of these latent Goals proliferating, each with a distinct Process of Motivation attributed to it. And I choose this particular latent Goal associated with virtues such as honesty, integrity, morality and respectability, to be related to a university setting. But I could have used other attributes, such as wisdom, lucidity, intellect, expertise, or perhaps impartiality or vigilance in an academic context.

By their nature, latent Goals remain inactive, although we are subconsciously aware of their existence. And this latent condition can be brought to life by the Impact from an interfering Reality. As such, Reality through its Impact can trigger these latent Goals, a phenomenon we will refer to later, notably when covering Chapter 11 and Chapter 12.

So, in this final example, a Phase of Impact triggered this particular latent Goal, and, in this Phase of Externally Evoked Self-Assessment, led to questioning the values that it contained: "Did I do well to have these high expectations of moral standards on autonomy to be present in a university? Or should I reconsider the adequacy of these latent expectations?"

To summarize, then, our observations on the Process of Motivation...

We define our Goals in a Phase of Expectancies, re-attuning those Goals in a cyclical Process as we invest Effort, while assessing its effects in a Phase of Internally Evoked Self-Assessment. And when this Process of Motivation is disrupted by an intruding Reality, we assess importance of this event in a Phase of Reality, and the extent of its consequences for the Process of Motivation in a Phase of Impact, as based on criteria defined in those Goals that are central in Motivation and constitute its 'raison d'être'. The Goal provides the criteria, upon which measurement occurs in a Phase of Impact, as expressed in observed Discrepancy.

And this measurement, in turn, leads to an assessment of adequacy of those criteria in a sixth Phase of the Process of Motivation, a Phase of Externally Evoked Self-Assessment.

Next comes the formulation of a plausible course of action, to be covered in Chapter 7.

But let us first determine in more detail what this Phase of Externally Evoked Self-Assessment consists of, and contemplate the repercussions of these assessments on feelings of adequacy, on competence and achievement, as they have been presented in literature both in theory and research.

The sixth Phase in the Process of Motivation is a Phase of Externally Evoked Self-Assessment.

Following the Impact from Reality and the perception of a small or large Discrepancy, three evaluative reactions occur.

A first reaction is aimed towards the Goal (and its parameters) in an assessment of adequacy: "Did I do well to define the Goal, the Effort and its outcomes the way I did?"

In this Phase, however, no actual amendments are yet to be made, as these are exclusively to occur (subsequently) in Phase 1 of the Process of Motivation.

*Phase 6 in the Model of Motivation is covered in detail on pp. 188-192. A summary is provided on p. 218.*

## 1 Definitions

After the Impact from Reality, a re-orientation occurs of the Goal versus Reality, and this re-orientation is aimed at three elements in which the interference found expression, as observed in Chapter 5: the Goal and its parameters, Reality, and Impact, as expressed in the Discrepancy between both constructs.

Referring to Fig 5.3., Chapter 5, the first assessment, then, is aimed at the Goal and its parameters.

Following the realization of Impact, we need to re-assess the Goal and its parameters on the consequences of this intruding Reality. "Did we do well in defining our Goal and its parameters the way we did?" In its most elementary form, a Phase of Externally Evoked Self-Assessment is an assessment of adequacy of the Goal and its settings, given the state of affairs following the interference from Reality in the Process of Motivation aimed at reaching that Goal.

Before proceeding to re-define the Goal and its parameters so as to minimize the interference, the confrontation sets in motion three preceding, passive, evaluative reactions. A Phase of Externally Evoked Self-Assessment, then, is the first of these three. And where it involves an assessment of adequacy of the Goal and its parameters as defined in a Phase of Expectancies, it is assumed this first re-appraisal proceeds in five distinct Stages. The first, a *Stage of Aspiration,* re-examines the Attitude towards the Goal in its newly perceived context with Reality. Does the urge, need, ambition still seem adequate and has the challenge remained the same in achieving the objective set? This Stage is followed by the most important Stage in this Phase, a *Stage of Contemplation,* where the Goal is re-evaluated not on its content (as this would initiate a new Process of Motivation), but rather on its properties of Attainability and Clarity, covered earlier in Chapter 1 and Chapter 2. Where Reality provides a new point of view, or a new perspective, one re-contemplates the feasibility of the Goal, notably in a re-assessment of its properties. A *Stage of Validation* re-evaluates the intended investments. And re-assessments of these initial Stages also lead to a re-appraisal of Achievement and Failure as initially set. How does one perceive chances of success once we are set to re-appraise the objective when confronted with Reality? A *Stage of Attainment* originates from the previous Stage, and re-evaluates Achievement and Failure associated with reaching the Goal. And finally, in a *Stage of Fulfillment*, this re-appraisal leads to a re-evaluation of Satisfaction and Frustration levels.

A Phase of Externally Evoked Self-Assessment is initiated to eventually neutralize the effects of Impact on the Goal and its parameters. It is a 'reflective' assessment between the Attitude, Energy, Achievement-Failure and Satisfaction-Frustration parameters initially set, and the Goal now encountered in light of Reality. This 'reflection' towards the Goal is visualized in Fig. 6.1., by the arrows enclosing the initial parameters, on one side, and the Goal as perceived, on the other.

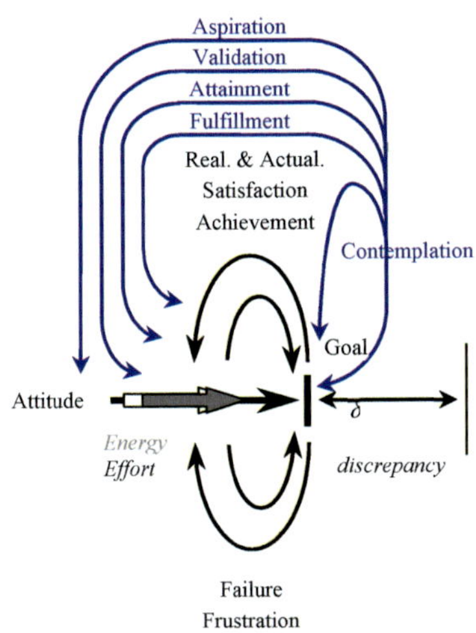


*Fig. 6.1.*
*A visualized overview of Phase 6,*
*a Phase of Externally Evoked Self-Assessment*
*in the theoretical Model of Motivation,*
*consisting of:*

11. A Stage of Aspiration
12. A Stage of Contemplation
13. A Stage of Validation
14. A Stage of Attainment
15. A Stage of Fulfillment

The outcome of this evaluative re-appraisal can be expressed in terms of a negative or a positive outcome. If the Goal and parameters are found to be less adequate, outcomes of the evaluation are negative; If these are found to be adequate, the evaluation turns out to be positive.

Summarizing this sixth Phase in the Process of Motivation within the sequence of preceding Phases, it follows directly upon Impact, initiating the first of three passive, evaluative reactions, as visualized in Fig. 6.2.

Now, what effects are occurring, according to the various options we observed earlier in Chapter 5? Which options are likely to produce positive outcomes, and which can be considered to be detrimental to the Process of Motivation? To put these questions in a slightly different perspective: "What would make me reconsider my initial objectives? What 'opens me up', and what causes me to withdraw?"

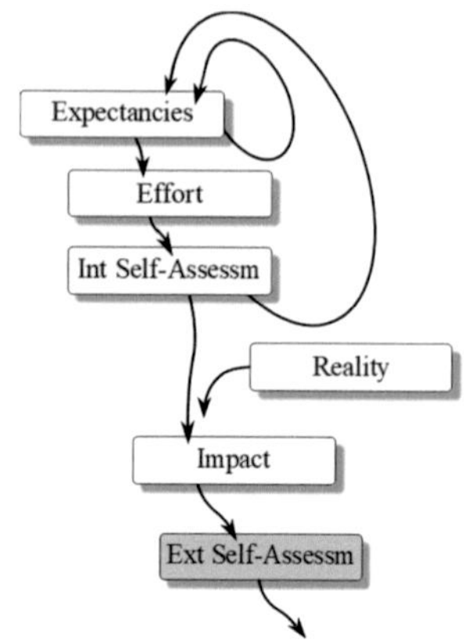


*Fig. 6.2.*
*A Phase of Externally Evoked Self-Assessment Visualized as part of successive Phases in the description of the Model of Motivation*

In Chapter 5, we saw there were eight main options to consider. From these, the ones having highly Significant Goals, facing Reality with low perceived Significance (options 1 and 3, p. 123) are likely to yield little effect, as Reality has insufficient 'standing' to make me reconsider the adequacy of my Goal and its settings. The same applies to both options with low Significance of the Goal and low perceived Significance of Reality (options 5 and 7, p. 124). In both cases, the Process of Motivation proceeds through the various Phases without much effects occurring. The situation changes somewhat when both options are confronted with a high perceived Significance of Reality. Effects remain rather low when a Goal with low Significance is contrasted with such a Reality when perceived Discrepancy is high (option 6, p. 124), but these effects increase when perceived Discrepancy is low (option 8, p. 124). Still the effects remain modest because the Goal lacks 'weight' justifying a reconsideration of adequacy, but this small

Discrepancy adds 'persuasion' from a Significant Reality, making it an interesting venue to explore when considering *addressing* the Process of Motivation through Reality, i.e. in a Process of Interference.

Which leaves us, as observed earlier in Chapter 5, with two options that deserve attention for the effects they produce in the Process of Motivation: a highly Significant Goal versus a perceived highly Significant Reality, with a first option of high Discrepancy (option 2, p. 123). The option is highly disrupting. The thoughts, notions, ideas that made me define this Goal the way it is in a Phase of Expectancies, consolidated subsequently in a Phase of Effort and a Phase of Internally Evoked Self-Assessment, these same Processes now make me resist the input provided from Reality. The perceived Discrepancy between this Goal and Reality is simply too large. The Significance of my Goal, the Processes that let me to define the objective, now prevent me from reconsidering their adequacy in a direction that is to favor Reality, which, in addition, is perceived to oppose my attempts at reaching this highly desired Goal. Reality becomes 'the enemy'. The re-assessment of adequacy in this Phase is most unlikely to favor this new, unforeseen and disruptive input from Reality. *Thus, when a Goal of high Significance is confronted with a highly Significant Reality, the effects in reconsidering the adequacy of the Goal are assumed to favor the Goal rather than Reality when perceived Discrepancy between both is large.* And the option causes me to withdraw.

Fortunately, when perceived Discrepancy decreases between a highly Significant Goal and a highly Significant Reality (option 4, p. 123), the chances to reconsider the Goal and my settings increase considerably, as Reality in its full Significance provides an acknowledgement of my treasured ambitions, giving support to the Process of Motivation aimed at reaching this Goal. We turn to such a supportive Reality so as to further enhance its positive effect on the Process. *In contrast, then, when a Goal of high Significance is confronted with a highly Significant Reality, the effects in reconsidering the adequacy of the Goal are assumed to favor Reality in accord with the Goal when perceived Discrepancy between both is small.* It is the option that 'opens me up' and makes me reconsider my initial objectives.

So, effects occur mainly when Significance of the Goal and Significance of Reality are high. And these effects are aimed primarily at anticipating on protective measures in case of perceived high Discrepancy, and on increasing the positive effects from Reality when Discrepancy is low.

These effects of Impact, of anticipating on adequacy of the Goal, of investments made and their assessments, especially in both cases when Significance is high, not only affect the subsequent steps that are made in the Process of Motivation. Impact from Reality and assessments of adequacy have a much broader effect that has been the subject of extensive research in the social sciences, particularly in areas covering competence and achievement.

These assessments also affect perceptions of ability, aptitude and proficiency on a personal scale. And research in this field has provided many insights that help us to further understand the depth of the effects of Impact.

In a Phase of Externally Evoked Self-Assessment, external cues come to interfere with our personal observations and deductions. And the effects of this interference will profoundly determine not only our assessments of competence and achievement, but also of the way we perceive ourselves, in what has been referred to as 'self-concept', to be covered more extensively in Chapter 8.

Assessment of one's competence and achievement, as provided through the Impact from Reality, has been extensively studied in relation to a concept referred to in literature as 'self-efficacy'. Theory and research in the field of self-efficacy will provide not only further insights into mechanisms involved in these assessments, but will also provide a confirmation for the effects that are assumed to occur in a Phase of Externally Evoked Self-Assessment, especially when Significance is high, both in the Goal that is set and in perceived Significance of an interfering Reality.

## 2 Theories

These insights in success, in perceptions of adequacy, in abilities, competence and achievement are central in a Phase of Externally Evoked Self-Assessment. And their effects on affective, cognitive and behavioral processes and outcomes (defined in the field as 'nomological networks') have been the source of further development in both theory and research. A number of theories have been prominent: *goal-orientation theories*, *social cognitive theories, expectancy-value theories* and *self-determination theory.*

A first field of study that provides further insights in effects of Impact is the field of *goal-orientation theories.* As reflected on previously (first in Chapter 3, and further extended in Chapter 5), goals aimed at performance were thought to lead to mixed or negative outcomes, as the effects of Impact from an interfering Reality are more prominent when goals are aimed at demonstrating competence or avoiding demonstrating incompetence (one either 'wins' or 'loses'). And goals aimed at mastery were assumed to produce positive outcomes, as the effects of Impact from an interfering Reality are less pronounced when goals are aimed at developing competence and task mastery.

The theory was further refined with a diversification in mastery-approach and mastery-avoidance goals, producing a 2x2 achievement goal model.

*See exhibit next page* ➔

Even more than in the previous trichotomous achievement goal model, this further refinement laid emphasis on the effects of Impact, and especially on perceived adequacy of standards used, not only in performance-oriented but also in mastery-oriented goals. The distinction in approach and avoidance not only implies an outside interference (as covered in Chapter 5), it also (at least partly) presumes an awareness of the consequences occurring from the interference: one either 'approaches' or 'avoids'. In parallel, the Model of Motivation suggests, in a Phase of Externally Evoked Self-Assessment, a similar awareness, assuming an assessment of adequacy producing positive or negative effects, in terms of affective, cognitive and behavioral processes and outcomes. And with the distinction extending to mastery-oriented goals, a further refinement in assumed effects can be made.

With mastery-oriented goal pursuit producing less interference, as covered in Chapter 5, a distinction in mastery-approach and mastery-avoidance goal orientation is expected to produce outcomes that follow an incremental scale in terms of perceived interference, hence Impact and perceived Discrepancy.

Mastery-oriented goals that are assumed to be less susceptible to outside interference are expected to range from a highly positive Impact with small perceived Discrepancy for mastery-approach goals, to moderate forms of Impact with higher perceived Discrepancy for mastery-avoidance goals. And these would be followed on this incremental scale by performance-approach, respectively performance-avoidance goal orientations, with an increase in perceived Discrepancy and Impact on the Process of Motivation according to the Model, and increased negative outcomes.

These refinements in the trichotomous achievement goal model produced results in research that will provide further confirmation for the assumptions made with regard to the effects of Impact and perceived adequacy, covered subsequently in Section 3.

But this distinction did not receive unreserved agreement in the research field (Niemivirta, Pulkka, Tapola & Tuominen, 2019), leading again to further diversifications into mastery-intrinsic and mastery-extrinsic goals (Niemivirta, 2002, 2004). And results from research on these refined 3x2 achievement goal model diversifications, in turn, produced further confirmation for the model.

The diversification in mastery-intrinsic and mastery-extrinsic goals enables further insights into the effects

### 3.3. Goal-orientation theories

The 2x2 achievement goal model extends the trichotomous model with a distinction in approach-avoidance for mastery-oriented goals.

Thus, in the 2x2 achievement goal model, a distinction is made in:

- *Performance-approach goals,* aimed at demonstrating competence relative to others (as conceptualized in the trichotomous model, see exhibit p. 132). These goals are assumed to produce mixed outcomes;
- *Performance-avoidance goals,* aimed at avoiding demonstrating incompetence relative to others (equivalent to the trichotomous model, p. 132). These goals are expected to produce negative, maladaptive outcomes;
- *Mastery-approach goals,* aimed at developing competence and task mastery (conceptualized as mastery-oriented goals in the dichotomous model, see p. 132). These goals are expected to produce positive outcomes;
- *Mastery-avoidance goals,* aimed at avoiding task-based or intrapersonal incompetence. These goals are assumed to produce less positive outcomes than mastery-approach goals, but more positive than performance-avoidance goals.

(Elliot, 1999; Elliot & McGregor, 2001; Pintrich, 2000a).

*(Continued)*

of Reality and Impact assumed by the Model of Motivation. At the basis of the 3x2 achievement goal model is a distinction previously made in Chapter 3 and Chapter 5, between standards of competence defined entirely by the individual (referred to as 'mastery-intrinsic' or 'self-based goals' in the 3x2 model, with intrapersonal standards of competence) and standards defined externally, either in an absolute sense (defined as 'mastery-extrinsic' or 'task-based goals' in the 3x2 model, with absolute standards of competence) or by comparison to others (defined as 'other-based goals' in the 3x2 model, with interpersonal standards of competence, comparable to the performance-oriented goals in both 2x2 and trichotomous models).

*See exhibit* ➔

A further refinement is made in Goal-orientation theories in a so-called 3x2 achievement goal model, where besides the dichotomy in performance-approach and performance-avoidance goals (referred to as 'other-approach' and 'other-avoidance goals'), a further distinction is made in mastery-oriented approach and avoidance goals, which make use of either mastery-intrinsic goals aimed at a standard which is entirely self-defined (thus following a so-called 'intrapersonal standard') or mastery-extrinsic goals aimed at an absolute standard of competence.

### 3.3. Goal-orientation theories

Thus, the 3x2 achievement goal model consists of:

- *Performance-oriented goals* (other-based goals with interpersonal standards of competence):
  - *other-approach goals,* (performance-approach goals), are aimed at demonstrating competence relative to others;
  - *other-avoidance goals,* (performance-avoidance goals) are aimed at avoiding demonstrating incompetence relative to others;
- *Mastery-intrinsic goals* (self-based goals with intrapersonal standards of competence):
  - *self-approach goals,* are aimed at developing self-based competence;
  - *self-avoidance goals*, are aimed at avoiding self-based incompetence;
- *Mastery-extrinsic goals* (task-based goals with absolute standards of competence):
  - *task-approach goals,* are aimed at developing task-based competence;
  - *task-avoidance goals,* are aimed at avoiding task-based incompetence.

(Elliot, Murayama & Pekrun, 2011).

For an overview of these achievement goal models, see: Elliot & Hulleman, 2017. For an historical overview: Urdan & Kaplan, 2020.

As such, the 3x2 achievement goal model provides a demarcation between the self-based, or mastery-intrinsic, goals defined and verified in the first three Phases of the Model, and the task- or other-based goals where effects of Reality and Impact are assumed to lead to assessments of adequacy proposed in the Model. One either gains confidence in self-defined goals that have evolved through successive cycles in the Process of Motivation to what has been conceptualized as self-based approach goals, or these assessments have resulted in negative assessments through successive cycles, leading to self-based avoidance goals. So results from research findings are expected to reflect these approach-avoidance strategies. And the subsequent distinctions involving external influences are assumed to follow equivalent patterns according to the Model, in Phases of Reality and Impact, and assessments of adequacy in a Phase of Externally Evoked Self-Assessment. Where absolute standards are aimed for in task-based goals, the cyclical experience should produce either approach or avoidance strategies where perceived small or large Discrepancies interfering with one's Process of Motivation are thought to be generated by the outcomes from Impact, and therefore expected to lead to positive or negative outcomes, respectively. Where interpersonal standards are used in other-based goals, the cyclical experience that is being built-up according to the Model should produce equivalent approach or avoidance strategies when Discrepancies are perceived to be small or large and Impact is expected to lead to positive or negative outcomes, respectively. And within this distinction, the absolute standards, given their objective and neutral connotation, are expected to produce more moderate effects than interpersonal standards, where a more explicit 'win or lose' connotation is expected to produce more pronounced outcomes.

Research findings on the 3x2 achievement goal model are to follow in Section 3.

Although originating from a differing perspective, these further distinctions made in goal-orientation theories, progressing from a 2x2 to a 3x2 achievement goal model, appear to confirm the assumptions made in the Model of Motivation, where a cyclical Process of Motivation is assumed to yield strategies comparable to the approach and avoidance constructs proposed in both achievement goal models.

What is the outcome of these various approaches in goal pursuit when observing one's competence?

In the Impact from Reality and the assessment of adequacy of the Goal that has been set, as postulated in the Model of Motivation, a phenomenon occurs that has been the subject of intense study, especially in the field of educational psychology.

As time goes by, the encounters with Reality multiply in the various Processes of Motivation that are initiated. Moreover, as we will come to realize later in Chapter 8, the Process of Motivation is not static, as it progresses over subsequent Phases. Rather, the Process is dynamic, and, as it happens, will appear to be even cyclical in nature, where the encounter with Reality will reoccur at several occasions as the Process gradually progresses towards reaching the Goal that has been set.

In this multiple exposure to the Impact from Reality and the assessments of adequacy of one's Goal and one's aspirations, there is also a progressive buildup in awareness and insights about one's competence and ability in reaching this particular Goal. This gradual 'accumulation of knowledge' about one's proficiencies, in turn, not only has consequences for the way the individual gradually comes to perceive him or herself in various areas ("I am really good at playing tennis, am I not?"), but also leads to expectations, to confidence or doubts, as one extrapolates these outcomes to future achievements ("I am confident on winning this match, shall we make a bet?"). And when these experiences lead to all kind of statements, these, in turn, manifest themselves as expressions of Reality for others that could even affect their Processes of Motivation as well ("I'll have to be careful, this fellow seems so confident of winning, I doubt if I'll meet up with the challenge").

These experiences and reciprocal interactions following Impact are complex and have been the subject of study in no less than three major theories of motivation: *social cognitive theory, expectancy-value theory,* covered earlier in Chapter 1, and *self-determination theory,* covered in Chapter 3 and Chapter 5.

*Social cognitive theory* was developed by Albert Bandura in the late 1970s, and has been further developed over the years. As discussed earlier in Chapter 1, in the mid-twentieth century, the individual was perceived to be a passive and reactive organism. As Bandura later stated, "(...) brains [are] merely repositories for past stimuli inputs and conduits for external stimulations, but they can add nothing to their performance" (Bandura 1999, p. 22). From the perspective that it was "(...) ironic that a science of human functioning should strip people of the very capabilities that make them unique in their power to shape their environment and their destiny (...)" (p. 21), he proposed a theory where the individual was proactively engaged in development and pursuit of success, influenced by, and, in reciprocity, influencing his or her environment. Central to the theory was that human thought and behavior were the product of a dynamic interplay of both personal, behavioral and social/environmental factors or influences. As commented on later by Pajares: "How people interpret the results of their own actions informs and alters their environments and the personal factors they possess, which, in turn, inform and alter future actions" (Pajares, 2006, p. 340). These beliefs are central to social cognitive theory, and are perceived as the foundation for motivation, well-being and personal accomplishment. As stated by Pajares: "This is because unless (...) people believe that their actions can produce the results they desire, they have little incentive to act or to persevere in the face of the difficulties that inevitably ensue" (Pajares, 2006, p. 339).

*See exhibit* ➔

So we pursue tasks and activities which we believe are within our capabilities, and we tend to avoid those that we believe are beyond our competence.

As a direct consequence of these assumptions, the belief that one holds about one's capability to succeed in an endeavor becomes a vital force in attaining such an objective; or in failing to do so. Among these beliefs, none is more central or pervasive than beliefs of personal efficacy. As commented on by Bandura: "[People] are self-examiners of their own functioning. Through functional self-awareness they reflect on their personal efficacy, the soundness of their thoughts and actions, and the

A central concept in social cognitive theory is 'self-efficacy'. It is a generative concept that refers to people's beliefs in their capabilities to address a particular situation, given the skills one has and the circumstances one faces. As such, it refers to a reflective, proactive process (Bandura, 1997).

### 5.1. Social cognitive theories

Social cognitive theory emphasizes the role of self-beliefs (Pajares, 2006). And these are the product of reciprocal interactions between three factors.

Individuals are viewed as proactive, self-reflecting and self-regulating within a dynamic interplay, where *personal factors* (such as cognition, affect and biological events), *behavioral factors* and *environmental influences* create interactions that mutually affect each other. This framework, defined as a so-called '*triadic reciprocality*', defines how people interpret the result of their actions, which, in turn, affects these personal, behavioral and environmental factors, to further influence and alter future actions.

This reciprocality is a central tenet of social cognitive theory.

These self-beliefs, as products of the triadic reciprocality, provide the foundations for motivation. And among these beliefs, the most central or pervasive are beliefs of personal efficacy. These beliefs are referred to as perceptions of '*self-efficacy*'.

Self-efficacy is defined as one's "(...) beliefs in one's capabilities to organize and execute the courses of action required to manage prospective situations" (Bandura, 1997, p. 2).

*(Continued)*

meaning of their pursuits, and they make corrective adjustments if necessary" (Bandura, 2006c, p. 3).

This reflection on personal efficacy through functional self-awareness has become known as the concept of 'self-efficacy'. Self-efficacy refers to one's beliefs, or one's subjective judgments of one's capabilities "(...) to organize and execute courses of action to attain designated goals (...). It is a belief about what a person *can* do rather than personal judgments about one's physical or personality attributes" (Zimmerman & Cleary, 2006, p. 47). As eloquently stated by Reeve: "Self-efficacy is a more generative capacity in which the individual organizes and orchestrates his skills (...). It is the capacity to use one's personal resources well under diverse and trying circumstances" (Reeve, 2005, p. 228).

So self-efficacy is a personal reflection that extends beyond a mere noticing of one's capabilities. It also involves translating those capabilities into effective performance in multiple circumstances. And having the means to adapt favorably to those circumstances, in turn, affects one's perception of self, as we will cover in Chapter 8.

Where do these beliefs in one's self-efficacy come from? According to social cognitive theory, they originate from four main sources. A first source, is through mastery experiences, also referred to as

### 5.1. Social cognitive theories

In social cognitive theory, beliefs of personal efficacy play an essential role and form the foundation of motivated action.

In general, then, social cognitive theory is rooted in the core belief that one has the power to influence one's functioning and the course of events by one's actions. This is referred to as a so-called '*agentic perspective*' (Bandura, 1986, 1989, 2001, 2006a, 2018). "In this conception, people are self-organizing, proactive, self-regulating, and self-reflecting. They are contributors to their life circumstances not just products of them" (Bandura, 2006c, p. 3).

There are four functions through which human agency is exercised: *intentionality* (a proactive commitment to induce a course of action), *forethought* (an anticipation on subsequent events and likely consequences), *self-reactiveness* (initiating self-regulatory processes to maintain a course of action), and *self-reflectiveness* (the ability to evaluate the effectiveness of actions). And it is by engaging in self-reflectiveness that one develops perceptions of self-efficacy.

For further reading on social cognitive theory: Bandura, 1982, 1986, 1991, 1993, 1997, 2000, 2001, 2011, 2018.

*Next related thread 5.2. ➔ p. 283*

'performance accomplishments'. These are the gradual 'accumulation' of experiences referred to earlier, where success builds a robust belief in one's efficacy and failure undermines these beliefs. A second source is through so-called 'vicarious experiences' observed in social models. And it appears that the more one perceives similarities with those role models, the more persuasive their successes and failures, and the more pronounced their impact on self-efficacy. A third source is 'social persuasion', where verbal feedback and instruction serve to strengthen one's beliefs that one has the potential to succeed. A fourth and final source is 'emotional arousal', where emotions and physiological arousal can impact self-efficacy (Bandura, 1986, 1997).

These sources reflect the various forms in which Reality manifests itself, as proposed in the Model of Motivation. There are a number of additional observations to be made as based on the ideas put forward by social cognitive theory, both on these expressions of Reality and on the effects of Impact in a Phase of Externally Evoked Self-Assessment as proposed in the Model of Motivation.

First, following the assumptions about reciprocality, people appear not only to act on the Impact from Reality, but also to react towards Reality and their environment in return. As we shall see in coming Chapters, notably Chapter 8, we not only assess and act upon Impact, but Reality itself is, in turn, 'impacted' by these events, especially as the Model will appear to become cyclical after these assessments in reaction to the Impact from Reality have been made. The Impact is not unidirectional, but rather appears to be reciprocal and interactive.

Secondly, following the cyclical nature in the Process of Motivation as proposed in the Model, social cognitive theory also provides insights into the gradual buildup not only of knowledge pertaining to one's capabilities, but also, and, more prominently, into the consequences of this 'accumulation' for future action and the endeavors we are likely to pursue. This gradual buildup of an adequate belief in one's personal resources provides a portfolio on which basic choices are made on ventures people are likely to pursue.

So, the insights from social cognitive theory expand on the evaluative approach of assessments of adequacy in a Phase of Externally Evoked Self-Assessment as proposed in the Model of Motivation. And it also extends the unidimensional character of the Impact from Reality into a reciprocal interaction that evolves as the Process of Motivation progresses over subsequent cycles.

As such, the insights from social cognitive theory 'enrich' the propositions from the Model. It provides an impressive account of the complexities in determinants of human behavior captured in the constructs it defines. However, in doing so, social cognitive theory has also encountered considerable difficulties in misconceptions and methodological issues in studies that have been published.

*See exhibit next page* ➔

## *Related Topics: on Constructs and Concepts*

In defining social cognitive theory, Bandura used a remarkable approach in theorizing on what he called "(...) the plurality of determinants and the intricate and dynamic interaction between them" (Bandura, 2018, p. 132). In his attempt at building a theory of human behavior, it appears he captured the complexities of those determinants and dynamics into single constructs (such as a 'triadic reciprocality' or an 'agentic perspective', see exhibits pp. 198-199), and used these integrated constructs to provide further insights in deeper strata of human functioning. Thus, in a sense, these constructs have been used as foundations, or building blocks, for further theorizing.

This sophisticated approach and the variety of insights it produced also had a downside. In research, studies were being published using faulty measures as those concepts, in their complexity, have frequently been misunderstood...

Serious threats occur to the integrity of research findings when misinterpretations are made in concepts and constructs used. Problems have been reported in several areas of study in motivation.

Although Bandura provided specific guidelines for the construction of appropriate scales and measurements (Bandura 1997, 2006b), he reported on misconceptions of self-efficacy theory and faulty measures in an article reflecting on the field of social cognitive theory and human agency (Bandura, 2018).

Referring to research related to self-efficacy theory, Klassen and Usher (2010), state: "Measurement problems continue to taint self-efficacy research, and faulty conceptualization of the construct was widespread in the research we reviewed. The pervasiveness of mismeasurement creates a serious threat to the future of self-efficacy research. When more than half of studies published in influential journals include flawed or atheoretical measures, the future of self-efficacy research as a theoretically grounded means of understanding human behavior is threatened" (p. 20).

Issues in methodology and conceptualization have been reported in other areas of study in motivation, such as expectancy-value theories (Wigfield & Eccles, 2000), goal-orientation theories (Elliot, 2005) and self-determination theory (Patall & Hooper, 2019), as we commented on earlier in an exhibit, p. 81.

Competence is a central concept in goal-orientation theories. At the start of the millennium, the classic *Handbook of Competence and Motivation* by Andrew Elliot and Carol Dweck (2005) had an ambitious aim "(...) to refocus the achievement motivation literature using the concept of competence (...)", and to establish competence as its conceptual core (Elliot, Dweck & Yeager, 2017, p. 3.).

So, the concept of competence gradually replaced the concept of achievement. Competence is defined as: "(...) a condition or quality of effectiveness, ability, sufficiency or success" (Elliot, Dweck & Yeager, 2017, p. 3).

And likewise, the inherent need conceptualized earlier in a 'need for achievement' and 'achievement motivation' (see p. 42, 43) has been shifted towards 'competence motivation'.

Competence and competence motivation are usually associated with an urge, or a will, usually defined as a *need,* to achieve competence. And goals that are aimed at fulfilling this need are (still) defined as 'achievement goals', having "(...) the purpose for engaging in competence-relevant behavior" (Elliot & Hulleman, 2017, p. 44). Hence the emphasis on achievement goals in goal-orientation theories, as central constructs, in tracing their origin and effects (Elliot & Hulleman, 2017).

## *Example 1 ~ 'Competence'*

*Issues in measurement and conceptualization have affected research on motivation.*

*To illustrate the difficulties arising when using concepts and constructs to capture complex phenomena, let us refer to a concept that has been frequently used in theories of motivation: the concept of 'competence'.*

*We already referred to the concept on many occasions. But what is 'competence'?*

*And what are differences with other concepts, such as 'confidence', or the concept of 'self-efficacy' we just covered?*

A number of theories on motivation have focused on competence, and their origins and effects, notably on perceptions of self.

For a current extensive overview on competence, see: Elliot, Dweck & Yeager, 2017.

*Competence* is a condition or quality of effectiveness, ability, sufficiency or success.

## :ample 2 ~ 'Confidence' and 'Self-efficacy'

*In using concepts capturing the processes that make us aware of our abilities, talents, proficiencies, we refer to the concept of 'competence', but why not use 'confidence' or 'self-efficacy' instead? Are all these concepts not capturing the same notion, idea or thought that we all use to refer to how we make use of our capabilities, skills or talents?*

*The fact of the matter is, that theories use specific concepts and constructs to refer to (thus conceptualize) specific notions, ideas, thoughts that we tend to use within a much broader context of everyday life.*

*To illustrate, let us observe in a second example the difference between 'confidence' and 'self-efficacy'.*

*Confidence* is a colloquial construct, indicating a (positive) end-result, as an outcome of competence-oriented pursuits...

*Self-efficacy* is a personal estimation of one's confidence that one can successfully complete a task at hand.

In informal, colloquial use of language, 'confidence' and 'self-efficacy' are often used interchangeably. But self-efficacy, in its use as a central concept in social cognitive theory, is different from the concept of confidence...

Recall that self-efficacy was not a simple expectation of outcomes, or estimate that one's behavior will lead to a certain outcome (Pajares & Schunk, 2005). Rather, "an efficacy expectation is the conviction that one can successfully execute the behavior required to produce the outcomes" (Bandura, 1977, p. 193). It is, in its strictest sense, a perceived capability to produce given attainments (Bandura, 2006b). As such, "self-efficacy is a competence-based construct and represents personal estimation of the confidence toward the task at hand" (Ahn & Bong, 2019, p. 65).

So there is a relation with confidence, but it is used in a very precise and restricted connotation.

In general, the concept of confidence is used in a broader context. It is a colloquial construct, indicating a (positive) end result, as an outcome of competence-oriented pursuits (Elliot & Hulleman, 2017).

The difference illustrates the difficulties encountered by theoreticians in choosing suitable designations for the constructs they use, as these constructs often also have a colloquial meaning.

# Constructs and Concepts in Motivation

So, a study of the complex expressions in which motivation manifests itself, necessitates that these expressions be captured in ideas, thoughts and notions, that we refer to as concepts, or constructs.

And to have research yield precise results, those concepts and constructs need to be defined as accurate as possible. As commented on by Pajares and Schunk (2005): "Social science constructs are always at the mercy of the researchers who define and use them. When researchers' conceptions of the same construct differ, one can expect that comparing findings will be a challenging, perhaps hopeless, enterprise" (p. 107).

As we cover those concepts and constructs progressively in the Chapters covering the Process of Motivation, confusion can easily arise. To assist in maintaining an adequate overview, here are the main concepts and constructs used in theories and research from literature in the field of motivation. A number of these have been covered previously, and to maintain a complete coverage, the overview includes some that are still to be covered more extensively.

A number of constructs and concepts are central to the study of motivation.

To illustrate, a selection is provided, with reference to related concepts and constructs, as they have been covered so far throughout the text:

- *Achievement*
- *Need for achievement*
- *Achievement goals* are goals having the purpose for engaging in competence-relevant behavior

*More on these concepts* ➔ *p. 42, 43, 202.*

- *Curiosity*
- *Interest* is the motivation to seek and learn new information linked to some form of existing knowledge

*For these concepts* ➔ *p. 48, 77, 179.*

- *Competence*
- *Confidence*
- *Self-efficacy*

*For these concepts* ➔ *p. 198, 202-203.*

In coming Chapters, we will add further concepts, including:

- *Attributions*

*More on 'attributions'* ➔ *p. 234-242.*

- *Self-concept*
- *Academic Self-concept*

So, in the attempts at reaching an objective, there is not only a series of assessments that occur as proposed in the Model of Motivation, there is also an 'accumulation of knowledge' on one's potential and competence as a result of these assessments. And this knowledge further increases as the Process of Motivation progresses through successive cycles. And as distinct Processes of Motivation evolve over time, these Processes provide further growth in this increasing knowledge as the evidence accumulates. Thus, it is a dynamic 'accumulation' within distinct Processes of Motivation, as well as between the whole of these Processes as they evolve over time.

This reflection on and progressive awareness of personal efficacy also affect and shape people's outcome expectations. In a further development to a theory we observed earlier, *expectancy-value theories* have provided further insights in how these expectations further progress. Recall from Chapter 1 that in these theories, so-called 'expectancies for success' were defined as one's beliefs about how well one would perform on future achievement tasks. As such, there is a distinct link between findings just observed in social cognitive theory, and those proposed in expectancy-value theories.

In a more recent version of the expectancy-value model in achievement motivation, achievement-related choices and performance are influenced directly by expectancies and values. And these "(...) are influenced by individual's task-specific beliefs, such as their self-concepts of ability, and their goals and self-schemas, along with their affective memories for different achievement-related events. These (...) are in turn influenced by individuals' perceptions of other peoples' attitudes and expectations for them, and by their own interpretations of their previous achievement outcomes" (Wigfield, Rosenzweig & Eccles, 2017, p. 117; see also: Rosenzweig, Wigfield & Eccles, 2019)[1].

*See exhibit next page* ➔

Although it is important to acknowledge that these suggested concepts and constructs come from a different theoretical model that emphasizes different aspects of motivation, there are distinct analogies with the Model of Motivation proposed. Moreover, it adds further insights through these specific achievement-related constructs. Where the Model of Motivation focuses on the genesis and development and growth of a specific Goal as it progresses towards its

[1] It must be noted that a number of these constructs were also contained within the earlier version of the expectancy-value model as presented by Eccles-Parsons et al. in 1983. However, as recent diversifications to the model focused on these external oriented constructs, which bear resemblance to a Phase of Externally Evoked Self-Assessment following Impact from Reality, these elements are covered presently, distinct from those reported on in relation to a Phase of Expectancies in Chapter 1. Nonetheless, it must be noted that in the expectancy-value model, these constructs that appear to be both intra- and interpersonal in their manifestation, are less articulate than the demarcation made in the Model of Motivation between Phases preceding, and Phases following Impact from Reality.

achievement, expectancy-value theory focuses on where these expectancies and values originate from and how they are being influenced.

Previously, in Chapter 1, we covered conceptual similarities occurring between expectancy-value theories and the distinct Stages proposed in a Phase of Expectancies. If we extend the Model with insights pertaining to a Phase of Externally Evoked Self-Assessment, we can assume, in accord with these propositions made especially in the more recent and extended version of the expectancy-value model of achievement motivation, that an assessment of adequacy following the Impact from Reality leads to a gradual increase, or 'accumulation of knowledge'. This, in turn, not only leads to insights on competence and self-efficacy, as previously seen, but also to so-called 'self-schemas', perceptions of 'ideal self' and 'task demands', as well as a 'self-concept of one's abilities', as further defined in the expectancy-value model. And in the proposed succession of subsequent Phases in the Model of Motivation, these produce affective memories, giving rise to new 'short-term' and 'long-term goals'.

In addition, insights from the expectancy-value theory could extend the concept of Reality to include not only external and situational influences, but also cultural and gender role stereotypes and perception

### 1.2. Expectancy-value theories

Most prominent amongst recent expectancy-value theories of motivation is the Eccles et al. expectancy-value model of achievement choice.

In their model, Eccles and colleagues built on previous work (see exhibit pp. 43-44) to determine "(...) how students' values predict their choices in a variety of domains, and (...) the developmental course of individual's expectancies and values" (Wigfield, Rosenzweig & Eccles, 2017, p. 117).

In their model, achievement-related choices and performances are directly influenced by: *subjective task value* and *expectancies for success.*

Task value is perceived to consist of four components:

- *intrinsic value,* the extent to which the task is interesting, or completing a task is attractive;
- *attainment value,* the extent to which a task is perceived to be important or meaningful, and central to one's sense of self;
- *utility value,* the extent to which a task is useful for current or future goals or plans;
- *cost,* a fourth distinction considered more recently to be a distinct construct, defined as the extent to which engaging in a task has negative aspects.

(Barron & Hulleman, 2015).

*(Continued)*

of socializer's beliefs, expectations and attitudes[1].

Despite the less articulate demarcation between the various concepts used in the expectancy-value model of achievement motivation and the constructs used in the Model of Motivation, both models have noticeable similarities in these concepts, in the relation between these concepts, and in the assumptions about the dynamic nature of the processes involved.

More recently, the model has been extended further, by observing the 'cost' construct as a separate entity[2]. By defining cost as a factor influencing value, rather than one of its constituting components, the concept of cost in its present form bears resemblance to elements of Reality as conceptualized in the Model of Motivation (For overviews, see Barron & Hulleman, 2015; Johnson & Safavian, 2016; Wigfield, Rosenzweig & Eccles, 2017)[3].

[1] Contrary to the previous comment, these observations reflect not as much on similarities between constructs, but rather on their various manifestations.

[2] The construct had emerged as a separate factor distinct from the concepts of expectancies and values (Conley, 2012; Kosovich, Hulleman, Barron & Getty, 2015; Trautwein, Marsh, Nagengast, Ludtke, Nagy & Jonkmann, 2012).

[3] In its present conceptualization, the concepts of so-called 'psychological cost', 'social cost' and 'economic' or 'financial cost' make explicit reference to a concept similar to Reality (See Wigfield, Rosenzweig & Eccles, 2017).

### 1.2. Expectancy-value theories

In expectancies for success, no such distinct components are discerned.

But both expectancies for success and task values are believed to be instigated by task-specific beliefs, such as:

- *self-concepts of ability,*
- *self-schemas,*
- *short-term goals,*
- *long-term goals,*
- *perceptions of ideal self,*
- *perceptions of task demands.*

(Wigfield, Rosenzweig & Eccles, 2017).

And these, in turn, are influenced by one's perceptions of other peoples' attitudes and expectations, and by one's interpretations of previous achievement outcomes.

For further reading, reference is made to: Wigfield, Tonks & Klauda, 2016; For recent reviews, see: Rosenzweig, Wigfield & Eccles, 2019.

For general overviews on expectancy-value theories, see: Eccles & Wigfield, 2002; Schunk, Pintrich & Meece, 2008; Wigfield & Eccles, 1992, 2000, 2002.

Overviews on the history of expectancy-value theories are provided in Wigfield & Eccles, 1992; Wigfield, Tonks & Klauda, 2009; Wigfield & Cambria, 2010a; Rosenzweig, Wigfield & Eccles, 2019.

So, the Process of attaining one's Goal, and the assessments made following Impact, not only leads to an 'accumulation of knowledge' on one's potential and competence, it also labels and values the attempts that are made, and shapes one's perceptions and expectations for future action, and the strategies involved. Most importantly, this wide array of resultant findings is to affect the way we perceive ourselves, as we will see in Chapter 8, when observing the outcomes of all these repercussions occurring following Impact from Reality on the Process of Motivation.

In brief, all these intricate outcomes appear to center around the construct of competence. Competence not only generates an array of effects, it also ignites ambitions and strivings to succeed and grow, to intervene in one's surroundings and master the opportunities that occur. From this perspective, *self-determination theory* perceives competence to be one of its three basic psychological needs: universal needs that represent "(...) innate requirements rather than acquired motives" (Ryan & Deci, 2002, p. 7), where competence in and of itself is a source of satisfaction contributing to one's well-being.

*See exhibit* ➔

Competence, then, appears to play a crucial role, not only as an essential resultant of the evaluative Phase in the Process of Motivation occurring following Impact, but it also constitutes a need whereby we seek to master our environment.

### 4.3. Self-determination theory

In self-determination theory, three basic psychological needs must be satisfied for psychological interest, development, and wellness to be sustained: *autonomy, relatedness* and *competence* (Deci & Ryan, 1985; Ryan & Deci, 2000, 2018, 2020).

*Competence* is defined as the need to have control over one's environment. The experience of effectance in one's pursuits (Patall & Hooper, 2019).

As such, "the need for competence leads people to seek challenges that are optimal for their capacities and to persistently attempt to maintain and enhance those skills and capacities through activity" (Ryan & Deci, 2002, p. 7). As a result, "the need for competence is evident as an inherent striving, manifested in curiosity, manipulation, and a wide range of epistemic motives (Deci & Moller, 2005)" (Ryan & Deci, 2018, p. 11). Which implies that "(...) the experience of competence in and of itself is a source of satisfaction and a contributor to well-being (...)" (Deci & Ryan, 2000, p. 257).

Competence, then, is not "(...) an attained skill or capability, but rather is a felt sense of confidence and effectance in action" (Ryan & Deci, 2002, p. 7).

For more on competence: Ryan & Deci, 2018 (notably Chapter 6).

*Next related thread 4.4.* ➔ *p. 290*

In summary then, observing the adequacy of the Goal that has been set, in a Phase of Externally Evoked Self-Assessment, sets in motion a chain of associated assessments that have been the subject of study in a number of major theories on motivation. Observing one's achievements within the interplay with Reality appears to center around perceived competence, where these theories have proposed a number of concepts and constructs that provide an insightful expansion of the Model.

These concepts and constructs are briefly summarized within the context of this sixth Phase in the Model of Motivation. A number of observations, however, are to precede this highly condensed, and schematic overview.

First, and as previously covered, in conceptualizing the various concepts and constructs, there has been confusion in the field both in formulations and in interpretations that have been used. To avoid confusion in the schematic overview provided, we refer to the definitions used throughout the text and the accompanying references to the literature for an overview of the conceptualizations that have been made there.

In addition, it must be noted that these theories have covered these areas from different conceptual and historical perspectives. And although in the various formulations an attempt has been made to preserve as much as possible the character and essence of these theories, it is recommended to refer to the various sources mentioned to fully appreciate the extent of the thoughts they imply.

And, finally, the Model of Motivation aims at capturing Motivation by searching for the most elementary ingredients by which the Process gradually progresses towards reaching a specific Goal the individual aims to attain. As mentioned in the Introduction, it is meant to illustrate the Process in its elementary form, capturing its essentials. The theories that were observed extend on this rudimentary representation by adding the complexity of environmental and interpersonal interactions and the prospective consequences they have for future actions. Adding this expanded view to the Model of Motivation is to be perceived as adding a 'molecular' view to a Model that is meant to provide insights at a different level, into the particles or 'atoms' or ingredients of this intricate and complex Process.

To summarize, then, where a Phase of Externally Evoked Self-Assessment in the Model of Motivation provides an assessment of adequacy of the Goals that are set, theories from literature have extended insights in three main areas, with a number of concepts and constructs that are related to perceptions of potential and competence.

*See exhibit next page* ➔

## *Outcomes of a Phase of Externally Evoked Self-Assessment*

Theories from literature have extended insights in three main areas, with a number of concepts and constructs that are related to perceptions of potential and competence:

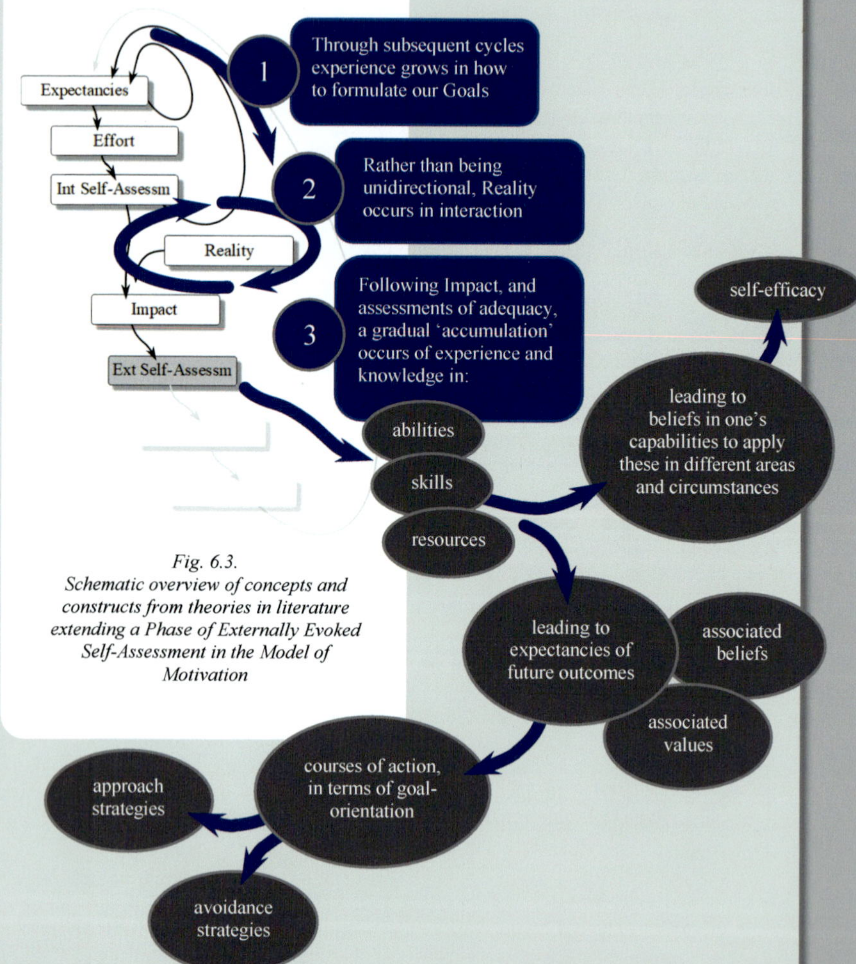


*Fig. 6.3.*
*Schematic overview of concepts and constructs from theories in literature extending a Phase of Externally Evoked Self-Assessment in the Model of Motivation*

## 3 Research

A vast body of knowledge has been produced by research in the respective fields of study associated with the four major theories we covered. An overview of findings is provided, as obtained from research on *goal-orientation theories*, *social cognitive theory*, *expectancy-value theories*, and *self-determination theory*, with an emphasis on the third of the basic psychological needs: the need for competence.

As previously mentioned, when covering outcomes obtained from research in *goal-orientation theories*, the approach-avoidance distinction used in performance-oriented goal strategies was subsequently also applied to mastery-oriented goals, leading to the 2x2 achievement goal model. Thus, the diversification in performance-approach and performance-avoidance categories was supplemented by mastery-approach and mastery-avoidance categories. In parallel with the observations made using the Model of Motivation, it was hypothesized by researchers that the pattern of effects in terms of affective, cognitive and behavioral processes and outcomes would produce a pattern ranging from positive (for mastery-approach goals), to moderate (for mastery-avoidance goals), mixed (performance-approach goals) and negative outcomes (performance-avoidance goals), thus following an assumed incremental scale in terms of perceived interference, or Impact and perceived Discrepancy according to the Model of Motivation. And although systematic empirical work capturing all operationalization issues for the 2x2 achievement goal model has yet to be conducted (Elliot & Hulleman, 2017), the overall tendency reveals these assumed patterns. Where performance-avoidance and performance-approach have previously been covered in Chapter 5, the empirical pattern for mastery-avoidance tends to be negative and indicative of anxiety, procrastination and maladaptive forms of perfectionism and reduced performance levels (Baranik, Stanley, Bynum & Lance, 2010; Hulleman, Schrager, Bodmann & Harackiewicz, 2010). These tendencies thus appear to confirm the assumed effects anticipated on in the Model of Motivation.

As observed in Section 2, a subsequent further diversification into mastery-intrinsic and mastery-extrinsic goals (Niemivirta, 2002, 2004) produced further refinements in these outcomes. Although only a small number of studies have tested links between the diversification in goals and their effects in terms of processes and outcomes (Elliot & Hulleman, 2017), a number of findings have emerged providing outcomes that appear to confirm these earlier observed tendencies.

An overview of these findings is provided, using the 3x2 achievement goal model (Elliot, Murayama & Pekrun, 2011), where a distinction is made in other-based goals, task-based goals, and self-based goals, each further refined in approach and avoidance categories.

Where other-approach goal-orientation is aimed at demonstrating competence relative to others (performance-approach goal-orientation), these goal-orientations are a positive predictor of performance attainment (Diseth, 2015; Elliot, Murayama & Pekrun, 2011) and perceived competence (Diseth, 2015; Elliot, Murayama & Pekrun, 2011; Mascret, Elliot & Cury, 2015). Where other-avoidance goal-orientation is aimed at avoiding demonstrating incompetence relative to others (performance-avoidance goal-orientation), these goal-orientations are a negative predictor of performance attainment (Elliot, Murayama & Pekrun, 2011; Johnson & Kestler, 2013). These findings are in agreement to outcomes from research on performance-approach and performance-avoidance goal pursuit, as previously covered in Chapter 5. And in parallel with observations previously made, these findings are in accordance with assumptions made in the Model of Motivation. After experiencing success over subsequent cycles in a Process of Motivation, confidence increases that one can successfully attain one's objective, leading to higher perceived competence enabling a more daring strategy as observed in performance-approach goal pursuit. Findings reflect those assumptions in positive correlates with performance attainment. After experiencing failure or negative interference from Reality, where performance attainment is frustrated, these strategies are more likely to manifest themselves in the form of performance-avoidance goal pursuit. And having experienced over subsequent cycles in a Process of Motivation that one meets standards of competence in absolute terms, in so-called mastery-extrinsic goals aimed at developing task-based competence, these task-based goals, defined as task-approach goals, are likely to become a positive predictor of task interest and satisfaction (Gillet, Lafrenière, Huyghebaert & Fouquereau, 2015; Mascret, Elliot & Cury, 2015), and perceived competence (Diseth, 2015; Elliot, Murayama & Pekrun, 2011; Mascret, Elliot & Cury, 2015). In contrast, when one has experienced that one fails to reach those standards of competence in mastery-extrinsic goals, these task-based goals turn into avoidance strategies aimed at avoiding task-based incompetence, defined as task-avoidance goals. When these standards of competence become self-based, in so-called mastery-intrinsic goals aimed at developing self-based competence, the findings are confirmed that were observed earlier in Chapter 5 on mastery-oriented goal-setting strategies, and appear to be positive predictors of task interest and satisfaction (Gillet, Lafrenière, Huyghebaert & Fouquereau, 2015; Mascret, Elliot & Cury, 2015). Those findings appear to be less pronounced when goal strategies are aimed at avoiding self-based incompetence, in so-called self-avoidance goals in mastery-intrinsic goals.

In recent years, researchers have focused not only on further isolating these various goal-orientation strategies, but have shifted attention also to combinations in new emerging profiles. In addition, goal-orientation theorists now propose that a person may benefit from endorsing multiple goals (Barron & Harackiewicz, 2000; Harackiewicz, Barron, Pintrich, Elliot & Thrash, 2002; Midgley, Kaplan & Middleton, 2001; Pintrich, 2000b). In doing so, a further level of complexity is added to current research, an overview of which exceeds our present scope[1] [2].

Pastor, Barron, Miller and Davis (2007) analyzed these newly emerging sets of profiles, to provide evidence as to whether those more complex models of goal-orientation were needed to justify their use over the more simple ones, distinguishing the patterns of processes and outcomes as proposed by the Model of Motivation. The suggested dichotomy in perceived Discrepancy, defined as being low or high, and conceptualized in goal-orientation theories in terms of approach or avoidance strategies, appears to find confirmation, together with the assumed mastery and performance dimensions. As was commented: "(...) our results add support to the idea that more complex conceptualizations utilizing approach and avoidance dimensions in addition to mastery and performance dimensions can be useful in educational practice and research" (Pastor, Barron, Miller & Davis, 2007, pp. 40-41)[3].

[1] In summary, five main clusters appear to emerge which largely coincide with our previous observations made in Chapter 5, when covering findings from research on goal-orientation theories:

- Mastery-oriented: students displaying a predominant tendency towards mastery;
- Success-oriented: students displaying a predominant tendency towards both mastery and performance;
- Performance-oriented: students displaying a predominant tendency towards performance with low mastery. It must be noted, however, that this profile did not emerge in several recent studies (for overviews: Tuominen, Niemivirta, Lonka & Salmela-Aro, 2020);
- Avoidance-oriented or disaffected: students displaying a predominant tendency towards avoidance, low mastery, low performance;
- Indifferent or moderate: students without a dominant tendency towards a specific goal-orientation.

For general overviews on these profiles: Niemivirta, 2002; Niemivirta, Pulkka, Tapola & Tuominen, 2019; Tuominen-Soini, Salmela-Aro, Niemivirta, 2008, 2011, 2012; Wormington & Linnenbrink-Garcia, 2017.

[2] In addition, it has been found that these goal-orientation profiles appear to be rather stable over time (Jansen in de Wal, Hornstra, Prins, Peetsma & van der Veen, 2016; Meece & Miller, 2001; Middleton, Kaplan & Midgley, 2004; Niemivirta, Pulkka, Tapola & Tuominen, 2019; Pulkka & Niemivirta, 2013; Tuominen, Niemivirta, Lonka & Salmela-Aro, 2020; Tuominen-Soini, Salmela-Aro, Niemivirta, 2011, 2012).

[3] Currently there is a discussion on these models of goal-orientation. The debate appears to center on a number of topics: whether more complex definitions of the goal-orientation construct are needed or whether more parsimonious conceptualizations can suffice (Harackiewicz, Barron, Pintrich, Elliot & Thrash, 2002; Midgley, Kaplan & Middleton, 2001; Pastor, Barron, Miller & Davis, 2007). And (Continued)

Having made these observations, on approach and avoidance dimensions in the dichotomy between performance and mastery in goal-orientations, and having obtained confirmation for a progressive pattern ranging from positive (for mastery-approach goals) to moderate (for mastery-avoidance goals), mixed (performance-approach goals) and negative outcomes (performance-avoidance goals), following an assumed incremental scale in terms of perceived interference as proposed in the Model, we can now finalize our observations and those made in previous Chapters, on the profound effects of performance-oriented goal-related strategies.

*See exhibit next page* ➔

Research in the field of *social cognitive theory,* notably on self-efficacy, has been found to confirm those findings from research in goal-orientation theories. The broad range of positive effects associated with mastery-oriented goals appears to extend in effects related to self-efficacy (Schunk & Ertmer, 1999). Students displaying higher self-efficacy are more likely to endorse mastery-oriented goals and set higher standards than students with low self-efficacy (Pajares, 1997). Performance-oriented students show slightly lower self-efficacy (Niemivirta, 2002). More in general, studies have systematically shown positive relationships between mastery-goals and self-efficacy (Ainley & Patrick, 2006; Bong, 2001b; Harackiewicz, Barron, Tauer, Carter & Elliot, 2000; McGregor & Elliot, 2002; Nolen, 1988; Pajares, Britner & Valiante, 2000; Pekrun, Elliot & Maier, 2006; Schwinger, Steinmayr & Spinath, 2016; Tuominen-Soini, Salmela-Aro & Niemivirta, 2012).

In observing the four sources from which self-efficacy is assumed to originate, past achievements (defined as 'mastery experiences'[1]) have been shown to be the most powerful and consistent predictors of self-efficacy (Joët, Usher & Bressoux, 2011; Usher & Pajares, 2008). In line with the assumptions previously made in Section 2, where a Phase of Externally Evoked Self-Assessment contributed to a progressive increase and 'accumulation of knowledge' on one's potential and competence, these past experiences when perceived as successful, appear to further nourish and enrich one's beliefs of self-efficacy (Britner & Pajares, 2006), and when those are perceived to be unsuccessful, they appear to weaken and lower those beliefs (Pajares, 2003). As stated by Ahn and Bong: "What is most important in self-efficacy estimation (...) is not the success and failure in an objective sense but one's subjective recognition and interpretation of one's own prior experiences" (Ahn & Bong, 2019, p. 67).

whether observed variations are the resultant of the timing of observations, choice of measures and research methods (see: Tuominen, Niemivirta, Lonka & Salmela-Aro, 2020).

[1] With reference to the exposé in Section 2, the four major sources of information from which efficacy beliefs were acquired were: mastery experience, vicarious experience, social persuasion, and physiological states (Bandura 1986, 1997).

## *Related Topics: The Thought of Winning...*

We live in times in which we seek to be 'best', rank at the 'highest levels', 'exceed expectations', and appear 'successful' in all undertakings we set ourselves to do.

*Do we?...*

All these expressions of success are aimed at demonstrating competence, and where others are involved to compare us with, these appear to be expressions of performance-oriented strategies that were found to come at a heavy price, referring to what we observed in Chapter 3 (p. 83) and Chapter 5 (pp. 154-155).

Which is remarkable, when we consider that other approaches appear to have much better prospects when applied. Strategies that we are equiped with in the earliest days of our lives: mastery-oriented strategies. It was found in a vast majority of findings that mastery-oriented strategies were related to a range of positive outcomes related to well-being, as observed in Chapter 3 (p. 83), Chapter 5 (pp. 156-157), and this Chapter (p. 212).

Consider the case of pursuing excellence...

A performance-oriented approach to pursuing excellence can be expressed in one word: *winning!* If that is your thing, fine, but it does come at a price. Defined in slightly different terms, one could state that in this approach *others define the criteria of competition.* The 'loss' is that we are dependent on those others for winning, but the 'gain' is clarity in 'who wins' and 'who loses'.

A mastery-oriented approach to pursuing excellence is quite different. This time, *you are the one who defines the criteria of competition.* The 'loss' is that clarity of winning appears a bit 'blurry' (for who knows that you are 'winning'?), the 'gain' is, however, that you are independent of others, as you are the only one deciding on whether you have been successful or not...

*Pursuing excellence means finding strategies to adequately fight against the restraining forces of our fear to fail in our attempts.*

Addressing these strategies requires a personalized approach. And there appear to be two options, each with their specific pros and cons...

And the gradual buildup of these convictions for successfully executing a course of action based on prior experiences leads to a belief and confidence in, and an effective judgment of, one's accomplishments, as postulated in the Model of Motivation. Empirical evidence confirming those effects have been obtained in research findings, where self-efficacy appeared as a strong predictor of learning, (academic) achievement and performance (Alivernini & Lucidi, 2011; Bandura, 1997; Bandura & Schunk, 1981; Caprara, Fida, Vecchione, Del Bove, Vecchio, Barbaranelli & Bandura, 2008; Honicke & Broadbent, 2016; Joët, Usher & Bressoux, 2011; Klassen & Usher, 2010; Multon, Brown & Lent, 1991; Pajares, 1996, 1997; Pajares & Schunk, 2001; Sadri & Robertson, 1993; Schunk, 1981, 1995; Schunk & Miller, 2002; Schunk & Pajares, 2009; Stajkovic & Luthans, 1998; Zimmerman, 2000; Zimmerman, Bandura & Martinez-Pons, 1992).

It is not a simple buildup of past experiences, it is a gradual assessment and self-awareness, where experiences obtained from all previous Phases contribute to the Process of Motivation in attaining the Goal that has been set. As eloquently summarized by Bandura and Locke, commenting on the beliefs of personal efficacy: "Whatever other factors serve as guides and motivators, they are rooted in the core belief that one has the power to produce desired effects (...). Self-efficacy beliefs regulate human functioning through cognitive, motivational, affective, and decisional processes (Bandura, 1997). They affect whether individuals think in self-enhancing or self-debilitating ways, how well they motivate themselves and persevere in the face of difficulties (...)" (Bandura & Locke, 2003, p. 87).

And these experiences, perceptions and interpretations, in turn, lead to subsequent perceptions of self, as we will come to find when covering subsequent Phases in the Process of Motivation, notably in Chapter 8.

These findings from research in social cognitive theory, confirming the effects of self-efficacy beliefs, are reflected in findings obtained from studies associated with *expectancy-value theories*. Recall from Section 2 that achievement-related choices and performances were assumed to be influenced by subjective task value and expectancies for success. And these expectancies for success refer to the subjective estimated probability of success, which is considered conceptually similar to self-efficacy (Ahn & Bong, 2019)[1]. Where these expectancies for success appear to be highly correlated to subjective task value, as previously covered in Chapter 1 in findings from research on expectancy-

[1] Referring to earlier observations made in Section 2, notably in the exhibit on p. 203, it must be noted that self-efficacy is not only concerned with the expectation that given performances will produce particular outcomes, but especially with a 'prognostic' conviction that one can successfully execute behavior required to produce certain outcomes: "(...) people act on their beliefs about what they can do as well as their beliefs about the likely outcomes of performance" (Bandura & Locke, 2003, p. 92).

value theories, many studies, in turn, have also attested to the positive relationship between self-efficacy (and related expectancies for success) and task value (for an overview, see: Bong, 2001a). Recall that task value refers to the value that one places on the expected outcome when engaging in a task, and the more one has the belief to successfully complete a task, the more those tasks are valued (Lee, Bong & Kim, 2014; Wolters, Yu & Pintrich, 1996)[1]. And, subsequently, the more those tasks appear to instigate interest (Bandura & Schunk, 1981; Zimmerman & Kitsantas, 1997); although it has also been hypothesized that interest is an important prerequisite for developing self-efficacy beliefs (Bong, Lee & Woo, 2015), or occurring in reciprocal interaction (Niemivirta & Tapola, 2007; Rottinghaus, Larson & Borgen, 2003). Within this context, an interesting finding with children is that those task values, expectancies, and competence beliefs increase with age (Wigfield, Eccles, Yoon, Harold, Arbreton, Freedman-Doan & Blumenfeld, 1997), thus suggesting also that children progressively come to value what they are good at.

One might conclude from these findings that expectancy-value and self-efficacy beliefs show reciprocal tendencies, where a progressive and gradual increase can eventually lead to self-propelling effects, in terms of performance, achievement, interest and perseverance, which is in line with assumptions proposed in the Model of Motivation, in effects produced in a Phase of Externally Evoked Self-Assessment.

Given the centrality of the construct of competence in all these theories, it follows that a need for competence, as defined within *self-determination theory* as a "(...) felt sense of confidence and effectance in action" (Ryan & Deci, 2002, p. 7), has emerged as the strongest need satisfaction predictor of performance in a meta-analysis of the literature on the subject (Cerasoli, Nicklin & Nassrelgrgawi, 2016), where effects appeared to be even larger than those associated with autonomy and relatedness needs[2].

[1] However, it appears that these perceptions of greater task value also induce higher levels of test-related stress, both among students with strong self-efficacy beliefs and among those with weak self-efficacy (Lee, Lee & Bong, 2013).

[2] Referring, however, to differences in conceptualization of the competence construct between self-determination theory and social cognitive theory (Elliot, McGregor & Thrash, 2002).

## Summary

The sixth Phase in the Model of Motivation is a 'Phase of Externally Evoked Self-Assessment', where an assessment of adequacy is made of the Goal and its settings, given the new state of affairs following Impact from Reality in the Process of Motivation.

The assessment occurs in five successive Stages. In a *Stage of Aspiration,* the initial Attitude towards the Goal is re-examined in its newly perceived context with Reality. The Stage is followed by the most important Stage in this Phase, a *Stage of Contemplation,* where the Goal is re-evaluated in adequacy from this new perspective following Impact from Reality. A *Stage of Validation* re-evaluates the intended investments. And re-assessment of these initial Stages leads to a re-appraisal of Achievement and Failure, as initially set, in a *Stage of Attainment,* and of Satisfaction and Frustration levels in a *Stage of Fulfillment.*

What are the effects of these assessments of adequacy? The re-evaluation follows a positive route when adequacy of the Goal and its settings is perceived to be in line with Reality, while it is negative when both are found to be in disaccord. And these effects are more pronounced when both are perceived to be Significant.

The consequences of Impact from Reality as expressed in a Phase of Externally Evoked Self-Assessment have been elaborated on by a number of theories on motivation. Where the Model in this Phase of Motivation proposes an assessment of adequacy of the Goals that are set, theories from literature have extended insights, especially in the effects of those assessments on perceptions of competence. Effects of Reality and Impact occur in reciprocal interaction, where awareness of those effects leads to reflection on one's personal efficacy, the soundness of one's thoughts and actions, and the meaning of one's pursuits.

In line with the assumptions made in the Model, a Phase of Externally Evoked Self-Assessment thereby contributes to a progressive increase and 'accumulation of knowledge' on one's potential and competence, where past experiences when perceived as successful appear to further nourish and enrich those efficacy beliefs, and when perceived to be unsuccessful, appear to weaken and lower those beliefs.

Theory and research from literature have thus expanded the elements of Impact and Reality provided in the Model to more intricate and pluriform expressions.

# Chapter 7
## *Making Sense (and Sensibility)*
## *Phase 7 - A Phase of Anticipated Change*

From our frame of reference we are observing this new Reality, which imposed its authority on our attempts at reaching our Goal in the Process of Motivation. Our 'field of view' was shaped in the first initializing Phases of this Process: from these Phases came the criteria against which we are now to assess the Impact from Reality in subsequent Phases. And the more Significant our objective, the more it affects our perception of the event.

In Chapter 5, we used the analogy of a gauge, where the initial Phases determined the settings, or the scale, and thereby defined the criteria. We extended the analogy, with readings equal to, below or above an imaginative 'red line', providing measures of perceived Discrepancy as manifested in a Phase of Impact. And these settings, in turn, led us to assess the adequacy of those initial criteria, as previously seen in Chapter 6, covering a Phase of Externally Evoked Self-Assessment in the Process of Motivation.

The question is: what happens next in this Process? We found that we did not respond at once, by changing either the Goal, the levels of Satisfaction we seek, or the investments in terms of Effort we make. As we saw in Chapter 5, a number of essential steps are made preceding the response.

In a subsequent Phase, defined as a *'Phase of Anticipated Change'*, we are to define our strategy based on these previous observations of adequacy. Following the Impact from Reality and the Discrepancy with the Goal that has been set, are we to maintain, increase or decrease the gap we have detected between the Process of reaching the Goal and this imposing Reality?

Chapter 6 addressed adequacy; Chapter 7, then, is to define direction.

This Phase of Anticipated Change is to add to the new mindset obtained following the confrontation with Reality in a Phase of Impact and the assessment made in a Phase of Externally Evoked Self-Assessment. If you contemplate a change in Goal-setting to accommodate Reality and thus anticipate on reducing its Impact, the perspective this creates is different and much more positive than if you decide *not* to make any amendments, let alone to further increase Discrepancy and head for a full confrontation with Reality in a next encounter.

Let us observe these various effects in which we anticipate on things to come in the Process of Motivation.

Monserrate. My assessment of adequacy was rather clear, and urgent corrections were expected to be made. And those amendments are now to be defined in this Phase of Anticipated Change. But which amendments are there to consider? Reality interferes; but exactly what *causes* this interference? How does Reality manifest itself? If we want to anticipate on addressing the gap, or Discrepancy, between the Goal we have set and this interfering Reality, we must determine its precise nature first. Recall that the Goal was to have 'a-great-and-romantic-experience-of-amazement-and-wonder' by visiting the Palace and Gardens at Monserrate. What *precisely* is interfering and discouraging the attempt to reach this objective? Is it the traffic, the noise, the people, their behavior, their conduct? Let us concentrate on the people. They *are* annoying. Is it one person, the gentleman guiding this group, this *'crowd'?* Chances are, it is not one person, but rather this *'crowd'* disrupting my trip, my carefully planned journey. Note how this *'crowd'* is anonymous; they have no face. Observe how indiscriminate I am: they are all to blame, they are all disturbing my attempts at reaching my objective, *they are all the same!* And also note how carefully I thereby prevent myself from subsequently following alternative options to address people in particular, or engage in interacting, talking to these folks. Preserving anonymity, turning people indiscriminately into 'crowds', cleverly anticipates on preserving my Goal intact. And the more Significant my Goal, the more ingenious those strategies become... However, when every nuance disappears, the way it does in my approach, it leaves no room to maneuver. How to address and neutralize interference coming from 'crowds'? Well, we can't. We cannot possibly diminish or even maintain the Discrepancy. The alternative that is left is to increase the gap. To bail out. A retreat is imminent, and this is what I anticipate on in the approach taken. We increase the gap beyond repair, by anticipating to withdraw in a subsequent step in the Process of Motivation. But not without the assistance of some accommodating strategy or mechanism to help us cover up the damage that is inflicted to our Process of Motivation. And note how this strategy leads to extremes and polarizes the situation. More to come on these mechanisms in the next Chapter, when covering the repercussions of the approach and perceiving Reality in this manner...

So, this is the price we pay when nuance disappears. But it will ease subsequent action when the time comes...

Fortunately, things were rather different in my tennis exploits. And now comes the time to affirm the splendid achievements I made. I had intended, in a previous Phase, to further increase my Efforts so as to get more Satisfaction from the results obtained. Of course, with increased investment, the risks of Failure would also rise, but given the success these chances were perceived as negligible. Therefore, in this Phase of Anticipated Change, I plan to further decrease a perceived Discrepancy between the Goal that has gradually evolved from 'having-fun' to 'winning', and the acknowledging Reality affirming this intention. So, the strategy of 'decreasing the gap', in effect, is to anticipate on the prospect of participating in more contests. Previously, in Chapter 5, reference was made to the subsequent perceptions not only of Reality, and the noble sport of tennis, but also to the fine qualities of my opponents and to the splendid occasions provided in those contests to increase one's confidence. These reactions capturing the positive Impact from Reality on the Process of Motivation, will be covered subsequently in Chapter 8.

My third example.

How am I to react to the call of duty in grocery shopping? In this third example, the decision I take on the road to follow is prompted by the perceived Significance of the Goal as a frame of reference, by the perceived urgency called for in a Phase of Reality, by the Discrepancy that occurs between both perceptions, and by the resulting assessment of adequacy of my initial stand in this state of affairs. Certainly, perceived Significance to do the 'moral-and-decent-thing' is high; which rather complicates things further, as I have to (somehow) defend my unrightful postponement (which is the strategy I followed in the first three Phases, determining my frame of reference against which I assess the Impact from Reality), while at the same time I will have to (somehow) come to accept that I need to come to action and do this 'moral-and-decent-thing-to-do'. Opposites that need to come together, as concluded in the assessment of adequacy made in the previous Phase. Two options now emerge. If I decide to increase the Discrepancy by following my own ways in postponement, we will come to realize that my perception of Reality in a subsequent Phase 8 will have a different outcome than if I am to decide to decrease the Discrepancy. To put it bluntly, in the first instance 'I win', at the expense of a further and most probable clash with Reality later on; in the latter, 'Reality wins', at the expense, however, of a subsequent and most probable clash with my own previous standards to postpone. Being a decent fellow and a most dependable partner (note how personality, competence, perception of self affect these choices, but are left out of our analysis), I choose for the option to do 'the-decent-thing' and *decrease* Discrepancy. Thus, 'Reality wins'. And this sequence of steps following the Impact from Reality is to determine my mindset towards Reality in a subsequent Phase 8, and will have its repercussions in the perception I have of this interference in my 'wise-and-sensible-plans' to postpone; more on this in Chapter 8.

And then there is the prospect of going to Hong Kong.

In the previous Chapter, we found that the Processes of Motivation associated with these last three examples appear to influence each other gradually, in a rather confusing mixture of parallel Processes of Motivation. And in this intermingling of Processes it gradually becomes clear that we have an extraordinary occurrence obscuring our analysis and observations: *we have a single manifestation of Reality protruding in three Processes of Motivation producing two opposite reactions!*

Here is the situation.

We have a dormant Goal to travel to Hong Kong, which has now surfaced because of an emerging Reality in the person of my supervisor. In this Phase of the Process, this option now leads to a most convenient, thus positive outcome, which we will reveal in a moment.

Then we have the same superior causing (in my perception) intrusion into my decision to delay a paper, which in this Phase of the Process will eventually lead to an uncompromising, thus negative reaction.

And, finally, we have the same Reality, personified by my superior, intruding and affecting my latent Goal to be part of a university environment that supposedly was to preserve my autonomy, which, in the present Phase of Anticipated Change, will lead to a similar obstinate reaction.

Let us observe these three examples, and the respective courses of action they lead to, in more detail.

First, the prospect of going to Hong Kong. We have alluded to this dormant Goal already many times, but it is only at this point in the Process of Motivation, in a Phase of Anticipated Change, that we come to contemplate and consider an alternative strategy of returning to Hong Kong. Recall that my frame of reference until now has been to postpone; events that occurred in a Phase of Reality made me re-assess in a previous Phase the adequacy of the decision, and they now bring me to examine the possibility of an alternative option. And the urge to do so, originates from events occurring in a parallel Process of Motivation, where my superior appears to interfere in a course of action where I feel obliged to write an article (example 5), which goes against my principles (example 6). Contemplating a departure to Hong Kong would serve both strategies set out in those next two examples, to further increase the perceived Discrepancies between this imposing Reality and the Goals I seek to reach or maintain in these examples. *Observe how this intruding Reality has no direct apparent relation to the Goal that was initially set to go to Hong Kong, which was subsequently postponed. It now provides direction and a change in strategy, and thus interferes in this Process of Motivation.* And its interference is positive. This Reality, which will prove to have a detrimental effect on the Processes occurring in these next two examples, now, in the present example, increases the urgency to go, and thereby serves and propels the Process of Motivation.

This strategy, then, to consider a return to Hong Kong, reverberates in those next and final examples...

In the example of postponing the article for fear of failure, following the intrusion of my superior, the strategy in a Phase of Anticipated Change could follow three alternative routes. I could consider taking appropriate action to start writing my paper and thus diminish the Discrepancy I (erroneously) perceive between my policy to postpone and the urge to publish conveyed by the email sent by my superior. Or I could decide to ignore the event and retain the status quo that I initiated from the start. So, no change in

Discrepancy. Or, third alternative, I could consider increasing the Discrepancy even further, anticipating on actively taking up the challenge by 'refusing to obey' (at least from my point of view). As observed, taking this course of action would serve two purposes: it would affirm my strategy to postpone (and thus conveniently serve my cleverly concealed fear of failure), and it would support my going to Hong Kong, as considered in the previous example. However, it goes without saying that this 'call to arms' will have its repercussions on my assessment of Reality and the perceived intrusion by my superior, in a subsequent Phase of the Process...

And this 'refusal to obey', which is lacking any form of verification and appears to be highly irrational, in turn is further strengthened by the connection to a prominent latent Goal that had made me join the academia. In this sixth and final example, we observed earlier how a Phase of Impact triggered this hidden and implicit Goal, where universities were expected to be the epitome of highest principles and moral values, and where autonomy was to prevail in every respect. And, as we saw in a Phase of Externally Evoked Self-Assessment, it gave rise to questioning those values: "Did I do well to have those high standards or should I reconsider those values in the position I now have within the university, and accept that no such absolute autonomy can exist?" Now, latent Goals such as these are seldom made to reconsider. A position that is thought to represent 'highest principles and moral values' is not likely to be meddled with. Latent Goals, in general, are expressed in strongly held beliefs; they constitute our 'moral compass': justice, equality, tolerance, honesty, integrity, trustworthiness... Those are the standards we adhere to. So, latent Goals are strict, in a sense, and in reflecting on a strategy to follow in this last example, I will not reconsider those values that made me enter the academic world. So, decreasing the perceived Discrepancy appears to be an unlikely option. Two alternatives remain, then: I will maintain a present status quo or I will increase Discrepancy further by considering leaving the university. Maintaining the objectivity and correctness of the moral judgments I made could be an option. But given the Significance of my latent Goal, and given the evaluative reactions I had in the parallel Processes of Motivation occurring, by preserving my strategy to postpone my article and the attractive opportunity of 'leaving everything behind and going to Hong Kong', the option to *increase* Discrepancy further and consider leaving the university, now becomes most likely to occur...

So there you have it: I am to reconsider my present position among the academia. And the more I am engaged to 'adhere to the highest of moral standards' (at least, from my point of view), the less flexible I become to reconsider the correctness of my judgment... This intransigent attitude, reflecting the Significance of a latent Goal, and serving so conveniently both parallel Processes of Motivation, leaves me no alternative, and is to determine my future. And beyond...

An almost dogmatic point of view has been created, instigated by a series, a 'constellation', of Significant Goals. It has made me almost inaccessible, not open to any form of reason. What a waste! This is where conflicts are born: the interpretation of an email, the Significance of highest standards and noble pursuits. It appears that disharmony beyond repair originates from objectives we seek and achievements we strive for, where we adhere to 'latent standards' that leave us no other choice but rejection, as we seek to preserve those values and ideals. This obstinate, inflexible, uncompromising attitude is meant to protect these Significant Goals, instigated by strategies that originate in this Phase of Anticipated Change.

And yet, those strategies are made to fail when they, in turn, evoke parallel, new Processes of Motivation centered around new latent Goals, in which they emerge most unexpectedly. These are the mechanisms which, in the end, through cascading disharmony, produce inflexible attitudes and intolerance, and allow it to proliferate.

And thus, protective measures, aimed at preserving Significant Goals, appear to be at the root of inflexibility and intolerance.

These effects are remarkable, especially when one realizes that they serve to preserve pursuits that appear, in themselves, to be perfectly harmless: the intention of traveling to Hong Kong, the postponement of writing a paper, the adherence to noble standards. It is a 'constellation' of Goals and their respective Processes of Motivation that appear to produce, in an almost inescapable end result, a poisonous outcome where 'the whole is greater than the sum of its parts'...

And although these 'constellations' of Processes of Motivation can also produce an equivalent positive result, where comparable mechanisms may serve to propel the individual to memorable achievements, because of their excessive nature they do have a tendency, nonetheless, to frequently produce these negative outcomes...

The seventh Phase in the Process of Motivation is a Phase of Anticipated Change.

Following the Impact from Reality and the perception of a small or large Discrepancy, three evaluative reactions occur.

The second of these reactions is aimed towards this Discrepancy: Am I to retain, decrease or increase the Discrepancy?

In this Phase, only a course of action is defined and no actual amendments are made, as these are to occur (at a later stage) exclusively in Phase 1 of the Process of Motivation.

*Phase 7 in the Model of Motivation is covered in detail on pp. 229-233. A summary is provided on p. 249.*

This is where intolerance starts and from which prejudice leading to harm beyond repair originates. But there is more to this mixture to come to these provocative outcomes. The roots of which are laid in a next Phase of the Process of Motivation...

First, however, a summary of definitions and an overview of related theories and findings obtained from research in literature.

## 1 Definitions

Following the Impact from Reality, it was found that a re-orientation occurs of the Goal versus Reality. This re-orientation is aimed at the three essential elements involved in the interference: the Goal and the parameters that were set, the gap or Discrepancy, and Reality.

In reference to Fig 5.3., Chapter 5, the second assessment we make is aimed at the gap or Discrepancy.

In the Process of Motivation, we do not directly proceed towards action or a conclusion when the Process is affected by the Impact from an interfering Reality.

Following the realization of Impact, we re-assessed the Goal and its parameters on their adequacy in Phase 6, a Phase of Externally Evoked Self-Assessment. And now comes a Phase in which the consequences are considered. Whereas Phase 6 is a critical assessment, with the standards, or criteria, provided in the first three Phases of the Process acting as a reference, Phase 7 defines the master plan upon which amendments are to be made.

Phase 7, then, is a Phase aimed at preserving the integrity of the Goal as much as possible, given the confrontation with Reality in a Phase of Impact. Are we to retain the Goal and its settings as defined in a Phase of Expectancies, or are we anticipating on changes that are either increasing or decreasing the Impact from Reality that has been observed? Given the state of affairs as reported on in the previous Phases, Phase 7 is characterized by prospective amendments: it is a *Phase of Anticipated Change.*

This second Phase, following the Impact of Reality, again, is a passive, evaluative reaction which precedes a course of action. It is an evaluative Phase in which an appraisal is made of the potential readiness to decrease Discrepancy and to close the gap that has been observed between the Goal and Reality. The appraisal of the Discrepancy can be positive, negative or neutral. It is positive when we decide Discrepancy needs to be reduced. It is negative when we do not expect a reduction but an increase. It is neutral when no further action is foreseen[1].

[1] A positive assessment does not mean the gap is evaluated as 'not so very large'. This assessment has previously been made in a Phase of Impact, where the 'seriousness' of the matter was considered. Here, a positive assessment means: the intention is expressed to reduce perceived Discrepancy.

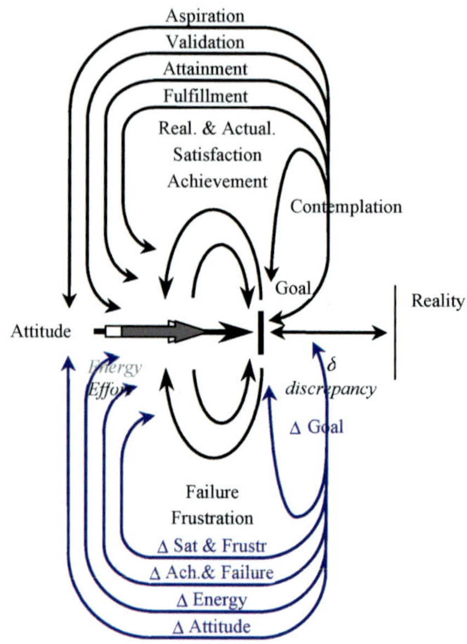


*Fig. 7.1.*
*A visualized overview of Phase 7,*
*a Phase of Anticipated Change*
*in the theoretical Model of Motivation,*
*consisting of:*

16. Δ - Attitude
17. Δ - Goal
18. Δ - Energy
19. Δ - Achievement and Failure
20. Δ - Satisfaction and Frustration

A Phase of Anticipated Change, then, is a re-evaluation of the Discrepancy after Reality has presented itself, given the previous re-evaluation of the Goal and its parameters in a Phase of Externally Evoked Self-Assessment. This re-evaluation consists of an 'anticipating reflection on change'. In visualizing this next Phase, in Fig. 7.1., the elements are assumed to remain the same, as the Process at this point is anticipatory and reflective in nature. Only the implications of the Discrepancy for each element are observed. Again, arrows visualize this 'contrasting' of parameters, evaluating the Goal versus the Discrepancy with Reality, as observed.

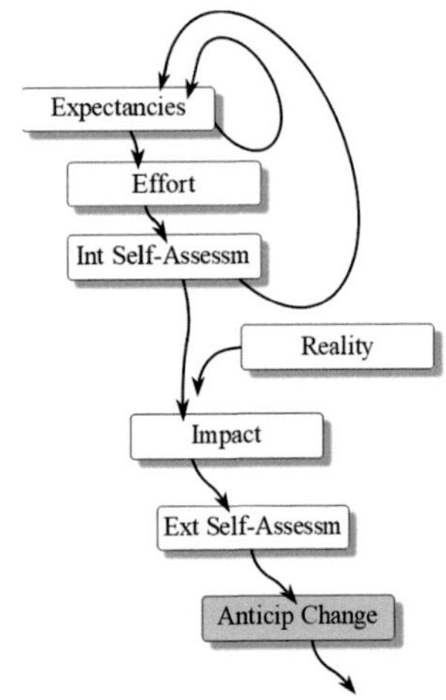


*Fig. 7.2.*
*A Phase of Anticipated Change Visualized as part of successive Phases in the description of the Model of Motivation*

And as the re-evaluation is aimed at the elements defined in a Phase of Expectancies, versus the Discrepancy, it is assumed that a Phase of Anticipated Change also consists of five Stages. To stress both the aspect of change and its association with the Discrepancy, the symbol 'Δ' is added to designate those separate Stages. The first Stage *(Δ - Attitude),* assesses and anticipates on an active change in Attitude aimed at closing, increasing or maintaining the Discrepancy between Goal and Reality. The second Stage *(Δ - Goal)* anticipates on an active change in properties of the Goal. An anticipated change would aim at closing or increasing the Discrepancy between Goal and Reality, as an outcome of the previous Stages in the Process. An anticipated absence in change would be aimed at maintaining the observed Discrepancy. Both Stages are followed by a Stage *(Δ - Energy)* in which an assessment is made if one is inclined to invest more, less or the same amount of Energy now that the Goal appears in a new perspective. Re-investing more Energy, as an option, seems very much related to the Attitude brought to the Process on the one hand, and Significance attached to Reality on the other. The more ambitious the individual, and the more Significant Reality is perceived to be, the more one would be inclined to consider a higher investment in Energy so as to 'protect and preserve' the objective initially set[1]. A subsequent Stage, then, defined as *Δ - Achievement and Failure,* assesses and anticipates on subsequent intentions to re-define Achievement and Failure ratios in achieving the Goal, aimed at closing, maintaining or increasing the Discrepancy; followed by a final Stage *(Δ - Satisfaction and Frustration)*, where an assessment is made of the willingness to re-define subjective outcomes initially set, aimed at decreasing, maintaining or increasing the Discrepancy between the Goal and Reality.

In summarizing this fifth Phase of Anticipated Change within the sequence of Phases already observed in the Process of Motivation, Fig. 7.2., visualizes the Phase as it follows the input previously made on adequacy, in a Phase of Externally Evoked Self-Assessment, and initiates this second of three passive, evaluative reactions, following the Impact from Reality.

Now, earlier we observed the various expressions in which the Process of Motivation manifests itself, according to the three essential constructs that largely determine its outcome. In Chapter 5, eight options were distinguished. And as observed in Chapter 6, the question is: what effects are likely to occur in each of these variations? In Chapter 5, it was assumed that two distinct options would yield the highest effects, both positive and negative, on the Process of Motivation. But do these effects remain the same for all these various manifestations, as the Process of Motivation gradually progresses in this next Phase of Anticipated Change?

Clearly, we can see that the effects following Impact from Reality with low perceived Significance do not justify contemplating a change in properties of the Goal, especially when the Goal is perceived as Significant (options 1 and 3, p. 123). But even if the Goal is low in Significance, Reality provides no incentive to consider any changes (options 5 and 7, p. 124). This leaves us with both alternatives mentioned, together with a combination of low Significance of the Goal. The option with low Significance of the Goal, high perceived Significance of Reality and a high Discrepancy (option 6, p. 124) appears to bring us further away from considering any changes, as it appears unlikely that a Goal with low Significance leads to action aimed at altering high perceived Discrepancy. Effects are therefore expected to be minimal. At first sight, the next option, the combination of low Significance of the Goal, small Discrepancy and high perceived Significance of Reality (option 8, p. 124), could instigate an anticipated change in properties of the Goal, but the effects will only be substantial when the Goal is 'upgraded' to higher Significance. It is a good start, though, and the option could lead to promising outcomes over time, but effects at this point in the Process are still likely to remain marginal.

[1] Although there can be exceptions to this rule, depending on the Impact from Reality. See Chapter 10.

Which leaves us, again, with both combinations mentioned earlier in Chapter 5 and Chapter 6. Let us observe both more closely.

Again, effects are likely to be high when a Significant Goal is confronted with a Significant Reality and perceived Discrepancy is high (option 2, p. 123). Given the previous input from a Phase of Externally Evoked Self-Assessment on adequacy, this Phase is now aimed at taking protective measures intended to preserve the Goal. And these protective measures are not likely to include elements to accommodate Reality, as we observed in Chapter 6. As occurred in the previous Phase, the ideas, notions, ambitions that led me to define a Significant Goal now prevent me from having such an adaptive attitude, especially when Reality is perceived as highly disruptive and Discrepancy is high.

On the same grounds, however, orientation towards Reality dramatically increases when Discrepancy is perceived to be small (option 4, p. 123). Where my attempts at reaching this Significant Goal are acknowledged and supported by a Significant Reality, I will do anything to maintain these positive conditions. The ideas, notions, ambitions that made me define the Goal the way it is now urge me to seek the support I need in reaching the Goal that I set. Especially when this support comes from a source with such a high Significance. A Significant Goal combined with a Significant Reality in a setting perceived to have a small Discrepancy makes the amendments that are considered in a Phase of Anticipated Change, aimed at further diminishing Discrepancy, most likely to occur, in order to further enhance these positive effects in reaching the important Goal.

As previously observed in a Phase of Externally Evoked Self-Assessment, these effects occurring in a Phase of Anticipated Change also extend beyond the course of the Process of Motivation alone...

As we are to observe next, we seem to discard a negative Impact on the Process of reaching a Goal as foreign and often beyond our control. And in considering amendments, we deny having responsibility for the effects occurring to the Process. And, in contrast, we seem to embrace positive effects that occur from Reality as originating from our own accord, to the extent that we often experience having considerable influence on the course of events that appear to have been favorable to the Process through these external influences.

In the field of motivational psychology, important insights into these phenomena have been provided by findings obtained from a field, commonly referred to as 'attribution theory'.

In the next Section, an overview is provided where these findings seem to confirm the various assumptions made about a Phase of Anticipated Change in the Process of Motivation.

# 2 Theories

Evidence of the occurrence of intended change in a Phase of Anticipated Change has been indirectly provided by theory and research on perceived causes, originating from studies in social learning and personal responsibility. If one reflects on the causes of one's actions or achievements, following input obtained in a Phase of Reality and a Phase of Externally Evoked Self-Assessment, and on amendments to be made based on this input, this provides further insights into the 'anticipated reflection on change', as assumed to occur in the Model of Motivation, in a Phase of Anticipated Change.

In previous Chapters, we observed how theories and research have focused on goal pursuit and on the patterns of affect, cognition and behavior (the so-called 'nomological networks', mentioned in Chapter 6), in generated outcomes and processes. And these goals had a purpose for engaging in competence-relevant behavior. Hence, the concept of 'achievement goals', and the central concept of competence in the theories we covered previously in Chapter 6.

We observed a gradual 'accumulation of knowledge' on one's potential and competence, but looking at competence from the perspective of an 'anticipated reflection on change', as assumed to occur in a Phase of Anticipated Change, introduces the concept of *causality* in competence appraisal. "I have reached an understanding as to the abilities, capacities and levels of competence I have in reaching a specific Goal, but if I am to invigorate a course of action to increase, decrease or maintain a Discrepancy observed, I have to come to terms with why this Discrepancy has occurred. Am I to blame for any lack of abilities, capacities or competence, or is it the external agency, the outside actor causing the interference? And what are the implications, in terms of necessary amendments to be made to the Goal that I set?"

Theories that aim at a causal search to identify an explanation for an occurrence or event are defined as *'attribution theories'*[1]; and a most prominent

[1] As it happens, a subtle distinction in this field of study is made between *attribution* and *attributional* theories. Attribution theories focus mainly on how causal attributions are reached, by observing the antecedents of causal attribution and the factors that lead to a particular cause. As such, they are primarily concerned with the process of causal inferences. Attributional theories focus mainly on the consequences of these causal inferences on motivation, subsequent behavior and experience, and as such, are concerned with the outcome, or product, of causal inferences (Kelley & Michela, 1980).

For reasons of convenience, however, no distinction is made between both groups of theories, the more so since Weiner's theory in our coverage contains elements of both conceptualizations. Moreover, in current literature the distinction appears to have become less prominent.

attribution theory is Bernard Weiner's *attributional theory of motivation and emotion* (see, among others: Dweck, 2018; Försterling, 2001; Graham, 2020).

In one of his first writings introducing this theory, Weiner stated: "Why this constant pursuit of 'why'? A number of explanations come to mind (...). We might just want to know, that is, to understand the environment, to penetrate ourselves and our surroundings. This familiar motivational interpretation is known as the principle of mastery (White, 1959). In addition, it clearly is functional to know why an event has occurred. (...) Once a cause, or causes are assigned, effective management may be possible and a prescriptive or guide for future action can be suggested" (Weiner, 1985, p. 548). If an outcome appears to be successful, then clearly a renewed attempt would be likely to proceed along comparable lines. If, however, the outcome or event is undesired, then most likely an attempt to alter the causes of such an outcome would be made to produce a different and hopefully more positive result.

These two expressions, or desires, the desire for mastery and the desire for functional search, are perceived by Weiner as the two generators of causal exploration (Weiner, 1985, 1986, notably Chapter 2).

In 1967, on the memorable Nebraska Symposium of Motivation, Harold Kelley authored a chapter that introduced the first attribution-related ideas into mainstream social psychology (Kelley, 1967), notably those of Fritz Heider, who had proposed the conception of attribution theory (together with balance theory) ten years before (Heider, 1958). The following year, Kelley approached Bernard Weiner and Edward Jones and proposed to establish a working group on attribution theory, which led to the 1972 publication on attribution that finally positioned it to a dominant conception within social psychology (Jones, Kanouse, Kelley, Nisbett, Valins & Weiner, 1972). In a modest and eloquent recollection of the history of attribution theory, Weiner memorized these events that marked the start of his work on attribution: "There also was a sad consequence of our meetings. Many years later I was having dinner with Ned Jones and he confessed that the meetings elicited a deep depression. He felt the young assistant professors had 'taken over' and he was no longer up to the mental tasks of his position. Of course, this was a totally unwarranted conclusion and quite the opposite of our beliefs - we greatly admired and envied Ned" (Weiner, 2008, p. 153).

In following years, Weiner was to introduce his attributional theory of motivation and emotion to the field of motivation psychology and education (Weiner, 1979, 1985, 1986). And although, in his account, "(...) there are many attribution-based theories and attribution is better characterized as a field of study rather than a theory" (Weiner, 2008, p. 154), we will give prominence to his theory in covering the concept.

To fully understand and appreciate the extent of Weiner's attribution theory, let us first provide examples to illustrate its basic principles and introduce some of the key concepts.

Consider the outcome of an action or event. It could be positive, and give rise to feelings of happiness, pride, joy, and consequently to action and effort in order to repeat the expected successful course of events. And when things turn out to be negative, the process turns in the opposite direction, with feelings of unhappiness, shame, or guilt, and where actions lead to a different array of subsequent outcomes.

Thus, actions and events can lead to a vast amount of possible outcomes. Why is it that some outcomes lead us to persist, and others to disengage? Is it only driven by positive or negative feelings, or do expectancies on possible outcomes also play a role?

Subsequent behavior, following the outcomes of an action or event, starts with causal exploration. Once we know the reasons for the perceived outcomes of a train of events, we have the means to manage and guide future actions.

Now, here is a first and important distinction to be made in thinking about causality. Any event, action, or occurrence can lead to a search of causes, but in attribution theory, only *achievement outcomes* are considered, especially those that have led to unexpected or negative results. Beliefs as to why people engage in certain activities is not the subject of study. As stated by Weiner: "(...) in my work and those of others in the achievement domain, (...) attributions are elicited for achievement *outcomes*. That is, in achievement settings there is a desire to find causes of success and failure. Thus, I do not address beliefs regarding why individuals undertake achievement activities, i.e., why one plays baseball, or goes to school, or accepts a particular job. However, I do examine perceptions regarding why one struck out at baseball, dropped out of school, or was fired from a job (...). Notice that these are negative end results, which elicit more search and attribution-related activity than do positive outcomes" (Weiner, 2008, pp. 154-155)[1] [2].

[1] As such, attribution theory is not concerned with causal determinants of a Goal, or antecedents leading to the formulation of a Goal, as defined according to the Model of Motivation. Rather, it progresses on the assessments made in a previous Phase 6 and observes the causes of these achievement outcomes.

[2] In addition, Weiner makes a distinction between *reasons* and *causes*, which has been neglected in literature (Weiner, 2008). As stated, in attribution theory the primal focus is on causes. Reasons have an explanatory connotation: "If a person is asked why he or she went to Movie X, the likely answers will be what are called reasons, such as: 'I heard it was good'; 'I was given free tickets'; 'I love mysteries'; and so on. These explanations or justifications make the choice understandable and intelligible. In explaining everyday actions, people focus on reasons (...)" (Weiner, 2008, p. 155; see also: Weiner, 1986, notably Chapter 2; Weiner, 2006, notably Chapter 1).

So, attribution theory observes the causes of achievement outcomes. In line with assumptions made in the Model of Motivation, these achievement outcomes can be seen as the resultant of a previous Phase of Externally Evoked Self-Assessment. Following an examination of these outcomes, there is a desire for a subsequent course of action. And in defining this course of action, causality and causal exploration play an essential role.

In this search for causality, attribution theory has attempted not only to classify these causes, but also to provide insights into why certain outcomes lead to certain courses of action by identifying certain properties within these various causes: "Inasmuch as there are an indefinite number of perceived causes of positive and negative outcomes, attribution theorists have attempted to identify their common properties and arrange causes within a taxonomic scheme" (Weiner, 2009, p. 62).

In this 'taxonomic scheme', attribution theory makes a distinction into specific elements, or *causes*, and specific properties, or *dimensions*, within those causes. Weiner proposes four main perceived elements, or causes, of achievement outcomes: ability, effort, task difficulty and luck. And each of these is assumed to differ in three specific properties, or causal dimensions.

*See exhibit* ➔

### 6.1. Attribution theories

Attribution theories aim at describing the processes involved in assigning causes to (achievement-related) events.

Within these theories, Bernard Weiner's attributional theory of motivation and emotion is "(...) recognized for its stature, elegance and logical precision (...)" (Perry & Hamm, 2017, p. 65).

In his theory, Weiner observes four important *causes,* or *elements*, within achievement-related settings:

a) *Ability:* often in a social comparison with others, abilities are derived from past experiences;
b) *Effort:* perception of investment on an activity or task;
c) *Task difficulty:* in a comparison with others;
d) *Luck:* in performing a task over which no control can be exercised.

These four elements differ along three *properties*, or *causal dimensions:*

1) *Controllability:* refers to the extent at which an event is perceived as being controllable or uncontrollable;
2) *Stability:* refers to the likelihood the cause can be altered over time: unstable where the cause can be altered, stable where the cause remains unchanged;
3) *Locus:* refers to the source the cause is believed to originate from: either internal or external to the individual.

*(Continued p. 239)*

Let us illustrate these elements, or causes, and how they differentiate along these specific properties, or causal dimensions.

If one tries to succeed in passing a test, and fails in the attempt, one tends to attribute the failure to (a lack of) ability, (insufficient) effort, the difficulty of the test, or (bad) luck. And conversely, if the outcome is successful and one succeeds in passing the exam, one tends to attribute the cause of success to the same set of elements, or causes, in positive connotation.

Now in each of these attributed causes, specific causal dimensions play a role. Suppose one fails in this attempt to pass a test, and tends to attribute the cause to a lack of ability. Ability, according to Weiner, is an 'uncontrollable' disposition: one either has the necessary skills, or capacities, to pass this test or not. Moreover, the disposition is 'stable', and doesn't change overnight: it is most likely to reoccur under same circumstances in the future. A third dimension, according to Weiner, would define ability as being 'internal', where causality is perceived to be within the individual, without any external influence playing a role. So, by attributing failure to pass the exam to a lack of ability, one attributes the reason for failure to a cause that has an uncontrollable, stable, and internal property, or dimension. And this, in turn, according to Weiner, will prove to have implications in terms of affect and emotions, and in subsequent behavior, which we will cover in a next Phase of the Process, when observing these responses.

Likewise, one could attribute the cause of failure to insufficient effort, which tends to be perceived as having different causal dimensions. Effort, according to Weiner, differs from ability in that it is a 'controllable' property: one has the choice to either spend sufficient effort or not. Furthermore, in contrast to ability, effort is 'unstable' as the investment of effort can fluctuate over time. Finally, as with ability, effort is considered to be 'internal', with causality perceived to be situated within the individual, and external influences play no substantial role. From this perspective, the reason for failure is attributed to controllable, unstable and internal properties, associated with the investment of insufficient effort. From this 'taxonomic scheme', it follows that the consequences are most likely to be different from those occurring when attributed to a lack of ability.

Furthermore, a cause of failure to pass the exam could be attributed to task difficulty. This might, at first sight, coincide with a lack of ability to perform according to required standards, but there is an essential distinction, according to Weiner, in that it is imposed, and therefore 'external'. Such an external influence enforces, as it were, the issue[1]. And this 'external' dimension makes it different from ability, which was assumed to be 'internal', leading most likely to yet another course of action. Which is further affected by an assumed 'stable' or sustained

[1] Note how this dimension also makes it 'uncontrollable', as in ability.

condition that is likely to intensify these effects. And note how these characteristics reflect the perceptions of the individual, where perceptions can change from one person to another and, in turn, can lead to differing outcomes.

Finally, when a failure is attributed to a lack of luck (or, more appropriately, when success is attributed to sheer luck), causes are perceived as 'uncontrollable' and beyond one's influence. It is assumed to be an 'unstable' condition, or a causal dimension that is not likely to last. Its 'external' properties further add to perceptions of causality that are beyond reach, affecting, in turn, the extent of subsequent action and outcomes.

So, in the perceived attributed causes of achievement outcomes, ability, effort, task difficulty and luck, there is a 'three-dimensional' characteristic in their various manifestations, ranging from 'controllable' to 'uncontrollable', from 'stable' to 'unstable', and from 'internal' to 'external'[1] [2].

*See exhibit* ➔

[1] For this conceptualization, Weiner uses the metaphor of a "three-dimensional taxonomic space" (Weiner, 2010, p. 32).

[2] Weiner commented on these causal dimensions that are conceived as located on a bipolar continuum: "however, it has (...) been contended that humans think in terms of dichotomous constructs (...), rather than continua (...). Hence, this issue certainly is not settled" (Weiner, 1986, p. 44; see also: Passer, Kelley & Michela, 1978).

### 6.1. Attribution theories

Thus, the four elements that determine the interpretation of an achievement-related event each have a unique profile of causal dimensions:

- Ability: uncontrollable, stable, internal;
- Effort: controllable, unstable, internal;
- Task difficulty: uncontrollable, stable, external;
- Luck: uncontrollable, unstable, external.

"Causal dimensions have psychological consequences, being related to both expectancy and affect. (...) Finally, expectancy and affect are presumed to determine action (...)" (Weiner, 1985, p. 566). High ability or great effort generates expectancies of success; low ability or insufficient effort decreases those expectancies. These expectancies lead to affective consequences such as pride or shame. And the combination of these expectancies and resulting affective consequences, in turn, determine subsequent action, to be covered in Chapter 8.

For further reading: Weiner, 1986 (notably Chapters 6 and 9); 1992 (notably Chapter 6).
For a shorter overview: Weiner, 1985, 2010, 2018.
For an analysis of causal structure: Weiner, 1986 (notably Chapter 3); 1992 (notably Chapter 6).

*Next related thread 6.2.* ➔ *p. 279*

And it is in these specific causal dimensions that an indication appears to be provided, not only of a subsequent course of action with associated effects and emotions, but also of the strategies involved that lead to these actions and emotions.

Both outcomes, behavioral and emotional, are addressed in a next Chapter, when we cover the consequences of the assessments and strategic inferences made in a Phase of Anticipated Change. But at this point in our coverage of causal inferences as proposed by attribution theory, *it is in those strategies of assigning causal attributes that we find important insights into how this Process appears to evolve within a Phase of Anticipated Change.*

For when one chooses (most likely subconsciously) the ingredients of causality, one not only defines causes and explanations, but also justifications, pretexts, alibis, for these achievement-related events with negative or unexpected outcomes, and confirmations, approvals and acknowledgements for those that turn out to be positive.

Elaborating on the example of an unsuccessful test: if one would attribute a cause of failure to ability, which is, among others, an 'uncontrollable' disposition, the behavioral consequences are likely to be quite different than when a cause of failure is attributed to effort, which is 'controllable'. With insufficient effort, the causes are within one's reach, whereas with a lack of ability, one is less accountable for the outcome: "I couldn't really help this from happening, now could I? Unfortunately I am not that smart". Observe the clever use of a causal dimension that, in spite of being 'internal', clears all suspicion of guilt for failing the attempt by attributing the outcome to an 'uncontrollable' causal dimension; whereas insufficient effort brings full responsibility as it is, in contrast, a fully 'controllable' causal dimension. The price, however, for this ingenious solution of having failed the exam, comes in the emotional consequences it entails: shame and embarrassment, as we shall observe in the next Chapter.

Comparable effects occur when attributing causes to 'external' dimensions, where task difficulty, with its 'uncontrollable' properties, appears to clear us from having full responsibility for unfortunate outcomes, and a lack of luck positions the reasons for failure even more beyond our control. As such, by attributing causes one also orchestrates the possible outcomes in terms of subsequent action, behavior and motivation. And by using the causal dimensions instead of the vast array of possible perceived causes, one can dramatically reduce the complexities of this intricate process. Thus, the 'taxonomic scheme' used in attribution theory, especially in relation to achievement-related outcomes, enables deeper insights into the behavioral consequences and subsequent effects on motivation, as we shall see in the next Chapter.

Although causal beliefs thus appear to provide the ingredients for strategic planning in a Phase of Anticipated Change, it must be noted that the attributional theory of motivation and emotion takes a slightly different stand, in that it emphasizes the behavioral and emotional consequences of causal beliefs, rather than pursuing the possible backgrounds where those causal beliefs originate from. The theory only indirectly refers to the origins of causal beliefs in research performed on the effects of changing one's causal beliefs and resulting influences both on performance and on motivation in general, as we shall observe in the next Section covering research findings from the field.

Attribution theories, then, and notably Weiner's attributional theory of motivation and emotion, primarily provide insights into causal attributions in achievement-related contexts. Where we are seeking to compare the proposed Model of Motivation with prominent current theories of motivation, a strong liaison appears with a Phase of Anticipated Change, where causal thinking is assumed to occur as a subsequent step in the Process of Motivation, based on prior assessments of potential and competence that lead to anticipated measures on increasing, sustaining or decreasing a perceived Discrepancy between the objectives we seek and the Impact from Reality.

*See exhibit next page* ➔

And although Weiner's attributional theory of motivation and emotion focuses primarily on causal beliefs, it appears also to shed light on the ingredients we use in our strategies to anticipate on cognitions, affects and subsequent courses of action. These consequences are covered more extensively in a next Phase in the Model of Motivation, to be addressed in the next Chapter.

## *Outcomes of a Phase of Anticipated Change*

Attribution theories, notably Weiner's attributional theory of motivation and emotion, provided further insights into processes involved in attributing causes to (achievement-related) events, following Impact and its related assessments:

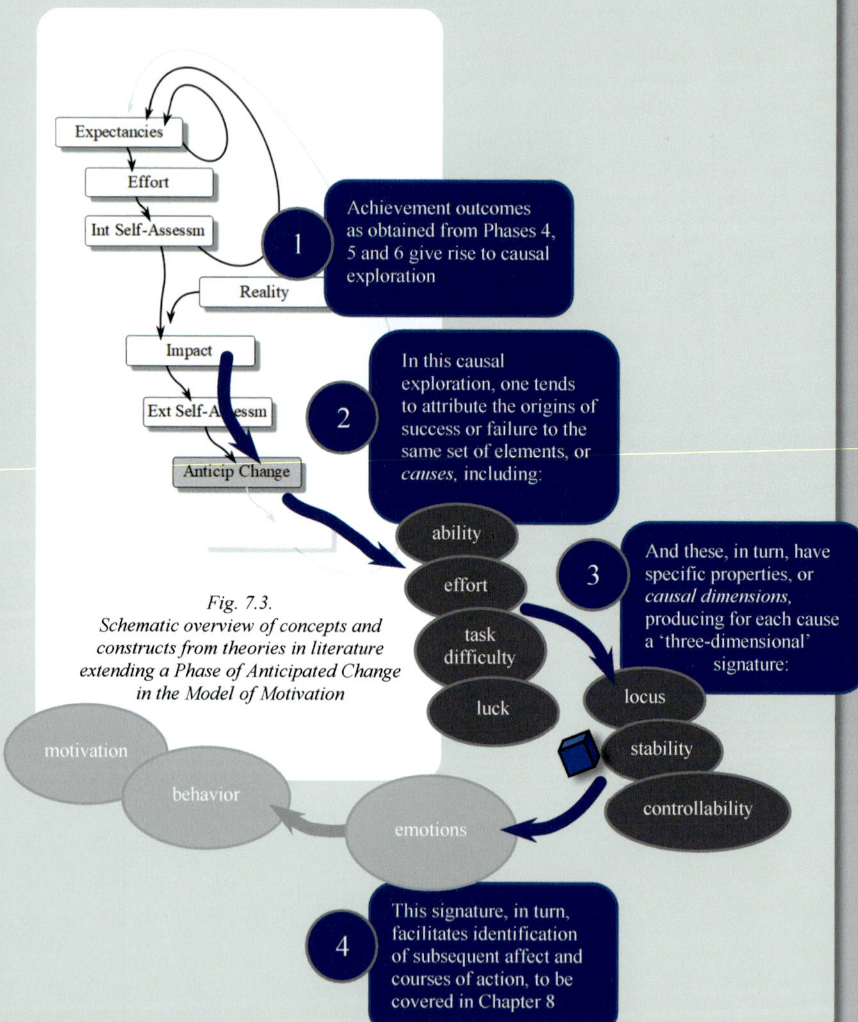


*Fig. 7.3.*
*Schematic overview of concepts and constructs from theories in literature extending a Phase of Anticipated Change in the Model of Motivation*

## 3 Research

From the onset, Weiner's attributional theory of motivation and emotion has been based on research findings that aimed at defining dominant causal attributions of success or failure within the achievement domain.

Research on attributional beliefs was first initiated with studies aimed at isolating perceived causes of success and failure especially in achievement-related situations. The experimental settings that induced conditions of success or failure had participants recall real-life situations of success or failure, or had them imagine related positive or negative outcomes. These studies, at first, were assumed to provide evidence for the importance of attributional thinking (see: Kelley & Michela, 1980, Weiner, 1980a, 1986, notably Chapter 1). "It was only after many such investigations that psychologists began to raise doubts about the methodology being used. The basic dissatisfaction was that the experimental procedure was reactive: that is, the responses of the subjects were believed to be influenced by the experimenter's introducing the notion of causality (...)" (Weiner, 1986, p. 23).

Subsequently, research concentrated on spontaneous attributional activities by coding written material notably from newspaper articles and comments. One of the first studies investigating spontaneous attributions was performed by Lau and Russell (1980), using 107 newspaper articles covering 33 major sporting events. In subsequent years at least 19 additional articles systematically investigated spontaneous attributions (see: Weiner, 1986, notably Table 2-1, pp. 34-35). Based on these data, Weiner concluded, "there is consistent evidence of a great deal of attributional exposure and thinking in everyday life, and this is exhibited in very diverse written material (...)" (Weiner, 1986, p. 27).

Once evidence of attributional thinking was established, Weiner aimed at defining common features in those attributions. At first, more than 40 studies investigated the four elements, or causes (Whitley & Frieze, 1983), which Weiner and his colleagues had proposed (Weiner, Frieze, Kukla, Reed, Rest & Rosenbaum, 1971); as he later commented, "subsequent investigators accepted this analysis and did not consider broadening their attributional net to include other possible subjective causes of achievement-related outcomes" (Weiner, 1986, p. 37). However, when subsequent studies observed a greater range and diversity of perceived causes in achievement-related contexts, findings emerged that appeared to confirm the four dominant attributions of ability, effort, task difficulty, and luck (see: Weiner, 1985, 1986, notably Tables 2-2 and 2-3, pp. 38-39, referring to: Anderson, 1983; Bar-Tal, Goldberg & Knaani, 1984; Burger, Cooper & Good, 1982; Cooper & Burger, 1980; Elig & Frieze, 1979; Frieze, 1976; Frieze & Snyder,

1980; Wilson & Palmer, 1983). "The most dominant of these causes are ability and effort. That is, success is ascribed to high ability and hard work, and failure is attributed to low ability and the absence of trying" (Weiner, 1985, p. 549; see also Cooper & Burger, 1980)[1].

From these observations on elements or causes attributed to achievement-related outcomes, the taxonomy of causal structures was derived. Weiner had defined the causal dimensions, of locus and stability by elaborating on the works of Rotter (1966), applying observations made by Atkinson on the effects of the experience of pride on achievement performance[2], and then by "filling in the blanks" and adding controllability, "perhaps the most important addition" (Weiner, 2010, p. 32), to join these dimensions of locus and stability.

Initially, Weiner had largely based the choice of the three causal dimensions, locus, stability and controllability, on outcomes of research performed at the time on causal structure (see: Weiner, 1985, 1986, notably Table 3-5, pp. 66-67, referring to: Meyer, 1980; Meyer & Koelbl, 1982; Michela, Peplau & Weeks, 1982; Passer, 1977; Passer, Kelley & Michela, 1978; Wimer & Kelley, 1982)[3]. As he commented in a later revision of his earlier textbooks on motivation (Weiner, 1972, 1980b): "The data from these empirical approaches support the contention that there are three dimensions or properties of perceived causality (see review in Weiner, 1986). These data also indicate that the structure of causality is not merely a convenient classification system imposed by attribution theorists. Rather, these dimensions are part of lay psychology, indicating that there is a relative simplicity in the organization of causal thinking, just as there is in the selection of specific causes" (Weiner, 1992, p. 253). Or, as he later commented: "It has been argued that causality, just as time and space, is a basic category of human thinking, inborn and 'ready' for use" (Weiner, 2006, p. 11). Thoughts that were reiterated more recently: "No other causal property has been consistently documented across situation and motivation domains. Hence, locus, stability, and controllability appear to be *the* general characteristics of causes (...)" (Weiner, 2018, p. 6).

[1] It must be noted, however, that at present it is not known "(...) whether ability-like or effort-like attributions are the most dominant causes in other parts of the non-western/non-industrialized world (...)" (Graham, 2020).

[2] See: Weiner, Frieze, Kukla, Reed, Rest & Rosenbaum, 1971. An interesting overview of his reasoning at the time was provided in an address given at the American Psychological Association Convention in Toronto, Canada, in August 2009 (see: Weiner, 2010).

[3] For a brief background on the choice of these three causal properties, see: Weiner, 1985; for a more general analysis of causal structure, see: Weiner, 1986, notably Chapter 3; Weiner, 1992, notably Chapter 6.

So given these findings, there appears to be evidence for the structures and taxonomies in causal attributions, as proposed by Weiner's attributional theory of motivation and emotion[1].

From the perspective of the Model of Motivation, this, in turn, provides an indication for the assumed Processes involved which, following assessments made in achievement-related contexts in a Phase of Externally Evoked Self-Assessment, eventually lead to strategies used within a Phase of Anticipated Change. The confirmation of findings on the ingredients of causal thinking, provides a foundation for further understanding on how these strategies are conceived, as suggested in Section 2.

Extending on these assumptions made in Section 2, let us briefly anticipate on evidence accumulating in literature that causal beliefs generate a predictable range of psychological consequences which lead to a variety of expressions in behavior and emotions, to be covered more extensively in the next Chapter.

Notably, it has been found that changes in causal beliefs can indeed lead to alternative forms of behavioral outcomes. In some instances, these alternative expressions have been found to be more adequate and effective, not only in terms of performance but on a broader scale, affecting motivation more in general. "Most encouraging concerning the applicability of the theory is that changes in causal beliefs alter achievement-related performance, although this conclusion is in great need of further empirical confirmation and elaboration" (Weiner, 2010, p. 34). In spite of these words of caution, attempts to alter causal beliefs, especially that failure is regarded as unstable (and therefore changeable), rather than stable (thus unchangeable), have produced positive results in performance, ranging from college students (Perry & Hamm, 2017; Perry, Hechter, Menec & Weinberg, 1993; Wilson, Damiani & Shelton, 2002) to elderly people, who were inclined to attribute failure to exercise to their (stable and unchangeable) 'old age'... (Sarkisian, Prohaska, Davis & Weiner, 2007). As summarized, "(...) stable beliefs about the causes of failure are important impediments to motivation, whereas unstable ascriptions for failure result in hope, which facilitates motivation" (Weiner, 2010, p. 35).

*See exhibits next pages* ➔

Changing one's strategies in causal beliefs, then, generates changes in behavior and emotions, and appears to also provide an indication for the assumptions made on underlying strategies.

[1] However, disagreement appears to remain in literature about the dimensional properties of ability. As commented by Graham: "(...) the mindset literature maintains that ability can be conceptualized as either fixed (stable) or malleable (unstable) (Dweck, 2006)" (Graham, 2020, p. 2.), where cross-cultural research also provides an indication of diverse results (Schuster, Forsterlung & Weiner, 1989).

## *Related Topics: On 'Learned Helplessness' and 'Self-handicapping'*

Attributing causes of failure to lack of ability (stable beliefs) rather than lack of effort (unstable beliefs), or ascribing failure to the self and causes of success to external factors, are important impediments to motivation (Weiner, 2010). Two areas of research have generated much interest and have been referred to as *'learned helplessness'* and *'self-handicapping'*.

*Learned helplessness* was developed in the mid-eighties by Peterson and Seligman (Graham, 1991), following experimental investigations by others that dramatically illustrated the adverse effects of loss of control. (Hiroto & Seligman, 1975; Seligman, 1972, 1975; for an overview: Weiner, 1992). It led to revisions advanced by Abramson, Seligman and Teasdale (1978), which make use of an attributional analysis of depression (Weiner, 1985). "According to this reformulated theory, depression follows uncontrollability when a person explains an uncontrollable event with causes that are internal ('it's me'), [and] stable ('it's going to last forever') (...)" (Seligman & Peterson, 2001, p. 8585; see also: Abramson, Metalsky & Alloy, 1989).

For overviews, see: Au, Watkins, Hattie & Alexander, 2009; Peterson, Maier & Seligman, 1993.

*Self-handicapping* uses similar strategies, although it is more explicitly aimed at the outcomes of this process, providing through careful orchestration an excuse (or explanation) for potential poor performance (Martin, Marsh, Williamson & Debus, 2005).

Self-handicapping is the strategy to select impediments to successful performance so that a cause of failure can be directed to those impediments rather than one's lack of competence. "Thus, if the individual fails in some way, he or she has a ready excuse: the lack of effort, for example, is seen as the cause rather than the individual's lack of ability" (Martin, Marsh, Williamson & Debus, 2005, p. 358).

An important reason for using these strategies lies in protecting one's self-worth. If one is inclined to attribute outcomes to external causes, and is uncertain as to one's ability to perform, self-worth is jeopardized and needs protective measures: "(...) When students see success and failure as externally caused, they perceive little control over their ability to maintain success or avoid failure (...)" (*ibid.,* p. 377).

For overviews, see also: Hattie & Marsh, 1996; Higgins, Snyder & Berglas, 1990; Martin, Marsh & Debus, 2001, 2003.

## Related Topics: On Positive Psychology

Altering causal ascriptions not only changes performance, but also appears to have a profound impact on a wider scale, ranging from affecting self-esteem to having a new perspective on one's perceptions of self, which has been at the core of the positive psychology revolution (see: Bandura, 2008; Hunter & Csikszentmihalyi, 2003; Lopez, 2008). However, the origins of positive psychology are not to be found in causal ascriptions, but rather in a new vision of psychology that was formulated around the start of the millennium...

*Here is an example of a resilience exercise:*
*"Home life: You phone your girlfriend when it is late at night (...) and she does not answer. Worst outcome:*

- *She's out on a date (...).*
- *She's having an affair.*
- *It's all over.*

*Best outcome?*

- *She's asleep (...).*
- *She's staying overnight at her mother's house.*

*Most likely outcome?*

- *She's gone out drinking with her girlfriends.*
- *She's tempted by other guys.*

*Now formulate a plan for dealing with the most likely outcomes" (Seligman, 2019, p. 14).*

Early 1998, the newly appointed president of the American Psychological Association, Martin Seligman, asked Mihaly Csikszentmihalyi to spend the first week of 1998 "(...) spelling out the elements of a new field and how to found it" (Seligman, 2019, p. 3). Their message was to remind the field "(...) that psychology is not just the study of pathology, weakness, and damage; it is also the study of strength and virtue. Treatment is not just fixing what is broken; it is nurturing what is best. Psychology is not (...) just concerned with illness or health; it is much larger" (Seligman & Csikszentmihalyi, 2000, p. 7).

Positive psychology started out with major tests on well-being (Seligman, 2019). At first, "people assumed that favorable external conditions such as employment, safety, health, and community participation would result in higher well-being" (*ibid.*, p. 12), but it gradually became clear that happiness itself, also caused these desirable outcomes. "Positive psychology holds that one of the best ways to help suffering people is to focus on positive things" (Seligman & Pawelski, 2003, p. 162). But it is more than just 'positive thinking', it is 'undoing' the negative emotion in order to build strength and resilience.

For more, see: Peterson, 2006; Seligman, 1998, 2002; 2018; Seligman & Csikszentmihalyi, 2000.

In summarizing these findings from research, then, there are two conclusions to be drawn. First, as with previous theories of motivation, it appears that Weiner's attributional theory of motivation and emotion has a liaison with the Model of Motivation, in that it highlights the Process that goes beyond the assertions of competence we saw in a Phase of Externally Evoked Self-Assessment, and provides evidence for the occurrence of causal thinking, as assumed to be prominent in a Phase of Anticipated Change. Moreover, in a second conclusion, it appears to also provide insights into the constituents or ingredients we use in defining strategies to address the approach at increasing, sustaining or decreasing a perceived Discrepancy between the Goals we set and the Impact from Reality, as assumed to occur in a Phase of Anticipated Change.

The outcomes of this sequential Process in which Motivation appears to progress following Impact will prove to have repercussions, as stated, on cognitions, affect, and behavior, as we are to uncover next in a Chapter that appears to contain the last Phase in this Process of Motivation.

## Summary

The seventh Phase in the Model of Motivation is a 'Phase of Anticipated Change', where the consequences are considered, following the assessment of adequacy of the Goal and its parameters after the Impact from Reality.

Phase 6 is a critical re-assessment; Phase 7 defines the master plan upon which amendments are to be made.

In a Phase of Anticipated Change, an appraisal is made of the potential readiness to decrease Discrepancy and to close the gap that has been observed between the Goal and Reality. The appraisal of the Discrepancy can be positive, negative or neutral. It is positive when one aims at reducing Discrepancy, it is negative when a further increase is intended, and neutral when no further action is foreseen.

The assessment is made in five successive Stages: The first Stage *(Δ - Attitude)* assesses and anticipates on an active change in Attitude aimed at closing, increasing or maintaining Discrepancy between the Goal and Reality. The second Stage *(Δ - Goal)* anticipates on an active change in properties of the Goal, where an anticipated change would likewise aim at closing, increasing or maintaining Discrepancy. Both Stages are followed by a Stage *(Δ - Energy)* in which a similar assessment is made aimed at potential changes in investment. Subsequent Stages, defined as *Δ - Achievement and Failure* and *Δ - Satisfaction and Frustration*, anticipate on subsequent intentions to re-define objective and subjective ratios, respectively, in achieving the Goal, aimed at closing, maintaining or increasing the Discrepancy.

The perspective of an 'anticipated reflection on change', as assumed to occur in a Phase of Anticipated Change, introduced the concept of causality in the sequential appraisals made. Within theories that are aimed at causal search, Weiner's attributional theory of motivation and emotion was considered to be the most prominent. Although the theory was primarily aimed at providing insights into causal attributions in achievement-related contexts and in subsequent associated effects and emotions, it also appeared in the analysis to shed light on the ingredients we tend to use in our strategies to anticipate on cognitions, affects and subsequent courses of action. These consequences are covered more extensively in a subsequent Phase of the Model of Motivation, to be addressed in the next Chapter.

# Chapter 8
## *In Search of Redemption*
## *Phase 8 - A Phase of Dedication*

So, *finally,* we come to respond to the intrusion that occurred in the Process of Motivation through the Impact from Reality...

As we observed in Chapter 5, in the Process of Motivation the reaction doesn't occur immediately after this confrontation. It manifests itself progressively through successive Phases: first, by comparing our previous intentions as defined in the first Phases of the Process with this new input emerging from Reality, then followed by an appraisal of a suitable course of action. And it is only then, that we come to respond to the Impact in the Process. It is not 'simply emerging'; the reaction follows from these previous Phases that determine its appearance and its intensity.

So it is the perspective, as it were, created by the objective that has been set that determines our reaction and the emotional expression it entails.

And the expression comes in pairs.

First appears the emotion experienced through the Impact from Reality towards the Process of Motivation. "Do I feel supported, acknowledged, recognized, or discouraged and obstructed in the attempt I was making at reaching my objective?" And the more Significant the objective, the more intense these primary emotions.

Let us, again, observe the examples we used.

So, here I am at Monserrate. And these folks are *ruining* my day. I feel *not at all* "supported, acknowledged, recognized". Note how simple and straightforward my reaction is. And recall how this was initiated by the indiscriminate perception from the previous Phase. These folks are *all* to blame, they are all disturbing my precious attempts, which evokes this primary reaction of non-support. There is no rationality involved. The emotions stream out. The idea that these people have every right to be there never enters the picture, and the idea that their presence, in fact, should be acclaimed for having such great taste to come and visit the Palace does not cross my mind: these rational thoughts *may* come, but they come later. And by then, they appear largely affected by these primary emotions emerging from the experience.

For now, then, the expression is simple and straightforward. And the more Significant my objective, the more explicit these feelings are likely to be. The intensity and tenacity, in both negative or positive expressions, can often serve as an indicator for an external observer of the severity of the Impact and the Significance of the objective that has been interfered with. Recall how we can often be caught by surprise with the intensity of someone's reaction on a seemingly trivial event. It should make us aware, not only of the (often unintended) Impact of our actions, or those of others, but also of the (often unintended) interference they cause in highly Significant Goals that are more often than not carefully kept away from being disclosed to others. The same applies to me. Through my unpleasantness, and especially the intensity of my reaction, I reveal how much I am affected and disappointed in my visit to Monserrate, and more prominently, how Significant the event is for me, and how carefully I have concealed its true meaning in the expression of my temper.

And these 'derivatives', serving to protect the integrity of a Significant Goal, can thus become indicators to provide insight to an external observer (and to ourselves) into in their hidden meaning.

Now, these emotions came in pairs.

And my primal reaction was one of being not at all supported, and denied, disrespected in my attempts at having a long-awaited 'romantic-experience-of-amazement-and-wonder' at Monserrate. Now comes this strange, almost revengeful 'tit-for-tat' secondary reaction: I feel disdain and contempt towards my fellow visitors, in return. The impression of being disrespected by Reality (which is by no means apparent in any of the reactions of those visitors) leads to disrespect from my side, in return. And these feelings have largely been initiated by the assessments made in both previous Phases that led to this final outcome.

A bad day, indeed...

So let us change our repertoire, with our second example... Remember how well I did at the tennis match? How uplifting this experience has been! It makes one feel revitalized: this is 'the world of success', this is *'the world of tennis!'* Now, it almost seems that I'm exaggerating (and of course, I am), but there is more to it than simple exaggeration. What I also achieve by overstating the experience is that I 'boost' and enhance the positive effects on my morale, my confidence, my self-worth; it has an almost therapeutical effect. It seems a simple exaggeration, but it is a 'mental medicine' that helps intensify the positive effects on the Process of achieving the objective, the Goal that I had set. And, in fact, as we saw, it wasn't about just 'playing a nice game': it gradually, through this cyclical Process in Phases 1, 2 and 3, evolved into a more Significant Goal, where elements of confidence and self-worth gradually came to play an implicit role; and these very elements are now the ones that are being accentuated in the emotional assessments that are made in this present Phase. The primary reaction following the Impact from Reality is generated by the input from previous Phases 6 and 7: I feel "supported, acknowledged, recognized" in my achievements in this match. And, *in return,* in a secondary reaction I recognize, appreciate and even identify with this 'acknowledging world', which is 'the world of tennis'. Just as demeaning wordings about the visitors at Monserrate served to reduce a negative Impact on the Process of Motivation, so does an overstatement of 'the world of tennis' now serve to enhance its positive Impact on what I try to accomplish in this Process of Motivation.

*It is as if these primary and secondary emotions occurring in this Phase are not simple 'derivatives' of the Process of Motivation. They also serve to protect the Process; to prevent us in our attempts from harmful interference.* It is a 'cordon sanitaire' against 'the world out there'; a mechanism that serves to protect the integrity of the Process of Motivation as it progresses towards reaching the Goal that has been set.

Let us take a next step in the examples we have set, and observe these protective mechanisms as they materialize in primary and secondary reactions.

Here is the third example. The wicked groceries... I had thought the criteria were clear; the deal was set. And in a subsequent Phase of Anticipated Change, I realized I had to proceed to action. So what are the emotional repercussions now? The two prior Phases provide exposure for my negligence. I had intended to postpone (no sufficient return on investment), but now both prior Phases following Impact show me I will have to act. These prior Phases of evaluation following Impact from Reality brought me to choose for the decent option and decrease Discrepancy. But having made this choice, my perception was that 'Reality won'. In this present Phase it leads to feelings of 'being exposed', as I should have provided a follow-up. These feelings are personal and could have been different for someone else. These reactions highly depend on the individual. Note also that no action is being taken at this point: a follow-up on these feelings and observations comes later. So, to recapitulate, my primary reaction to the interference from Reality in my carefully orchestrated postponement in this Process of Motivation is one of 'being exposed', leading to a 'sense of guilt' and embarrassment. To compensate, I would gladly see my beloved (who thus interrupted my plans) have equal feelings towards me (to feel at least a 'little guilty' would be most helpful indeed). And to ascertain that she does, I express frustration in a secondary reaction, which is one of 'annoyance'. And these secondary feelings, in turn, can lead to subsequent reactions from her that further add to the experience...

Again, these 'reactive mechanisms' serve to protect me, in this case from guilt. And note how the expression is likely to induce *quite an opposite reaction from others, thus from Reality...*

Finally, let us examine the complex constellation of interrelated Processes of Motivation in the last three examples, sharing a common Reality and producing a variety of reactions in the last Phases, as we observed in the previous Chapter.

Somehow these interrelated Processes will have to lead to a common expression of feelings towards this interfering Reality, that is to serve as an adequate protection in this last Phase of the Process.

Let us observe, first, the trip to Hong Kong, where we considered a return for the first time. What are the effects on perceptions of Reality? Recall that the interference had a positive outcome: it produced, in a Phase of Anticipated Change, this appealing alternative of going to Hong Kong. One would expect at least a positive reaction, but recall that Reality *did not provide support.* It merely *enabled* this course of events to occur, but was in no way responsible for the alternative that presented itself: there was no offer of any sort to make this trip. On the contrary, the occurrence of an interfering superior (in the next example) led to considering an alternative. *Emphasizing this negative occurrence in this parallel Process of Motivation would serve the cause of going to Hong Kong in this present example. So the Process of Motivation is well-served by expressing negative feelings to this interfering Reality, which is (literally, strangely enough) supporting my intentions to go in this present example.* Primary feelings, then, acknowledge the (perceived) rejection that is caused by the interfering Reality, which serves my intentions to go; and these primary feelings, in turn, evoke secondary feelings expressed in the form of a rejection in return, for "such a flagrant interference in one's academic activities". The worse my portrayal of my poor manager, the better it serves my purpose, and the sooner I'll be on my way to Hong Kong. Note again that this portrayal is *not at all* served by having at least checked the underlying assumptions that the interference by my superior has been deliberate and that it was explicitly aimed at frustrating my attempts to publish. The less refined my judgment, and the less subtle the nuances I make, the better my Process of Motivation is served; but, in return, the more prejudiced I become, the more forceful and resistant I become to any nuance, any hesitation, or doubt. My presentation of the state of affairs thus becomes rigid and lacking.

Reconsidering my trip, and all these subsequent deliberations, was instigated by the confrontation with Reality in my fifth example: my superior inquiring on the status of a publication. And I was on high alert, as I had postponed writing a paper because I feared that I would fail in the attempt. This unfortunate addressing of my dormant Goal led me to decide to maintain my original objective in an assessment of adequacy made in a Phase of Externally Evoked Self-Assessment; and subsequently to a 'call to arms', in a Phase of Anticipated Change, thereby affirming my strategy to postpone (and thereby also cleverly concealing my fear of failure), and conveniently emphasizing the need to go to Hong Kong and "leave all troubles behind". And both Phases now determine my mindset in an emotional reaction and appraisal of Reality in the present Phase. I feel belittled and exposed in my fear: no sense of support whatsoever from Reality, from my superior "in these trying times". Again, I do not verify these allusions, as they serve the protective measures I took in both preceding Phases. And these primary feelings of non-support experienced from Reality now lead to this strange, almost revengeful, 'tit-for-tat' secondary reaction: I feel disrespect towards my superior in return. *As observed earlier, the impression of being disrespected by Reality (which has not been verified, and in the example happens to be an incorrect assumption) now leads to disrespect from my side, in return.*

But how convenient this representation of Reality now becomes!

These primary and secondary emotions are not merely an outcome of the Process of Motivation, they also serve, as observed, to protect us from an intruding Reality; to protect the integrity of the Process of reaching the objective that was set. In having these primary and secondary reactions, I neutralize the perceived interference from Reality in the Process of Motivation that, in this example, was aimed initially at postponement of writing a paper. Reducing through feelings of disrespect an interfering Reality now prevents me from being pressurized. Turning Reality through these feelings of disrespect into an unobtrusive, inconspicuous version, a new representation of Reality, subsequently reduces the extent of a perceived interference. This new representation of my superior thus conveniently reduces the perceived threat to reconsider my postponement of writing the paper.

And all these mechanisms are intertwined. If I can have one Process of Motivation assist me to enhance these neutralizing effects in another Process, I will not hesitate to do so, as illustrated in the example of going to Hong Kong: the prospect of going there now gives me an entirely new perspective, and could, in addition, serve as a further deterrent for the exposure I experience to a forceful superior pressurizing me to publish, and to defy my fear of failure in writing this article: "I'm out of here, and Hong Kong may serve the cause!"

Lastly, then, let us observe how this 'intertwined constellation of Processes of Motivation' is further served in protecting our sixth and final example, which involved latent Goals: those Goals that were addressing the way 'the world ought to be'. Recall that my latent objective was "to be part of a university with highest principles and moral values", and "where autonomy was to prevail in every respect". From the multitude of latent Goals that I have, this one was made to trigger. The email from my superior occurring as a perceived Reality in an adjacent Process of Motivation has now influenced the setting in which I perceive and evaluate my university. As previously observed, it first led to questioning the values contained in my latent Goal in a Phase of Externally Evoked Self-Assessment: "Did I do well to adhere to these highest moral standards, or should I drastically reduce these expectations, in considering my present position?" Now this, of course, was highly unlikely, given the Significance of my latent Goal, and the pervasive and urgent need to adhere to those highest standards, as we saw next in observing a Phase of Anticipated Change.

So, the perspective I had has now been supplemented by a frame of reference shaped in these two previous Phases. And this frame of reference leaves me no alternative but to be highly critical of my academic surroundings imposing a moral obligation to submit a paper (at least in my perception). My primary reaction is one of disapproval, referring to this ominous email: "They do not act towards me according to my standards of integrity and freedom of mind", and as a result my secondary reaction mirrors my rejection of this perceived Reality: "I do not wish to be part of this anymore". And thereby, I conveniently adhere to the feelings of disrespect I developed towards this perceived Reality, in both preceding and related examples.

Previous Phases, then, have produced a frame of reference, which now leads to primary and secondary reactions towards Reality, creating a picture that has, literally, lost a sense of realism and is lacking a basic verification of the underlying assumptions it suggests.

These successive Phases thus provide the ingredients that can make us rigid and prejudiced, intolerant in our perceptions; and the more Significant the objective, the Goal to which we refer, the more inclined we are to follow its perspective as *the* principal reference in our perception of Reality. Conversely, this reaction towards Reality can also be aimed at enhancing and amplifying positive aspects of

Reality that serve or sustain the Process of Motivation, as we saw in our second example in a 'world of tennis'.

So, in summary, here is the sequence once again.

A Goal has been set, and attempts have been made to reach that Goal with subsequent assessments in the first three Phases of the Process of Motivation. Now, Reality interferes in this Process, and its Impact is not directly reacted upon. Instead, these initial Phases of the Process provide a perspective to react in two subsequent Phases, thereby creating bias in the perception of Reality.

*Reality in its Impact, then, is not observed the 'way it is', but is perceived through the perspective of the Goal with which it interferes. And the more Significant the Goal, the more pronounced the perspective, and the more predisposed a twofold reaction towards Reality. This next Phase in the Process of Motivation is a Phase where we contemplate and react on the effects of Impact through Reality: it is a 'Phase of Dedication'.*

Now, after these primary and secondary reactions in a Phase of Dedication, are we finally to proceed towards making those amendments that we have anticipated on when assessing adequacy of the Goal and the settings that were made, after the Impact of Reality?

Not quite...

There is a last phenomenon occurring prior to us doubling back on our tracks and carefully re-attuning the Goal and its parameters, as we observed in the first Phases of the Process. This phenomenon is referred to as a *'Mechanism of Representation'*.

These primary and secondary reactions we develop towards an interfering Reality leave a trace, an impression. It is in a sense a 'visualization' of what we believe Reality stands for, either in its negative or in its positive Impact on the Process of Motivation. And it is this image, this 'Representation', that we will use to anticipate on, once we return to a first Phase of Expectancies, in which the intended re-amendments are made.

*So, in a Phase of Dedication we not only define our perceptions of and feelings towards Reality in response to its Impact, we also generate a 'visualization', or 'Representation', of Reality in Mechanisms of Representation. And it is in those Mechanisms associated with the Impact from Reality that profound effects are to appear in the Process of Motivation...*

Let us observe these effects in the examples used so far.

'Crowds of people' interfering with the pleasures of my day, and I need a clever way out, following the awareness that I cannot get even with such an adversary, with primary feelings of being denied and being disrespected, and secondary feelings of disdain and contempt in return. In the Representation of Reality, my fellow visitors become an anonymous 'crowd', cleverly reduced to a gathering of folks with whom you cannot reason and (consequently) where the elegant solution is to act "as any sensible person would do", and leave the place.

Now, the opposite occurs when Reality recognizes and ascertains my Significant Goals. Where *downgrading* Reality served to reduce a negative Impact on the Process in the previous example, *overstating* Reality in our second example now serves to enhance the positive effects. 'The world of tennis' is made into a Representation that articulates high standards, following primary and secondary reactions of experiencing and expressing recognition. And being successful within such a setting extends and amplifies my winnings. It comes as no surprise that expressions (more often implicit than explicitly made) of being part of such a world associated with success often serve to confirm and consolidate the positive Impact it provides to our personal Goals, and reveal together with a vast array of materialized tokens, such as cars, clothing, jewelry, a need for such expressions that symbolize and confirm our success.

But Representations can take other forms as well that reveal their hidden meaning in highly concealed and suppressed ways. Those groceries... As an outcome of Phase 6 and Phase 7, I am going to do something that I do not want to do. And I am to neutralize these 'pressurizing-influences-against-my-will' originating from Reality: following the primary reaction of 'being exposed', combined with a 'sense of guilt' and embarrassment as we observed, those feelings in turn lead to a secondary, compensating reaction where I feel 'annoyed'. And I could extend on those feelings, where I express my frustration and annoyance by pretending to be 'amused' by the situation. I now have a Representation of Reality that perfectly suits my needs. Reality becomes 'a trivial incident' so as to 'downgrade' its influence. The embarrassment I experience is reflected in the intensity of my conduct. To state it explicitly: the more I feel embarrassed, the more 'amused' I pretend to be, and the more I compensate with an unreasonable demeanor against my better judgment. In short, the more I care, the *less* serious I become. And these expressions, in turn, are most likely to lead to subsequent reactions that further add to the confusion that is caused.

These mechanisms, then, are made to neutralize a Significant Reality and the Impact it causes, by creating a Representation. And these Representations, surprisingly, are thus often made to conceal how much (in fact) we care, as in the example: to gain approval from those that are essential to us. *Mechanisms of Representation often appear at the basis of seemingly incomprehensible actions or expressions aimed in particular at those that are Significant to us.*

Let us increase complexity further with the last three examples.

Reality interfering in a dormant Goal of going to Hong Kong served to propel this pleasurable prospect, as it conveniently combined with feelings towards my superior, aimed at concealing my fear of failure to write a paper, and thereby sustaining feelings of disapproval concerning my latent Goal of being part of a university with highest principles where autonomy was to prevail. This perception of Reality, interfering as we saw in multiple Processes of Motivation, now materializes in a Representation of my superior, turning an inconvenient Reality through these feelings into an unobtrusive, inconspicuous version, thereby reducing its interference. And this Representation cleverly supports the course of action set out in both previous Phases to consider leaving for Hong Kong. In addition, it consolidates the outcomes to maintain postponing this paper from the perspective that "with such directives I take control of my own priorities", thereby further decreasing this perceived input from Reality. *Which, incidentally, remains to be Significant.* The inconvenient Reality is simply replaced by a Representation that better suits my courses of action initiated in both previous Phases. And, finally, this same Representation serves to defuse the Impact that triggered my latent Goal and made me determined not to "admit defeat" and surrender to "lesser moral standards", where, again, the Representation conveniently neutralizes the intrusion that occurred from Reality.

And these Representations often result in strange 'amalgamations' that serve these Processes of Motivation to preserve and protect Significant Goals that have been set, be it explicit, dormant or latent in their expression.

*So, this is where the intricate Process of Motivation leads us to when the Goals that we set are perceived as Significant. The successive Phases following a Phase of Impact lead to assessments that eventually, through primary and secondary reactions, make us adapt and change a perceived Reality into a Representation that better suits our needs.*

*Mechanisms of Representation are aimed at neutralizing Reality, either by enhancing its positive effects or reducing its negative effects, and in these effects they profoundly influence the way we perceive Reality, especially when its Significance is high.*

> In Phase 8, primary and secondary reactions eventually lead to a replacement of Reality through a so-called 'Mechanism of Representation'.

*And it is only then that we, finally, make the amendments anticipated on when we encountered Reality in its Impact, and successively assessed its effects on the Process of Motivation.*

*A Phase of Dedication marks the end of the sequential Process of Motivation, as it returns to make these amendments in a previous Phase in which these intentions initially materialized: a Phase of Expectancies. And by returning to these original Stages, the Process of Motivation has now become cyclical, where the sequence of successive Phases is re-initiated.*

As we will observe in the next Chapter, there is a distinctive feature that makes this second cycle different from its previous version: we now come prepared for the upcoming renewed confrontation with Reality. And a most essential ingredient in this second cycle is provided through a Mechanism of Representation. For the Representation that was made as an outcome of the first cycle is now introduced in lieu of its original.

So, in this new cycle of the Process of Motivation, Reality has changed, and the more Significant the objective, the more it is changed to a Representation, creating circumstances for discord and conflict to emerge... A perfectly innocent group of visitors thus turns into a 'crowd' ruining the day; a tennis match turns into a glamorous event; a 'moral-and-decent-thing-to-do' is being challenged and turned into an unpleasant obligation; and an interfering superior is made into an unobtrusive, inconspicuous character.

Although in portraying those negative pictures, it appears that Mechanisms of Representation often produce the most disturbing effects, it is to be noted that these Mechanisms can also produce a positive and staggering portrayal of a Significant Reality that has enhanced and supported our attempts at reaching a desirable Goal: these Representations then take the form of the 'perfect' teacher, coach, lecturer, the 'best ever' performer, film, actor or actress, author, composer, and these are but a few examples of how a Mechanism of Representation can outperform its uplifting effects on the Process of Motivation.

But although these represent a positive side of the picture, negative implications nonetheless appear to prevail. And the uneasy, apprehensive conclusion is to be maintained that many of our problems, arguments and conflicts originate from this Mechanism of Representation. This is where prejudice, irrationality, exaggeration originate from. This is how unverified assumptions, mis-interpretations based on the disruptive Impact from Reality on dormant and latent Goals bring dreams to a halt and can affect one's future beyond repair...

The eighth Phase in the Process of Motivation is a Phase of Dedication.

Following the Impact from Reality and the perception of Discrepancy, three evaluative reactions occur.

And the third, and final, of these reactions is aimed at an assessment of Reality. In a primary reaction ("How do I experience the Impact from Reality?") and in a secondary reaction ("What is my response in return?") the assessment is made.

After this Phase, the Process proceeds towards making the necessary amendments anticipated on, by returning to the first Phase, a Phase of Expectancies, thereby turning the Process of Motivation into a cyclical system of recurring Phases progressing sequentially towards Goal attainment.

*Phase 8 in the Model of Motivation is covered in detail on pp. 264-273. A summary is on pp. 300-301.*

# 1 Definitions

In a sequence of Phases following the Impact from Reality, a re-orientation occurs of the Goal versus Reality. This re-orientation aims at the essential elements that are involved: the Goal and its parameters, the gap or Discrepancy, and Reality.

In reference to Fig 5.3., Chapter 5, the third and final assessment we make, then, is aimed at Reality...

One would assume that following the Impact from Reality, we react directly to the new situation at hand; and it often seems that we do. But the reaction, even if it appears to occur almost instantaneously, is always preceded by this stepwise assessment Process we first came to observe in Chapter 5. As without these steps, there would be no reaction: we first have to have awareness of the occurrence (in Phase 4) and the effects it has on our attempts at reaching an objective (Phase 5); then we need to assess adequacy (Phase 6) and consequences (Phase 7), before we can make the actual amendments needed to address the situation.

So, a Phase of Impact was found to set in motion three reactions, previously described as 'preceding passive, evaluative reactions', before we are set to re-attune the Goal and its parameters. The third of these three reactions constitutes the eighth and last Phase in the Process of Motivation.

In this Phase, a *Phase of Dedication*, after having observed the Goal and the gap that emerged, the attention now turns back to Reality. Thus, it is assumed in the Model of Motivation that the individual, after having assessed the Impact from Reality on the Goal that has been set, now in turn evaluates Reality. In this respect, a Phase of Dedication differs drastically in nature from the previous Phases in the Process of Motivation. *All preceding Phases were centered around the Goal. A Phase of Dedication, in contrast, focuses on Reality*[1].

[1] From this perspective, one could argue that a Phase of Dedication should be excluded from the Model. It does not belong in a Process of Motivation, for the Process evolves around a Goal, as defined initially in the Introduction. A Phase of Dedication appears to be rather a product, or an outcome, of the Process. But there is an important reason to include the Phase within the Model of Motivation, for it will prove to provide essential input for a subsequent active reaction towards Reality, when a re-formulation of the Goal and its associated parameters is made in a subsequent renewed cycle of the Process. As we shall observe, the perception the individual holds of Reality is to determine to a large extent these renewed amendments that are essential in re-establishing an adequate balance within the Process. A Phase of Dedication is therefore included as an integral part, and a distinct Phase, within the Model.

This third evaluative reaction has two distinct features: it evaluates Reality, but this evaluation also produces a specific outcome, referred to as a 'Representation'.

First, the evaluation.

In a Phase of Dedication, then, it is not the Goal but Reality that is at focus. *Given the input provided by the previous two Phases, in a Phase of Dedication an assessment is made in terms of perceived 'support', or 'non-support', for the Goal, which is central to the Process, and for the various parameters initially set.*

It is assumed that a Phase of Dedication progresses in four Stages, as opposed to the previous evaluations that occurred in a Phase of Externally Evoked Self-Assessment and a Phase of Anticipated Change. In this third evaluative Phase, one Stage is excluded: a Stage evaluating Reality versus the Goal. The Stage is excluded as it has been evaluated earlier in a Stage of Impact. In this Stage, or Phase, an assessment was made of implications for the Process of reaching the Goal, given the introduction of Reality. The Impact of Reality was defined as a 'Discrepancy' experienced by the individual between a perceived Reality and the Goal that had been set, which expresses an assessment in terms of perceived 'support' or 'non-support' towards this Goal.

So, an analysis of the effects of Reality specifically addressed towards the Goal that has been set, is to be excluded from this Phase of Dedication, as the assessment has previously occurred in a Stage, or Phase, of Impact, thereby expressing the prominent position of this Stage within the Process of Motivation.

The passive, evaluative reaction in a Phase of Dedication, then, is aimed at the four remaining Stages that were instrumental in defining the Goal. The first of which consisted of a Stage of Attitude. Earlier, Attitude was defined as a 'mental status' aimed towards the Goal and thus, starting the Process of Motivation. This mental status has now been re-evaluated after Reality interrupted the Process of Motivation. How then is Reality, in turn, being evaluated after the event? In the first Stage of a Phase of Dedication, a *Stage of Appreciation* is defined as a passive, evaluative reaction towards Reality, from a perspective of the Attitude initially set. Basically, Reality can be perceived as 'supportive', 'non-supportive' or 'neutral' to the initial Attitude, and this perception is largely influenced by both re-assessments in previous Phases of Externally Evoked Self-Assessment and Anticipated Change. Likewise, a *Stage of Approbation* can be defined as a passive, evaluative reaction towards Reality from a perspective of the 'Energy' or investment needed to reach the Goal, thus reflecting its perceived value. In addition, a *Stage of Affirmation* is a passive, evaluative reaction towards Reality from a perspective of Achievement and Failure, and a *Stage of Commitment* from a perspective of Satisfaction and Frustration.

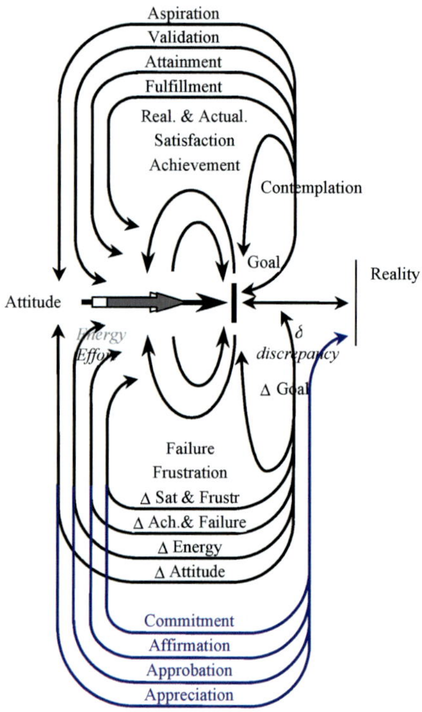


*Fig. 8.1.*
*A visualized overview of Phase 8,*
*a Phase of Dedication*
*in the theoretical Model of Motivation,*
*consisting of:*

21. A Stage of Appreciation
22. A Stage of Approbation
23. A Stage of Affirmation
24. A Stage of Commitment

These assessments are visualized in Fig. 8.1., for the four consecutive Stages comprising a Phase of Dedication. These four Stages, which reflect the Stages from a Phase of Expectancies, are assumed to remain the same, as the Process is anticipatory and reflective in nature. Only the assessments for each element are observed, thus, 'contrasting' the four parameters with Reality as observed. In addition, from Fig. 8.1., this 'contrasting' between the Goal and Reality can also be observed, as previously visualized in Chapter 5, Fig. 5.1., illustrating the observations made on the evaluation of the Goal in a Phase of Impact. The evaluation previously made in this Phase of Impact complements, as it were, those that were made in a Phase of Dedication.

But in this Phase of Dedication much more is happening than a mere assessment of perceived 'support' or 'non-support' from Reality at various levels. *This assessment of Reality within each of the four Stages proceeds in two steps, in what we referred to earlier as a 'primary' and a 'secondary' evaluation.*

In a Stage of Appreciation, the primary evaluation is mainly aimed at perceptions of 'support' or 'non-support' from Reality for the Attitude initially defined within a Phase of Expectancies. If Reality is perceived as 'supportive' to one's Attitude, this will lead to feelings of 'being appreciated' or 'acknowledged', in a primary evaluation. And, as a spin-off, this in turn will lead to feelings of 'appreciation' towards Reality in reaction, as a secondary evaluation. In parallel, if Reality is perceived as 'non-supportive', this could lead to feelings of 'being denied', or 'ignored', or 'rejected', in a primary evaluation. And these feelings, in turn, could lead to feelings of 'contempt' towards Reality, in a secondary evaluation. The more Reality is perceived as Significant, the more these feelings of 'being appreciated' or 'being ignored' emerge, and consequently, the more these will lead to feelings of either 'appreciation' or 'contempt' towards Reality in return.

In line with this, the Stage of Approbation is an evaluative reaction of Reality from a perspective of Energy, or investment needed to reach the Goal. From this perspective, one assesses perceived 'support' or 'non-support' for the investment one has made, which also reflects a perceived value one attaches to the Goal. A perception of Reality as 'supportive' or 'non-supportive' leads to feelings of 'being valued' or 'not valued', in a primary evaluation. And these feelings are intensified by the Significance attached to Reality. These primary evaluations, in turn, lead to secondary evaluations that are a reaction of these perceptions. When one feels 'valued' in case of perceived 'support', one is likely to 'value' Reality in return, thereby incidentally increasing its supportive properties. When one feels 'not valued', a reaction in the form of a secondary evaluation is likely to lead to similar feelings in return, thereby diminishing the effects Reality entails.

Likewise, in a Stage of Affirmation, an evaluation occurs of Reality from a point of view of initial Achievement and Failure ratios. In a primary evaluation, Reality is perceived as either 'confirming' or 'disapproving' one's choices. These perceptions of Reality being 'supportive' or 'non-supportive' for one's judgment, in turn, are likely to lead to secondary evaluations where these feelings of 'confirmation' or 'disapproval' from Reality, in turn, are echoed by feelings 'confirming' or 'disapproving' Reality, and thus affirming or questioning its integrity.

And finally, a Stage of Commitment concludes these evaluations. The Stage of Commitment is the 'end of the equation' and the 'grand total' of all the effects experienced from Reality in a condensed format. A Stage of Commitment either 'pushes one up or brings one down'. It provides the individual with the experience of 'worth', of being 'esteemed', depending on one's perception of Reality. When Reality is perceived as 'supportive' of one's subjective judgments, the primary evaluations will lead to feelings of 'worth', of 'making a difference', as instigated by Reality. The experience of 'non-support' from Reality often leads to extreme polarized reactions, with feelings of being 'unworthy'. And where one feels Reality as being either 'dedicated' or 'hostile' to one's cause, feelings of 'commitment' or 'hostility' are mirrored to Reality in return, in secondary evaluations.

So, these four Stages produce a variety of primary evaluations of perceived 'support', or 'non-support' in Reality. And these primary evaluations, in turn, generate a series of secondary evaluations towards Reality, in return.

This succession of evaluations, finally, results in a second remarkable feature occurring in a Phase of Dedication: the emergence of a 'Mechanism of Representation'.

Where primary evaluations lead to secondary evaluations, these effects are not only an outcome of the Process of Motivation, they also, and predominantly, serve to maintain this Process of reaching an objective. The primary and secondary evaluations emerge at all four Stages. In the Model of Motivation, it is assumed that these expressions, or feelings towards Reality, provide the input to further maintain the integrity of the Process. By evaluating Reality, the individual obtains the ingredients to either enhance or neutralize the influence of Reality on the Process. *In doing so, however, it is assumed a dangerous procedure is introduced in the Process of Motivation: the individual changes Reality in a direction that is most suitable to the Process. And the mechanisms that serve to produce these protective measures, as a resultant of evaluations in a Phase of Dedication, are referred to as 'Mechanisms of Representation'. These Mechanisms are an outcome of the evaluative Stages that occur in a Phase of Dedication, where the individual substitutes, or superimposes, an image obtained from these Stages in lieu of Reality. This image is referred to as a 'Representation'.*

In a Stage of Appreciation, where Reality is experienced as 'supportive', feelings of 'being appreciated' or 'acknowledged' are greatly served by an image expressing these feelings to further strengthen and 'propel' the Process. Where one feels Reality to be 'non-supportive', reactive feelings of 'contempt' towards Reality are likewise reflected in its Representation, which assists in neutralizing its importance, thereby diminishing the Impact it originally had on the Process.

In a Stage of Approbation, comparable Mechanisms serve to produce an image that either propels or neutralizes the perceived influence of Reality on the Process of Motivation. If one feels 'support' for one's investment, reflected in a perceived value of the Goal, a Representation expressing value towards Reality serves to enhance the positive Impact it produces. And if one feels 'non-support', an image expressing perceptions of a limited value attached to Reality will serve to diminish its importance, and hence its Significance, and neutralize its effects. A Significant Reality that acknowledges one's value system is valued even more, so as to further increase its effects on the Process of Motivation, as the increased Significance serves to further propel its effects. But the reverse also holds true. If one attaches great Significance to Reality and Reality is 'not supportive' of one's values, one 'degrades' Reality to neutralize or diminish its negative Impact. The more one perceives a Significant Reality as 'non-supportive', the more one tends to belittle its effects in the Representation generated as an outcome.

Likewise, in a Stage of Affirmation, the more one either confirms or questions the integrity of Reality, as an outcome of the evaluations, the more these perceptions are expressed in the Representation that is generated.

And finally, in a Stage of Commitment, the perception that one's emotional 'belief system' is either 'shared' or 'rejected' by Reality leads to profound feelings towards Reality in return, that are reflected in the Representation these evaluations produce. And these, in turn, serve to further propel the perceived positive effects, or neutralize the perceived negative interference from Reality in the Process of Motivation.

*So, a Phase of Dedication has two distinct features that produce a specific effect on the Process of Motivation: it evaluates Reality in a primary and a secondary sequence, and this, in turn, produces an image of Reality in a Mechanism of Representation.*

Now, do these effects associated with Mechanisms of Representation always occur or are there exceptions to the rule we observed earlier, in the previous Chapters, that Significance of the Goal and perceived Significance of Reality appear to control these outcomes to a large extent?

When do these effects occur? Previously, it was found that the various expressions in which the Process of Motivation could manifest itself, was largely determined by three essential constructs, Significance of the Goal, Discrepancy and perceived Significance of Reality. And combinations of these could be summarized in eight main options, as covered in Chapter 5. So to observe if, and when, effects occur in Mechanisms of Representation, we could, again, make use of these various manifestations in which the Process of Motivation reveals itself.

Let us proceed in the order used earlier, with highly Significant Goals, facing Reality with low perceived Significance (options 1 and 3, p. 123). If Discrepancy is high, the outcomes of a primary evaluation are expected to be negative; but Reality appears to have little importance and therefore produces a secondary evaluation that might have a negative connotation, but is not expected to lead to a pronounced Representation, as Reality lacks the status to leave a trace on the Process of Motivation. Despite its negative Impact and high Discrepancy, the Process needs no substantial amendments to further progress its course. If Discrepancy is low, the same outcome is likely to occur, despite the positive effects of low Discrepancy[1]. In parallel, effects are even further reduced when the Goal lacks Significance in combination with such a low perceived Significance of Reality (options 5 and 7, p. 124). The Process of Motivation proceeds through its various Phases without dramatic effects occurring. These effects could change slightly when perceived Significance of Reality increases. A first variation is when a Goal with low Significance meets a highly Significant Reality that is highly Discrepant (option 6, p. 124). This time, the Goal has little standing to justify further dramatic action in Mechanisms of Representation. But in this case, it could progress in two ways: either the primary evaluation (which is negative) could elicit a negative response, leading to a neutralizing Representation, or the primary evaluation could be perceived as an early warning ("think twice") to have one's Goal amended in time before a renewed confrontation occurs. However, the input provided in previous Phases, as observed in Chapter 6 and Chapter 7, makes this option less probable, as the Goal lacks 'weight' to justify further action, making it likely the situation remains unresponsive, with limited effects of Mechanisms of Representation. When Discrepancy decreases, however (option 8, p. 124), the effects are expected to be higher. A Significant Reality 'taps into' one's Process of Motivation, and although Significance of the Goal is low, perceived 'support' from Reality is welcomed, and the acknowledging effects obtained from a primary evaluation can lead to secondary reactions which, in turn, can serve to further propel these effects in a more pronounced Representation of Reality, especially as

[1] Although it is tempting to seek such Impact for the positive effects it induces on the Process, thereby raising the probability of a gradual increase in Significance of Reality. We will come to realize when observing a Process of Interference later in the Series that this is an effective technique used not only to address Motivation, but also to increase perceived Significance of an interfering Reality.

the Process of Motivation progresses through further subsequent cycles[1]. Nonetheless, the limited Significance of the Goal, prevents dramatic expressions in Mechanisms of Representation that could propel the Process of Motivation.

We hardly need to further elaborate on the last two options, and the effects they yield on the Process of Motivation. In line with the observations already made, when a Significant Goal is confronted with a Significant Reality and perceived Discrepancy is large (option 2, p. 123), the negative effects of a primary evaluation affect those of a secondary evaluation, which, in turn, lead to Mechanisms of Representation that are aimed at degrading and neutralizing the Impact from Reality. Likewise, the effects dramatically increase when Discrepancy is perceived to be small (option 4, p. 123), where the positive effects of Impact lead to a positive primary evaluation in reaction to perceived 'support', releasing positive reactions towards Reality in a secondary evaluation, which leads to Mechanisms of Representation that will underscore perceived Significance of Reality, thus propelling its positive Impact on the Process of Motivation.

So, effects associated with Mechanisms of Representation occur on a 'progressive scale', where Significance of the Goal and perceived Significance of Reality appear to regulate the extent of these effects, in parallel with what was observed before in both a Phase of Externally Evoked Self-Assessment and a Phase of Anticipated Change, preceding a Phase of Dedication.

*In summary, then, a Phase of Dedication finalizes a threefold passive, evaluative reaction towards Reality. It is a 'grand total' of the Process of Motivation, where all previous Phases play a role in determining a subjective experience of Reality. Reality is perceived as 'supportive', 'non-supportive' or 'neutral' to the way parameters were defined in a Phase of Expectancies in the Process of Motivation. These thoughts and feelings, emerging from a perceived 'support' or 'non-support', in turn, give rise to thoughts and feelings oriented towards Reality. And, as a result of these four Stages, a set of primary evaluations emerges stemming from a perception of Reality, with a set of secondary evaluations directed towards Reality in return.*

*And these 'intertwined' primary and secondary evaluations serve to produce an image, or Representation, of Reality on a 'progressive scale' that aims at either neutralizing or reinforcing the effects of Reality on the Process of Motivation.*

[1] Again, it seems likely that one seeks such Impact. Thus, in addition to the previous note, a technique where one aims at decreasing Discrepancy is likely to lead to a further increase in perceived Significance of Reality and is likely to be effective in addressing Motivation, through a Process of Interference.

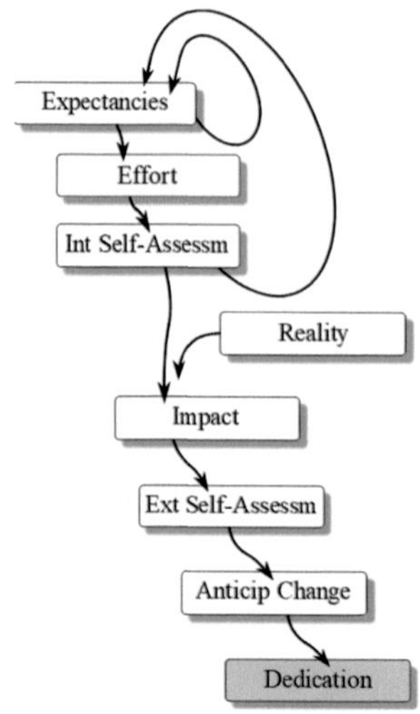


*Fig. 8.2.*
*A Phase of Dedication*
*Visualized as part of successive Phases*
*in the description of the*
*Model of Motivation*

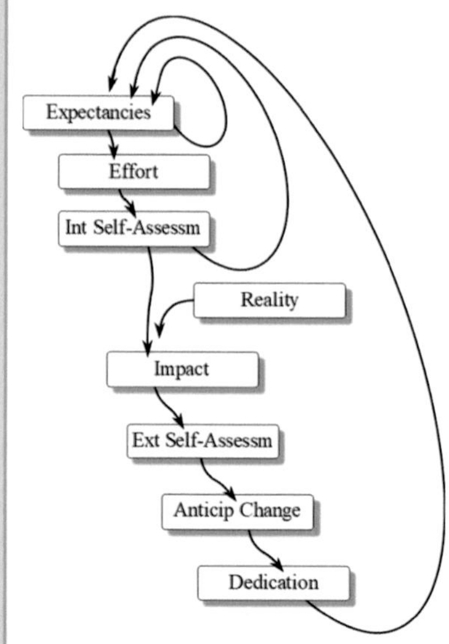


*Fig. 8.3.*
*A second cycle*
*Visualized as part of successive cycles*
*in the description of the*
*Model of Motivation*

This third evaluative Phase of Dedication is depicted in Fig. 8.2., summarizing the sequence of subsequent Phases as it continues to follow the input provided from a previous Phase of Externally Evoked Self-Assessment and a Phase of Anticipated Change, which are its 'predecessors' in the Process of Motivation.

And finally, then, the input provided by the successive evaluations in these three Phases following the Impact from Reality is used to make the subsequent amendments to the Goal and the parameters initially set in a Phase of Expectancies, thereby returning to the initial Stages of the Process, and thus turning the Process of Motivation into a cyclical Process where the sequence of Phases is re-initiated.

*Fig 8.3. illustrates this returning, final step, and therefore visualizes the Process of Motivation as it emerges in its final form: A progressive sequence of successive Phases that is predominantly characterized by its cyclical nature.*

These subjective and often highly emotional evaluations in a Phase of Dedication not only affect the Process of Motivation, but have a broader influence on many aspects of our lives. The Impact from Reality can make me more daring and ambitious, and can make me adapt my Goals accordingly. It can make me more confident and seek new challenges. But it can also make me doubt my performance and apprehensive to initiate new ventures.

The Impact from Reality can affect my perception of who I am, or how I would like to be perceived by this intruding and unexpected Reality.

Impact from Reality leaves traces that affect one's perception of adequacy and, extending on beliefs of one's potential and competence as observed in Chapter 6, the perception one has of oneself. In theory and research, these effects have been studied extensively in constructs referred to as 'self-concept' and 'academic self-concept'. These findings provide intriguing insights that seem to confirm the assumptions made in the Model of Motivation.

# 2 Theories

We have seen how Reality through its Impact affected us. We felt 'acknowledged', 'valued' and 'confirmed' or 'ignored', 'rejected' and 'disapproved'. We succeeded or we failed; we accomplished our Goal, in full or in part, where Impact interfered and could play a substantial role. And these assessments in terms of perceived 'support' or 'non-support' from the encounter we had with Reality, in turn, affected the way we experienced Impact from Reality, in what was referred to as 'primary' and 'secondary' reactions, or evaluations.

Finally, then, we are to cover theories from literature that could provide evidence for these conceptualizations that are part of a Phase of Dedication. Following our analysis in the previous Section, we should have two lines to observe in theories that cover the effects of a subjective experience of Reality and its Impact. In parallel with primary evaluations, or thoughts and feelings, emerging from perceived 'support' or 'non-support' from Reality, we can observe secondary evaluations, or those directed towards Reality in return.

Thus, and slightly re-defined to be more in line with conceptualizations in current literature, we need to observe:

- *Primary evaluations;* notably in theories on cognitive and affective reactions as a resultant of Impact, experienced *from* Reality;
  - To be extended with findings from literature on how we come to perceive ourselves, as a consequence, covering effects on what has been referred to as the 'self', with constructs of 'self-esteem' and, notably, 'self-concept'.
- *Secondary evaluations;* notably in theories on cognitive and affective reactions as a resultant of Impact, oriented *towards* Reality.

In observing primary evaluations, the ones we experience *from* Reality, two fields of study in literature have been prominent: attribution theory, previously covered in Chapter 7, and social cognitive theory, which was elaborated on in Chapter 6. Also, primary evaluations, by their nature, have been the subject of theories that center around perceptions of self and self-concept; and we will cover these fields of study subsequently at the end of the Section.

Now, secondary evaluations, the ones we tend to have *towards* Reality, have only occasionally been the subject of theories in the field of motivation. As confusion can arise with external interventions that we referred to as being part of a Process of Interference, *we will refrain from covering these presently, and will return to elaborate on these findings when addressing Interference.*

In observing the effects of Reality, we will extend our coverage also to the field of self-determination theory, in summarizing the effects of social and environmental causes on motivation, and its repercussions on the various ways it manifests itself.

So, we will emphasize theories from literature that have studied cognitive and affective reactions as a resultant of Impact and experienced *from* Reality, with either unexpected outcomes or outcomes that are perceived to be (partly) beyond our influence. As observed earlier, many studies related to motivation have been performed in the achievement domain. In observing theories on cognitive and affective reactions, only few have covered effects in the affective domain: "(...) Motivation surely is determined by affects. A fault with many current approaches to motivation, exemplified in self-efficacy theory, goal theory, intrinsic motivation theory, and many other conceptualizations, is they are devoid (or nearly devoid) of affects. (...) We desire to maximize good feelings and minimize bad ones, with actions guided by a cost-benefit analysis and hedonic desires" (Weiner, 2006, p. 34)[1].

In short, then, we will consider three theories: in observing cognitive and affective reactions, we will cover *attribution theories* and *social cognitive theory,* and in observing effects of Reality, in general, we will cover *self-determination theory.*

In covering attribution theories, we will focus again on *Weiner's attributional theory of motivation and emotion*, and proceed where we left off in Chapter 7. Recall that in Weiner's theory causal ascriptions play a central role. In achievement-related contexts there are a few dominant causal perceptions, and these were identified as: ability, effort, task difficulty and luck. These perceived causes of success and failure share three common properties, or causal dimensions: controllability, stability, and locus.

Now, in Weiner's attributional theory of motivation and emotion, these three causal dimensions "(...) affect a variety of common emotional experiences, including anger, gratitude, guilt, hopelessness, pity, pride, and shame. Expectancy and affect, in turn, are presumed to guide motivated behavior. The theory therefore relates the structure of thinking to the dynamics of feeling and action" (Weiner, 1985, p. 548). The theory "(...) assumes a sequence in which cognitions of increasing complexity enter into the emotion process to further refine and differentiate experience. (...) Following outcome appraisal and the immediate

[1] Weiner expressed these comments in 2006, despite promising observations made in the early 1990s, where he mentioned "(...) a tremendous increase (...) in the study of emotion in psychology, including the function of emotion as a motivator (...)" (Weiner, 1992, p. 301).

affective reaction, a causal ascription will be sought. A different set of emotions is then generated by the chosen attribution(s)" (Weiner, 1985, p. 560)[1].

Thus, according to Weiner, it is not so much the attributed cause, *but rather the causal dimension associated or connected to the cause that largely determines the emotional impact it produces or generates.*

To illustrate, let us use the example we used earlier in Chapter 7, and then observe the implications for the Model of Motivation, as well as the insight it provides into perceptions of the effects of Reality in a Phase of Dedication.

Recall how in Chapter 7 we discussed the example of failing a test. We had several options in attributing the cause of our failure: ability, effort, task difficulty, or luck.

As we saw, attributing the cause of failure to a lack of ability was to attribute the reason of one's failure to a cause that has an uncontrollable, stable, and internal property or dimension. Taking such a stand or perspective towards an unexpected achievement-related event (defined as an intruding Reality in the Model of Motivation) leads not only to cognitive, but also to affective reactions. Attributing a cause of failure to a lack of ability, according to attribution theory, brings about feelings of *shame*, as the uncontrollable property leads one to assume that success is beyond one's reach. In addition, and as a consequence of the stability dimension, these low expectations of future success are perceived to remain unchanged, which leads to feelings of *hopelessness.* And to make matters worse, assigning a failure to a lack of ability tends to affect one's *self-esteem*, as causality is perceived to be internal, where one sees oneself as the primal source of one's failure (Weiner, 1985; 1986, notably Chapter 5)[2]. And as mentioned in Chapter 7, these perceptions have consequences in terms of subsequent investment and motivation, as expressed in performance and persistence: "Expectations of future failure, paired with negative emotions and less self-responsibility, in turn, deplete motivation and erode performance, making persistence (...) much less likely" (Perry & Hamm, 2017, p. 63).

[1] Thus, within the attributional theory of motivation and emotion, Weiner makes a clear distinction in emotions that *directly* follow the outcome of an achievement-related event, in terms of a positive or negative reaction based on perceived success or failure. Those emotions subsequently initiate causal search (as covered in Chapter 7) and are defined as 'primary appraisals' and labeled as 'outcome dependent-attribution independent', as distinct from emotions that are to follow the attributional process and that are the subject of our present analysis (see: Weiner, 1985).

[2] Had the test been successful, these affective reactions associated with uncontrollable, stable, and internal properties would have been *gratitude, hopefulness,* and *pride,* respectively (where gratitude is usually perceived in affiliation with others (Weiner, 1985).

Things change, however, when one assigns a cause of failure to a lack of effort. Reactions as a consequence of attributing failure rather to a controllable, unstable, and internal cause lead to a range of differing emotional consequences, affecting, in turn, the outcomes in terms of subsequent investment and motivation. When the cause of failure is perceived to be controllable, attribution theory assumes one has failed in an attempt where one has had the opportunity to invest sufficient effort, but simply didn't, leading to feelings of *guilt* (being controllable, as opposed to shame, in the previous example); fortunately, however, these feelings are perceived to be unstable, where expectations about future performance lead to *hopefulness* (as opposed to hopelessness, in the attribute of ability), as the investment is perceived to have the property to fluctuate over time. The cause of one's failing is perceived to be internal, thus entirely in one's hands, and affecting *self-esteem*, which is expected to propel measures aimed at improvement: "Controllable causes (e.g. low effort) increase perceived responsibility for an outcome, as well as guilt, which together initiate actions to rectify the situation. Guilt is a motivating emotion and is less psychologically debilitating than shame or hopelessness" (Perry & Hamm, 2017, p. 63; see also: Weiner, 1985, 1986, notably Chapter 5)[1].

An observation referred to earlier in Chapter 7 can be made in summarizing these theoretical assumptions made in attribution theory: "Differences between ability and effort attributions in stability and controllability lie at the heart of many motivation and performance outcomes in achievement situations. Although both causes are internal, ascribing poor performance to low ability (stable, uncontrollable) decreases motivation, whereas low effort (unstable, controllable) increases motivation" (Perry & Hamm, 2017, p. 63), especially because the situation can be altered due to its perceived controllability.

As a (probable) consequence of these remarkable conclusions, literature has mainly focused on attributing causes to ability or effort, and its effects on performance, persistence, and self-esteem. However, for the purpose of observing theories on effects of Reality in terms of cognition and affect, we may attempt to extend these observations to include possible effects of the two remaining causes, task difficulty and luck, despite a modest coverage in literature.

When causes of failure are attributed to task difficulty, which is believed to be uncontrollable, stable, and external according to attribution theory (that is, from the perspective of an actor; see Weiner, 2018), the outcomes of the attributional process lead to affective reactions that may correspond to those just observed, with feelings of *shame* associated with the uncontrollable property. The stability

[1] As a consequence, success that follows upon a long-term period of effort expenditure results in a feeling of *calmness* or *serenity*, notably affecting *hopefulness* (stability, in a positive connotation) and *pride* (locus) (Weiner, 1985).

dimension could give rise to low expectations of future success leading to feelings of *hopelessness.* However, we need to recall that task difficulty, according to Weiner (2018), was assumed to be imposed from the perspective of an actor and therefore likely to be perceived as 'external'. Both dimensions 'external' and 'uncontrollable' associated with task difficulty, therefore make it less pronounced in its effects. Thus, these external causes, such as "(...) poor teaching, or test difficulty, may create less negative affect and are less harmful to pride and self-esteem, but they are likely to impair motivation nonetheless" (Perry & Hamm, 2017, p. 63; see also: Weiner, 1985, 1986, notably Chapter 5)[1].

Finally, we could speculate that these affective reactions become further defused when attributing causes of failure to bad luck. Where a cause of failure is ascribed to uncontrollable, unstable, and external factors, the affective reaction is likely to be minor. Feelings of *shame* (uncontrollable) are likely to be neutralized by the perceived combination with an external dimension that is likely to have minimal impact on *self-esteem.* And the unstable dimension, where a recurrent failure is perceived to be unlikely, further neutralizes these affective reactions, making feelings of *hopelessness* most unlikely (Weiner, 1985, 1986, notably Chapter 5)[2].

So a recurrent theme in the origin of these emotions is not so much the cause to which they are attributed: ability, effort, task difficulty, or luck; it is rather the property or dimension attributed to that cause that determines the expression and intensity of a subsequent affective reaction: perceived controllability, stability, and locus. Thus, we observed that guilt and shame (and gratitude in successful settings) "(...) are connected with the controllability dimension, (...) feelings of hopelessness (hopefulness) are associated with causal stability", and "the emotion of pride and feelings of self-esteem are linked with the locus dimension of causality" (Weiner, 1985, p. 561).

[1] In parallel with previous observations, successful completion of a difficult task would then lead especially to *hopefulness* (stability) and *pride* (locus), although the dimensions 'uncontrollable' in combination with 'external' are expected to influence these affective outcomes. As stated by Weiner: "Success and failure at skill tasks most usually are ascribed to ability and effort. (...) Inasmuch as the causes of a prior success are perceived as relatively stable given skill-related tasks, future success should be anticipated with greater certainty and there will be increments in aspiration level and expectancy judgments" (Weiner, 1985, p. 557).

[2] Likewise, when attributing success to luck, these feelings are equally moderated, especially by the unstable dimension of attributed causes. As commented by Weiner: "(...) success at chance tasks tends to be ascribed to an unstable factor. The actor is likely to reason, 'I had good luck last time, but that probably will not happen again'. Expectancy therefore should not rise and indeed could drop following a positive outcome" (Weiner, 1985, p. 557).

In observing the causal dimension of *controllability*, Weiner observes: "(...) Guilt arises from a particular act that is under volitional control and produces a desire to make amends (...). Shame, on the other hand, is elicited as a result of an act or a characteristic of the self that is not under volitional control and produces a desire to withdraw. Relating these differences to the dominant attributions of success and failure, (...) guilt follows when failure is ascribed to lack of effort, whereas shame is produced when failure is ascribed to lack of ability" (Weiner, 1986, pp. 152-153).

Referring to causal *stability*, Weiner states: "(...) if the future is anticipated to remain as bad as the past, then hopelessness is experienced" (Weiner, 1985, p. 563).

Commenting on the relation between causal *locus* and self-esteem: "A voluminous attributional literature (...) documents existence of a *hedonic bias,* or a tendency for individuals to ascribe success to internal factors and failure to external factors. As Harvey and Weary (1981) noted, 'by taking credit for good acts and denying blame for bad outcomes, the individual presumably may be able to enhance or protect his or her self-esteem' (p. 33). Pride and personal esteem therefore are self-reflective emotions, linked with the locus dimension of causality" (Weiner, 1985, pp. 561-562).

*See exhibit* ➔

### 6.2. Attribution theories

As previously mentioned in Chapter 7, Weiner's attributional theory of motivation and emotion proposes: "(...) that a motivational sequence is initiated by an outcome that the person interprets as positive (goal attainment) or negative (nonattainment). (...) If the outcome was unexpected or negative, a causal search is undertaken to determine why the outcome occurred. (...) The causal decision reached may elicit a unique affective reaction" (Weiner, 1986, p. 161, 163).

The reaction is elicited, not by the attributed cause but by the associated causal dimensions. "Causal dimensions have psychological consequences, being related to expectancy and affect" (Weiner, 1986, p. 163). Thus:

- *Controllability:* associated with the affect of guilt (controllable) and shame (uncontrollable);
- *Stability:* associated with the affect of hopelessness (stable-negative) and hopefulness (stable-positive) (however, see also: Weiner, 2018);
- *Locus:* associated with the affect of pride and self-esteem, where internal ascriptions elicit greater effects (positive, negative) than do external attributions.

(Weiner, 1986, notably Chapter 5).

For a shorter overview, see: Weiner, 1985; 2018.
For basic assumptions: Weiner, 1982; Weiner & Graham, 1984.

Let us position these thoughts, once again, within the Model of Motivation. According to the Model, the way we perceive the unexpected event from Reality following Impact not only produces a re-orientation in a Phase of Externally-Evoked Self-Assessment, as seen in Chapter 6, it also leads to strategies aimed at addressing these perceptions in a Phase of Anticipated Change, as covered in Chapter 7. And according to attribution theory, assigning attributions to these perceived events, in turn, leads to cognitive and affective reactions as a resultant of the Impact of Reality. And these reactions can be made to impair or improve subsequent action, behavior, motivation in what we defined as a renewed cycle in the Process of Motivation.

These findings in attribution theory could imply that affective reactions towards Reality, in a Phase of Dedication, may originate in the strategies we choose in a Phase of Anticipated Change, following the assessments we make of the extent in which the Process of achieving our Goal is affected by Impact, and of the repercussions it has on the initial parameters defined to achieve that Goal[1].

To summarize, then, it is not so much assigning failure to lack of ability or effort that appears to determine the emotion, but rather the property or causal dimension associated with the cause. In terms of the Model of Motivation, this would imply that in the sequence of events assumed to occur in the Process of Motivation (evaluation in a Phase of Externally Evoked Self-Assessment; defining subsequent strategies in a Phase of Anticipated Change) the affective reaction towards Reality in a Phase of Dedication would largely depend on the strategy defined in a Phase of Anticipated Change, or, in terms of attribution theory, on the causal attributes perceived and assigned by the individual. The specific properties of those attributes define whether Impact of Reality can be harmful or negative, or uplifting and positive, and thus supporting one's feelings of esteem (locus). And these specific properties can further degrade, sustain or increase those feelings (stability) or generate feelings of shame or guilt (controllability).

So, we observed Weiner's attributional theory on the personal causal inferences we make and the emotional effects they have, especially in achievement strivings, when either failures or unexpected outcomes bring us to contemplate the courses of our actions. In subsequent years, Weiner further extended his attributional theory of motivation and emotion from an *intra*personal perspective, to an attributional theory of *inter*personal or social motivation, where these causal

[1] However, as stated earlier in Chapter 7, it is to be noted that Weiner's attributional theory of motivation and emotion describes the process without making the assumption implicitly made here that there is intentionality in the strategies we use, and thus in the causal attributions we make, their associated dimensions and the outcomes they generate. As stated with precision by Weiner in summarizing his thoughts: "The theory (...) relates the structure of thinking to the dynamics of feeling and action" (Weiner, 1985, p. 548).

inferences are aimed primarily at others and their behaviors. This extended theory, however, exceeds the scope of our analysis in which we chose to focus only on the individual, hence the intrapersonal perspective in the Process of Motivation[1 2].

Although the theory had considerable impact on psychology and the field of motivation, its influence gradually decreased in the last decades. Reflecting on the history of attribution theory and research, fifty years after the first publication of *The Psychology of Interpersonal Relations* (Heider, 1958), Weiner stated in 2008: "It (...) is fair to state that attribution no longer is the dominant field of inquiry it once was, say in the 1970-1985 era" (Weiner, 2008, p. 151; see also: Graham, 1991; Weiner, 2019).

*See exhibit* ➔

[1] For an overview, reference is made to Weiner, 2006, where he commented on this extended theory: "(...) the interpersonal theory relates to social behaviors, primarily helping and aggression, and to social justice and punishment, but also to address other social phenomena including compliance, impression formation and stigmatization. In this theory, thoughts and emotions are about others, and behaviors such as helping, aggression, and punishment are directed toward these others" (Weiner, 2006, p. xvi).

See also: Weiner, 1985, 1986, 1995, 2000, 2006; Hareli & Weiner, 2002.

[2] It is noteworthy to observe that, within this Process of Interference, Weiner distinguished between the emotional reactions of an external interfering actor towards an individual, and those of the individual towards an actor, in response to interference. More on these subtle but essential differences when we cover Interference in subsequent Volumes of the Series.

### The Lifespan of Theories

Although attribution theory has had a prominent influence on psychology and the field of motivation, its influence gradually decreased in the last decades, to reappear however more recently in literature in the area of work motivation (Martinko & Mackey, 2019).

As commented on in a recent review of 65 papers: "(...) HR scholars have recently realized that understanding the process by which individuals explain the causes of behaviors and events provides insight into a host of HR-related issues" (Hewett, Shantz, Mundy & Alfes, 2018, p. 87).

It illustrates a phenomenon that has had only limited attention in literature: development in the field of motivation has not only been a gradually progressive expansion of knowledge, as insights obtained from research progressively grew in the field, but it has also been subject to shifts in interest and transitions in trends affecting development of theories in specific areas.

As in all human endeavors, science is not immune to changes incited by trends, interest, or personal preferences. *All too often, however, the unintended result of these shifts in attention also (and erroneously) suggests a decreased relevance of these areas in the field of motivation.*

For some interesting overviews on how personal relationships, history, interests have affected the field, see: Latham, 2007; Weiner, 2010, 2013.

How people behave, then, can to a large extent be predicted by the attributions they make and by the beliefs they hold. If one is inclined to perceive the effects of Impact from Reality (as proposed to occur in a Phase of Dedication) as more positive, they are reflected in the attributions made. And its repercussions on the Process of Motivation would be likewise; and vice versa.

One particular area that has been previously covered in Chapter 6, is on beliefs we hold about our capabilities, referred to as 'self-efficacy beliefs'. As we saw, depending on those self-efficacy beliefs, how people tend to act can often be better predicted "(...) than by what they are actually capable of accomplishing, for these self-perceptions help determine what individuals do with the knowledge and skills they have" (Pajares & Schunk, 2005, p. 100). One's set of beliefs, then, much as the attributions we make, determine not only what we do, but also to a large extent *how* we perform. In line with propositions made in the Model of Motivation, the assertions we have (as defined in a Phase of Externally Evoked Self-Assessment) and the inclinations we have (as defined in a Phase of Anticipated Change) determine the way we respond to Impact, notably in a Phase of Dedication. And these affective and cognitive reactions are reflected in our subsequent actions and achievements (conceptualized to occur in a renewed cycle of the Process of Motivation). And, as we shall see, how we subsequently come to perceive ourselves in the accomplishments we make.

These assertions we have, which typify our reactions to Reality, have been defined in *social cognitive theory* in terms of self-efficacy beliefs. If we are comfortable with the outcomes we perceive, subsequent experiences serve to further strengthen these beliefs, or, when in contrast to our expectations, lead to opposite reactions and subsequent amendments.

Thus, as covered in Chapter 6, we saw how self-efficacy not only brought us insights into how well we performed, but also how this 'accumulation of knowledge' of one's potential and competence, through self-reflection, led to proactive strategies and foresight in actions and behaviors. So, self-efficacy not only brought us a personal reflection on one's capabilities, it also meant translating those capabilities into effective performance in diverse settings and circumstances. It shaped our mind and made us persevere, or, in contrast, made us abandon our endeavors and give up in the face of failure, both at school (Pajares & Schunk, 2001) and in academic settings (Pajares, 1996, 1997).

If one is able to adapt adequately to a variety of circumstances, one has a "key personal resource in self-development, successful adaptation, and change. (...) Efficacy beliefs affect whether individuals think optimistically or pessimistically, in self-enhancing or self-debilitating ways. Such beliefs affect people's goals and aspirations, how well they motivate themselves, and their perseverance in the face of difficulties and adversity" (Bandura, 2006c, p. 4).

These reactions to Reality are thus manifested in our tendencies or inclinations. According to social cognitive theory one can differentiate between individuals with *high self-efficacy,* and those with *low self-efficacy beliefs.*

*See exhibit* ➔

The gradual 'accumulation of knowledge' on one's potential and competence, as observed in Chapter 6, then, not only fuels insights into one's capabilities and the feasibility of future accomplishments, it also has lasting effects on how we seize opportunities or refrain and renounce from new challenges: "One of the important characteristics of successful individuals is that failure and adversity do not undermine their self-efficacy beliefs. This is because self-efficacy is not so much about learning how to succeed as it is about learning *how to persevere when one does not succeed"* (Pajares, 2006, p. 345)[1].

As a consequence, these beliefs following Impact from Reality, in a reciprocal interaction according to social cognitive theory, also lead to subjective perceptions of the self. However, and distinct from constructs such as self-concept or self-esteem, these resulting subjective reactions are

[1] And consequently, as seen previously in the exhibits on 'learned helplessness', 'self-handicapping', and 'positive psychology', Chapter 7, not only causal attributes but also inaccurate self-efficacy beliefs appear to be responsible for people shortchanging themselves personally, socially and academically (Pajares, 2006).

### 5.2. Social cognitive theories

Self-efficacy, covered earlier in Chapter 6, can be defined as: "subjective convictions for successfully executing a course of action to achieve a desired outcome" (Ahn & Bong, 2019, p. 66, Table 3.1).

In these convictions, one can differentiate between individuals with *high self-efficacy beliefs* and those with *low self-efficacy beliefs.*

Those with high self-efficacy beliefs approach difficult tasks "(...) as challenges to be mastered rather than as threats to be avoided. (...) [They] set themselves challenging goals and maintain strong commitment to them, and heighten and sustain their efforts in the face of failure. Moreover, they more quickly recover their confidence after failures or setbacks (...)" (Pajares & Schunk, 2005, p. 101).

"Conversely, people with low self-efficacy may believe that things are tougher than they really are, a belief that fosters stress, depression, and a narrow vision of how best to solve a problem" (*ibid.,* p. 101). Thus: "People of low efficacy are easily convinced of the futility of effort in the face of difficulties. They quickly give up trying" (Bandura, 2006c, p. 4).

One's convictions thus have profound and lasting effects on the level of accomplishment that individuals finally attain.

clearly differentiated in social cognitive theory from the construct of self-efficacy. "Judgments of self-efficacy can (...) result in emotional responses but, unlike self-concept or self-esteem, these emotions stay as separate constructs and do not comprise self-efficacy beliefs (Bong & Clark, 1999; Bong & Skaalvik, 2003)" (Ahn & Bong, 2019, p. 65)[1].

So, much in line with the assumptions made about a Phase of Dedication, social cognitive theory perceives these subjective and emotional outcomes of these appraisals to be distinct entities.

In summary, then, achievements affected by context and circumstances, in the form of an intruding Reality as proposed in the Model of Motivation, appear to instigate a wide range of cognitive and affective psychological reactions, according to both attribution theory and social cognitive theory. Both theories extend insights by observing the effects of these psychological reactions, defined as 'primary evaluations' of perceived 'support' or 'non-support' following Impact from Reality.

These cognitive and affective reactions have a profound influence on the Process through which Motivation unfolds. They do not only proceed into subsequent behavior and performance as the Process progresses into a new cycle, as proposed in the Model of Motivation. Cognitions, affects and behaviors, instigated by Impact from Reality, also, and most explicitly, leave their trace on the way we come to perceive ourselves.

*Perceptions of self* refer to the construct of *self-concept,* which is one of the cornerstone constructs in the social sciences (Marsh, Seaton, Dicke, Parker & Horwood, 2019). But despite its centrality, it has been the source of debate and longstanding discussions both on the construct and on its far-reaching implications for self-perception and improvement of performance and achievement (Marsh & Craven, 2005).

[1] However, although both constructs are differentiated from each other and conceptually made into distinct entities, they are clearly related. As commented on by Pajares and Schunk: "Because one's self-concept includes a self-evaluation of competence, it is clear that, conceptually, self-efficacy is a critical ingredient of self-concept. How could it be otherwise? As we reflect on how we feel about ourselves, either in general or within a specified domain, we naturally will place great import on the confidence we possess to solve problems and accomplish the tasks at hand" (Pajares & Schunk, 2005, p. 104).

It must be noted that both concepts do not always relate to each other: "Some students may feel highly efficacious in mathematics but without the corresponding positive feelings of self-worth, in part because they may take no pride in accomplishments in this area" (*ibid.* p. 105).

To fully appreciate the extent of these implications, let us consider the two main options that have emerged from literature, when observing the self in relation to achievement: a number of studies have stressed the importance of high achievement on the self, whereas other studies, in contrast, emphasized effects of self-esteem and positive self-appraisal on subsequent achievement (Calsyn & Kenny, 1977)[1]. Controversies centered on the question of what appears to come first: a great experience of success that brings pride and a boost to the self and one's self-esteem, or rather the other way around, where nurturing one's self-esteem encourages us to engage on challenging tasks that would lead us to successful achievements. An answer to this question has profound implications, not only on motivation but also in the field of educational psychology, as it provides important insights into measures for improving achievement. Are we to seek great experiences of success by providing challenging environments, or should we rather aim at boosting self-esteem by providing circumstances and opportunities for self-enhancement that eventually lead to improved performance?

Although the question refers to a Process of Interference (as it aims at how to address Motivation), recent developments in thinking on the construct of self-concept have an important bearing on the Model in its approach to the Process of Motivation. According to the Model of Motivation, where Motivation is assumed to progress into a Process of circularity following a Phase of Dedication, the relation between achievement and self-concept is expected to emerge from this circular Process. Thus, the Model of Motivation proposes that in the relation between achievement and self-concept, *it is neither the one nor the other that is assumed to predominate, but both constructs in reciprocity.*

The Model of Motivation assumes that in the cyclical nature of the Process, experiences of success in seeking Goal attainment through various assessments in consecutive Phases lead to cognitive and affective reactions following Impact from Reality that enhance perceptions of self, which, in turn, in a renewed cycle of the Process, lead to further amendments to the Goal and investments in Effort and pursuit of further challenges, aimed at maintaining those achievements, as we shall come to observe in the next Chapters.

In findings from literature, this cyclical nature appears to be confirmed. Through works, especially by Herb Marsh and his colleagues (Marsh, 1990a, 1990b, 1993, 2008; Marsh, Byrne & Yeung, 1999; Marsh & Craven, 2005, 2006; Marsh & O'Mara, 2008; Marsh & Yeung, 1997), the reciprocal nature between

[1] A so-called 'skill development model' suggests that academic achievement influences self-beliefs, whereas self-beliefs do not influence achievement. A 'self-enhancement model' proposes that self-beliefs influence academic achievement, whereas achievement does not influence self-beliefs (Calsyn & Kenny, 1977; see reviews in Valentine & Dubois, 2005).

achievement and the concept of self has become increasingly prevalent in current thinking.

Developments leading to these insights have extended over years. For over a century, theorists had disputed the nature of self-concept (Marsh, Seaton, Dicke, Parker & Horwood, 2019). In discussions that started in the 1950s, it was initially argued that self-concept was unidimensional, with self-concept captured in single constructs such as self-esteem, self-appraisal and self-worth. The concept, however, appeared too broad in its conceptualization: "(...) By the 1970s the area was lacking in sound methodology, measurement instruments, definition, and theoretical perspectives (e.g. Shavelson Hubner & Stanton, 1976; Wells & Marwell, 1976: Wylie, 1979)" (Marsh, Seaton, Dicke, Parker & Horwood, 2019, p. 37). In response, Shavelson, Hubner and Stanton (1976) proposed a multidimensional model, with general self-concept divided into two components: academic self-concept (or ASC) and non-academic self-concept (non-ASC) (see also: Byrne, 1996; Marsh & Hattie, 1996).

From these refinements in the construct of self-concept, more precise and so-called 'domain-specific' conceptualizations emerged, diversifying the unidimensional representation of the self into the multidimensional construct it now is believed to be[1].

*See exhibit next page* ➔

And these refinements in turn, then, enabled a further understanding of the relation between self-concept and achievement. The first research results confirmed the reciprocal nature of both constructs (as we shall see in the next Section), indicating, as proposed by the Model of Motivation, that achievement-related outcomes affect perceptions of self; and these perceptions of self, in turn, influence performance and achievement in various contexts. As stated by Marsh and his colleagues: "Thus, not only does self-concept influence behavior, but behavior in turn influences one's perceptions, and how one views oneself is a function of one's interactions with others. In a sense, others are a mirror through which one catches glimpses of who and what one is" (Marsh, Seaton, Dicke, Parker & Horwood, 2019, p. 38; see also: Skaalvik & Skaalvik, 2002; Marsh, Trautwein, Lüdtke, Köller & Baumert, 2005).

[1] Despite this growing support, "(...) there exists a strongly held, contrary perspective suggesting that self-esteem in particular has little or no positive influence on achievement and other desirable outcomes, and may even be counterproductive (...)" (Marsh & Craven, 2005, p. 28, notably referring to Baumeister, Campbell, Krueger & Vohs, 2003). But these studies appeared to have focused on *global* measures of self-esteem and excluded research focusing on domain specific measures of self-concept (See review: Marsh & Craven, 2005).

## *Related Topics: on Self-Esteem and Self-Concept*

The various evaluations in preceding Phases of the Process of Motivation not only led to cognitive and affective reactions towards Reality, they also left their mark on perceptions of the self. In observing literature, three constructs appear to be central (Byrne, 1996): *Self-efficacy,* (described earlier in Chapter 6), *self-esteem,* and *self-concept.*

*Self-esteem* is defined as global evaluative judgments of oneself, which include relatively stable subjective perceptions in terms of satisfaction and recognition, acceptance or rejection of the self (Ahn & Bong, 2019; Marsh & Craven, 2005). A further diversification is made in literature into the concept of *academic self-esteem*, defined as: "evaluative judgments of oneself in achievements situations, which include one's feelings of and satisfaction toward oneself" (Ahn & Bong, 2019, p. 66, Table 3.1).

*Self-esteem* is a global evaluative judgment of oneself. *Self-concept* is more specific and related to perceptions of competence in particular domains of knowledge.

*Self-concept*, in literature, is more specific and related to particular domains of knowledge, notably the diversification into 'verbal' or 'mathematics'. It refers to relatively stable perceptions of one's specific competencies on these domains with resulting emotional reactions (Ahn & Bong, 2019). Self-concept is further diversified into two important constructs:

- *academic self-concept* (or ASC), defined as "knowledge and perceptions about one's competencies and attributes in achievement situations, along with resultant emotional reactions" (Ahn & Bong, 2019, p. 66, Table 3.1). A further partition is made in subject-specific self-concepts:
  - *math ASC:* math self-concept as one's ASC in math-related achievement situations;
  - *verbal ASC:* verbal self-concept as one's ASC in verbal-related achievement situations.
- *non-academic self-concept* (or non-ASC), covering a range of specified areas, including social self-concept, emotional self-concept, physical self-concept.

See also: Marsh, 2008; Marsh & Shavelson, 1985; Marsh, Byrne & Shavelson, 1988; Marsh, Byrne & Yeung, 1999.

So, in sum, these findings confirm the idea that Impact from Reality not only leads to cognitive and affective expressions, but also to perceptions of Self, which in turn, as the Process of Motivation progresses into a renewed cycle, affect not only the Goal that has been set, but also investments in Effort, and consequently in behavior, performance and achievement.

Now, these refinements to the conceptualization of the self revealed an additional and disconcerting effect, related to what we have observed earlier when analyzing the effects of Impact in Chapter 5. These effects in reaction to the Impact of Reality have been referred to in literature as the 'big-fish-little-pond effect', or BFLPE. In the study that laid the foundations of the BFLPE, Marsh and Parker (1984) found "(...) that students form their ASCs by comparing their academic achievements with those of their classmates. Thus, whereas there is a positive relation between individual ability and ASC, class- or school-average is negatively related to ASC (...)" (Marsh, Seaton, Dicke, Parker & Horwood, 2019, p. 47). This implies that effects of Reality are enhanced or magnified by the circumstances in which Reality manifests itself. To illustrate: If one attends a highly competitive school where only the 'best' are admitted to enroll, these magnifying effects of comparing to others that are 'equally good' have a *detrimental* effect on perceptions of the self. As stated by Marsh and his colleagues: "Consistent with the BFLPE, equally able students had lower ASCs in high-ability schools than those in low-ability schools. (...) Additionally, the BFLPE has been shown to exist at different levels of education, both in primary schools (e.g. Marsh, Chessor, Craven & Roche, 1995) and in high schools (e.g. Marsh, Köller & Baumert, 2001)" (Marsh, Seaton, Dicke, Parker & Horwood, 2019, p. 47; See also overviews in: Marsh & Craven, 2002; Marsh & Hau, 2003). And these findings appear to have a prolonged effect (Marsh & O'Mara, 2010) that is stable and persistent over time (Marsh, Köller & Baumert, 2001).

*See exhibit next page* ➔

Referring to the Model of Motivation, Reality in its Impact appears to provide achievement-related information *that extends beyond one's own accomplishments to include the achievements of important others, thereby serving as an extended frame of reference.*

These findings, together with previous observations made in Chapter 5, reveal an unexpected and disturbing outcome: that Reality in its 'multifaceted' appearance, ranging from a podium on which one seeks to demonstrate performance, to a stage consisting of individuals and groups with which one seems to compare oneself, that this wide range in which it manifests itself underlines *again* the importance Reality has, not only on the Process of Motivation, but on all aspects of our daily lives.

## *Related Topics: on Being a Big Fish in a Pond*

Effects of the big-fish-little-pond effect (BFLPE) are profound and far-reaching. An example to illustrate.

*As these effects appear to affect not only one's perceptions of self, but also other areas related to academic achievement with prolonged effects over time, the implications of these findings are many. However, to simply conclude avoiding highly competitive environments appears to be too simple, with very little evidence to support such strategies (Marsh & Seaton, 2015). Other factors appear to be involved, moderating those effects (for an overview of these 'counterbalancing effects', see: Marsh, Trautwein, Lüdtke, Baumert & Köller, 2007). But one conclusion can be drawn, however: "These findings imply that attending a high-ability school has negative effects on more educational outcomes than just ASC alone, meaning that such students may not be reaching their full academic potential" (Marsh, Seaton, Dicke, Parker & Horwood, 2019, p. 48).*

Attending highly selective educational institutions does not imply one will reach one's full academic potential.

In an extensive illustration of the BFLPE, Marsh and colleagues comment: "Consider this example: Alex and Bill are above-average mathematics students of similar ability, but Alex attends an academically selective school and Bill attends a mixed-ability school. (...) Bill's mathematics ability is extremely good compared to his classmates, so his mathematics self-concept is high, as he is a big fish in a little pond. However, in Alex's school there are many highly capable mathematics students and, compared to them, his mathematics ability is average. As a result, Alex's mathematics self-concept is low, as he is a little fish in a big pond. Here we see the frame of reference of the BFLPE at work: by attending the academically selective school Alex feels less competent in mathematics than Bill, even though they are both of similar mathematics ability" (Marsh, Seaton, Dicke, Parker & Horwood, 2019, p. 47).

These negative effects on perception of the self appear to extend to many other educational outcomes, including one's aspirations, college attendance and occupational aspirations (Marsh, 1991).

See also: Marsh, 1987; Marsh & Craven, 2002; Marsh & Parker, 1984; Marsh & Seaton, 2015.

Reality, then, plays an essential role in motivation. Not only influencing the courses of action we undertake, but also affecting us in the way we perceive ourselves.

Reality steers us, and influences us. It makes us perform, achieve and excel, but appears also to have distinct properties to obstruct, frustrate and deregulate. Clearly, there is a vast amount of variation in the way Reality can affect us.

In this interaction with Reality, we ourselves played a distinct role in the Process of Motivation, notably in the perceptions we have from Reality following Impact. But we saw from various theories in literature that Reality also plays a decisive role in this interactive, reciprocal Process.

To end our analysis of the literature on perceived effects from Reality, we return to one of the most widely cited theories on motivation (Adams, Little & Ryan, 2017; Boggiano, 1998; Deci & Ryan, 2000). *Self-determination theory,* which has been covered previously a number of times (notably on the three basic psychological needs of autonomy, relatedness and competence), has played a prominent role in observing these effects from Reality as they relate to motivation. In an extension to their theory, Self-determination theory has defined the effects of a variety of external influences on motivation, and provided a taxonomy for these effects.

*See exhibit* ➔

### 4.4. Self-determination theory

Self-determination theory is different from other approaches to motivation in its emphasis on the different types and sources of motivation. Rather than defining motivation as a 'unitary phenomenon', self-determination theory suggests that some forms of motivation are entirely volitional, whereas others can be entirely external. "Clearly, sources of motivation differ, as do the effects of being energized by these different motives. Put simply, different motives (...) vary in the phenomenal sources that initiate them, the affects and experiences that therefore accompany them, and their behavioral consequences (...) (Ryan & Deci, 2018, p.14).

Self-determination theory, therefore, clearly differentiates the concept of motivation in order to consider these effects of different types of motivation on these outcomes.

To differentiate these types of motivation, self-determination makes use of an *autonomy – control continuum,* where types of motivation are characterized in terms of the extent to which they represent autonomous versus controlled regulation. Within this taxonomy, three main types of motivation occur:

- *Intrinsic motivation;*
- *Extrinsic motivation;*
- *Amotivation.*

*(Continued)*

Depending on the way these external influences manifest themselves, self-determination distinguishes different expressions in types of motivation, depending on these differing sources[1].

Where Reality plays a role in addressing Motivation, there are several gradations one could observe in the extent to which this outside interference can affect the Process of Motivation. However, at the start of our study, we made a clear distinction between the Process of Motivation itself and the Process of Interference aimed at addressing Motivation in an extensive variety of manifestations.

This distinction that was made has been less prominent, or even absent, in the various theories that were observed in subsequent Chapters covering the Phases of the Model. Although the differentiation into various forms of motivation proposed by self-determination theory seems to diverge from the assumptions made in the Model of Motivation, we will come to realize that the expression in which Motivation uniquely manifests itself can be highly influenced by the form in which it is being addressed through a Process of Interference.

[1] In addition, reference is made to processes of internalization and integration of extrinsic regulations, see: Ryan & Deci, 2018, Chapter 8.

[2] The taxonomy of regulatory styles has also been referred to as *'the self-determination continuum'*, diversifying types of motivation and types of regulation (Ryan & Deci, 2002).

## 4.4. Self-determination theory

Within these main types of motivation, different styles of regulation prevail, ranging from autonomous to controlled regulation.

Within the three types of motivation, then, a *taxonomy of regulatory styles* can be made, distinguishing these various sources of motivation:

- Intrinsic motivation, with *intrinsic regulation* as main regulatory style, as expressed in interest, enjoyment, inherent satisfaction;
- Extrinsic motivation, with behavior ranging gradually from self-determined to non-self-determined, with progressively four sources of regulatory styles:
  - *Integrated regulation,* as expressed in awareness;
  - *Identified regulation,* expressed in conscious valuing;
  - *Introjected regulation,* expressed in self-control;
  - *External regulation,* expressed in compliance.
- Amotivation, with *non-regulation*, as in nonintentional expressions.

(Ryan & Deci, 2000, 2018).

Over the years, nomenclature has slightly changed, and the taxonomy of regulatory styles is also referred to as a *'taxonomy of motivation'*, diversifying extrinsic motivation into: *integration, identification, introjection* and *external regulation* (Ryan & Deci, 2020)[2].

See: Ryan & Deci, 2000, 2018, 2020.

Nonetheless, in the proposed Model of Motivation, the Process is assumed to progress through its Phases in a specific format, where differing expressions are only generated by the Goal that has been set. And distinct from this Process of Motivation, a large variety of possible approaches can be observed to address this Process. When we observe how this Process of Interference manifests itself later in the 'Series on Motivation', we will cover more extensively these propositions for a taxonomy made by self-determination theory.

We set ourselves to observe theories capturing what we defined as 'primary evaluations', experienced according to the Model in reaction to Impact, thus *from,* not *towards* Reality, which were defined as 'secondary evaluations', to be covered later in the Series.

These theories on cognitive and affective reactions experienced from Reality extended on our observations of attribution theories in Chapter 7, and social cognitive theories from Chapter 6. Weiner's attributional theory of motivation and emotion brought additional insights, notably into affective outcomes of the attributions in search of causality in achievement-related settings, which in turn led to subsequent behavior, or 'motivation'. Social cognitive theory appeared to be more inclined towards the cognitive reactions following Impact, as proposed by the Model. These cognitive and affective reactions determine what we do and how we perform.

These primary evaluations, these affective and cognitive reactions to Impact from Reality, also appeared to profoundly affect perceptions of self, and self-concept, in various layered 'strata' of awareness and different settings and 'domains'.

As in the preceding two Chapters, we can summarize how theories from literature thus extended insights into the assessment of Reality in a Phase of Dedication, as proposed by the Model of Motivation.

*See exhibit next page* ➔

At the end of our exposé in this Chapter, describing a Phase of Dedication and the nature of our reactions towards our surrounding Reality, especially when perceived as Significant, we came to realize the implications, not only at a personal level, but also for the effects it could have on our surroundings. We were surprised by the intensity of these expressions, and it appeared that the more Significant Reality was perceived to be, the more excessive our reaction, both in a positive, but also in a negative sense.

## *Outcomes of a Phase of Dedication*

Two theories provided further insights into the assumed evaluative effects in a Phase of Dedication: affective, as elaborated on by an attributional theory of motivation and emotion, cognitive, as further described in social cognitive theory.

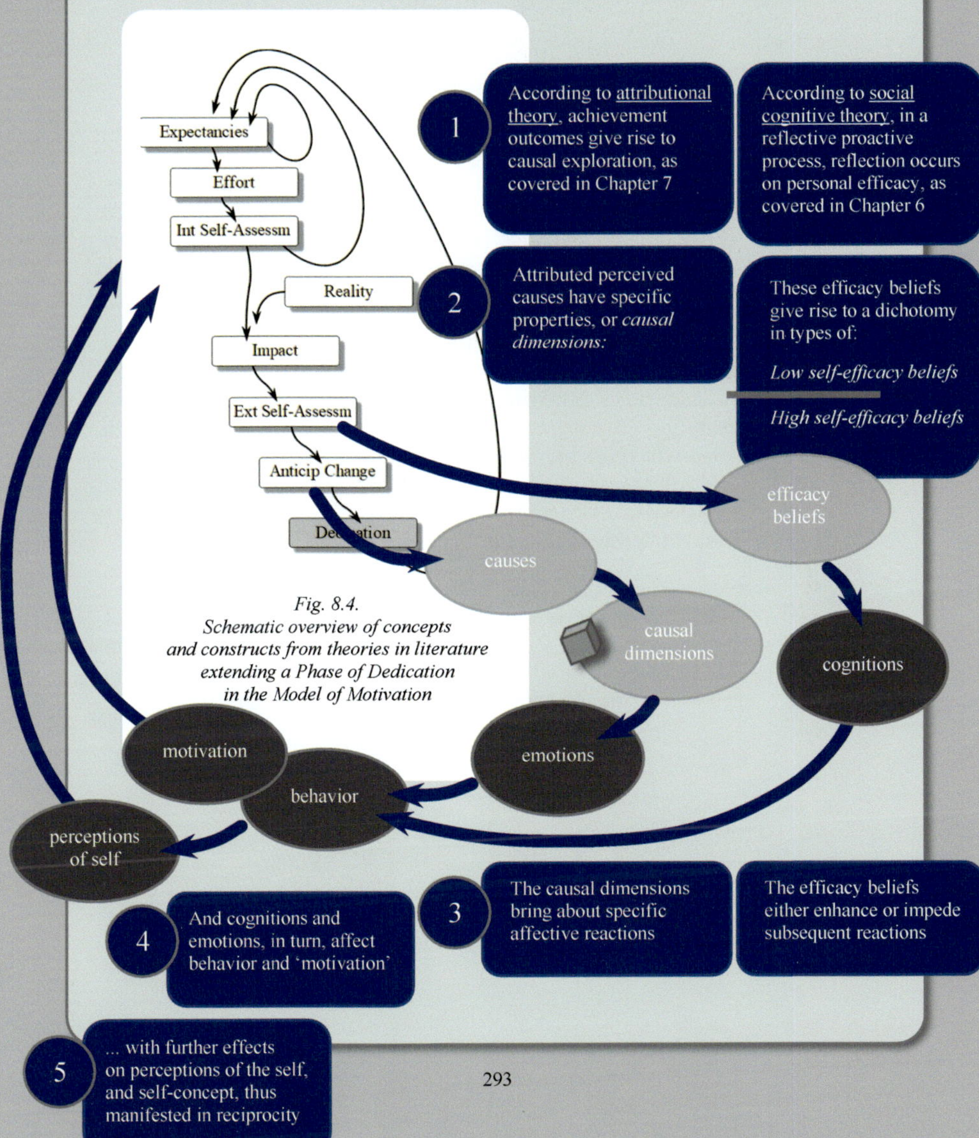


*Fig. 8.4.*
*Schematic overview of concepts and constructs from theories in literature extending a Phase of Dedication in the Model of Motivation*

# 3 Research

We have covered theories that not only provide a confirmation for the proposed Processes involved in a Phase of Dedication, but also present a more diverse view on the patterns of thinking, feeling and (eventually) acting that follows the Impact from Reality as suggested in the Model.

Findings from research on these theoretical insights are observed next. We will cover those from research on the *attributional theory of motivation and emotion*, on *social cognitive theory*, and on findings obtained from research on perceptions of *the self,* notably in achievement-related contexts. For research on *self-determination theory* and the taxonomy of regulatory styles (or motivation), we are to refer to coverage within the framework of a Process of Interference, as research explicitly related to the taxonomy has been mainly conducted from a perspective in which the individual is addressed according to these various regulatory styles (for overviews of findings over an extensive range of settings, see: Ryan & Deci, 2018).

As to the observed affective reactions in an *attributional theory of motivation and emotion*, Weiner (1985) noted: "(...) the bulk of the pertinent attribution-emotion research relates causal dimensions, rather than specific causes, to affects" (p. 561), in line with the observations previously made in Section 2. Although Weiner also observed affective states in interpersonal settings, we focus primarily on findings that are restricted to intrapersonal experiences, as interactions with others relate to a Process of Interference, as indicated earlier[1]. We thus observe findings on the causal dimensions of controllability, stability and locus.

First, however, research confirmed the emotion that initiates causal search (as covered previously in Chapter 7)[2]: studies revealed that "(...) success at achievement-related activities was associated with the affect of happy regardless of the cause of that outcome, and failure seemed to be related to frustration and sadness" (Weiner, 1985, p. 561; see also: Weiner, Russell & Lerman, 1978, 1979).

[1] These affective states are either non-related to achievement of a personal goal or instigated by activities of others. For more on these interpersonal affective reactions, see Weiner, 1982, 1985; Weiner & Graham, 1984.

[2] These emotions were briefly referred to in Section 2 as 'outcome dependent-attribution independent', following the outcome of an achievement-related event initiating causal search, that are distinct from emotions that are to follow the attributional process.

Findings from research on controllability where found to confirm a relation with the affect of guilt especially in controllable settings, where personal responsibility is felt (e.g. lack of effort), and shame in circumstances perceived to be uncontrollable (e.g. lack of ability) (Brown & Weiner,1984; Hoffman, 1976, 1982; Jagacinski & Nicholls, 1984; Weiner, Graham & Chandler, 1982; Wicker, Payne & Morgan, 1983). It must be noted, however, that cross-cultural differences in the expression and meaning of these attribution-related emotions have increasingly been reported in more recent literature (for an overview: Wong & Tsai, 2007)[1].

There are not many studies of stability-related emotions in achievement settings (Graham, 2020; Pekrun & Linnenbrink-Garcia, 2012). The association to the causal dimension of stability with the affect of hopelessness and resignation (stable-negative) and hopefulness (stable-positive) appeared in earlier research studies by Weiner and his colleagues (Weiner, Russell & Lerman, 1978, 1979).

The relation between causal locus and the affect of pride and self-esteem has been observed in research, linking positive outcomes to enhanced, and negative outcomes to decreased perceptions of the self (Stipek, 1983; Weiner, Russell & Lerman, 1978, 1979; see also: Oades-Sese, Matthews & Lewis, 2014; Tracy & Robins, 2007), where internal ascriptions elicit greater effects (positive, negative) than do external attributions. With further confirmation for the tendency mentioned earlier to ascribe success to an internal locus and failure to external factors (Harvey & Weary, 1981)[2].

A word of caution, however, is needed about these findings, as these linked emotions do not necessarily always follow causal ascriptions, and conversely, an emotion may be experienced in the absence of the assumed linked antecedent (Weiner, 1985). Nonetheless, findings give substantial reason to believe that the assumed linkages are prevalent in most achievement-related settings.

Which, subsequently, might add to our assumptions about causal ascriptions and the strategies used in a Phase of Anticipated Change as a possible source for the ways in which affect towards Reality is manifested in this Phase of Dedication.

[1] As summarized by Graham (2020): "The comparisons are primarily between collectivist Asian cultures like China and Japan and individualistic cultures as typified by the United States. For example, pride is less likely to be experienced for personal successes in collectivist societies and more likely to be felt in reaction to the successes of one's close ingroup members" (p. 9).

[2] As mentioned in Section 2, the phenomenon is referred to as 'hedonic bias', also known as 'self-serving attribution bias', 'ego enhancement', 'ego defensiveness', and 'beneffectance' (Weiner, 1992; see also: Bradley, 1978; Miller & Ross, 1975; Zuckerman, 1979; For a critical review: Malle, 2006).

Research on 'primary evaluations' experienced in reaction to Impact, as proposed by the Model of Motivation, has been predominantly focused on cognitive effects in studies related to *social cognitive theory.*

As observed, it is not so much our 'actual ability' that prevents us from performing and reaching an objective, but rather our beliefs and confidence to attain an objective that has been set (Bandura, 1997). Beliefs in personal efficacy are essential, not only in goal attainment and achievement, but also in a range of associated areas: "Do beliefs of personal efficacy contribute to human functioning? This issue has been extensively investigated by a variety of methodologies and analytic procedures. Nine large-scale meta-analyses have been conducted across diverse spheres of functioning. These spheres include work-related performances in both laboratory and field studies (Sadri & Robertson, 1993; Stajkovic & Luthans, 1998), psychosocial functioning in children and adolescents (Holden, Moncher, Schinke & Barker, 1990), academic achievement and persistence (Multon, Brown & Lent, 1991)(...). The evidence from (...) meta-analyses is consistent in showing that efficacy beliefs contribute significantly to the level of motivation and performance" (Bandura & Locke, 2003, p. 87)[1].

These self-efficacy beliefs influence the personal goals that one sets (Carson & Carson, 1993; Lerner & Locke, 1995; Zimmerman, 2000; Zimmerman, Bandura & Martinez-Pons, 1992; Zimmerman & Cleary, 2006). The higher one's self-efficacy beliefs in performing well on a task, the less difficult the goal is perceived to be (Lee & Bobko, 1992).

These self-efficacy beliefs, according to social cognitive theory, were thought to differentiate between individuals with *high self-efficacy* and those with *low self-efficacy beliefs*. Research findings appear to confirm these assumptions. As observed in research on goal-setting theory, it was found that people with higher self-efficacy are more willing to approach challenging tasks or goals (Berry & West, 1993; Pajares, 1996; Tang & Reynolds, 1993), exert more effort in those tasks (Zimmerman, 2000), find and use better strategies (Latham, Winters & Locke, 1994; Wood & Bandura, 1989; Zimmerman & Martinez-Pons, 1990), persist longer (Zimmerman, 2000), and experience lower levels of anxiety in those tasks (Bandura, 1997) than did people with low self-efficacy beliefs (Locke & Latham, 1990; Seijts & Latham, 2001). As stated in summary by Latham (2007), self-efficacy was "(...) positively associated with the difficulty level of the goals that are set, goal commitment, and subsequent performance" (p. 83).

[1] However, it has been noted that although efficacy beliefs have a generalized functional value, "(...) how they are developed and structured, the ways in which they are exercised, and the purposes to which they are put vary cross-culturally" (Bandura, 2002, p. 273). As concluded by Klassen (2004a, 2004b), individuals from collectivistic cultures tend to assess their self-efficacy lower than those from individualistic cultures (see also: Ahn & Bong, 2019; Pajares, 2007).

As a consequence, these self-efficacy beliefs, according to social cognitive theory, also affect subjective perceptions of the self. Although it must be noted that "(...) empirical efforts to distinguish between self-concept, self-esteem, and self-efficacy beliefs have met with only limited success (for a review, see Byrne, 1996)" (Valentine & DuBois, 2005, p. 55).

Research on perceptions of *the self* had at first reported moderate to weak relationships between self-concept and academic achievements (Hansford & Hattie, 1982; Shavelson & Bolus, 1982). As we saw in Section 2, however, "(...) in many studies during those years (...) researchers compared general, or global, self-concept with academic achievement" (Pajares & Schunk, 2005, p. 109).

Following the reconceptualization of the concept of the self into a multidimensional and domain-specific construct, research findings appeared that supported these diversifications (Marsh & O'Neill, 1984).

And this, in turn, as previously seen, enabled to demonstrate the relation between these domain-specific constructs related to academic self-concept and achievement (see overviews in: Marsh, 1993; Marsh & Craven, 1997). Differentiated measures enabled analysis of domain-specific responses. It was found that grades in English, mathematics, and science were correlated with matching areas of academic self-concept (Shavelson & Bolus, 1982). "Marsh (1992) extended these earlier studies by evaluating relations between more specific components of academic self-concept and school performance in eight core school subjects. (...) Consistently with predictions, Marsh found that correlations between matching areas of achievement and self-concept were substantial for all eight content areas (...) and substantially less than correlations between nonmatching areas of academic self-concept and achievement" (Marsh & Craven, 2005, p. 20). Thus, the higher one's mathematics self-concept (math-ASC) the higher one's performance in math-related contexts, or the higher one's verbal self-concept (verb-ASC) the higher the achievement in these areas. And vice versa, linking achievement to domain-specific ASC (see also: Marsh, Trautwein, Lüdtke, Köller & Baumert, 2006).

Having thus established that self-concept and achievement are substantially correlated, "(...) the key question became whether a causal link existed between the two: was one the cause or effect of the other?" (Marsh, Seaton, Dicke, Parker & Horwood, 2019, p. 44).

Refinements to the construct of self-concept enabled further research which confirmed a reciprocity between both constructs of achievement and self-concept (Chen, Yeh, Hwang & Lin, 2013; Huang, 2011; Pinxten, De Fraine, Van Damme & D'Haenens, 2010; Valentine, 2002; Valentine & DuBois, 2005; Valentine, DuBois & Cooper, 2004).

As recently summarized by Marsh and his colleagues: "The research evidence (...) has grown steadily, showing that prior self-concept and subsequent achievement are positively related, as are prior achievement and subsequent self-concept (...). Consistent with ASC theory and research, it is not surprising that prior achievement has an effect on ASC. However, [a] meta-analysis revealed that the effect of prior ASC on subsequent achievement, after controlling for the effects of prior achievement, was also highly significant overall and positive in 90 percent of the studies they considered" (Marsh, Seaton, Dicke, Parker & Horwood, 2019, p. 45, referring to a meta-analysis by Valentine, DuBois & Cooper, 2004, commented on in: Valentine & DuBois, 2005; see also: Marsh & Craven, 2005)[1].

Thus, research appears to confirm the effects that occur as proposed by the Model of Motivation, following Impact, the subsequent evaluations of achievement and the effects on perceptions of self, which in turn, through the assumed cyclical nature of the Process of Motivation, affects performance and achievement, which subsequently affects perceptions of self over subsequent cycles.

Finally, as observed in the previous Section, these findings appeared to extend further to what was referred to as the 'BFLPE', where the reciprocity between ASC and a student's own academic achievements appeared to be influenced also by the accomplishments of a student's classmates or peers (Marsh, 1987; Marsh & Parker, 1984). Since then, research has provided further support for these earlier findings (Marsh & Craven, 2002; Marsh & Seaton, 2015; Marsh, Seaton, Trautwein, Lüdtke, Hau, O'Mara & Craven, 2008; Zeidner & Schleyer, 1999). Research on the BFLPE suggests long-term effects (Marsh & O'Mara, 2010; Marsh, Trautwein, Lüdtke, Baumert & Köller, 2007) that appear stable and persistent over time (Marsh, Köller & Baumert, 2001; however, see also: Dai & Rin, 2008)[2].

So, these findings indicate not only that there appears to be a reciprocity between self-concept and achievement, but also that accomplishments of others, as expressed in the construct of Reality, serve as a frame of reference or standard of comparison used to form one's self-concept. And when these accomplishments are perceived to be more competent, the effects appear to be detrimental.

[1] In addition, research has provided support for a cross-cultural generalizability of the reciprocal effects between academic self-concept and achievement constructs (Marsh, Hau & Kong, 2002).

[2] Moreover, there is considerable support for the generalizability of negative effects of the BFLPE in cross-cultural studies (Marsh & Craven, 2002; Marsh & Hau, 2003; Marsh, Parker & Pekrun, 2018; Marsh, Seaton, Trautwein, Lüdtke, Hau, O'Mara & Craven, 2008; Nagengast & Marsh, 2012; Seaton, Marsh & Craven, 2009, 2010), thus, "demonstrating that the BFLPE is one of psychology's most cross-culturally universal phenomena (...)" (Marsh, Seaton, Dicke, Parker & Horwood, 2019, pp. 48-49).

Thus, these research results confirm the reciprocal nature of both constructs, indicating, as proposed by the Model of Motivation, that achievement-related outcomes affect perceptions of self; and these perceptions, in turn, influence performance and achievement in various contexts. But it also seems to extend the way in which Reality manifests itself far beyond its appearance as dictated by circumstances. In congruence with earlier findings from Chapter 5, the Impact of Reality as evaluated in a Phase of Dedication appears to be much broader, and to affect much more aspects of our being, than at first anticipated.

In the next Chapters, we will come to realize the extent of its influence, and the implications it has in our daily lives. And beyond.

## *Summary*

The eighth Phase in the Model of Motivation is a 'Phase of Dedication', which has two distinctive features: it evaluates Reality, and this evaluation also produces a specific outcome, referred to as a 'Representation'.

Given the input provided by the previous two Phases, in a Phase of Dedication, an assessment is made in terms of perceived 'support' or 'non-support' from Reality for the Goal and for the various parameters initially set.

And these evaluations, in turn, produce an image of Reality through a so-called 'Mechanism of Representation'.

A Phase of Dedication progresses, not in five, but four Stages, as opposed to the previous evaluations that occurred in a Phase of Externally Evoked Self-Assessment and a Phase of Anticipated Change. One Stage is excluded: a Stage evaluating Reality versus the Goal, as the assessment has previously occurred in a Phase of Impact, where perceived 'support' or 'non-support' was expressed in terms of Discrepancy. The centrality of this assessment in a Phase of Impact underlines the prominent position of this Stage within the Process of Motivation. Thus, the assessment previously made in a Phase of Impact complements those that are made in a Phase of Dedication.

And the assessment of perceived 'support' or 'non-support' from Reality in a Phase of Dedication occurs in four distinct Stages, proceeding at each Stage in two steps: a 'primary' and a 'secondary' evaluation.

In a first Stage, a *Stage of Appreciation,* an assessment is made of perceived 'support' or 'non-support' from Reality, from a perspective of the Attitude initially set. Reality can be perceived as 'supportive' to the initial Attitude, leading to a primary evaluation of 'being appreciated' or 'acknowledged'. And this, in turn, will lead to feelings of 'appreciation' towards Reality, as a secondary evaluation. In parallel, if Reality is perceived as 'non-supportive' this leads to feelings of 'being denied', or 'ignored', in a primary evaluation, in turn, leading to feelings of 'contempt' towards Reality in a secondary evaluation. Likewise, in a second *Stage of Approbation* an assessment is made of perceived 'support' or 'non-support' from Reality, from a perspective of the 'Energy' or investment needed to reach the

Goal, thus reflecting its perceived value. Perceived 'support' or 'non-support' leads to primary evaluations of 'being valued' or 'not valued', and these feelings, in turn, are reacted upon in secondary evaluations, 'valuing', or 'de-valuing' Reality in return, thereby affecting the effects of Reality on the Process. A third *Stage of Affirmation,* is a reaction towards Reality, from a perspective of Achievement and Failure. In primary evaluations, Reality is perceived as either 'confirming' or 'disapproving' one's choices in perceptions of 'support' and 'non-support', that are echoed by equivalent secondary evaluations. Finally, a *Stage of Commitment,* from a perspective of Satisfaction and Frustration, provides the individual with the experience of 'worth', versus feelings of being 'unworthy', depending on perceptions of Reality, which are likewise responded to with secondary reactions.

As a result of these four Stages, two sets of primary, and secondary evaluations emerge in perceptions of Reality. And these 'intertwined' primary and secondary evaluations serve to produce an image, or Representation, of Reality, that aims at either neutralizing or reinforcing the effects of Reality on the Process of Motivation. Perceived Significance of the Goal and Reality regulate and can intensify these primary and secondary evaluations, and thereby the nature of a Representation being made.

The input that is provided by successive evaluations in the three Phases following Impact from Reality, is used to make the necessary amendments to the Goal and the parameters initially set in a Phase of Expectancies, thereby returning to these initial Stages, and thus turning the Process of Motivation into a cyclical Process, where the sequence of Phases is re-initiated. As the Phase of Dedication initiates a return to the first Phases of the Process, it finalizes the sequence of successive Phases in the Process, and reveals for the first time the Process of Motivation as it emerges in its final form: A sequence of successive Phases, that is predominantly characterized by its cyclical nature.

Theory and research from literature on the effects of Impact, have further extended insights, notably in affective and cognitive reactions, that lead to behavioral consequences, which further influence these reactions.

These affective and cognitive reactions to Impact from Reality, appeared also to affect perceptions of self, and self-concept, in various layered 'strata' of awareness, and different settings and 'domains'. In addition, it was found that Reality in its Impact appears to provide achievement-related information, that extends beyond one's own accomplishments to include the achievements of important others, thereby serving as an extended frame of reference. These findings, together with previous observations made in Chapter 5, reveal an unexpected and disturbing outcome: that Reality as it manifests itself, profoundly affects the Process of Motivation.

*Preserving Balance - Ho Chi Minh City, Vietnam*

# Chapter 9
## *Preserving Balance*
## *A Second Cycle*

So, here I am... Or what's left of me...

I should have sat here under my tree, taking on the likes of a king. But instead my tree has lost its luster, and my good spirits have deserted me: Monserrate has been overruled by 'crowds', I am *forced* to do the groceries, my job needs serious reconsideration, and the only encouraging things that are left appear to be my tennis performance and the prospect of a trip to Hong Kong...

How am I to recover?

How am I to restore the Process of Motivation and regain the 'contours and splendors' of my original Goals?

Answer: by ingeniously using the assessments that were made following the intrusive Phase of Impact. Recall that after this Phase of Impact, assessments of adequacy were made in a Phase of Externally Evoked Self-Assessment, and courses of action were prepared in a Phase of Anticipated Change, providing a mindset which produced, in a subsequent Phase of Dedication, not only a twofold assessment of Reality, both primary and secondary, *but above all, a Representation reflecting all these sentiments towards Reality that will most effectively serve the purpose. Balance is restored through Mechanisms that are to make use of this Representation of Reality, rather than its original.*

And in doing so, the repercussions will prove to be considerable. But let us not digress on these effects at this point, and first analyze these Mechanisms by which the Process of Motivation is preserved, and whereby balance is restored in the attempts at reaching the Goal.

In this second cycle, then, balance is restored not by turning to Reality in its full and 'true' appearance, but by making use of its Representation instead. And the more Significant one's Goal, the more pronounced the use of this substitute.

At first sight, the approach appears to be remarkable. There are, after all, two options: by either 'adapting Reality' and accommodating our perception of Reality in the direction of the Goal (which is the approach we seem to follow), or by 'adapting the Goal' towards Reality. Why do we not tend to opt for the latter option, which is, literally, more 'realistic'? The approach seems surprising and even irrational, but on closer inspection, there is an inherent logic to be seen in this tendency. *The same strategies and intricacies that made me define the Goal in its 'splendor and Significance', now lead me to reject or oppose any form of influence aimed at 'adapting the Goal' towards Reality.* And the more Significance attached to the Goal, the more pronounced my strategies to retain all of its aspects that made it become the highly desirable objective I defined.

In addition, choosing for the other option ('adapting the Goal' towards Reality), constitutes a threat for something we (dearly) wish to obtain, as expressed in a specific manifestation: one's (Significant) Goal. So, why choose for the threat instead of the desire? Maintaining Reality the way it is and 'adapting the Goal' is therefore seldom an option. And *if* we are inclined to change, it often serves another purpose, mostly a Goal within an adjacent Process of Motivation.

And the same procedure applies when Reality has a positive Impact on the Process of Motivation. The same ideas, ambitions and strategies that made me define my Goal in its Significant manifestation, now prevent me from changing those properties in this highly desirable Goal, and instead bring me to choose to enlarge and magnify the positive aspects from Reality in a Representation;

aspects that underscore and acknowledge these highly appealing and Significant features of my Goal.

So, in this second cycle, balance is restored by making use of the input provided from a previous cycle, which, through subsequent assessments following the Impact from Reality, produced the ingredients to define a Representation. And this Representation reflects all the sentiments that will now most effectively serve the purpose.

Having said this, we are now on the verge of a new cycle in the Process of Motivation.

How are we to progress through the Stages and Phases of this second cycle? Do these steps remain the same, or are there differences emerging as the Process of Motivation progresses in this new cycle of reaching or consolidating the Goal?

Let us, again, turn to a number of examples that are different from the ones we have been using so far, to mark a brief departure from our storyline. And to assist us in observing the options emerging in the Process of Motivation in this second cycle, we will again turn to the story of the boy and the girl who went fishing; the story we used in Chapter 5 to illustrate progressive Phases after Impact in the Process of Motivation.

Recall, we had a little girl catching a fish, and being successful in the attempt, experiencing positive Impact from Reality. And next, we had a little boy who at first was less fortunate, with Reality intruding in a rather nasty way. Let us therefore choose for him the third example we used, where he was to meet a wizard fish, adding some complexity to the observations we make.

How do the various Stages and Phases emerge, then, together with Mechanisms of Representation in both cases? Here are the details, together with both portraits serving as a reference...

*See exhibits next pages* ➔

<u>What to do with a '10-inch-sized Catch'...</u>

So, here is the aftermath of the story of this little girl who wants to catch a great fish... Previously we saw that she caught a fish that exceeded her highest expectations. So, in a sense (and to slightly change the perspective in our context), this '10-inch-Reality' of a fish, had become a '20-inch-Representation' of its original...

But now things become a bit tricky...

If she sets her mind on catching an 'equal-sized' success, chances become rather grim, for this fish was truly an exceptional catch. So, again, she cleverly sets her expectations low, so that *with the knowledge she now has* the chance of Failure can be deflected, and success, or Achievement, retains its value. Note how the Goal and its parameters evolve in the same way as before in Phase 1. Again, she invests and goes to the river, Phase 2, and there she sits, waiting for things to come. Phase 3, again, has low profile, as the result is obtained only when Reality becomes apparent. So, there she sits patiently, cycling through Phases 1, 2 and 3 and maintaining hope as she did before...

Now, let us assume Reality comes in the form of a '5-inch-sized fish'...

Apparently, it is not the 'grand success' she previously had. Discrepancy between the Goal and this '5-inch-sized Reality' is larger. So, the criteria are as clearly set as before, and she obviously did not meet those criteria. But she cleverly arranged a contingency. In a subsequent Phase of Externally Evoked Self-Assessment, the adequacy of the (now modest) Goal and its parameters is assessed. As before. And a subsequent course of action is laid out in a Phase of Anticipated Change. As before. Leading to a conclusion as previously made in a Phase of Dedication.

So, the steps she makes coincide with the ones she made previously in a first cycle of the Process.

This time, however, one might say that *she gained experience.* She did catch a fish; in this, she was successful. But it was modest, which further emphasized the success of her strategy to stay reserved (as she does) in her expectations.

It goes without saying, things would have been different if she wouldn't have succeeded despite her efforts. Or if she would have caught two '20-inch-Representations' in a row...

## Gone Fishing!?

Earlier we met this exceptional boy, Matteo Motivation, and his encounter with the wizard fish, Proximo Providence...

Recall the fish had told him how to retain his place in a world that was devoted to him because of his gentle kindness. He had sent him a confusing message: “If thou art to seek glory and fame, thy eyes will remain without luster. But if thou art to seek kindness, in respect, dignity and trust, thy eyes are to shine upon wisdom and prosperity”.

So, after these memorable words, Matteo sat out to follow his advice, after granting Proximo the wizard fish the highest possible Representation in terms of honor, esteem and appreciation. And with this obvious tribute, a new cycle is initiated. The Goal is eminently clear, and has now been refined: to seek kindness, in respect, dignity and trust to everyone (and *certainly not* to seek glory and fame). So, as Phase 1 progresses into Phase 2, Matteo exercises exemplary kindness, which, in Phase 3, results in high self-confidence and pride in his accomplishments, *as far as he is concerned.*

Recall that he defined his Goal, anticipating the highly Significant Representation of the GREAT Proximo, who granted him, *‘bestowed upon him’,* the keys to retain his place in a devoted world (and acquire wisdom and prosperity). But alas, the moment Matteo became self-satisfied, he also became conceited and self-centered, seeking recognition and fame. And consequently, his eyes “lost their luster and became hollow in their sight”. In cycling through the first three Phases, he subsequently, in this second cycle of the Process, clashed with a Reality (or rather its Representation) which, most unexpectedly for him, proved to be highly Discrepant...

However, despite the Discrepancy, the sequence of subsequent Stages and Phases still remains the same. There is an obvious, highly Discrepant occurrence with the initial criteria as defined in the Goal. A subsequent assessment of adequacy in a Phase of Externally Evoked Self-Assessment leads him to reject Reality (in its current new perception), rather than the (refined) Goal he so anxiously set. And these assessments are further elaborated on in a Phase of Anticipated Change, in amendments to be made in a subsequent (third) cycle of the Process, leading to inevitable conclusions that are not aimed at honoring and preserving the glorious words of Proximo, and at admitting his Efforts had led him astray.

On the contrary, a *new* Representation is now formed, expressing deepest disappointment with Reality that “has been so cruel to him”...

And with these last disillusionments, the principal conclusion stands that this second cycle of the Process of Motivation, despite its intricacies, remains the same in the sequence of Stages and Phases in which it progresses over time.

Now, as we stated in Chapter 5, both stories in themselves are, obviously, not sufficient to adequately and convincingly determine the sequence of steps in this second cycle. But the case is more compelling when, again, we follow a more logical line of reasoning. Phase 1 is, by definition, the only Phase within the Process of Motivation where the Goal is re-defined, together with the assessments of investment needed, and the resultants in terms of objective and subjective effects of those investments. The occurrence of an actual Effort in Phase 2 of the Process is a logical consequence, and so is a subsequent personal assessment of outcomes in Phase 3, as the Process of Motivation has progressed through these Phases previously, and postponement or termination of the Process seems an unlikely alternative, especially since one comes prepared for having a renewed confrontation with Reality. And the Phases and Stages that follow awareness of a reoccurrence of the interference with Reality in Phase 4, and the realization of the nature of the intrusion on the Process of Motivation in Phase 5, are most likely to follow the logical sequence of *any* intervention as observed in Chapter 5. And these were: the existence of criteria (as obtained from the first three Phases, and especially the Goal), the assessment of adequacy of those criteria (as occurring in Phase 6), the decision on subsequent 'courses of action', either positive or negative (in Phase 7), leading inevitably to outcomes or conclusions from these various assessments (in Phase 8).

*So, the sequence of successive Phases (and related Stages) in a second cycle of the Process of Motivation is most likely to follow the same consecutive sequence as previously observed in a first cycle. There appear to be no specific circumstances that prevent the Process from progressing along similar sequential steps.*

So, we can safely assume that the sequence remains the same. Now, what happens to the Representation that is used to restore balance within the Process of Motivation in this new cycle?

Let us return to the examples we used in the previous Chapters, and observe the effects occurring especially in the various expressions following the Mechanisms of Representation.

To preserve the authentic and magical world of Monserrate, I had intended, in the last Phases of the previous cycle of the Process, to hold on to my initial settings and had fabricated a clever way out by leaving the premises in awareness of the 'crowds' that I was up against. So, it is these 'crowds' and not Monserrate that are to blame. And in this second cycle, I am to act accordingly: leaving the premises, to return later. And this second cycle will undoubtedly lead to a further downgrading of the poor tourists that happened to visit the place. I restore balance by creating a Representation blaming others, preferably in an anonymous and therefore neutral setting. Note again that the Representation is aimed at the intrusion, or intruders (which happened to be the interfering Reality), and not at Monserrate (which was part of the Goal that had been set).

Restoring, or rather preserving, balance in the second example is easier, as Reality, in the form of a victorious acknowledgement of my tennis achievements, needs only a proper consolidation. The only thing I need to be aware of is not 'to get carried away' and become overconfident in attempting to win all sorts of tennis matches in this wonderful 'world of tennis'. Fortunately, as we shall see in the next Chapter, I have all sorts of mechanisms at my disposal to take care of my buoyant optimism...

Now the examples of Monserrate and this tennis match are rather easy: the negative and positive experiences are properly addressed through both Representations ('crowds of visitors', and a wonderful 'world of tennis'), to restore balance and preserve the integrity of the Significant Goals I had set.

But things become different when we observe the effects in the remaining examples. The difficulties seem to add up on an almost progressive scale. How am I to restore balance when I become provocative by expressing amusement, as in the third example? The reaction is surprising, considering the agreements that were made on the issue. Moreover, it ends in resignation, which appears incomprehensible to an outsider, as not even a proper dialogue has been initiated to clear matters up. So how can a Representation that is provocative ('a trivial incident') lead to restoring balance? Recall that postponement in a Stage of Energy was the course I took, as the outcome did not provide the Achievement and Satisfaction, given the amount of anticipated Effort I would have to invest. Reality consisted of my beloved pointing me to the agreement we made, thus pressing me to action in this second cycle of the Process. And she was unmistakably right. The longer I postponed, the more uneasy the situation became. And now, in this second cycle, I feel 'exposed' and forced to go against my postponing strategies. And I restore balance by downgrading the incident and turning the situation into a hilarious episode, thereby decreasing its Impact. The effects of this provocative action are plain, and so is my uncomfortable exposure. For the less serious I seem to be, the more embarrassed I feel...

Mechanisms of Representation assist in restoring balance. In addition, the intensity of my reaction reflects the Significance of the Goal that needs this protective action. *The bewildering conclusion is that often these provocative actions reveal, in themselves, how Significant an underlying Goal appears to be to the one who causes the affront, and, caught in the act, reveal how carefully Significance in these Goals is concealed to prevent them from further interference.* And so, yes, these groceries happened to be Significant, or rather, these 'groceries-symbolizing-my-maintaining-the-deal-that-was-made', as demonstrated in the provocations that served to conceal my embarrassment...

Let us proceed on this progressive scale by observing the remaining examples.

We had an 'intertwined constellation of Processes of Motivation', where we anticipated on preserving three Significant Goals, restoring them from the interference caused by a 'common intrusion', captured in an adequate Representation of an 'inconspicuous-superior-infringing-on-academic-autonomy'. And in this second cycle the time has come to *act.* This Representation is further accentuated by reviving the dormant Goal of going to Hong Kong. Plans are initiated that will bring me there over subsequent cycles, thereby restoring balance on several levels: going there not only serves the long-awaited desire in the fourth example of going back to Hong Kong, it also consolidates my commitment to keep postponing my paper from the perspective that "with such directives, I take control of my own priorities", and, *in addition,* demonstrates my resolute intentions to defend my latent Goal to maintain highest principles and moral values, as expressed in 'academic autonomy', thereby defying the intrusion on this noble pursuit.

Well... Needless to say, the reaction in this second cycle, consolidating the earlier Representation, appears to be rather extreme, reflecting, as stated earlier, my prejudice and my intransigent mindset, which at this point in the Process has become rigid and devoid of good sense and judgment.

This is where not only an obstinate, inflexible, uncompromising attitude comes from, but also prejudice and intolerance. This is where irrationality and arrogance lead to discord and conflict. And again, the intensity of these expressions reveals the extent to which a Goal, in its Significance, needs to be protected at all costs.

At the root of these expressions, then, is the Mechanism of Representation we observed earlier in Chapter 8, which now emerges as a powerful, protective instrument of the mind.

The disruption that occurred in the Process of Motivation, then, is addressed in this second cycle, and balance is restored through these Mechanisms of Representation. The more Significant the Goal, the more manifest these Mechanisms become. The more Significant

The more Significant the Goal, the more explicit Mechanisms of Representation become, and, consequently, the less Reality is perceived in its 'true' manifestation...

the Goal, the more prominent the Representation substituting the original expression of Reality. And this Mechanism goes either way, not only when a perceived Impact has created high Discrepancy with the Process of Motivation in a Phase of Impact, but also when Reality provided positive Impact and affirmed the Process of reaching the Goal, acknowledging the Effort and leading to highly positive assessments in a Phase of Dedication. By emphasizing or even exaggerating these properties through Mechanisms of Representation, they are to further enhance their positive Impact in subsequent cycles of the Process.

Mechanisms of Representation are the Mechanisms that restore. But they can also lead us astray and position us at 'the center of the universe', or lead us to believe that 'the world is at our feet'; it can ruin careers and affect relations most dear to us.

Unfortunately, these effects are familiar to us all...

*But there is another outcome, which even exceeds those effects in severity.*

*The Process of Motivation, upon Impact from Reality, appears to lead to a series of reactions which, in turn, not only affect the Process, but also change our perception of this interfering Reality into an image, a Representation of its true manifestation. In its attempts to remain intact and unaffected in attaining the Goal that has been set, the Process of Motivation changes Reality in its appearance. And in these attempts at preserving the integrity of the Process, the more Significant the Goal, the more one is prepared to make adaptations to Reality and only perceive its Representation instead of the original.*

*These powerful Mechanisms that serve to protect the things we treasure most thus appear to have disturbing side effects that not only have the potential to lead us astray, they also make us inaccessible. As observed in intolerance, pride, obstinacy, prejudice, where we are determined to persevere in retaining the integrity of our Goal at all costs.*

*Thus, the more Significant the Goal, the more explicit these Mechanisms tend to become. And the less perceptible Reality becomes in its true manifestation. The implications are far-reaching, as we shall realize in the remaining Chapters, notably Chapter 11 that is to summarize these repercussions from various perspectives...*

As the Process of Motivation progresses into a second cycle, two observations are made.

The first is that the Process proceeds following a same sequence of Stages and Phases as previously occurred in a first cycle, thereby maintaining its cyclical character.

Within these cycles, attempts are made to preserve the integrity of the Goal, after the confrontation with Reality. The Representation that was made in Phase 8, a Phase of Dedication, reflecting all the sentiments towards Reality, now most effectively serves the purpose. Balance is restored through Mechanisms of Representation that make use of this Representation of Reality, rather than its original. Thus, the Goal and its parameters are re-attuned using this Representation as a reference.

*Mechanisms of Representation are covered in detail on pp. 315-316. A summary is provided on p. 317.*

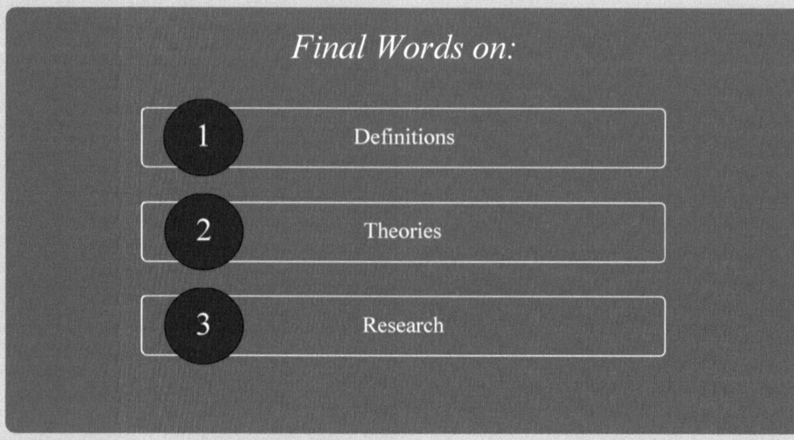


In the Introduction, we anticipated on having each separate Phase within the Model of Motivation described in separate Chapters. However, as we progressed through all Phases of the Model of Motivation, and have come to a renewed cycle in the Process, we will find ourselves reiterating the Definitions that have been discussed previously, while proceeding through these same Phases covered in preceding Chapters.

In addition, it appears that almost none of the theories from literature covered so far in Section 2 contains explicit references to the element of time, which also precludes a further coverage of findings from associated research in Section 3.

*As a result, no further references are made to theories and findings from research in separate Sections, as we observe the Process of Motivation in remaining Chapters. Instead, we will briefly refer to 'New Paradigms' that are emerging, in summarized overviews, capturing the essentials that are found as we observe new cycles of the Process. To differentiate this new Section from the main text in each Chapter, it is given a different background color (in gray) and a smaller font, as has previously been used for these Sections.*

## *New Paradigms: Mechanisms of Representation*

### How am I to restore balance?

### By using the Representation of Reality rather than the original.

### Let us define, in detail, the sequence of events.

We generated an idea, an intention which evolved into a Goal. We invested Effort. We even assessed Achievement and Failure, Satisfaction and Frustration. And then interference occurred: an unexpected event, or series of events, affecting our attempts at reaching this objective. We first assessed Significance of the intrusion, and its Impact. Then, we observed the repercussions of the occurrence on our attempts at reaching the objective, and subsequently contemplated the potential amendments to be made in order to preserve the integrity of the Goal as much as possible.

And then we came to assess the occurrence itself. Following a Phase of Reality and a Phase of Impact, the Phase of Externally Evoked Self-Assessment and the Phase of Anticipated Change provided the mindset whereby primary and secondary reactions towards Reality were made, leading, finally, to a Representation of Reality which further served as a reference. And it is this Representation that is to provide the primary input for our attempts at taking preemptive measures in a second cycle of the Process of Motivation.

*Balance is restored, then, by using the Representation of Reality, produced as an outcome of a previous Phase of Dedication through a Mechanism of Representation, and to use this outcome in a second cycle as input to make these necessary amendments in the first renewed Phases of the Process.*

What are the principal strategies that we tend to follow in these Mechanisms of Representation in a second cycle of the Process of Motivation?

Let us briefly return to the various expressions in which effects of interference manifest themselves in the Process. As we saw in Chapter 5, these manifestations were largely determined by three essential constructs: Significance of the Goal, Discrepancy and perceived Significance of Reality. From the eight options emerging, it was found over the last few Chapters that effects mainly occurred on two occasions: when Significance of the Goal and perceived Significance of Reality were high and Impact was either negative with large Discrepancy (option 2, p. 123) or positive with small Discrepancy (option 4, p. 123).

Now, recall that the effects observed using these constructs were observed as extremes on hypothetical continua, ranging from low to high Significance of the Goal and perceived Significance of Reality, and ranging from small to large perceived Discrepancy of Impact.

If we now, finally, reintroduce these ranges instead of extremes on our continua, we can summarize our observations on the principal strategies we tend to use in Mechanisms of Representation, and their effects on the Process of Motivation as it progresses into a new cycle.

Thus:

- When Significance of the Goal increases,
- and perceived Significance of Reality increases,

  Mechanisms of Representation become more pronounced,
  where Impact plays an important regulating role:

  - As Impact is perceived as increasingly positive, and Discrepancy therefore decreases:
    - Representations of Reality tend to be increasingly positive, as they are aimed at increasing the perceived positive effects on the Process of Motivation aimed at reaching or preserving the Goal. As a result, the individual tends to 'open up'.

  - As Impact is perceived as increasingly negative, and Discrepancy thus increases:
    - Representations of Reality tend to be increasingly negative, whereby an attempt is made at neutralizing and decreasing the perceived negative effects on the Process of Motivation aimed at reaching or preserving the Goal.
      As a result, the individual tends to become 'inaccessible'.

And consequently, the main effects on the Process of Motivation could be further summarized:

- The more Significant the Goal,
- and the more Significant a perceived Reality,

  the more pronounced the effects of Mechanisms of Representation.

*Which then leads to our final conclusion, that the more Significant our Goal, and the more Significant a perceived Reality, the more we tend to change this perceived Reality into a Representation of its original, and the less perceptible Reality becomes in its true manifestation...*

## *Summary*

As the Process of Motivation proceeds into a new cycle, it is prepared for a renewed confrontation with Reality, having had either positive or negative effects from Impact in a previous cycle.

To restore balance, following the Impact from Reality, we tend to make use of so-called 'Mechanisms of Representation'. These Mechanisms produce adaptations of a perceived Reality by making use of an image, or 'Representation', created in a Phase of Dedication as an outcome of consecutive Phases following Impact. The more Significant the Goal, the more pronounced these Mechanisms tend to manifest themselves in the Representations they produce.

Thus, when perceived Reality has created high Discrepancy with the Process of Motivation in a Phase of Impact, balance is restored in a second cycle of the Process through these Mechanisms by making use of the Representation of Reality rather than its original, thereby neutralizing its negative effects on the Process. And when perceived Reality has provided positive Impact and affirmed the Process of reaching the Goal, these Mechanisms of Representation serve to emphasize positive attributes of Reality, captured in its Representation, to further enhance their positive Impact in subsequent cycles of the Process.

Mechanisms of Representation are the Mechanisms that restore. But these powerful Mechanisms appear to also have disturbing side effects that not only have the potential to lead us astray in the image or Representation they create, they also make us inaccessible. As observed in intolerance, pride, obstinacy, prejudice, where we are determined to persevere in retaining the integrity of our Goal at all costs.

Thus, the more Significant the Goal, the more explicit these Mechanisms of Representation tend to become. And the less perceptible Reality becomes in its true manifestation... The implications are far-reaching, as can be observed in following Chapters...

# Chapter 10
## *Mechanisms of the Mind*
## *A Sequence of Subsequent Cycles*

How complicated the intriguing Process of Motivation now appears to have become!

As the Process unfolds and is re-initiated, the second cycle is characterized by a single asset, which was virtually absent when it began: through the Impact from Reality we were prepared for things to come. And this experience was optimized by making use of Mechanisms of Representation.

And as the Process of Motivation progresses over subsequent cycles, these Mechanisms are assisted by others that further improve these protective measures against intrusion from Reality.

'Mechanisms of the Mind'... And the more Significant the Goal they need to protect, the more pronounced they become.

What are these additional Mechanisms, and which strategies do they use? The Process of Motivation in subsequent cycles is characterized by a determination to enhance or reduce the interference caused by Reality in the balance obtained earlier in its first Phases. *These Mechanisms aimed at anticipating on an upcoming confrontation with Reality are referred to as 'Mechanisms of Anticipation'.*

In tracing which strategies these Mechanisms of Anticipation use, and which particular Stages or Phases in the Process of Motivation are involved, we turn again to the examples previously used of the girl and the boy in their encounter with Reality.

*See exhibits next pages* ➔

<u>A '10-inch-sized Catch'...</u>

Let us leave our speculations about the various options of success ("two near perfect 20-inch fishes in a row") for what they are, and focus on the strategy the little girl has followed, and where it originated from...

Recall this girl had cleverly devised a strategy to reduce expectations of catching a renewed '20-inch Representation' of her fish. This way, she could decrease chances of Failure, whereas success and Achievement could maintain their benefits. So, after having defined those 'settings' in Phase 1, she invested Effort in Phase 2, and sat patiently, cycling through the first three Phases, with Phase 3 providing only limited additional information. Thereupon she caught her fish, in this second cycle, followed by assessments of adequacy of her Goal and related 'settings' in Phase 6, anticipating on the necessary amendments to be made, Phase 7, and leading to renewed conclusions in Phase 8.

So, again, in the final Phases no strategies are made, only assessments. Which leaves us with the first three Phases as key to defining those strategies.

But we could make further refinements...

The input provided from the last Phases of the Process is now in a subsequent cycle used to set the necessary precautions both in the Goal, and in what we called 'her expectations'. In this third cycle of the Process, she had gained further experience. Her first catch was truly exceptional. So, this experience is now used to make further refinements in Phase 1 of this third cycle. And, again, she makes a clever move: instead of focusing on a praised catch, she moderates her expectations, *while keeping the anticipated investment in terms of Energy intact.* And when she subsequently proceeds through Phase 2, by investing an equal amount of Effort, assessing the merits of her approach in Phase 3, she comes to a favorable assessment of her strategy, initiated in Phase 1, to maintain her levels of Energy intact: "I invested hardly any Effort, and look what a great catch I had in the end! Moreover, I had great fun waiting for this next opportunity to emerge. *Fishing is great!"*

These clever anticipatory measures lead her to remain committed, despite the mediocre success she obtained in the '10-inch-sized beauty'. What's more: she is now up to the challenge of catching *no fish at all and still remaining enthusiastic...*

So, the strategy for subsequent steps appears to be laid out in Phase 1, with Phase 2, and to some extent Phase 3, providing additional options.

The Effects of Disillusionment...

Our second example to help us trace the strategies and roots of these Mechanisms of Anticipation is about the boy, Matteo Motivation, and his encounter with the wizard fish, Proximo Providence...

Recall that at first, Proximo was held in high regard: he had granted him "the keys to retain his place in a devoted world and acquire wisdom and prosperity". And Matteo had sat out to follow his advice and seek only kindness, in respect, dignity and trust to everyone, and *not* by seeking glory and fame. But as time (and the Process of Motivation) went by, he became more and more self-confident, and glory and fame became too attractive to resist. As we saw, his eyes "lost their luster and became hollow in their sight", thus leading to a clash with Reality. Proximo was no more the redemptive Representation he once had been. On the contrary, a renewed Representation expressed Matteo's deep disappointment.

How, then, will he anticipate on a next disappointment, and how are these Mechanisms of Anticipation to benefit from this new Representation expressing how life and especially Providence (Reality) "had been so cruel to him"?

Well, by *not investing* any more Energy and Effort...

The Representation of Reality in this third cycle of the Process is further enhanced by this unresponsive, indifferent attitude: "Whatever I did, this is an encounter that gave me nothing but disappointment. I am through with it." The poor boy tried so hard, and failed to see that in doing so, the attempt went terribly wrong...

And this new perspective is reflected in Phase 1 of the Process, in this third cycle, and subsequently refined through Phases 2 and 3, until the approach proved to be sufficiently effective to address the highly disappointing encounter: Proximo Providence (or rather: its perceived Representation) is unreliable, his prophecies are fallacies that deserve no further attention or investment and are to be neglected...

And as it so happened, the boy henceforth "became a disillusioned young man"...

Subsequent Phases following this dramatic clash do not appear to add further to the strategies that are set in place, primarily in Phase 1, and further refined in Phases 2 and 3. The Phases following Impact, as seen before, only offer a sequence of assessments on how to proceed vis-à-vis the renewed Representation of Reality, leading to a conclusion that, in turn, serves as input for a subsequent next cycle in the Process.

So, based on both these examples we appear to design our strategies aimed at defying the interference from Reality in the first three Phases of the Process of Motivation.

And although both examples are instructive, there is also a more logical approach, as we followed in Chapter 5 and Chapter 9. Since it is in the first Phases of the Process that we define not only the Goal we have in mind, but also its properties and its accompanying parameters in terms of the investments needed and its anticipated effects, which are tried out in practice in Phase 2, and re-assessed in Phase 3. Which Phases can be more appropriate to make amendments and a 'tailor-made design' to anticipate on a renewed confrontation with Reality (or rather, with its Representation), both in a negative as well as in a positive sense? The Phases that follow are assessments and preparations following Impact, and are to provide the input for renewed amendments to be made in these first three decisive Phases of the Process, where these settings are further refined.

*So Mechanisms of Anticipation, which make use of our prior knowledge of the effects of Impact, occur mainly in Phases 1, 2 and 3 of the Process of Motivation.*

Now, we could refine their 'locus of operation' even further, when we observe more closely the strategies they use...

At first sight, these strategies used in Mechanisms of Anticipation appear to be numerous: setting one's expectation low, withdrawing into apathy and indifference, having hopes and fantasies, trusting for the best, or losing courage, denying and renouncing. But at closer examination all these expressions are outcomes of thoughts, ideas, interpretations that *precede* those expressions. If we are to focus on Phase 1 of the Process of Motivation, a Phase of Expectancies, we can observe the sequence of steps, the Stages, that produce these various expressions. Hope, fantasy, confidence on the one hand, and losing courage, denying or even renouncing, on the other, are all outcomes and expressions of the Stages in which we make our assessments in terms of Achievement and Failure, of Satisfaction and Frustration. These expressions are outcomes, 'derivatives', of preceding Stages, where the Goal and investment in terms of Energy are defined. *If we are in search of the roots of the strategies we tend to use when we seek Mechanisms of Anticipation, it is in the design of our Goal and in the investment in a Stage of Energy that we find the key elements in the architecture of those strategies.*

So, in brief, we appear to anticipate on the effects from Reality and its Representation over subsequent cycles of the Process of Motivation, mainly by addressing specific properties of the Goal and/or by manipulating its accompanying levels of Energy in anticipated Effort.

Recall from the first steps we made in the Process, in Chapter 3 (and prior to this in the Definitions provided in Chapter 1 and Chapter 2), that three properties played a decisive role in the design of our Goals: 'Attainability', 'Clarity', and the 'Significance' or importance we attached to the Goal.

In a property defined as 'Attainability', the Goal can be defined as 'easy' or 'difficult' to reach. We saw in Chapter 3 that after gaining confidence in one's performance, the Goal could be re-defined in such a way that it became more within reach. And when expectancies of being successful were less positive, we could decide to set Attainability low and more distant, in order to protect ourselves against the risks of Failure: "This appears to be beyond reach, but let me at least give it a try". And this is precisely the approach we see in the first example: the little girl *re-defines the Attainability of the Goal* as (more) 'difficult' to reach. Consequently, her expectations are tempered, which prevents her from becoming frustrated, or even disillusioned, as in the example of Matteo. Observe how he, *in addition,* minimizes Energy, and consequently Effort, to further strengthen the strategy to deny a further intrusion from the Representation of Reality following the renewed Impact: "This encounter gives me nothing but disappointment. I am through with it, and will spend no more time on this..."

A second property that is used as a key element in defining a suitable strategy to adequately address Reality, or its substitute Representation through Mechanisms of Anticipation, is the property defined earlier as 'Clarity' of the Goal. As we saw in Chapter 3, high Clarity, as the name implies, makes a Goal precise and well-defined, while low Clarity makes it vague and indistinct. So, if we are less confident about the outcomes that may occur over subsequent cycles in the Process of reaching our Goal, we can, conveniently, decrease Clarity. The less precise we define our Goal, the less susceptible we become to outside interference. If my Goal would have been 'to have fun' on my daytrip to Monserrate, things would have been quite different. I would have simply left the place to find 'some fun' elsewhere. But instead my Goal, in terms of Clarity, was extremely precise. Recall, that in a cyclical succession of Phase 1 to Phase 3, the Goal increased in precision and Clarity, from a mere 'going-there' to 'going-there-to-have-a-great-and-romantic-experience-of-amazement-and-wonder'. As I felt more confident after having visited the place *twice*, my confidence increased, resulting in this increased Clarity. As we saw: the more precise we formulate the Goal the better we experience its success, and consequently, the higher the Achievement and Satisfaction of attaining such a Goal. But we also realized it came at a price: if we fail, we will fail *miserably*. The consequence of precision will turn against us, as we will become painfully aware of our Failure and Frustration. And this is what subsequently happened at Monserrate. We were fully exposed in our Failure and Frustration, leading to corrective action in the form of powerful Mechanisms of Representation, degrading my entourage to 'crowds of visitors' as the cause of the interference. A Mechanism of Anticipation would further empower this Mechanism by reducing Clarity in the Goal: "Let us seek distraction elsewhere, as the site is congested by *crowds of visitors*". And note how disdain and an intolerant attitude also sadly reveal the Significance of the events that deeply affected me.

Quite the opposite occurs in the second example, where increased Clarity, through successive cycles in Phase 1 to Phase 3, served to propel the experience of Achievement and Satisfaction. Luckily, an intruding Reality that further acknowledged my successes assisted to further increase the positive effects, conveniently expressed in a euphoric Representation, and consolidated in an even further increase in Clarity of the Goal. And possibly this, in turn, could even be supplemented with Attainability over successive cycles of the Process: "Let me participate in a few more matches, and let's see if I could reach the quarter finals, and perhaps win in the long run. Who can tell!"

A third, and final, ingredient in strategies used in Mechanisms of Anticipation is the property defined as 'Significance of the Goal'. Significance of the Goal is the importance we attach to the Goal. The third example we used was 'grocery shopping' which started as an obligation, with a minimal Significance, but as it happened, its Significance grew when I was exposed to a Reality which discreetly reminded me of my responsibilities. Despite my provocative behavior as expressed in my amusement, the Mechanism of Anticipation made use, in its strategy, of the property by *increasing* its Significance. And as a consequence, I now, in subsequent cycles of the Process, feel compelled to do the job *despite my attempts at pretending the opposite and turning the situation into a hilarious episode.*

*So in these strategies, Mechanisms of Anticipation make use primarily of the properties of Attainability, Clarity and Significance of the Goal, to anticipate on the effects from Reality and its Representation over subsequent cycles of the Process of Motivation.*

*In addition, they do so by directing Energy, and consequently the Effort invested.*

Let us briefly observe the remaining three examples, to illustrate.

At first, my plans to return to Hong Kong were set on hold. But then, the intertwined Processes of Motivation aimed at the presentation of a paper (which through its postponement out of fear had become a dormant Goal) and at being a representative of 'highest academic values', including academic autonomy (which was an implicit, latent Goal), these Processes were both disturbed by the interference of a common Reality, which had been conveniently addressed by creating an 'inconspicuous' Representation of my superior. And the neutralizing effects of this Representation could be dramatically improved by an *act of will,* thus by investing Effort, in this case a departure, "to an institution in Hong Kong that *truly* adheres to my academic standards of autonomy". Or at least, that is what I hope to find in this drastic exodus. So off I go. Investing Energy, and subsequently Effort, thus providing the ingredients for a Mechanism of Anticipation to withstand the unwelcome interference from Reality that has been neutralized through Mechanisms of Representation. The *act of will* and my departure underline, as it were, the Representation I made, which further assists in counteracting the intrusion in both remaining examples. By literally turning my back and defying an (alleged) intrusion that imposes upon me to write this paper, I assist *(by investing Effort in a parallel Process of Motivation)* in effectively realizing a postponement of my paper, in the fifth example. And note how in the sixth and final example, an *increased Clarity* of my hitherto latent Goal further sustains the effectiveness of both Mechanisms as they manifest themselves in these separate Processes of Motivation.

*So over subsequent cycles of the Process of Motivation, Mechanisms of Anticipation occur mainly in the first three Phases, notably in a Phase of Expectancies, where properties of Attainability, Clarity and Significance of the Goal are used, in conjunction with Energy and subsequent Effort, to counteract, or further propel, the effects of Impact from Reality and its Representation. And as we gain experience in the confrontation with Reality over these subsequent cycles, these Mechanisms are further refined over time.*

By using these properties of the Goal as main source, or elements in the design of strategies used in Mechanisms of Anticipation, the seemingly endless variations in which these strategies appear to manifest themselves in the Process of Motivation can be dramatically reduced, as we are to summarize in the next Section, covering these 'New Paradigms on Mechanisms of Anticipation'.

As the Process of Motivation, then, progresses over subsequent cycles, the balance that occurred in the first few Phases is gradually restored. First, by Mechanisms of Representation that produce convenient alternatives that serve as substitute for Reality. And second, by Mechanisms of Anticipation, where these Representations are used over subsequent cycles to further neutralize or enhance the effects of Impact on the Process.

And the more Significant our Goal, the more pronounced these Mechanisms become, not only in their

As the Process of Motivation progresses over subsequent cycles, so-called 'Mechanisms of Anticipation' gain prominence.

These Mechanisms, as the name implies, are aimed at anticipating on a renewed Impact from Reality, with either positive or negative effects on the Process.

Mechanisms of Anticipation occur mainly in the first three Phases of the Process of Motivation, notably in a Phase of Expectancies.

In this first Phase of the Process, where the Goal is defined, properties of Attainability and Clarity, and Significance of the Goal are used, in conjunction with Energy and subsequent Effort, to optimally anticipate, and thus counteract, a subsequent, renewed Impact from Reality on the Process of Motivation.

*Mechanisms of Anticipation are covered in detail on pp. 328-330. A summary is provided on p. 331.*

distinct expressions, but especially in the way they combine to form dynamics that produce powerful forces defying Reality as it manifests itself. And when the Process of Motivation progresses over subsequent cycles, these Mechanisms are further refined and attuned for the purpose, as experience builds up.

*However, as the Process of Motivation progresses, these protective measures have an unexpected outcome, as we referred to earlier at the closure of Chapter 9...*

*As Mechanisms of Representation and Mechanisms of Anticipation combine and blend to form protective measures preserving the integrity of our Goals, especially the ones that are perceived as Significant, they merge to form defenses that further enhance those strategies aimed at addressing Reality.*

*These powerful defenses are referred to as 'Stratagems of Coping', or 'Coping' for short.*

*All Goals that are Significant to us, in various degrees and expressions, are accompanied by these Stratagems of Coping. And as they are meant to address Reality and our surroundings, they are bound, sooner or later, to affect these surroundings, both on a small scale in our direct environment, family, friends, work, but also on a larger scale in groups or communities and social gatherings, which can even extend to affect society as a whole.*

*And it is in these expressions that Stratagems of Coping leave their traces, with repercussions that will prove to be beyond measure...*

## *New Paradigms: Mechanisms of Anticipation*

How am I to restore balance?

By using the Representation of Reality rather than the original, as observed previously in Chapter 9.

In addition, however, we now have a unique asset: we have, through the Impact from Reality in a previous cycle of the Process of Motivation, knowledge of the effects of this intruding Reality. And this knowledge even multiplies as time goes by and the Process progresses through multiple cycles.

So we come prepared for things to come. In the sequence of subsequent cycles of the Process, Mechanisms are made to anticipate on this renewed confrontation. And in doing so, there are recurrences and patterns to be seen in how the Process of Motivation makes use of our prior knowledge of the effects of Impact from Reality.

When progressing through subsequent cycles, the Process of Motivation has multiple encounters with an interfering Reality. And as time goes by, we increase our knowledge of these confrontations and optimize the Process as much as we can in our attempt to reach or preserve the objective that we have set. *Mechanisms of Anticipation are Mechanisms within the Process of Motivation that anticipate on an upcoming confrontation with Reality as the Process progresses over subsequent cycles.* And the more Significant the Goal, the more pronounced these Mechanisms of Anticipation become.

What are the tools we use in anticipating on a renewed Impact from Reality, and that serve to strengthen Mechanisms of Representation?

At first sight, there appear to be many. But at closer observation these expressions in Mechanisms of Anticipation can be reduced to only a few frequent occurrences in so-called 'Patterns of Motivation'.

One can deduce the primary roots of the Mechanisms of Anticipation, when observing the functionality of the different Phases in the Process of Motivation. Phase 1, a Phase of Expectancies, is basically where the 'settings' are defined, not only initiating, but also consolidating the Process as it progresses over time. Phase

2, a Phase of Effort, is where these intentions are executed, with follow-up on their outcomes in Phase 3, a Phase of Internally Evoked Self-Assessment. The Phases that follow, Reality in Phase 4 and Impact in Phase 5, are basically evaluative on the consequences and effects of the interference. So these Phases are outcomes, or derivatives, of the sequence of attunements made in the first three Phases of the Process. And when amendments need to be made, they more than likely occur within these first three Phases.

And from there, we could trace the origins to a first Phase of Expectancies, where Phase 2 and Phase 3, in turn, are in effect the resultants from this initiating Phase. And, proceeding further, from the five Stages that comprise a Phase of Expectancies, two Stages are also derivatives: a Stage of Achievement and Failure assessing the odds of investment as set in a Stage of Energy, and a Stage of Satisfaction and Frustration assessing these subsequent outcomes.

So that leaves us with the Goal, a Stage of Energy, and a Stage of Attitude. The latter serving only as instigator for thoughts, ideas, 'cognitions' that are subsequently materialized in the design of a Goal and in investment of Energy.

Now, given that the content of the Goal is to remain unchanged (as this would initiate a new Process of Motivation as defined in our Introduction), we can assume that we anticipate on the effects of Impact from Reality by only addressing the various properties of the Goal we set and/or by manipulating Energy, and consequently Effort. These properties of the Goal were defined earlier as Clarity and Attainability, together with Significance attached to the Goal, as defined in Chapter 1. *Where Mechanisms of Anticipation are mainly in effect when perceived Significance of the Goal is high, this brings us to the properties of Clarity and Attainability, together with investment levels of Energy and associated Effort, as principal parameters in which Mechanisms of Anticipation address the effects of Reality on the Process of Motivation following Impact.*

What are the various manifestations in which these parameters occur? If we recall the different expressions in which effects of interference manifest themselves in the Process, we could (as in Chapter 9) reintroduce our principal constructs (Significance of the Goal, Significance of Reality and Discrepancy) and observe ranges instead of extremes on respective continua proposed in Chapter 5.

Thus:

- When Significance of the Goal increases,
- and perceived Significance of Reality increases,

Mechanisms of Anticipation become more prominent, anticipating on Impact from Reality over subsequent cycles in the Process of Motivation, and where Impact therefore plays an important regulating role:

- As Impact is perceived as increasingly positive, and Discrepancy therefore decreases:
  - Mechanisms of Anticipation tend to anticipate on a positive Impact from Reality over subsequent cycles of the Process, where,
    - either properties of the Goal remain unchanged, and Energy investment tends to increase,
    - or properties of the Goal change towards increased Clarity and/or increased Attainability, and Energy investment tends to increase accordingly,

    thereby increasing the expected (positive) effects on the Process of Motivation. As a result, with an increase in Energy investment, one is likely to increase subsequent action in a Phase of Effort.

- As Impact is perceived as increasingly negative, and Discrepancy thus increases:
  - Mechanisms of Anticipation tend to anticipate on a negative Impact from Reality over subsequent cycles of the Process, therefore necessitating change, where,
    - either properties of the Goal change towards increased Clarity and/or increased Attainability, and Energy investment tends to increase accordingly, thereby necessitating pronounced Mechanisms of Representation to counteract this negative Impact from Reality,
    - or properties of the Goal change towards reduced Clarity and/or Attainability, and Energy investment remains at a same level or even decreases,

    thereby decreasing the expected (negative) effects on the Process of Motivation. As a result, with a decrease in Energy investment, the individual is likely to decrease subsequent action in a Phase of Effort, and is only likely to increase Effort at the expense of more pronounced Mechanisms of Representation.

And consequently, the main effects on the Process of Motivation could be further summarized:

- The more Significant the Goal,
- and the more Significant a perceived Reality,
  - the more pronounced the effects of Mechanisms of Anticipation.

*Which then leads to the conclusion that the more Significant our Goal and the more Significant a perceived Reality, the more we tend to accommodate various parameters to either enhance or diminish and neutralize the expected Impact from Reality.*

## Summary

As the Process of Motivation progresses further over subsequent cycles, the balance that occurred in the first few Phases is gradually restored using Mechanisms of Representation that produce convenient alternatives that serve as substitute for Reality.

In addition, insights obtained from previous cycles on the Impact from Reality now provide valuable input to counteract the effects on the Process of Motivation, either positive or negative. These measures aimed at restoring and preserving balance by anticipating on the Impact from Reality are defined as 'Mechanisms of Anticipation'. And these Mechanisms serve to further neutralize or enhance the effects of Impact on the Process.

Mechanisms of Anticipation occur mainly in the first three Phases, especially in a Phase of Expectancies, and tend to occur in recurring patterns, where properties of Attainability, Clarity and Significance of the Goal are used, in conjunction with Energy and subsequent Effort, to counteract, or further propel, the effects of Impact from Reality and its Representation. As we gain experience in the confrontation with Reality over subsequent cycles, these Mechanisms are further refined over time.

And as the Process of Motivation progresses over subsequent cycles, Mechanisms of Representation and Mechanisms of Anticipation thus combine and blend to form protective measures preserving the integrity of our Goals, especially the ones that are perceived as Significant. These combined defenses are referred to as 'Stratagems of Coping', or 'Coping' for short.

Stratagems of Coping leave their traces on many aspects of our lives. And as referred to in previous Chapters, their repercussions will prove to be most profound...

# Chapter 11
## *The Quest for Expression*
## *Stratagems of Coping*

The Process of Motivation, then, appears to be not only a means to an end as a sequential stepwise Process towards achieving one's objective, but now reveals itself as a powerful medium to protect ourselves against an intruding world.

The Process of Motivation makes an effective weapon aimed at restoring balance, but it now also appears to hold powerful Mechanisms with fearsome implications. These Mechanisms replace Reality by a Representation, in lieu of its original, while simultaneously using pluriform expressions of Anticipation, in attempts to restore balance as summarized in Chapter 10. And when both Mechanisms thus combine to form protective measures to preserve our Goals, these combinations become powerful defensive Mechanisms that are referred to as 'Stratagems of Coping', or 'Coping' for short.

A Stratagem of Coping changes our perspective of Reality; it makes us intolerant towards our surroundings and fellow visitors who happen to share our interest, it inflates our expressions of self to be noticed to the point of becoming an embarrassment to others, it even turns us against our loved ones on uneasy grounds, and makes us question the integrity of superiors without any reasonable grounds.

Is there anything positive about those Stratagems of Coping? And of course there is! But, regrettably, the ones who benefit from Coping are mainly ourselves. Coping protects. It preserves our Significant objectives, our dreams, passions, the things that are our 'raison d'être', and as such it protects us, it is our 'medicine' against the disillusions, the fears, the obstructions we are faced with. And likewise, it ignites the positive occurrences that give us feelings of worth, of meaning, of happiness.

*So, Stratagems of Coping not only appear to have clear advantages in our attempts to protect the Goals that we treasure most from interference, be it positive or negative, but they are also a necessity for survival in an often difficult, formidable or even fearsome and hostile world.* Recall that even in those positive instances, we demonstrate a necessity to inflate the positive support that is 'bestowed upon us', and by merely demonstrating this necessity, we also reveal the extent to which it affects us and the Significance it has, and therefore, the extent to which we are vulnerable to that same Reality that appears to favor us its support.

Stratagems of Coping have distinct advantages. They are 'part of life', and are a necessity for survival.

But at the same time, these Stratagems are at the root of controversies and conflicts. Of intolerance, pride, obstinacy, prejudice, as we saw in the examples used. As such, Stratagems of Coping determine to a large extent, not only our well-being and the way we perceive ourselves in feelings of worth, but also how we are perceived by others, our relatives, friends, colleagues, in the effects these Stratagems induce on our surroundings. The world is filled with expressions of Coping. *Coping is at the root of the 'human condition' and therefore deserves our full attention, both in the way it is generated through the underlying Processes of Motivation, but also in the effects it produces, where we often reveal ourselves from an entirely new and unforeseen perspective...*

The world is filled with Stratagems of Coping; and they deserve our full attention, not only in their negative, but also in their positive connotation. These expressions of Coping are not only doom and gloom, they also emerge as ingredients in 'essentials of life' such as friendship, where they provide positive and sustaining effects.

*To illustrate, see exhibit next page* ➔

## *Related Topics: What Friends are For ...*

What are friends for?

What a question!

They bring us comfort, we can relate to them, exchange our deepest thoughts and emotions, they give us support, as we give ours as best as we can; and this is just to name a few...

Some of us find deep gratification in their relations with friends; in fact, to a certain extent, we all do. For friends provide us with another unique feature: we can *talk* to them; and not only in the sense of having a 'conversation' or a simple 'chat'. When we *talk,* we also convey unique messages. And one of the most important features in these messages *is that we seek acknowledgement, understanding, approval, rapport...*

But what exactly do we pursue in those interactions?

*A counseling technique that makes extensive use of properties that provide support for one's Coping is paraphrasing. In paraphrasing, a listener repeats, briefly and in different words, the message received. And by doing so, provides the unique features of 'assistance in Coping'. However, as it involves a Process of Interference, it is beyond our present coverage...*

Communicating is one of the most complex activities we can engage in. And one of the most remarkable and powerful properties in communication is that we use it with our friends and loved ones *when we seek support in the strategies we use to counteract an interfering Reality. For when we talk, it often assists us in our Coping...*

Here's an example we may all recognize...

I have this exam coming up. And I've worked like crazy on the subject, but I am far from confident on the results. So what happens? The Stratagem of Coping first makes me skillfully reduce the scary Reality of the exam into a 'minor detail' in a Mechanism of Representation; next, I reduce Clarity: "As long as I pass, that's fine with me". In addition, I invest huge Efforts. And then comes the important part: I talk to a friend, *and in doing so, I seek 'assistance in Coping'...*

And my buddy, this 'comrade in arms' *knows* what to say to provide me with the comfort I need at these trying times: "Yeah, sure, I didn't really do enough either, but you know, who cares, as long as we pass, that's good enough for us, isn't it?"

Acknowledging our Coping... Now, that's what friends are for!

Let us, then, provide some final observations on the nature and on the effects of Coping, following the exposé in preceding Chapters on their origins, as Mechanisms of Representation and Mechanisms of Anticipation combine and merge to form these Stratagems. We have sufficiently covered how these Stratagems emerge and evolve over successive cycles of the Process of Motivation, as illustrated in the examples from the past few Chapters. But there are a number of important additional observations to be made on the nature of Coping.

First and foremost, as we observed, they are instigated by Goals that are Significant. The more Significant, the more expressive the preemptive measures displayed in Stratagems of Coping. And the (often) excessive nature originates from the perceived necessity to protect these Significant Goals.

And second, as a result, despite their 'overpowering' display, Stratagems of Coping serve to protect a vulnerable cause. They originate from anxiety, distress, or even fear. Emotions that are involved when Impact from Reality occurs. Even when the Impact comes in a positive appearance, we still need to further enhance its positive effects, wrapped in Stratagems of Coping, and somehow need these approvals, endorsements and confirmations. Needless to say, what the effects are when Impact is perceived as negative. Coping originates from experienced vulnerability, although the expressions of Coping (profoundly) suggest otherwise. *If we are to be so expressive in the nature of our defenses against an intruding Reality, it reveals not only the power of these Mechanisms, but also the extensive need and the necessity for protection. We will go to any length to preserve those Goals that are Significant. And in these, at times desperate expressions, we also reveal, how vulnerable we are...*

We can make a third observation while examining the origin of Coping and its expressive nature. In Chapter 8, we found that in Mechanisms of Representation we had a tendency to produce

Representations of Reality that mirrored its effects through primary and secondary reactions in a Phase of Reality. When we felt overwhelmed by 'crowds of visitors' we responded 'overwhelmingly', when we felt 'embarrassed' we tried to make fun of the situation, and when we felt 'controlled' we took control ourselves, reaching for extreme measures. *Stratagems of Coping are often echoes that reflect how Reality has been perceived, thereby (unintentionally) creating circumstances that are likely to produce an opposite effect of what one intends to achieve through Coping: when 'overwhelmed' or impressed, we impress in return, thus creating a situation that is likely to escalate; when we feel 'controlled', we take control in return and, often, are to suffer the consequences that we intend to avoid*.

*Fear to protect our Goals often instigates the things we are most fearful about...*

*A fourth observation, and possibly the most important in the formation and nature of Stratagems of Coping, is the concealed effect of Goals with high, but implicit, Significance.* Recall how we discussed the various manifestations in which we tend to define our Goals. Most of them were obvious and unambiguous. But there appear to be quite a number of Goals that are less articulate. Among those are Goals that we came to define as 'dormant' Goals, lying in wait, sometimes for many years. And 'latent' Goals, containing a more implicit meaning, with Goals or intentions that express strongly held beliefs: that justice 'will always prevail', or equality, tolerance, honesty, integrity. And these latent Goals are strict, irrevocable; and by nature therefore often appear as the 'hidden causes' of many expressions of Coping. *When confronted with an interfering Reality that constitutes a flagrant denial of one or more of these 'pursued virtues' or latent Goals we hold, Stratagems of Coping emerge. The highly Discrepant Realities are neutralized in whatever way seems fit, to counteract these highly Significant intrusions into our belief system. When inequality, intolerance, injustice befalls those in our society who are less fortunate, these perceived excesses that contradict our latent Goals need addressing to reinstate the Process of Motivation that holds these beliefs in high regard. And instead of turning to those who are in need, and who urge us to act, we 'turn away', in lethargy or indifference. Seemingly. As the surprising fact is, that we 'turn away' because we care.* An intruding Reality, coming to us through television, newspapers, social media, that is in excessive Discrepancy to the latent Goals we hold in high esteem (that justice 'will always prevail', or tolerance, or honesty and integrity...), this Reality needs to be neutralized at all costs to preserve the integrity of these strongly held beliefs, or latent Goals. Subsequent expressions of indignation and outrage serve to consolidate the 'truth'-fulness of these beliefs, or Goals, as effective expressions of Coping, whilst nothing happens to address the issues that are at hand. These Stratagems of Coping not only serve to neutralize the attack on these beliefs, but also, most often inadvertently, lead to the distressing fact that subsequent actions also fail to materialize.

*We 'turn away' because we care...*

Stratagems of Coping, then, have many unexpected manifestations that often conceal their true meaning. We have seen in the various examples used in the preceding Chapters how Coping is generated, and leads us into situations where we hardly recognize ourselves in expressions of intolerance, pride, obstinacy, prejudice, and in instances just mentioned, of indifference we appear to display, for which we have no fundamental and convincing justification.

If these expressions are often hidden, what happens when Reality, in return, provides us with a reaction? As indicated many times in the various examples, the effects of interactions resulting from these Stratagems of Coping are far-reaching, especially due to the intense and often disproportionate nature of Coping.

In a fifth and final observation, then, what are the effects of these expressions of Coping *when they are directed towards an intruding Reality?*

As stated in Chapter 8, although Stratagems of Coping unmistakably have positive effects, especially when perceived Discrepancy is low (i.e. when displaying appreciation, admiration, devotion, love towards Reality, to name but a few), negative effects nonetheless seem to prevail. Many of our unintended problems, arguments and conflicts originate from Coping and from the effects occurring in capturing Reality in forms of overstated Representations.

Recall, for example, the nasty Representation I gave of my superior in the last three examples we used, where he sent me an email which, from his perspective, was meant as a simple inquiry. Coping brought me on high alert. I didn't even check. Now, imagine the whole affair would have led to a discussion... Fortunately, no further interaction was initiated, but it brings back memories of occasions and incidents with less fortunate outcomes...

Could it be that we have all witnessed such reactions, both in our private lives with our loved ones and in our surroundings, at work, both with employees and their immediate managers, let alone top management? Not to mention the many thoughts we hear that are expressed anonymously in public or on social media, or when watching talk shows on the various networks? Chances are that those reactions we witnessed were reactions to expressions of Coping, which led to unintended outcomes, both in our private lives and in social venues.

And as these various interactions involve those that are close to us, or meant to be exemplary in a social context, chances further increase that these people become, literally, Representations of a Reality perceived as highly Significant. And when these events evolve into interactions that affect us personally, and come to intervene in the Goals we set that are important to us, chances are that these interactions, in turn, generate expressions of Coping from our side...

Stratagems of Coping appear to surface everywhere...

These Stratagems of Coping deeply affect not only the ordinary course of events in our everyday lives, but also determine to a large extent how we perceive ourselves and our surroundings from a broader, at times even 'existential', perspective. And, on an even larger scale, these perceptions and interactions affect not only the smaller circle of our private lives, but can also spread to define how we connect and communicate in groups and communities, and even society in general.

*So Stratagems of Coping affect and determine to a large extent our lives, and are therefore at the root of the 'human condition'.*

To conclude these first observations on the nature and effects of Stratagems of Coping, let us provide a number of examples that illustrate their broad range of expressions, and how they affect and determine our lives.

The examples are meant to illustrate progressive states of complexity in the expressions of Coping. What all examples have in common is a perceived Significance of the Goal that has been set. Without Significance of the Goal there would have been no Coping. And, consequently, in their distinct manifestations, they reflect the personality of an individual, within a specific environment and (historical) context. And a specific interpretation of Reality.

Therefore, when reading those examples, a cautionary note is in order. As not only do people differ in their expressions of Coping, an observer can also easily be misled in interpreting perceptions and attributing them to Coping, when, at closer look, they need not be expressions of Coping at all... Let alone the vast range of alternative interpretations that can be made...

These examples, then, are only meant to illustrate the Mechanisms involved in particular expressions of Coping, and are not intended to generalize to comparable situations.

With these restrictions in mind, four Cases are presented...

*See exhibits next pages* ➔

## *Case 1 ~ Coping*

*Let's start out with a Case we're all familiar with...*

*Arrogance!*

*This is what we do...*

"I ignore you! You are *pathetic!*"

*and why...*

For both examples, some reactions:

"He is just such an arrogant character... I have no idea why he picks on me. So what I do is I *ignore* him".

"And as I feel I am doing the wrong thing all the time, one of these days, I am going to tell him what I think. But somehow, I feel this will make things worse. Is it right to speak your mind? Everybody tells me so"...

"I feel bad about it. I didn't ask for this to happen. I try to do everything the best I can. And this is my reward"...

What all these reactions have in common is that *they respond to an expression of Coping (arrogance),* although the expression of Coping is primarily meant for the interlocutor.

And to make matters worse, the reaction we have is also one of Coping, *our Coping in response to his Coping ...*

So in this Case, things will probably become rather confusing...

*Here's what we may do (if we can)...*

In one word: nothing!

In his Coping, he is not talking to you, but to himself. And mind you, don't tell him so: you *will* be in trouble...

Why? *You* are the source of his Coping. For some reason he takes the trouble to let you know, *explicitly,* that you are *small and insignificant.* Why are people taking this trouble and going to such lengths *if this would really be the case?* Would you?

And in this Case, as you are the source of his Coping, whatever you do or say will be 'used against you'...

If you really insist on doing something to help the guy out: *be impressed,* be *truly* impressed (if you can). Why? Because that is (in its essence) what he seeks: uplifting words from someone he looks up to!

Recall that Coping often leads to opposed reactions. Arrogance aimed at neutralizing an impressive Reality instigates a reaction to be ignored. The one thing he is trying to avoid...

## rogance, and its whereabouts

*How can arrogance be an expression of Coping? And why are we inclined to react the way we do in these instances?*

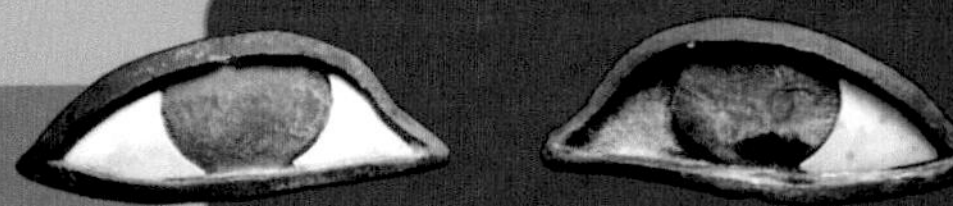

*This is what we see...*

"An arrogant character"...

*This is what is happening...*

Let's make it a 'he', shall we? Now, let us hear what no one is supposed to hear: we will listen to what he truly feels in the expression of his arrogance...

We will give two examples, one more 'neutral' and the other filled with emotions ...

First example:
"I have this young man in my team, and he is a *bloke*. Mind you, he is good at his job, *very* good even. But the thing is: he knows it. And that irritates me. I have 25+ years of experience in the field, and he should ask me my opinion, at least once in a while. Acknowledge my expertise...
After all, I am his *supervisor"*.

Second example:
"There's this wonderful woman. And she makes me nervous. I don't know what it is, but she makes me insecure. In fact, she is *so perfect*, I can hardly look at her (and I actually don't: I dare not look her right in the eye. I wonder if she has noticed).
I feel so imperfect, so clumsy, compared to her... And I hate this. But I'm not in love, mind you!"

*What he must do...*

Well, to start with: accept and acknowledge that he is downgrading another person. Downgrading Reality. And in doing so, in going to such lengths, *he should acknowledge its Significance first.* So, this person (in both occasions) *is* Significant to him. Both he and she have Impact.

Next, he should notice his reaction. He is *downgrading*, making them 'look small'. Acknowledging this will make him feel exposed... But the approach is *not meant to criticize*, but simply to observe. It 'happens to be what it is'. There is an 'interesting reason' why he acts the way he does. So, no corrective actions at this point. They distract...

Third, why does he have to make them look small? Why does he go to such lengths to even actively address them? This should alert him. He is convincing himself of the fact that they are small, *because they impress him. They impress in matters he finds important. And perhaps in matters, he feels he is failing, or at least floundering...*

This is where a personal reflection on causes starts...

*This is what we do...*

"I try to help her to overcome her fear of failure, by stimulating her wherever I can. She is so good at things! I hate to see her being so uncertain..."

*and why...*

Now, this is what we feel, don't we?

But we have to reluctantly admit that we are (inadvertently and with the best of intentions in mind), *addressing our own Coping.* The objective cannot be more Significant for us, and this Reality we now perceive (our daughter) is both highly Significant and Discrepant. One might even say: the better mom or dad you are, the more you *hate* to see her so frightened, and the more you'll try to comfort her, telling her that she shouldn't be afraid. But, most regrettably, *that is your Coping telling you to do so...*

And the result, strangely enough, is just the opposite, because from her frame of reference, she feels *she's not been taken seriously in whatever it is that frightens her so...* And although you *feel* you do, *you are (from her perspective) not acknowledging the dramatic interference in whatever Goal she has set...* Ignoring her feelings, gives her no support. And support is what she desperately needs at this point...

And here, again, we see that what we try to achieve, *through our own Coping,* leads to an opposite reaction.

## *Case 2 ~ Coping*

*Let us increase difficulty...*
*Here's the next Case...*

*Your daughter, aged 6, is having a terrible time...*

*Here's what we may do (if we can)...*

In one word: wait!

And perhaps (if we feel up to it): express *her* feelings (not ours): "Now this is scary, isn't it?" (For her that is, not for us)...

Why is this? In the waiting lies the acknowledgement of what she feels. She *is* frightened, and she needs all the help she can get. 'Voicing' her feelings is a good start (recall the exhibit on p. 179). *Never ever* tell her "not to be frightened, dear!" as it completely ignores her feelings, *and her Coping with the situation at hand.*

So, 'voicing' it is. And then wait. See what happens, and where you (when the time is ripe) could serve as 'role model' to try out an alternative: "Mmm, what do you think, it is scary now isn't it? But let me try something here... Are you okay with that?"

And then? You wait again, and see what happens...
Difficult? It is almost impossible...
But it's worth a try!

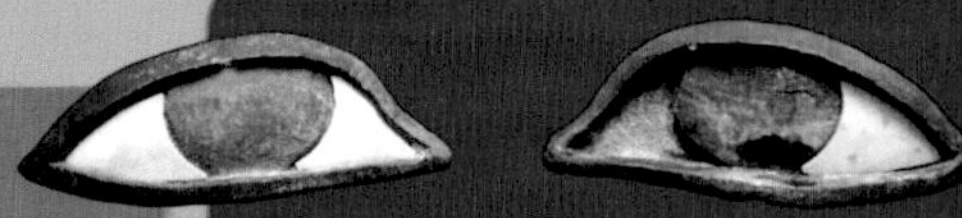

## *Girl and her Fear of Failure*

*Here's a Case to illustrate how fear of failure (and Coping) works in children at the start of their lives...*

*This is what we see...*

"A frightened little girl, withdrawn and even a bit dull, having lost all initiative..."

*This is what is happening...*

Here, again, let us hear what no one is supposed to hear, and listen to what she truly feels...

"I just started school... I was so much looking forward to this, but now everything seems so overwhelming. And I feel everyone is watching me. Watching what I do, and if it is all good enough... I feel I am not up to this. And to make matters worse, my teacher told me to focus more on what I do..."

*What she must do...*

Well, if she were a little older, things would be easier to explain, for the clue is to understand that *this is Coping*. This is how she protects herself and most importantly: how she prevents herself from taking action, which is the safe thing for her to do. So, it starts with *acknowledging*.

But in the end, it would lead her nowhere, because no action means you won't be experimenting to find other ways to address this fearful Reality. And in doing so, she would (in due course) be wise to simply *observe, without judgments.*

And thirdly, when the time comes, she will proceed to find out that preventing herself from taking action does indeed provide protection, but will not bring alternatives in the end. These insights (together with a safe environment) will eventually bring her to start experimenting...

And, in due course, to seek alternatives in her approach to her fear of failure...

## *Case 3 ~ Coping*

*Here's the next Case... Where we are to learn how to act when the going gets tough!*

*This is what we do...*

We interfere...

*and why...*

Basically, because most of the time we do not know how to react, and "I can't have her behave the way she does, now do I?"

As we saw in both previous Cases, what we tend to do is to *react to her expressions of Coping,* which is to state (and convince herself) that she is "perfectly capable to live her life the way she does, and incidentally, that she does not need *any* input from *anybody*, thank you very much!" This articulates *her* uneasiness with what life throws at her at this young age... Through Coping she convinces herself...

And then we react. With our Coping...

As we previously saw, these reactions, where we tend to react to someone's Coping through expressions of Coping from our side, are most likely to 'confuse the interaction'...

*Here's what we may do (if we can)...*

*Acknowledge their expertise...*

"What expertise?" That's where you're wrong… They *do* have acquired expertise in their 15+ years of living. For surely, they know best what they want (they are the sole expert in setting their Goals). These Goals may not be the wisest, strategically smartest, and best attainable Goals. But they certainly are worth trying to develop proficiencies, strategies, skills. And they won't be doing so if you keep interfering as a 'non-supportive' Reality. With high Significance...

*"High Significance?"* By all means! Otherwise, she wouldn't be demonstrating such perfect Coping. Imagine the investment it takes on her part to act the way she does...

She now needs all the help she can get... And to adequately assist her, *ask her expertise.* Acquaint yourself with *her* perspective. She will feel acknowledged. And with time, she will appreciate your input, or even ask your advice... *It needs a shift in mindset, that at least equals hers...*

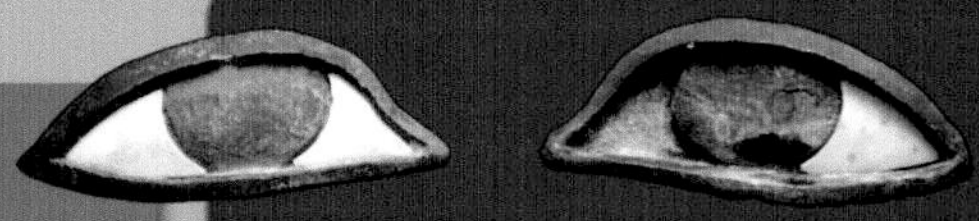

## *he Wonderful World of Puberty*

*Welcome to the wonderful world of puberty, or: how to get reacquainted with your daughter (or son)…*

*What she must do…*

Here, again, time is not on our side...

For the sequence we saw in previous Cases (acknowledge your fears without judgment, and then observing where Coping points us to), this sequence of self-reflection is (literally) the subject of her Coping...

She *knows* her insecurity, her 'inadequacy'. It is *the* Reality she is addressing.

The only thing she can do is start this 'Great Adventure'. Start the experiment. And in experimenting (if life hopefully presents itself as supportive), in years to come, she will gain confidence to eventually start this self-reflection into the causes of her Coping. And overcome her fears.

*This is what we see…*

The insolence! The impertinence! "And *rude* towards those who love her most!"

*This is what is happening…*

So, here is what no one is supposed to hear, let's listen to what she truly feels...

"I am 15 years old, and I know what is best for me... At least that is what I think. But then, when I realize that I can't even take care of basic needs such as doing the groceries or living on my own, I feel worthless, at times"...

"And then my parents... They have a way of telling me that I can't even support myself, that they know best... And that doesn't really help, does it?"

"And then my uncertainty about everything grows further, and breaks me down"...

*This is what we do...*

"He DOES make me nervous... And in addition, I am not at all taken seriously in a job, I was pretty sure I did rather well..."

*and why...*

Despite what we sometimes seem to feel, *no manager starts the day thinking how to be a nuisance to their employees.* Having said that, no manager seems to be aware of the impact they have, *given their position,* on the well-being of those they are paid to guide, steer, inspire, and foster in their talents.

Could this also be the case with our manager?

And here, again, we all tend to react to the expressions of Coping of the manager. And again, it is essential to realize that his expression of Coping (control) is meant primarily for himself, the interlocutor, to address an intruding Reality.

Instead of reacting (with our expressions of Coping) to his expressions of Coping, we would be well-advised to analyze where this Coping from our manager originates from.

If it is an 'option 1 reason' we will experience so, right away. And can act accordingly.

If it is an 'option 2 reason' we will also experience this, and we may be in trouble. And also..., act accordingly.

## *Case 4 ~ Coping*

*Here's a final compelling Case...*

*Here's what we may do (if we can)...*

*Talk!...* Always. But not in an offensive way: it would be a reaction to his Coping, which ignites your reaction (Coping) in return. Which, as we saw, tends to make things worse.

In that case, act as if *convinced* (I mean: *convinced*) he means you *no* harm. That he's seeking for the best. And your approach, your wording, your tone of voice, will change. From this perspective, describe objectively what you see. Give examples. And... show appreciation.

Then, describe *objectively* what effects are on your side: "Somehow, it makes me feel uncertain. That I am not performing the way I did in the past. Keeping up to my standards. I do not know how to change the situation. Do you have any ideas that might help?"

And then observe. Truly observe. If your boss acts according to 'option 1', he will come up with the right answers. If he's an 'option 2', then things call for more drastic approaches. Seek further counsel, discuss with those you trust and who are familiar with the situation.

## ne Control-Freak Boss ...

*The boss with ideas of his own, who's an expert in all areas. And controlling whatever we do…*

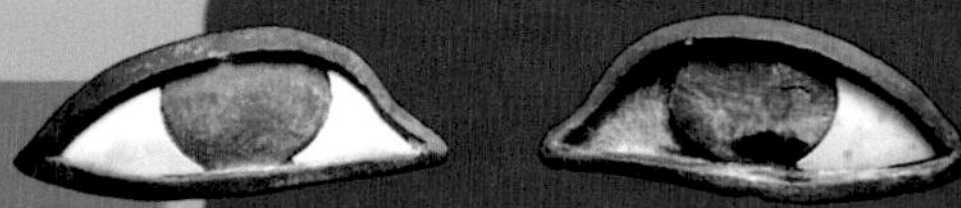

*This is what we see...*

Well, a superior that is constantly on top of things...

*This is what is happening...*

Here's what no one is supposed to hear, and we'll listen to what he truly feels...

"I have this new employee. And I'm worried. I do not trust her. And I don't know why"...

Two options could lead to this lack of trust...

Here's Option 1:
"She is very talented, and I like her. She is open-minded, and she has a way of interacting with people. I'd like her to be successful, but I'm worried that her approach could turn her to become a bit negligent... I will try to keep 'on top of things', and will check regularly how she is doing"...

Now, here's Option 2:
"This new employee is talented...
She is *very good* at her job. Sooner or later, I will find her opposing my authority. She *is* a threat, and I need to control what she is up to.
I am not jealous, though.
I know my own talents!"...

*What he must do…*

We have seen the sequence of a 'persuasive introspection', starting with acknowledging our Coping. Without being judgmental.

And this self-reflection, guided by our expressions of Coping, would point the manager, *in both options 1 and 2,* in the right direction. Why this stringent control? What is the threat that needs to be neutralized?

In the first option, it originates in 'true' intentions, fueled by a 'true' sense of concern with the well-being of one's employees. A subsequent question this form of Coping points to is: why this concern? And this could originate from a more 'selfish' cause, "to be manager of the best team, where everybody thrives".

The second option is of great concern. For these managers (through their uncertainties) seldom address these deeply rooted fears... They are indeed disruptive as leaders, for they lack the essence of leadership: a self-reflective attitude for the effects of their personal Coping strategies.

In the expressions of Coping, we see a large variety extending over many aspects of our lives. We had already observed a number of these expressions in the examples covered over previous Chapters, leading to intolerance, pride, obstinacy, prejudice. And we can now add the outcomes from these four Cases to this elaborate display.

In observing the effects in those Cases, we come to the disquieting conclusion that it is in these Stratagems of Coping that the causes can be found of many forms of miscommunication, dispute and conflict. When these Stratagems serve to neutralize the involvements of others, because they are perceived as intruding, those 'intruders', in turn, not only tend to react to the intense and often extreme nature of the interaction, as we can see from these examples, but also to the often uncompromising and irrational *content* of the message. *As illustrated in these Cases, it is essential to realize that the contents of those expressions are meant primarily for the interlocutor and only serve to neutralize or enhance external input.* And although the topic of how to address Stratagems of Coping exceeds the present context (aimed at a Process of Motivation and its expressions, and not at a Process of Interference), it is important to note that these expressions, be it negative or positive, primarily serve the cause of the individual, and not that of an external observer, who is often called to react, and thereby drawn into a debate which (as an almost inevitable resultant) often leads to the conflicts and misunderstandings we just referred to.

In addition, these disagreements are often started with persons who are important to us, or at least who hold an important position, important enough to be able to obstruct the course of a Process of Motivation that is aimed at reaching or sustaining important objectives. And although expressions of Coping can also produce positive effects in those relations with others, there seems to remain an undertone of 'self-oriented constraints' in these positive reactions towards a Reality that appear to predominantly serve a mainly self-centered cause.

So, in the effects they generate, the negative outcomes of Stratagems of Coping appear to exceed the positive benefits it contains.

Are we, then, to condemn these Stratagems of Coping and prevent ourselves from using them?

On the contrary!

They make us survive the hardships we encounter, and treasure the achievements we make. When joy, pleasure or happiness is called for, they inspire and strengthen these wonderful moments. When modesty or sobriety is more appropriate, they induce these necessary dispositions. And when protection, defense or even aggression is needed, they legitimize these expressions.

Stratagems of Coping are part of the 'human condition'. They serve to protect the ambitions, objectives, the Goals we treasure. They are our medicine, a panacea for all that life throws at us. But, as we saw, they can easily lead us astray, in expressions of intolerance, pride, obstinacy, prejudice, indifference...

Stratagems of Coping are our medicine. But they can very well turn against us. These powerful Mechanisms call for introspection; but a different kind of introspection we are perhaps accustomed to. This introspection contains a duality: we have to treasure and preserve Coping, *but at the same time we have to be fiercely aware of their existence, and be prepared to trace their whereabouts in the effects they produce on our surroundings.*

In this twofold introspection, it appears we stand alone. As the inherent exposure also contains the danger of renewed Coping when someone else steps in.

It is an activity, an act of will, where no distraction is to catch us by surprise.

In this, we have, in a sense, to transcend ourselves...

When Mechanisms of Representation and Mechanisms of Anticipation combine to form protective measures to protect a Significant Goal against an intruding, hence Significant Reality, these combinations become powerful defensive Mechanisms referred to as 'Stratagems of Coping', or 'Coping' for short.

Where Coping changes our perspective of Reality, it has profound implications...

*Stratagems of Coping are covered in more detail on pp. 352-354. A summary is on pp. 355-356.*

Stratagems of Coping, then, call for a personal form of 'persuasive introspection'. Not intended to avoid Coping and thereby disabling the indispensable remedies it provides, but to create awareness for the effects it inevitably causes to our surroundings.

*Let us recapitulate where we stand...*

*Stratagems of Coping are Mechanisms aimed at preserving a Significant Goal against an intruding Reality. They consist of combinations of Mechanisms of Representation and Mechanisms of Anticipation. They serve to protect the Goals we perceive as essential, and thereby serve a greater cause.*

*But Stratagems of Coping change our perspective of Reality, and hence have profound and even severe effects on ourselves and our surroundings. Coping makes us less open, or even inaccessible to Reality in its true manifestation. It bears the signs of intolerance, pride, obstinacy, prejudice, and indifference.*

*Stratagems of Coping are at the root of the 'human condition', and therefore deserve our full attention in the effects they produce.*

*But there is another profoundly important reason to address further awareness for the effects of Coping. Uncovering its implications is to conclude our study on the Process of Motivation, in the next and final Chapter...*

*The introduction of a Stratagem of Coping will prove to have profound Implications that extend far beyond the limitations set to the analysis in the present Volume of the study.*

*For further details, reference is made to Volume III in the 'Series on Motivation'.*

*Within the Series, Volume VIII is to further address the construct in more detail, notably as it refers to so-called 'Stratagems of Collective Coping', to be covered in the next Chapter.*

## *New Paradigms: Stratagems of Coping*

The Mechanisms seen in the previous Chapters, aimed at restoring balance, now come at a price...

Progressing through the subsequent Phases of the Process of Motivation, various Mechanisms appear that are aimed especially at addressing a Reality that interferes with the Process of Motivation aimed at reaching a Goal, and where a certain balance was reached in its first three Phases. Two Mechanisms appeared to be prominent, and both have been covered extensively: Mechanisms of Representation, in Chapter 9, and Mechanisms of Anticipation in Chapter 10.

When both Mechanisms combine to form protective measures to preserve our Goals, these combinations become defensive Mechanisms that are referred to as 'Stratagems of Coping', or 'Coping' for short[1] [2].

[1] This is the definition of Stratagems of Coping, used throughout Volume I, as a first introduction to the construct. This definition, however, slightly differs from the definition in its strictest sense, as used in the formal and more detailed overview on the Process of Motivation, as presented in Volume III of this 'Series on Motivation'.

It is assumed in the more formal definition of the construct that Mechanisms of Representation and Mechanisms of Anticipation produce, over subsequent cycles of the Process of Motivation, recurring patterns in the measures and strategies undertaken to increase or decrease the effects of an intervening Reality. Strategies that become more prominent as Significance of the Goal increases. These recurring patterns are referred to as so-called 'Patterns of Motivation'.

Following the formulation used throughout this introductory Volume, Mechanisms of Representation and Mechanisms of Anticipation produce a myriad of strategies that evolve into coherent patterns, defined as those recurring Patterns of Motivation. *In the more formal definition of the construct, then, a Stratagem of Coping is the combined manifestation of those Patterns of Motivation occurring as the individual, through a Process of Motivation, aims to reach a certain Goal.*

For further details, reference is made to Volume III of the Series, notably Chapter 5.2., Chapter 5.3., and summarized in Chapter 6.5.6. and Chapter 8.2.3.

[2] Within the 'Series on Motivation', Volume VIII is to address the construct in more detail, where we are to extend on its definition: Stratagems of Coping are 'the narratives we use to hide our deepest fears'.

Coping is the approach we seem to take when the Goal in its Significance necessitates protective measures against Reality. A Stratagem of Coping consists of both these Mechanisms, carefully attuned to one another. The more perceived Significance of the Goal increases, the more it reaches the heights of its 'protective potential'. In the Goals that are protected (especially in those referred to as 'latent' Goals), the effects of Coping can be concealed, as they find expression in intolerance, pride, obstinacy, prejudice, indifference, and many other related forms.

Previously, in Chapter 9 and Chapter 10, we found a number of recurrent tendencies in both these Mechanisms of Representation and Mechanisms of Anticipation. Thus, when both Mechanisms combine to form Stratagems of Coping, we can extrapolate those previous findings into two distinct states in which these Stratagems are likely to occur as the Process of Motivation progresses over subsequent cycles.

In summary:

- When Significance of the Goal increases,
- and perceived Significance of Reality increases,

  Mechanisms of Representation and Mechanisms of Anticipation become more prominent,
  merging into Stratagems of Coping as the Process of Motivation progresses over subsequent cycles,
  where Impact plays an important regulating role:

  - As Impact is perceived as increasingly positive, and Discrepancy therefore decreases:
    - Mechanisms of Representation tend to produce a Representation of Reality that is increasingly positive, where it is aimed at increasing these perceived positive effects on the Process of Motivation;
    - Mechanisms of Anticipation tend to anticipate on this positive Impact from Reality by progressively making use of this positive Representation over subsequent cycles of the Process, where,
      - either properties of the Goal remain unchanged, and Energy investment tends to increase,
      - or properties of the Goal change towards increased Clarity and/or increased Attainability, and Energy investment tends to increase accordingly,

      thereby further increasing the expected (positive) effects on the Process of Motivation.

- As Impact is perceived as increasingly negative, and Discrepancy thus increases:
  - Mechanisms of Representation tend to produce a Representation of Reality that is increasingly negative, whereby an attempt is made at neutralizing these perceived negative effects on the Process of Motivation;
  - Mechanisms of Anticipation tend to anticipate on this negative Impact from Reality by progressively making use of this negative Representation over subsequent cycles of the Process, where,
    - either properties of the Goal change towards increased Clarity and/or increased Attainability, and Energy investment tends to increase accordingly, thereby necessitating, however, more pronounced Mechanisms of Representation anticipating on the negative Impact from Reality,
    - or properties of the Goal change towards reduced Clarity and/or Attainability, and Energy investment remains at a same level or even decreases,

    thereby decreasing the expected (negative) effects on the Process of Motivation.

And, consequently, the main effects on the Process of Motivation can be further summarized:

- The more Significant the Goal,
- and the more Significant a perceived Reality,
  - the more pronounced the effects of these combined Mechanisms as manifested in Stratagems of Coping,
    - aimed at enhancing effects from Reality on the Process of Motivation, when Impact and Discrepancy are low and perceptions of 'support' are high,
    - aimed at neutralizing effects from Reality on the Process, when Impact and Discrepancy are high and perceptions of 'support' are low.

*Which then, in parallel with previous findings in Chapter 9 and Chapter 10, leads to our final conclusion that the more Significant our Goal, and the more Significant a perceived Reality, the more we tend to change this perceived Reality through these combined Mechanisms in Stratagems of Coping, and the less perceptible Reality becomes in its true manifestation...*

*In shortest summary: the more Significant our Goal, the more prominent these Stratagems of Coping, the more we change Reality, and the more we become inaccessible and intransigent to its influences.*

## *Summary*

Progressing over subsequent cycles, the Process of Motivation emerges as an intricate and powerful defense aimed at protecting the Goals it seeks to attain against outside interference.

Mechanisms of Representation and Mechanisms of Anticipation progressively combine and blend into these protective measures, which preserve the integrity of Significant Goals. These 'Mechanisms of the Mind' are referred to as 'Stratagems of Coping', or 'Coping' for short.

Stratagems of Coping are the outcome, the product of all Phases working together producing Mechanisms of Representation and Mechanisms of Anticipation that combine to address the intrusion from Reality on the Process of Motivation, for better and for worse. For better, as they preserve the integrity of the objectives we treasure most; for worse, as these Stratagems change our perception of the world around us.

The more Significant the Goal, the more Reality is encapsulated through Stratagems of Coping. And the less we perceive Reality in its true form, the less we are influenced, if at all, through its true and intended manifestation.

Those 'Mechanisms of the Mind' not only affect us and the way we perceive our world. In their 'Quest for Expression', they in turn profoundly influence our surroundings, the way we interact, affecting both our direct environment, family, friends and work-related, but also, on a broader scale, the communities we live in, extending even to society as a whole.

Stratagems of Coping protect and preserve. But these Mechanisms come at a price, as they appear to be the primal source, the origin, of expressions of intolerance, pride, obstinacy, prejudice and indifference. In the effects they generate, Stratagems of Coping call for an exceptional form of introspection. A personal form of 'persuasive introspection'. Not intended to avoid Coping and thereby disabling the indispensable remedies it provides, but to create awareness for the effects it inevitably causes.

This introspection therefore contains a duality: we have to treasure and preserve those Stratagems of Coping, *but at the same time we have to be fiercely aware of their existence, and be prepared to trace their whereabouts in the effects they produce on our surroundings.*

*Insight into the Process of Motivation can assist in this persuasive introspection. It can thus serve to preserve these protective measures, and at the same time guide a deliberate and forceful attempt aimed at their exposure, and as a testimony of their existence.*

# Chapter 12
## *The Abyss of our Time*
## *Stratagems of Collective Coping*

Although the advantages of Stratagems of Coping are clear and self-evident, we came to view the Process of Motivation from a new and unexpected angle through these expressions, and especially in the effects that appeared to occur.

Stratagems of Coping not only often produce dramatic outcomes for ourselves by changing the perceptions we have of Reality, but also appear to profoundly affect our surroundings. And these effects not only extend to our direct surroundings, but also, and most unexpectedly, to larger audiences, affecting the groups and communities we live in, and reaching even further, and in more general terms, to our present society as well. And these developments seem to have taken us by surprise.

The phenomenon, to some extent, exceeds the limits of our present study on the Process of Motivation, but deserves mentioning as we reach the final pages of our venture, because of the profound impact it appears to generate.

For the last hundred years, or so, we have witnessed numerous developments in science and technology that have led us to witness exceptional improvements in our daily lives on an unprecedented scale, ranging from education and communication to health and prosperity. *But these developments also brought upon us a sequel with consequences hitherto unknown to any society before us.*

When we interact, we not only communicate our day-to-day events, activities, affairs and concerns. We also, as observed, communicate expressions of Coping, which affects our surroundings, and, in turn, can initiate subsequent reactions. The incomparable speed at which technology has developed since the appearance of the radio in the early twentieth century, has now brought us means to be heard and to express ourselves to an extent that has increased exponentially over the last decades. First, through radio, newspapers and tabloids, then through television and a progressive increase in available channels, followed by the introduction of computers, the internet, which provided a new forum to an increasingly diverse audience, and extending even further into means of communications through digital technologies and online applications. And all these developments have led through journalism, commentaries, talk shows, films and documentaries, together with an extensive variety of social media, to an abundance of personalized expressions. And although these means to communicate serve a great cause, in which we are allowed to express ourselves as we are, they also create a platform to convey, often unintentionally, the Processes associated with Stratagems of Coping to a larger audience. Often larger than we would have intended.

One-liners that are used to reflect one's personal Coping are shared at exponential rates with many, and seized by others to address Coping strategies of their own. The excessive nature of these expressions often serves to evoke and propel corresponding ideas among many that share a necessity to protect and preserve Goals that are perceived to be exposed by a common Reality.

And when these Stratagems of Coping thus synchronize on a larger scale, these expressions unite to form powerful Mechanisms that work in synergy to enhance or neutralize Reality and thereby collectively change its true appearance. *When Stratagems of Coping coalesce to form these shared defensive strategies, collective forms of Coping emerge.*

*These expressions are referred to as 'Stratagems of Collective Coping', or 'Collective Coping' for short. Stratagems of Collective*

*Coping are the expression of shared Mechanisms originating from Processes of Motivation using identical or comparable strategies to address, and enhance or neutralize, shared perceptions of Reality, thereby protecting a Goal that is explicitly, or implicitly perceived as Significant.*

*Developments over the last hundred years have opened the world to these forms of Collective Coping on an unprecedented scale. And the effects it has on our daily lives are beyond measure.* When Stratagems of Coping synchronize to form Stratagems of Collective Coping, this unifies all the properties we observed so far. As we saw, it is characterized by a Reality perceived as Significant affecting a Goal that is also held in highest esteem. As with Stratagems of Coping, it emerges as a combination of a less open, or even inaccessible stand towards a perceived Reality in its true manifestation, and a Significant Goal that can be more diverse, but where the urge for protective measures is shared.

Let us observe a number of these expressions towards Reality, to acquaint ourselves with the phenomenon.

Effects take on a variety of forms. First, the expressions towards Reality need not be all harmful or destructive and can have a positive connotation. We see these expressions of Collective Coping during sports events, underlying an alleged supremacy of joint perceived Reality: "We stand united behind our invincible heroes or heroines!" In addition, we see these expressions in the shared feelings we have for our university, our 'alma mater', further enhanced in the position it holds in the numerous rank-ordered listings that often serve to accentuate these underlying expressions of Collective Coping.

But in their excessive nature, it is a small step from here to the negative images we are all familiar with, that also appear to characterize these same sports events. And we can extend these experiences to politics and elections. The slogans used in the various debates. They may have a benign nature at the start, but as the campaign progresses, the expressions of Collective Coping, initially aimed at expressing a shared belief and a common Reality, gradually tend to become negative and even turn evil as they progressively serve to neutralize a Reality that takes the form of 'the enemy', with all the unfortunate extremes we are called to witness every day.

Stratagems of Collective Coping can manifest themselves in harmless manifestations, but can easily turn into expressions towards Reality that brings a disquieting and even fearful attribute to the phenomenon. And in these negative expressions of Collective Coping lie the origins of evil.

These Mechanisms appear to have supremacy when driven to neutralize and change the appearance of Reality, thereby enabling actions that are beyond imagination and that open the door to tragedy. Where we are familiar with expressions of intolerance, pride, obstinacy, prejudice, and indifference at a personal level, these expressions now merge to form the seeds not only for arguments and dispute, but even for conflict and war; not only for misplaced chauvinism, which finds its fearful ways to xenophobia and discrimination, but even for excesses that can end in persecution and atrocities of genocide. It can merge into collective displays of indifference that lead to shared neglect of poverty and injustice that fall upon those who happen to be less fortunate in the circumstances in which they need to find their existence.

These effects obstruct, in turn, initiatives aimed at addressing these excesses of human nature. Here is where the inaccessibility of these Mechanisms plays an additional destructive role, frustrating dialogue, compromise and reconciliation.

In the impact stratagems of Coping appear to generate, an additional problem emerges. Recall that at the end of our first introduction to the phenomenon of Coping in the previous Chapter, it appeared that at a personal level a form of 'persuasive introspection' was needed. Not to avoid or disable Coping and the indispensable remedies it provides, but to create awareness for the repercussions it has for ourselves and our surroundings, before they turn into irrevocable consequences and courses of action. And this persuasive and strictly personal introspection becomes nearly impossible when Collective forms of Coping emerge. Where the one calls for reflective action, the other reacts to protect and maintain these expressions of Coping. The very Mechanisms that serve to protect our needs now become the machineries aimed at preventing exposure when expressed in a Collective form. Numerous discussions and debates appear to be reflections of these Mechanisms of Collective Coping. The intransigence of dialogues, the expressions of offensive nature, are the expressions of Collective Coping that often find fertile ground in the audiences they attract. And on the other side of the spectrum, when confronted with the atrocities of war and genocide, of poverty and injustice, we join to meet in Collective forms of Coping through the indifference we display, often to our own dismay. And even when we appear to come to a form of action, the forces of Collective Coping in similar expressions often prevent these initiatives from materializing into structural measures to adequately address these excesses.

These are expressions we are familiar with. These are the various manifestations of a Significant Reality that needs Collective forms to neutralize its Impact.

But what are the Goals that need such protection? They appear more diverse in nature. It could be Goals that find their roots in pride, or personal gain. Or in doctrine and dogma. Or in fear. These Goals are explicit in nature. But most of the Significant Goals that underlie and instigate these Collective forms of Coping are implicit in nature. Goals that we are often unaware of. We defined these Goals earlier as 'latent' Goals, Goals that were aimed at maintaining high principles and moral values in the way 'the world ought to be'...

Let us observe two examples that are familiar to us all, to illustrate not only how Stratagems of Collective Coping seem to work, but also how these Significant and often latent Goals play an unintended role in the subdued effects they produce.

*See exhibits next pages* ➔

*This is what we do...*

We 'turn away'...

*and why...*

Our venture into the origins of these Mechanisms has just started.

But this is what we seem to have uncovered so far...

These effects are rooted in neutralizing Mechanisms. Neutralizing Impact from Reality. If we appear to 'turn away', *it is not in indifference, it is in the awareness that we are facing a flagrant denial of those Goals we seem to treasure most. That life is 'mendable', that 'justice prevails'...*

When we are confronted with opposing forces to those so-called 'latent' Goals we treasure, we have but one option: to neutralize their Impact.

In this act to neutralize these fearsome forces lies the formidable challenge to find adequate venues and strategies to counteract these atrocities of our times...

## *Case 5 ~ Collective Coping*

*Here's the Case of a little child we saw a few years ago...*

*Reappearing time and time again, in different settings...*

*What must we do?...*

Although addressing this issue falls beyond the scope of this Volume, and we will need all our resources to (at least) venture into addressing these curses, we can make a first, modest start at this point *by acknowledging the workings of Stratagems of Collective Coping, and especially the effects they tend to generate.*

*At a later stage in our venture, when we found the essentials in tracing and addressing these Mechanisms, (especially in Volume VIII and Volume IX of the Series), we will extend on these reflections, to act accordingly.*


*This picture, which appears in the Prologue, at the start of Volume III of the 'Series on Motivation', made a deep personal impact when it appeared in August 2005. A picture of a child, barely alive and floating defenselessly, suspended on a scale as it was weighed in a refugee camp of Médecins Sans Frontières / Doctors Without Borders in Zinder, Niger. It is reproduced here, again, in deep appreciation to its author, Silver Camera and ICP Infinity Award laureate Geert van Kesteren.*

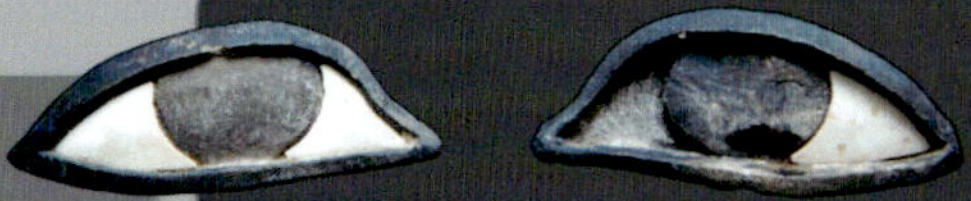

## Curses of Indifference ~ Refugees

*We watched...*

*And nothing happened.*
*Why this indifference?*

*This is what we see...*

A picture
that we can barely look at...

*This is what is happening...*

But it affects us
beyond words...

And fills us with shame and guilt...

As the facts are plain and simple: this child simply had the misfortune to have its cradle (or what is left of it) at the wrong place, at the wrong time...

## *Case 6 ~ Collective Coping*

*Final Case*
*And this one affects us all…*

*The ongoing debate on Climate Change…*

*This is what we do...*

We wait. We wait for governments to step in with initiatives...
We postpone...
At best we *'turn green'*...

But are we substantially doing what is needed?

*and why...*

As in our previous Case, we are opposing formidable forces...

These postponements, or 'cosmetic' actions, serve a cause. A cause aimed at neutralizing an 'inconvenient truth': that we are facing peril, or rather, that those who come after us will face imminent threat.

And here again, it appears that latent Goals that need protection at all costs are at the root of these Stratagems of Collective Coping. But this time, the expressions of these latent Goals are many. A most obvious latent Goal is to 'remain alive' and to 'be protected from impending disaster'. But they extend further, ranging from *guilt* (which leads to Collective expressions that "we can't help to address these forces that are beyond our measure"), to *being devastated* (as expressed in Collective forms to downgrade the events in various forms: "We have time, we can address this, and must find agreement amongst nations first to adequately take appropriate action").

Negligence and postponements are the inevitable result...

*What must we do?...*

To follow our metaphor:
Invest boldly and bravely, and *substantially*, to provide a full and adequate insurance against an imminent threat (without discussing the various expressions of this threat, as these are expressions of Collective Coping).

Better still: dive into the many forms already known to us in which we could invest, and then *act accordingly* by investing.

And thus, become accustomed to the changes in (household) expenditure that are necessary for this vital insurance...

*Again, we will extend on these reflections later in the Series when we found the essentials to address these Mechanisms, notably in Volume VIII and Volume IX.*

## Postponements ~ Climate Change

*And we watch...*
*As nothing substantially seems to happen...*
*Why the postponement of good intentions?*

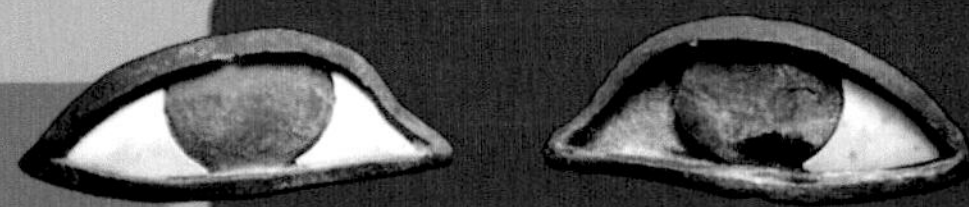

*This is what we see...*

For some: a perceived change in climate.
For all: a (heated) debate on climate.

The facts (e.g. see: IPCC 2021, 2022): a serious threat of imminent catastrophe...

*This is what is happening...*

In one word: *not much.*
If we observe what is at stake...

Consider a metaphor...
It is as if we remain without a proper insurance policy to cover the threat of fire, theft, or (in our case) imminent catastrophe facing, *not us (we hope), but the children of our children's children (for sure).*

This insurance policy will cost us dearly, and we somehow seem to hesitate, and thus remain uninsured... Thereby, unintentionally, exposing future generations...

And our offspring, *our kin...*

In both Cases, let us find common ground in the expression of a Reality we Collectively aim to neutralize: the atrocity of an image which is unbearable to look at, and the issue of our climate of which we know that the repercussions could be enormous and even irrevocable for generations to come.

So, Significant it is. Now, let us turn to the examples of the Goals that need such desperate protection.

They range from being explicit to implicit and latent in nature. From the previous Chapter, we are familiar with the explicit nature of Significant Goals that lead to expressions of Coping. So here we have chosen in both examples latent expressions of Significant Goals to illustrate the workings of these Stratagems of Collective Coping.

The first Case, Case 5, illustrates the effects of shared expressions which are, sadly, known to us all: the effects of a *seemingly* indifference to the unbearable images we face every day in the media. 'Seemingly', because previously we came to realize that these expressions are the product of Stratagems of Coping that aim to neutralize the effects of a highly intruding Reality which disturbs us deeply. This Reality overwhelms us because of its exposure, revealing a flagrant inadequacy when contrasted with a highly Significant latent Goal: our deeply rooted desire or need to live in a 'just' world, or at least a world that is 'mendable', or a world where 'justice and fairness prevail', or any other noble Goal that we desperately wish to be 'true and everlasting'. And these latent Goals deserve to be protected at all costs. Because, if we don't, "what else is there left for us?" or "what else would be the use of living?" or whatever else these images and perceptions evoke as reactions in us. And these latent Goals in their diversity are, inadvertently, at the root of subsequent Collective expressions, where they serve the cause to find a shared purpose in defending and maintaining these ideas and moral virtues captured in these latent Goals.

Stratagems of Collective Coping, then, serve to maintain and preserve these latent Goals, as Mechanisms of Coping do at an individual level. And these Stratagems of Collective Coping find expression in shared statements that this is "the sad story of our time", "which can't be helped", or "which has been with us for as long as we can recall". These bewildering expressions of indifference, in fact, *are meant to preserve the integrity of a highly Significant latent Goal, a deeply rooted urge, need, objective, by means of shared expressions of Coping.*

As we came to realize earlier, in Chapter 7, these latent Goals are seldom made to reconsider, as they represent our highest principles and moral values, as expressed in our beliefs not only that 'justice prevails', but also that we live in a world where equality, tolerance, honesty, integrity, trustworthiness are protected at all costs. And when faced with inescapable proof that flagrantly contradicts those latent Goals, we find ourselves confronted with a Reality that needs to be neutralized at all costs, in order to maintain our standards and preserve these Significant Goals.

These Collective expressions, then, synchronize to emphasize, and justify, the individual expressions of our own Coping. Stratagems of Collective Coping are shared defensive Mechanisms against a collectively perceived expression of Reality, as in the form of a picture in our example, in images that come to us every day; images that interfere with diverse expressions of Significant, often latent, Goals. In synchronized expressions, we find Collective grounds to neutralize the effects of these perceptions. *And these shared Mechanisms make us neutralize and seemingly turn indifferent to a plethora of Realities that come to us, extending not only to images but to witnessing through all possible media the recurring curses, and even atrocities of our time. From intolerance, pride and obstinacy, to arguments and dispute, to conflict and war. From prejudice to discrimination, to the atrocities of persecution or even genocide. And indifference and neglect towards the many forms of injustice, and poverty that we witness every day.*

Stratagems of Collective Coping can thus be made to protect and maintain latent Goals in areas that even affect the socio-economic and political agendas of our time.

Our second example, Case 6, further illustrates these effects.

Although it might seem at times to be only a vehement debate, the issue of climate change also contains elements that originate from Stratagems of Collective Coping.

As we saw, a common Reality needs to be neutralized in its potential Impact at all costs. But which latent Goal contains such Significance, and needs protective action from so many, that it generates shared Stratagems of Coping in such a vast number of expressions? A majority of these expressions of Collective Coping are likely to find their origin in a latent existential Goal we all share (and with good reason): to 'remain alive' and to 'be protected from evil', or 'impending disaster'. And 'to remain so and live happily ever after'. And exposing all kinds of threatening scenarios, is likely to affect this urge, that characterizes us all as a necessity of our very existence. The danger that our climate might change beyond repair is a perceived Reality that profoundly affects this most Significant Goal for survival. And this latent Goal is most likely to produce Stratagems of Coping that seek for shared expressions to further reinforce these protective measures. These Stratagems of Collective Coping directly, and indirectly, find their way in shared expressions and statements neutralizing the intrusion, either by disregarding or questioning its effects ("All these stories are speculations"), or by overstating its consequences ("Can you imagine the implication this has in personal expenditures, let alone on our economy?"), articulated in often emotional statements, discussions and debates on a range of available media. And when these expressions of Coping, which serve to protect these highly Significant latent Goals, come to synchronize into Collective forms of Coping, a plethora of expressions conveniently progresses us away from the central issue that desperately needs attention in the existential threat it imposes.

And such are the effects that Stratagems of Collective Coping often lead to postponement, frustration and delay.

Stratagems of Collective Coping appear to affect many of the current issues of our time, where we find ourselves in debates, discussions and polemics instead of securing ourselves with master plans to ensure safety for the latent Goals that are at the origin of most of these expressions. There is no master plan for when the lights go out on the children of our children's children...

*When Stratagems of Coping evolve into forms of Collective Coping, it enables the acceptance of the unacceptable, the turning away from concerns that directly affect future generations. And they not only involve these issues of climate change used as an example, but extend also to our attitude and the limited measures we take in addressing distribution of wealth and abuse of scarce resources, to name but a few.*

Stratagems of Coping and Collective Coping are part of the human condition, and justify further study, not only into their origins, as part of the Process of Motivation, but even more prominently, into the means to address these powerful defenses.

In the 'Series on Motivation' the issue of Coping and Collective Coping will be studied in its various expressions, emerging in subsequent Volumes, and seeking the steps that are needed to get there.

After having finalized our assumptions and findings in Volumes II and III, subsequent Volumes IV, V and VI are to lay a foundation for addressing the Mechanisms of Coping in an extensive analysis of the Process of Interference, with research findings to be elaborated on in Volume VII. And from these findings, we are to seek implications for Stratagems of Coping and Collective Coping in Volumes VIII and IX, and, from a different perspective, in Volume X.

When Stratagems of Coping find expression to larger audiences through a gradual and exponential increase in present-day media that we find at our disposal, these expressions can synchronize into collective forms of Coping, defined as 'Stratagems of Collective Coping'.

In these Stratagems of Collective Coping, the effects of Mechanisms of Representation and Mechanisms of Anticipation are prominent. With far-reaching implications, as observed in preceding Chapters...

*Stratagems of Coping are covered in more detail on pp. 372-373. A summary is on pp. 374-375.*

To conclude, then, expressions of Collective Coping appear to be found are everywhere. Where the Process of Motivation profoundly defines our lives, these shared and synchronized expressions also appear to be an essential part of the 'human condition' as well, where they provide us, in shared forms, with the protective measures needed to address the complexities of our present-day societies. For better and for worse.

Tracing the origins of these expressions has brought us here. And having made a first step in exposing these Stratagems, it now falls upon us to further extend on these findings.

However, providing further insights into these Mechanisms is one thing, addressing those Stratagems is another. As stated, it extends beyond the scope of the present introduction into the Processes involved in Motivation. Addressing Stratagems of Coping means addressing essential Mechanisms that lie at the heart of these Processes. And addressing Motivation needs further knowledge in the Processes we referred to in the Introduction as 'Processes of Interference'.

If we are called to meet the challenge of addressing the very Mechanisms that affect our present-day lives in the form of these Stratagems of Collective Coping, we first need to find our way to disclose the fundamentals of these Processes of Interference.

The end of this first introduction of a Model which aims at unveiling the Processes of Motivation, marks the start of a new venture as we progress through the next Volumes of this 'Series on Motivation', into unveiling the essential elements of these Processes of Interference.

## *New Paradigms: Stratagems of Collective Coping*

Let us recapitulate the essentials.

When Mechanisms of Anticipation and Mechanisms of Representation combine to form protective measures to preserve our Goals, these combinations become defensive Mechanisms that are referred to as 'Stratagems of Coping'.

The more Significant the Goal, the more pronounced these Stratagems of Coping become. And the more Reality becomes encapsulated by protective measures, and the less we perceive Reality in its 'true' form, and the less accessible we become for expressions of Reality in its 'true' manifestation.

When through present-day media these expressions are shared on a large scale, Stratagems of Coping can synchronize into shared defensive strategies against a commonly perceived Reality. When Stratagems of Coping coalesce to form these shared defensive strategies, collective forms of Coping emerge.

These expressions are referred to as 'Stratagems of Collective Coping', or 'Collective Coping' for short. Stratagems of Collective Coping are the expression of shared Mechanisms originating from Processes of Motivation using identical or comparable strategies to address, and enhance or neutralize shared perceptions of Reality, thereby protecting a Goal that is explicitly, or implicitly perceived as Significant[1].

Where Stratagems of Collective Coping originate from Stratagems of Coping, a number of distinctive characteristics can, at this point, be observed from the preliminary conclusions drawn in the previous Chapter:

[1] These Stratagems of Collective Coping are to be covered, together with Stratagems of Coping, in Volume VIII of the 'Series on Motivation'.

Two distinct states in which Stratagems of Coping are likely to occur were previously summarized:

- The more Significant the Goal,
- and the more Significant a perceived Reality,
    - the more pronounced the effects of Stratagems of Coping,
        - aimed at enhancing effects from Reality on the Process of Motivation, when Impact and Discrepancy are low and perceptions of 'support' are high,
        - aimed at neutralizing effects from Reality on the Process, when Impact and Discrepancy are high and perceptions of 'support' are low.

As Coping is expressed towards Reality, it is in the expression of a shared Representation that commonality is most likely to be found through present-day media.

As observed previously in Chapter 9, the more Significant the Goal, and the more Significant a perceived Reality, the more pronounced these Representations tend to become. Consequently, these expressions of Collective Coping find common ground in shared Representations, that tend be characterized by pronounced forms.

Two consequences are most likely to occur, as based on our conclusions from previous Chapters:

- The more expressions of Coping are shared in Collective forms of Coping,
- and the more they find common ground in shared Representations that are characterized by their pronounced form,
    - the more excessive these Stratagems of Collective Coping become,
    - the less a shared perception of Reality in its 'true' form becomes,
    - and the less one becomes accessible for effects intended to occur through expressions of Reality in its 'true' form.

*In shortest summary, the more prominent these Stratagems of Collective Coping, the more they change Reality, and the more one becomes inaccessible and intransigent to its influences.*

## *Summary*

Stratagems of Coping are the outcome, the product of all Phases working together in a Process of Motivation, producing Mechanisms of Representation and Mechanisms of Anticipation that combine to address the intrusion from Reality, thus protecting the Goals we treasure against interference, either positive, or negative.

Those Stratagems of Coping, protect and preserve. They are bound to the Process of Motivation, for better and for worse. For better, as they preserve the integrity of these Significant Goals, as we observed in Chapter 11. For worse, as these Stratagems of Coping not only change our perception of the world around us, but also, in reciprocity, appear to have profound effects on our surroundings, and even affect our society and the socio-economic and political agendas of our time. This final Chapter was to address these repercussions.

In the last decades, we have witnessed numerous developments in science and technology that have led us to improvements in our daily lives, ranging from education and communication to health and prosperity. But these developments also brought upon us a sequel with consequences that has been unknown to any society before. And it appears that we failed to observe and fully grasp the depth of these consequences.

For these developments, have also brought us ways to be heard and to express ourselves to an extent that has increased exponentially through means of communication, providing a forum to an abundance of personalized expressions. And although these means to communicate serve a great cause, they also create a platform to convey, often unintentionally, the Processes associated with Stratagems of Coping to a larger audience. Often larger than we would have intended.

When these expressions of Coping spread through the extensive forms of present-day media, they are shared at exponential rates with many, and can be seized by others to address Coping strategies of their own.

When these Stratagems of Coping thus synchronize on a larger scale, these expressions unite to form powerful Mechanisms that work in synergy to enhance or neutralize Reality and thereby collectively change its true appearance. *When Stratagems of Coping coalesce to form these shared defensive strategies, collective forms of Coping emerge. These expressions are referred to as 'Stratagems of Collective Coping', or 'Collective Coping' for short.*

*These Stratagems of Collective Coping, then, synchronize the individual expressions we observed and turn them into shared expressions. And when these Stratagems of Coping thus meet to coalesce into Stratagems of Collective Coping, they seldom come to bear the fruits of good, but rather turn into seeds of evil, where individual expressions of intolerance, pride, obstinacy, prejudice and indifference turn into shared expressions of conflict, discrimination, and collective displays of indifference and neglect towards injustice, poverty and even genocide, where initiatives addressing these atrocities fail to materialize.*

Tracing the origins of these expressions has brought us here. And having made a first step in exposing these Stratagems, it now falls upon us to further extend on those findings.

The end of this first introduction of a Model of Motivation is to mark the start of a new venture, as we progress in further Volumes of this 'Series on Motivation' into unveiling the essential elements to address this Process of Motivation and the Mechanisms they appear to contain.

To be able, in due course, to provide insights into addressing these Stratagems that profoundly affect the world we live in.

# Summary
## *Motivation:*
## *Mechanisms of the Mind and their Quest for Expression*

In their 'Quest for Expression', 'Mechanisms of the Mind' appear to manifest themselves in many forms, which not only include positive expressions, but also expressions of intolerance, pride, obstinacy, prejudice and indifference, which can extend into shared forms that are at the root of complex issues of modern-day society.

The Process of Motivation appears to play a central role in all of these expressions. And this conclusion is both disturbing and hopeful. Although the unmistakable outcome is that these expressions are made almost inaccessible by clever and intricate Mechanisms, the good news is that they appear to be construed as composites, or expressions of one and the same recurring Process of Motivation. If, in time, we want to address these issues, a fundamental knowledge of this Process of Motivation appears to be essential.

We are, then, in search of an overall 'architecture' of this Process of Motivation.

In summarizing major findings, a Model of Motivation is proposed, in which Motivation appears to be a stepwise, sequential Process that is centered around an objective the individual seeks to achieve, as it progresses over time. The Process of Motivation consists of a sequence of eight successive steps, or 'Phases', in which various Mechanisms play distinctive roles. In following pages, these Phases and Mechanisms are briefly described and summarized in their specific expressions and in the effects they produce.

# Phase 1 - A Phase of Expectancies

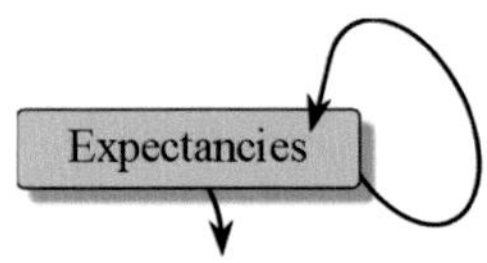


*Fig. 13.1.*
*A Phase of Expectancies*
*Visualized as part of successive Phases*
*in the Model of Motivation*

The Process of Motivation can be visualized in its distinct progressive Phases, as depicted in Fig. 13.1. and in successive figures that are provided in Fig. 13.2. to Fig. 13.8.

The first Phase of the Process of Motivation is a *Phase of Expectancies.* It is a Phase consisting of subsequent Stages in which, in progressive, circular steps, a Goal is defined. It is a cognitive, mental, evaluative Phase, in which no overt action occurs. In this Phase, not only the Goal, but also its importance or 'Significance' is defined.

A Phase of Expectancies, in turn, initiates a train of subsequent Phases, some of which are characterized by a similar circularity, whereas others progress more straightforwardly, in successive order.

And this sequence of subsequent steps, or Phases, will lead to an intricate Process which evolves around a specific Goal that has been designed, or 'generated', in this first Phase of Expectancies. This set of distinct, subsequent Phases centered around a Goal is what characterizes the Process of Motivation, where each Goal has its own distinct sequential Process.

# Phase 2 - A Phase of Effort

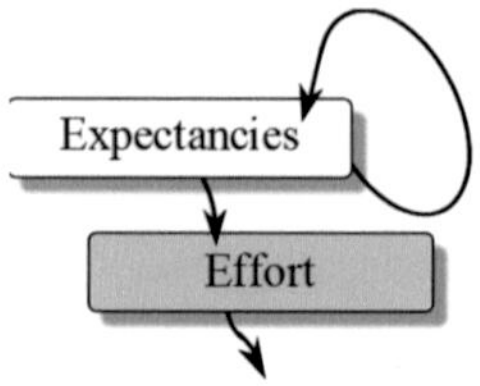


*Fig. 13.2.*
*A Phase of Effort*
*Visualized as part of successive Phases*
*in the Model of Motivation*

Everything changes in the second Phase of the Process. Phase 2, a *Phase of Effort,* is a Phase of action, of behavior and overt activity.

Once the action occurs, there is 'no way back'...

So, by its nature, this Phase is to lead to subsequent Phases that form a reaction to the explicit action that is displayed.

Not all Processes of Motivation progress into this second Phase. As many Goals that we set ourselves fail to materialize, and no follow-up in subsequent action occurs, the Process of Motivation in these instances remains as a 'fantasy', or 'dream', confined within a first Phase of Expectancies.

When action occurs, however, in a Phase of Effort, the Process of Motivation progresses into a third Phase.

# Phase 3 - A Phase of Internally Evoked Self-Assessment

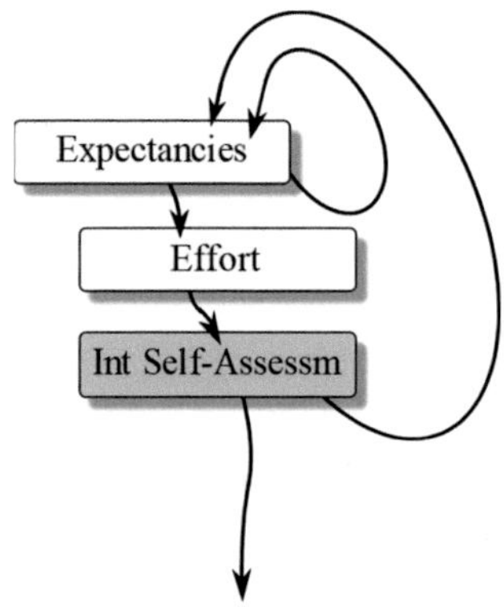


*Fig. 13.3.*
*A Phase of Internally Evoked Self-Assessment*
*Visualized as part of successive Phases*
*in the Model of Motivation*

Phase 3, a *Phase of Internally Evoked Self-Assessment,* evaluates the outcomes of the display of action from the previous Phase of Effort.

And it does so at a personal level; at a point in the Process of Motivation where no outside, external influences from others, or from interfering events, have yet occurred. It is a personal assessment by the individual, leading to further amendments made in a Phase of Expectancies; and as such, it turns the first three Phases of Motivation into a circular Process.

This 'cyclical attunement' eventually leads to a form of balance, or 'stasis', where the Goal, the investment, and the revenues it yields are gradually perceived to be in accord with each other.

## Phase 4 - A Phase of Reality

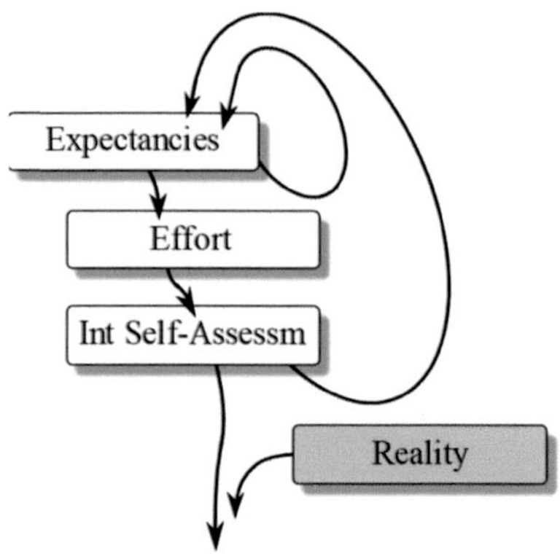


*Fig. 13.4.*
*A Phase of Reality*
*Visualized as part of successive Phases*
*in the Model of Motivation*

As balance occurs within this 'cyclical attunement', our intention is to maintain a status quo where invested Effort progressively yields the revenues we seek in attainment of the Goal.

Unfortunately, however, this 'cocooned' balance, is in most cases to be disrupted by input from an external event, or series of events. Phase 4 of the Process of Motivation is appropriately referred to as a *'Phase of Reality'*. It is the unforeseen event, actor, action, occurrence that, in one's perception, affects the Process of Motivation as it has progressed so far.

In a Phase of Reality, this perception is expressed in terms of importance, or Significance of Reality.

# Phase 5 - A Phase of Impact

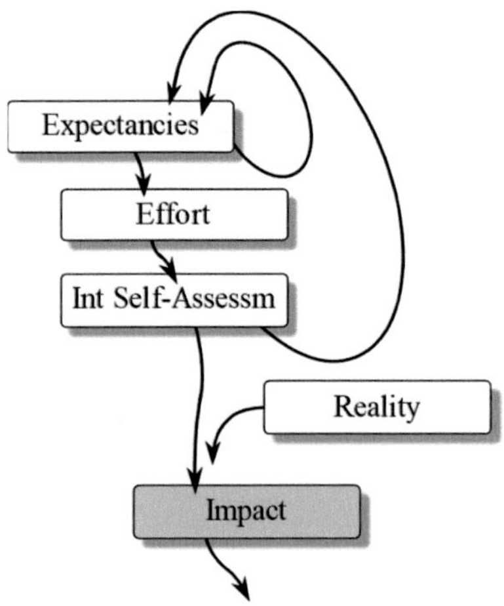


*Fig. 13.5.*
*A Phase of Impact*
*Visualized as part of successive Phases*
*in the Model of Motivation*

In a subsequent Phase, following the introduction of Reality, the consequences are assessed of this intrusion in the Process of Motivation: the fifth Phase in the Process is a *Phase of Impact.*

Given this new perspective, following the introduction of Reality, is there a mismatch, a gap, between the Goal that was carefully attuned in the first Phases of the Process and this 'confrontation with the unexpected'?

A Phase of Impact is expressed in terms of 'Discrepancy': when the Impact has a positive effect on the Process of Motivation, in one's perception, Discrepancy is small; when the Impact is perceived to be negative, Discrepancy is large.

## Phase 6 - A Phase of Externally Evoked Self-Assessment

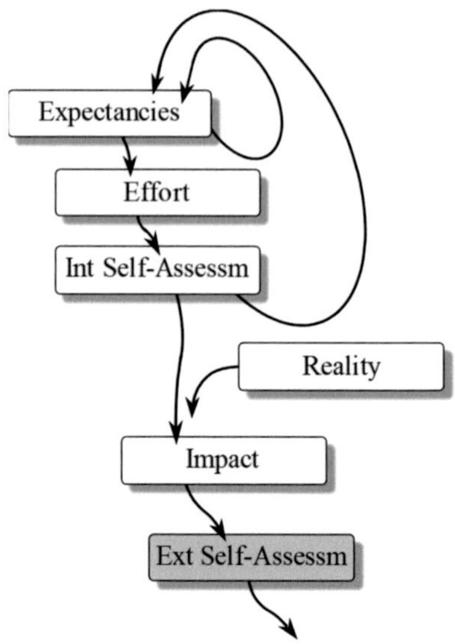


*Fig. 13.6.*
*A Phase of Externally Evoked Self-Assessment*
*Visualized as part of successive Phases*
*in the Model of Motivation*

This new state of affairs calls for subsequent re-assessments, the first of which is a *Phase of Externally Evoked Self-Assessment.* In this first re-assessment, the adequacy of the Goal and its properties is observed: "Did I do well to define the Goal the way I did, and the investment I made, with its various subsequent assessments?" However, no actual amendments are made in this Phase yet, as adjustments are only to be made in a Phase of Expectancies...

# Phase 7 - A Phase of Anticipated Change

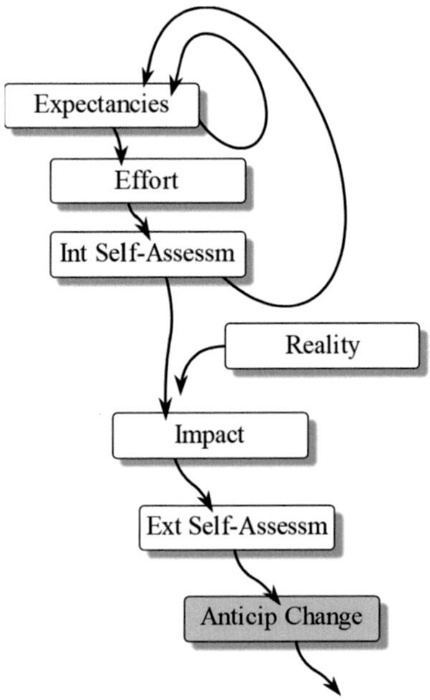


*Fig. 13.7.*
*A Phase of Anticipated Change*
*Visualized as part of successive Phases*
*in the Model of Motivation*

And this first assessment is followed by a second, in which an appropriate strategy is defined for potential amendments. As in the previous Phase, it is a Phase in which we only anticipate on these potential courses of action: it is a *Phase of Anticipated Change.* In this Phase, we focus not on the Goal, but rather on the Discrepancy between our intentions captured in our Goal and Reality: Are we to maintain, increase or decrease the perceived Discrepancy?

# Phase 8 - A Phase of Dedication

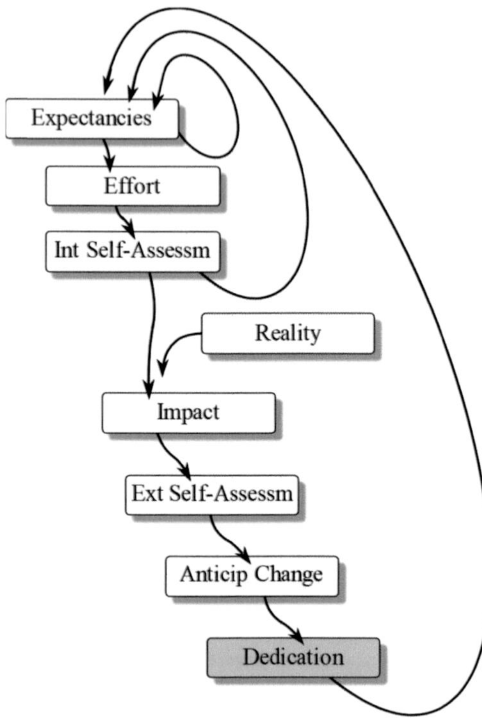


*Fig. 13.8.*
*A Phase of Dedication*
*Visualized as part of successive Phases*
*in the Model of Motivation*

The two assessments made in both previous Phases finally lead to a third and final assessment, following the Impact from Reality: a *Phase of Dedication.*

After having re-assessed the Goal, and the Discrepancy that has occurred, we now come to assess Reality.

And there are two important outcomes.

First, in a primary and secondary evaluation of the Impact from Reality that has occurred, we observe, in a passive sense, the effects from Reality: do we feel supported, acknowledged, respected by Reality? And subsequently, in a secondary evaluation, we actively return these sentiments: do we support, acknowledge, respect Reality, in return?

And second, these primary and secondary evaluative reactions lead to the fabrication of an image, a notion, or impression we have of Reality, defined as a 'Representation', that is heavily based on both evaluations in our perceptions of Reality.

The Phase of Dedication is the final Phase in the Process of Motivation. As the threefold assessment that has occurred in the last three Phases provides the basis for a renewed definition of the Goal and its various associated parameters, the Process of Motivation now progresses to implement those amendments.

As a result, the Process of Motivation returns to its original settings, made in a Phase of Expectancies, and thus becomes cyclical.

The Process of Motivation, then, is a stepwise, sequential Process that evolves around a Goal, and gradually progresses towards attainment in eight distinct Phases, where interference from Reality is assessed and counteractive measures are anticipated upon. As the Process progresses through these Phases, it returns to its initial settings to implement these measures, and becomes cyclical.

Each Goal thus has its own Process of Motivation. And all these Processes of Motivation coexist and influence each other in multiple reciprocities, where each Process of Motivation proceeds in comparable Phases, but retains its specific character instigated by the Goal that defines each separate Process.

# Emerging Mechanisms

In this sequence of successive Phases, which progresses over subsequent cycles, the Process of Motivation becomes increasingly complex.

In disentangling these intricacies, two Mechanisms are essential: a *Mechanism of Representation* and a *Mechanism of Anticipation.*

### *A Mechanism of Representation*

Emerging as a principal outcome of the last Phase, a Phase of Dedication, one has had one's experience with Reality confirmed and captured in a Representation.

We do not see Reality as it is, we see Reality in an image, a notion, or impression, defined as a 'Representation'. Mechanisms of Representation make adaptations of Reality produced as an outcome of consecutive Phases following Impact. The more Significant our Goal, the more pronounced these Mechanisms of Representation.

In Mechanisms of Representation, two outcomes predominate:

- When the effects of Impact from Reality are perceived as positive for the Process of Motivation, one tends to overstate or even exaggerate these effects, thereby accentuating Reality: a manager, teacher, lecturer or friend who acknowledges our input, performance, creativity or intellect becomes "the best *ever* manager, teacher, lecturer, friend"...
- When the Impact is perceived as disruptive to the Process of Motivation in reaching a particular Goal, one tends to do the opposite by degrading or even caricaturizing Reality: "The *worst* manager, teacher, lecturer, friend I have ever had"...

### *A Mechanism of Anticipation*

As the Process of Motivation progresses over subsequent cycles, experience is gradually obtained on how Reality interferes with one's attempt to reach the Goal. And as experience builds up, one can anticipate on events to come.

Mechanisms of Anticipation manifest themselves in two forms:

- When effects of Impact from Reality are perceived to be positive for the Process of Motivation, the Mechanism is aimed at further increasing those effects, as they are likely to occur in a renewed cycle, and can thereby serve to propel the Process towards reaching the Goal;
- When the Impact is perceived as negative and disruptive to the Process of Motivation, the Mechanism is aimed at neutralizing these effects.

Mechanisms of Anticipation can take on many forms, three of which are prominent: by increasing or decreasing *Clarity* of the Goal, or its perceived *Attainability*, one can anticipate on minimizing interference from Reality. In addition, by re-attuning *Investment in Effort,* both Mechanisms can be further improved in these effects.

# Stratagems of Coping

As the Process of Motivation progresses over subsequent cycles, Mechanisms of Representation thus produce convenient alternatives that serve as substitute for Reality. And Mechanisms of Anticipation are used to further neutralize or enhance the effects of Impact on the Process.

And the more Significant the Goal, the more pronounced these Mechanisms become, not only in their distinct expressions, but especially in the way they combine to form dynamics that produce powerful forces defying Reality as it manifests itself. And over subsequent cycles these Mechanisms are further adjusted and attuned to serve this purpose, as experience builds up.

Thus, Mechanisms of Representation merge with Mechanisms of Anticipation to form compelling forces against outside interference. These powerful expressions of combined protective Mechanisms are referred to as *'Stratagems of Coping'*, or *'Coping'* for short.

All Goals that are perceived to be Significant lead to these protective measures in the form of Stratagems of Coping.

The emergence of Stratagems of Coping in the Process of Motivation, has a number of profound implications.

Through Stratagems of Coping, perceptions of Reality in its 'true' manifestation are inevitably affected, and can create distance and confusion in the Representation of Reality they propagate. Moreover, as these expressions of Coping are meant to address Reality and our surroundings, they are likely to affect those surroundings as well, in reciprocity, where they can cause further distance and confusion in our interactions with our direct environment, family, friends, or in work-related settings.

But these individual expressions of Coping can also, on a larger scale, affect groups, communities and social gatherings, even to extend into affecting our present society.

Stratagems of Coping, in their expression, can be shared with larger audiences and made to proliferate through an extensive increase in available media in modern-day society. And when these Stratagems of Coping synchronize on a larger scale, these individual expressions unite to form powerful Mechanisms that work in synergy to enhance or neutralize Reality, and thereby, collectively, change its true appearance. When Stratagems of Coping coalesce to form these shared defensive strategies, Collective forms emerge, that are referred to as *'Stratagems of Collective Coping'*, or *'Collective coping'* for short.

Stratagems of Collective Coping are the expression of shared Mechanisms, using comparable common strategies to address and enhance or neutralize shared perceptions of Reality, thereby protecting a Goal that is explicitly, or implicitly perceived as Significant.

Developments over the last hundred years have opened the world to these forms of Collective Coping on an unprecedented scale. And the effects it has on our daily lives appear to be extensive.

# *The Model of Motivation: Definitions*

Let us summarize in more detail the Process of Motivation, as it unfolds according to the Model of Motivation that has been proposed.

The Process of Motivation is assumed to consist of a series of successive Phases, partly cyclical in nature, where the individual gradually progresses towards an objective that has been set.

A description of each Phase and its constituting Stages is presented in Chapter 1 to Chapter 8, covering each of these distinct Phases in the Model of Motivation. It is assumed the Process of Motivation evolves and proceeds in eight distinct Phases, each comprising of separate Stages:

- *1. A Phase of Expectancies;* The Process of Motivation is initiated by a Phase of Expectancies, consisting of five Stages that are part of a cognitive Process that is anticipatory in nature, where the objective, or 'Goal', is defined which characterizes the Process of Motivation, and where a careful assessment occurs of levels of investment and expected outcomes. The Process in these first Stages is cyclical in nature, where the Goal is progressively fine-tuned and optimized to meet the needs of the individual.
- *2. A Phase of Effort;* This Process of mentally balancing investment and expected gains and losses in a Phase of Expectancies is assumed to lead in a number of cases to an actual, concrete and physical investment. In a Phase of Effort, the intentions materialize into action that is aimed at reaching the Goal that has been previously defined.
- *3. A Phase of Internally Evoked Self-Assessment;* After having invested the actual Effort, a twofold evaluative Phase of Internally Evoked Self-Assessment assesses the outcomes of these concrete activities in two Stages, both in objective, economic terms and from a subjective, emotional point of view.

  And this third Phase, in turn, leads to a re-assessment of the parameters that were initially set in a first Phase of Expectancies, thus turning the Process of Motivation into a cyclical system. These first three Phases of the Process of Motivation are 'self-propelling', gradually progressing into a balanced system, carefully matching intended and actual Effort to expected outcomes.

  Within this 'cocooned balance', however, interference is likely to occur.
- *4. A Phase of Reality;* within this balance, then, an external, unexpected

event is likely to occur and to disrupt this self-regulated Process. It is in this subsequent confrontation that the Process of Motivation dramatically changes into a Process aimed at neutralizing these effects. In a Phase of Reality, the individual is confronted with an unexpected event, or chain of events, that is experienced as interrupting the Process of Motivation and the balance reached within the first three Phases. In a Phase of Reality, an assessment is made of the importance, or 'Significance' of this occurrence interrupting the Process of Motivation.

- *5. A Phase of Impact;* The Model of Motivation assumes Reality has two dimensions: its 'Significance' or importance, as previously defined in a Phase of Reality, and its Impact, or 'Discrepancy'. In a Phase of Impact, the effects are assessed that are experienced by the individual, and expressed as a Discrepancy between the Goal that has been set and Reality interfering.
- *6. A Phase of Externally Evoked Self-Assessment;* Preceding possible re-adjustments in the Goal and its associated parameters in reaction to the confrontation with Reality, a threefold assessment occurs.
The first of these three focuses on the Goal and the Assumptions initially made. In a Phase of Externally Evoked Self-Assessment, the initial settings made in a Phase of Expectancies are assumed to be re-assessed in five Stages on their effectiveness and adequacy, given the Impact that has occurred with Reality.
- *7. A Phase of Anticipated Change;* The second of the three passive evaluative Phases, a Phase of Anticipated Change, can be defined as an 'anticipating reflection on change'. It assesses in five Stages a readiness for change in these initial settings, in an attempt to diminish the Discrepancy observed. It focuses, then, on Discrepancy given the Impact that occurred with Reality.
- *8. A Phase of Dedication;* The Process of Motivation ends in a Phase of Dedication, finalizing in four Stages the threefold passive evaluative reactions towards Reality, where the individual is assumed to assess effects of Reality in terms of perceived 'support' or 'non-support'.
Thus, a Phase of Dedication focuses on Reality, given the Impact that has occurred on the Process. It is a 'grand total' of the Process of Motivation, where all previous Phases play a role in determining this experience of Reality.

The Process of Motivation subsequently progresses into making the adjustments anticipated on in the threefold assessment in reaction to the unexpected confrontation with Reality. By reverting to a Phase of Expectancies, the Process of Motivation reaches its final state and becomes cyclical.

As the Process of Motivation progresses into a second cycle, the individual deals with the effects encountered in the confrontation with Reality observed during a first cycle of the Process.

In this second cycle of the Process of Motivation, the various Stages of a Phase of Expectancies are carefully re-attuned in a cyclical Process, following the previous experience with Reality. In re-defining the Goal and intended investment versus gains and losses, the individual anticipates on the interference from Reality that is expected to re-emerge in a renewed confrontation. So-called 'Mechanisms of Anticipation' are being introduced to either enhance the influence of Reality when its Impact is perceived as positive for the Process of Motivation, or to further reduce the influence of Reality when its Impact is perceived as negative.

Perceptions of 'support' or 'non-support' that have previously been made in a Phase of Dedication, initiate so-called 'Mechanisms of Representation' where the effects of Reality are thus neutralized to preserve the integrity of the Process in its attempts to reach the Goal.

These Mechanisms of Anticipation and Representation work together in synergy to address Reality, neutralizing or enhancing its Impact on the Process of Motivation, and both Mechanisms thereby combine their forces to form so-called 'Stratagems of Coping', or 'Coping', through which the Goal is thus protected from exposure and interference. The more Significant the Goal, the more pronounced these Stratagems of Coping become.

These expressions of Coping in the Process of Motivation, by their nature, can lead to expressions that range in extremes from positive to negative, in recurrent forms of behavior or activities as they tend to be manifested in reaching one's objectives. And as these expressions of Coping serve to protect and preserve the objectives we treasure most, they are often used to conceal these inner desires from interference from a surrounding Reality. Insights in one's expressions of Coping can lead to insights in our hidden drives, intentions or 'motives'. In short, insights into Stratagems of Coping reveal, in the strictest sense, 'why we do the things we do'.

Fig. 13.9., then, summarizes these distinct Phases that constitute the Process of Motivation, as proposed by the Model. A brief description is provided of these Phases as they progress towards Goal attainment in successive cyclical steps, characterizing each Process of Motivation.

*See exhibit next page* ➔

## *A Summarized Overview of the Model of Motivation*

A summarizing overview of the Process of Motivation, as proposed by the Model of Motivation, visualizing its successive Phases and its cyclical nature:

The Process of Motivation originates from a *Phase of Expectancies*, where the Goal is defined in its distinct properties, on some occasions leading to concrete action in a *Phase of Effort*, which in turn is assessed on its inherent Achievements or Failures, its Satisfactions or Frustrations. This subsequently leads to re-amendments of the initial Goal and its properties. Leading eventually to a status quo where a cyclical balance is achieved between Goal attainment and invested Effort...

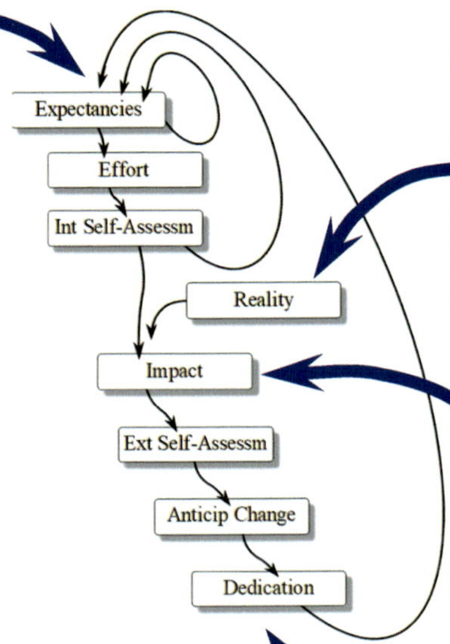


*Fig. 13.9.*
*An overview of successive Phases in the Model of Motivation*

A *Phase of Reality* disrupts this 'cocooned' balance. And an appraisal of Significance of the interference is made...

In a subsequent *Phase of Impact*, the effects on the Process are observed in terms of Discrepancy. When effects are negative, Discrepancy is large, when positive they are perceived as small...

And these observations, in turn, lead to re-appraisals of one's Goal and the settings that were made, and of the interference that occurred in subjective evaluations of Reality in a *Phase of Dedication.*

## *The Model of Motivation: Related Theories*

The Model of Motivation, then, provides insights in the Process of Motivation, characterized by its stepwise cyclical nature.

Major theories from literature have been observed, not only to search for parallels and corresponding views in their respective approaches to Motivation, as compared to the proposed Model, but also to provide additions that could supplement our observations.

These theories were clustered according to six major categories, as further commented on in the Introduction of this Volume, pp. 19-21:[1]

- Expectancy-value theories;
- Goal-setting theories;
- Goal-orientation theories;
- Self-determination theory;
- Social cognitive theories;
- Attribution theories.

Four major observations were made.

First, it was found that none of these main clusters of theories appeared to cover all aspects included in the Model of Motivation. Instead, each major theory highlighted one or more separate Phases from the Model. As such, distinct elements from these theories were covered in the respective Chapters covering each of the Phases of the Model.

Second, the insights emerging from these theories brought depth and complexity to the Process of Motivation, and extended on the insights proposed in the Model. These insights included concepts and constructs that have been the subject of studies covering several decades. A number of areas stood out, and are briefly mentioned as examples.

The literature extended our views on the assessments of adequacy occurring in a Phase of Externally Evoked Self-Assessment. These assessments appeared also to lead to a progressive increase and 'accumulation of knowledge' and experience about one's potential and competence. And this, in turn, affected self-efficacy beliefs and expectancies for engaging in future activities, reflected in

[1] Referring to the Introduction, it is noted that only theories related to the Process of Motivation were observed, thereby excluding theories aimed at *addressing* Motivation, as those are assumed to be related to a Process of Interference (see the Introduction, notably pp. 7-9).

designs of goal-orientation that were captured in constructs expressed in approach and avoidance strategies. A brief visualized summary of these elaborate findings is provided on p. 210.

Furthermore, by adding insights in perceptions of causality and their origin, the literature extended on the proposed assessments made in a Phase of Anticipated Change, anticipating on appropriate strategies for potential amendments aimed at decreasing perceived Discrepancies. It was found that reflecting on the causes of one's actions or achievements, exposed crucial attributes used in achievement-related contexts. And these were to shed light on the ingredients we tend to use in our strategies to anticipate on subsequent courses of action. A visualized summary is provided on p. 242.

In addition, theories from literature extended on the proposed assessments assumed to occur in a Phase of Dedication. These thoughts elaborated on affects and cognitions following Impact from Reality, and on subsequent effects, in terms of performance and behavior in general. And these, in turn, extended even further to include perceptions of who we are in constructs capturing the self, and related self-esteem and (academic) self-concept. Visualized overviews are provided on p. 293.

These are but a few of the examples emerging as we progressed through the various Phases of the Model, enriching and elaborating on our views.

In a third observation, we were able to provide an alternative view to controversies that had risen in the field, (especially between goal-setting theory, self-determination theory, and goal-orientation theories). Three conclusions were proposed based on the Model of Motivation for the differences that have occurred not only in theoretical conceptualizations, but more prominently, in research findings obtained in these three areas of study. Details on these opposed views are summarized on p. 138, and summaries of principal conclusions in an alternative view are provided on p. 177.

Fourth, and as a final conclusion, it was found that no contradictions appear to exist between views articulated in these major theories from literature, and those proposed in the Model of Motivation.

## *The Model of Motivation: Related Research*

Each Chapter covering these major theories as they related to the successive Phases of the Model, extended further on these findings by providing an overview of empirical evidence that had been advanced by researchers in the respective fields of study.

As connections could be made between those major categories of clustered theories and the Model of Motivation, findings obtained from research in those fields of study confirming the plausibility of those theories also reflected on assumptions made in the Model and its related areas.

However, it is noted that finding confirmation from research in those fields is not meant to provide evidence, or validation, for the assumptions proposed in the Model of Motivation. They are merely what the French eloquently indicate as *'des indices concordants'*, research findings that do not seem to contradict the assumptions made in the Model, and thereby provide indications as to their plausibility.

In this respect, it is to be noted that no references have been made in the present introductory Volume to research that has been conducted over the years directly related to the Model of Motivation. These findings are to be reported on extensively in Volume VII of the Series, as further commented on in the Introduction of this Volume, notably p. 14.

## The Model of Motivation: The Essentials and their Implications

In this introductory Volume, a Model of Motivation has been presented that provides a new perspective in our thinking on human Motivation.

The Model of Motivation adds dynamic properties to the construct, by suggesting that Motivation is a sequential, stepwise, cyclical Process, and by introducing the element of time, as this 'Process of Motivation' progresses in successive cycles towards achieving its objective.

In addition, it provides a new perspective, by making a distinction between the Process of Motivation itself, and the techniques and methods needed to address this Process, through so-called 'Processes of Interference', and by making it imperative to clearly differentiate between both.

In this introductory overview, the focus has been on the Process of Motivation, proposing a Model consisting of distinct steps covered in separate Chapters of the study, and elaborated on in preceding pages.

The Process of Motivation appears to be an 'inner dialogue', a Process, largely evaluative in nature, evolving around an objective, or 'Goal', the individual seeks to achieve. Within this Process interference occurs from perceived surroundings, defined as 'Reality', leading to evaluative, counteracting measures. The Process of Motivation is assumed to progress in a number of distinct, consecutive steps, or 'Stages', which can be organized in a number of groups, defined as 'Phases'. These Phases appear to follow a specific sequence, each successively evolving into another, at times becoming cyclical before proceeding to a next Phase.

This Process that centers around the Goal in successive Phases, thus aims at reaching this objective and at preserving its integrity.

And once these Phases aimed at addressing an intruding and interfering Reality have been completed, the Process returns to its original settings to initiate revisions and amendments, whereby the Process of Motivation becomes cyclical.

In this second cycle, so-called 'Mechanisms' emerge that serve to preserve the integrity of the Goal. The more important, or 'Significant', the Goal is perceived to be, the more profound the effects of these Mechanisms.

The first, a 'Mechanism of Representation', is based on the experience obtained following the confrontation with Reality. Effects that are experienced following this confrontation result through intricate Processes into perceptions of Reality that either enhance or neutralize its effects. These Mechanisms of Representation are thus aimed at preserving the integrity of the Process of Motivation in its attempts to reach or maintain the Goal that has been set.

In addition, the experiences obtained from a previous cycle can also serve to anticipate on the interference from Reality that is expected to re-emerge in this new cycle of the Process of Motivation. So-called 'Mechanisms of Anticipation' are introduced to either enhance the influence of Reality when the Impact is perceived as positive to the Process of Motivation or to reduce the influence of Reality when the Impact is perceived as negative.

*The Process of Motivation, then, is assumed to be a sequential, cyclical Process that intentionally orients the individual towards a desired status quo of a Goal that has been set, leading to evaluative activities aimed at minimizing the effects of an interfering Reality.*

And as these Mechanisms of Representation and Mechanisms of Anticipation combine and blend to form protective measures preserving the integrity of our Goals, especially the ones that are perceived as Significant, they merge to form defenses that are referred to as 'Stratagems of Coping', or 'Coping' for short.

All Goals that are Significant to us, in various degrees and expressions, are accompanied by Stratagems of Coping. And as they are meant to address Reality and our surroundings, they are bound, sooner or later, to affect these surroundings, not only on a small scale in our direct environment, but extending their impact to even affect society as a whole.

It is in these expressions that Stratagems of Coping leave their traces, with profound repercussions. At a personal level, they appear to be the primal cause for expressions of intolerance, pride, obstinacy, prejudice. These are expressions in which we figure as instigator, as performer in the act. But it appears that we can also play a more passive, observant role where Stratagems of Coping are found to be the primary Mechanisms that make us 'turn away', and become seemingly indifferent for a surrounding world that appears to intrude our lives to an extent that calls for powerful counteractive measures.

Stratagems of Coping were found to be the unexpected outcomes of this Process of Motivation, when Significance increases in the Goals we tend to set. Where Motivation is defined in the act of will to intervene in one's destiny and surroundings, Stratagems of Coping appear to be essential elements of the human condition to strive and prosper in a better world, for better and for worse. For better, as they preserve the integrity of the Goals that we treasure most; for worse, because these Stratagems make us change Reality and our perception of the world around us, affecting both our direct environment, family, friends and in work-related settings, but also, on a broader scale, the communities we live in, and extending even further to affect society on an extensive range of essential issues.

Where the study of the Process of Motivation has, in its 'Quest for Expression', led us to disclose not only the roots of good, but also these origins of evil, it now falls upon us to provide further insights into these Mechanisms, as called for in the Prologue to this introductory Volume in the 'Series on Motivation'.

The Model of Motivation provides a new perspective to our thinking on Motivation. It adds dynamic properties and provides an essential distinction between the Process of Motivation and the techniques and methods needed to address this Process. It introduces specific Mechanisms that lead to profound repercussions in the way we act, and the way we are acted upon.

Further studies are needed to extend our knowledge, not only on these techniques and methods aimed at addressing Motivation, but most explicitly on the measures that can be used to affect these Stratagems as an outcome of this Process of Motivation.

Successive Volumes in this 'Series on Motivation', are to cover these topics progressively.

*Remember,*
*A tree that fills a man's embrace grows from a seedling,*
*A tower nine stories high starts with one brick,*
*A journey of a thousand miles*
*begins with a single step...*

Lao Tzu, Tao Te Ching, verse 64
(Star, 2003)

# Epilogue

In nearly all activities one sets about, a purpose, an intention, an act of will can be seen. And all these intentional acts appear to have a common origin in the will to intervene in our destiny and surroundings, both mentally and physically.

Why do we do the things we do?

Motivation is the all-inclusive concept in which all expressions are captured of what we referred to, in the Prologue to this Volume, as 'the will to intervene in one's destiny and surroundings'.

Motivation can be seen from the perspective of an individual, but also, in more general terms, from a perspective involving others, relatives, family, friends, or in work-related settings, and at an even larger scale, involving communities or society in general.

In our venture into the unknown, we focused on the individual. And even at this level, we made a further distinction that proved to be essential. We differentiated the constructs and mechanisms involved in how Motivation works, as being part of a 'Process of Motivation', and made a distinction between this Process of Motivation and the methods and procedures that are used to address and manage Motivation, and we defined these as being part of a 'Process of Interference'.

The distinction made it possible to clearly differentiate the intricacies of how Motivation works and evolves over time, from the technicalities of addressing or managing this Process.

In this introductory Volume, we focused on the Process of Motivation. The Process appeared to be an 'inner dialogue', a stepwise successive series of sequential 'Phases', where one Phase follows the other, providing input as it progresses towards an objective, or 'Goal', that is set. This Process appeared to be cyclical in its attempts at reaching the Goal, producing adjustments as it progresses. All Processes of Motivation thus evolve around a Goal, with each Goal having its own distinct Process. And all these Processes together interact to produce 'Motivation', the act 'to intervene in one's destiny and surroundings'.

It was found that in this sequential Process aimed at reaching a Goal, at a certain moment an unforeseen intrusion is likely to occur, either in a positive or negative sense, either encouraging these attempts or discouraging them. We defined this often unforeseen event as 'Reality'. Reality captures these external, unexpected events, and can either represent an external actor or a physical environment, but can also manifest itself in more abstract terms, in the form of perceived constraints or imposed restrictions. And Reality was found to set in motion a series of subsequent Phases aimed to address the intrusion on this Process of reaching the Goal that had been set, either in its positive, but also in its negative effects.

And as we ventured into these new grounds, we unexpectedly came upon forces that had been mentioned in the Prologue to this Volume. Compelling forces, which had been found to lead us astray and "to prevent the human condition to strive and prosper in a better world", despite the deep sense of urgency felt by most, if not all, in our urge to intervene and counteract these influences.

It was found that these powerful Mechanisms emerge and serve a cause in protecting the Goals we treasure most. At first, these Mechanisms appeared to only moderate the Impact from Reality on our attempts at reaching these Goals. But as we ventured further, in analyzing the intricacies of these Mechanisms within the Process of Motivation, implications emerged that seemed to provide first insights on these unintended and opposing forces.

Not only do we appear to counteract and neutralize Reality and our surroundings, but we also actively change its manifestation, its appearance in a direction that most conveniently meets our needs in the attempts to reach our objective, either emphasizing its features when these are found to be assisting, or minimizing these, when they appear harmful or detrimental to our cause. And the more important and 'Significant' our Goal, the more explicit and dramatic these amendments appeared to be. Not only in their distinct expressions, but especially in the way they were found to combine and to form dynamics that produce powerful forces defying Reality as it manifests itself.

It made us less accessible, intransigent for external input and disturbing intrusions that affect our attempts at reaching our objectives.

These protective measures, over subsequent cycles of a Process of Motivation, appeared to progressively shield these Goals of high Significance, as, with time, they are fine-tuned and adjusted to the purpose, as experience builds up. When these Mechanisms combine and blend to form protective measures preserving the integrity of our Goals, especially the ones that are perceived as Significant, they merge to form defenses that were referred to as 'Stratagems of Coping', or 'Coping' for short.

All Goals that are Significant to us, in various degrees and expressions appeared to be accompanied by these Stratagems of Coping. And as they are meant to address Reality and our surroundings, they were also found to affect these surroundings, both on a small scale in our direct vicinity, with relatives and friends, and in our work, but also on a larger scale affecting groups and communities, and extending on an even larger scale to affect society as a whole.

For when these expressions of Coping tend to spread through the extensive forms of present-day media that we find at our disposal, they can be shared by others to address Coping strategies of their own, to protect and preserve Goals that are perceived to be exposed by a common Reality. The excessive nature of these expressions often serves to evoke and propel corresponding ideas among many, and spread to neutralize the Impact of Realities that are essential on the socio-economic agendas of our time.

When these Stratagems of Coping meet to coalesce into shared expressions, that were referred to as 'Stratagems of Collective Coping', they turn individual expressions such as intolerance, pride, obstinacy, prejudice, and indifference into shared expressions that provide the seeds not only for arguments and dispute, but even for conflict and war; not only for misplaced chauvinism, which finds its fearful ways in xenophobia and discrimination, but even for excesses that can end in persecution and atrocities of genocide. It can merge into collective displays of indifference that lead to shared neglect of poverty and injustice falling upon those who happen to be less fortunate in the circumstances in which they need to find their existence.

And these shared expressions, in turn, can be made to obstruct initiatives that are aimed at addressing these excesses of human nature, frustrating dialogue, compromise and reconciliation.

When Stratagems of Coping meet to join in synchronized harmony, they thus provide us with forms of justifications in acts in which we, often inadvertently, play an active role. But these shared expressions can also be found in more passive, observant roles where Stratagems of Collective Coping make us ignore the essentials of our times. They make us 'turn away' from issues that will affect our children and the children of our children's children, generations to come, in issues such as climate change, distribution of wealth, and abuse of scarce resources.

'The will to intervene in our destiny'...

If Motivation is at the heart of it all, and we appear to have unveiled important aspects of its working, we are called to meet the challenge to further trace these forces mentioned in the Prologue to this study.

What is it that prevents us from having conflict, discrimination, genocide, poverty and injustice reoccur over the course of time? What are the crucial elements of the human condition that somehow seem to force us into witnessing these atrocities, time and time again?

It appears, that in our journey to the roots of 'the will to intervene in our destiny', these strong and compelling forces originate from the expressions of Stratagems of Collective Coping that seem to produce these fierce counterproductive and evil outcomes.

When Stratagems of Coping evolve into forms of Collective Coping, it enables the acceptance of the unacceptable, the turning away from essentials.

Stratagems of Collective Coping enable us to accept that war exists as a 'fact of life', it enables that we submit to injustice, and it opens the road to neglect, or denial, to discord and polarization. These Stratagems are made to neutralize the Impact from Realities that produced the darkest pages in human history, and makes that we are still witnessing human suffering that remains largely ignored.

To face Collective Coping is to look evil in the eye.

It transcends the purpose of this book to elaborate on the implications of these unexpected findings.

Investigating these venues falls beyond the scope of the present introduction to the origins of the Process of Motivation. But it provides a basis upon which we may better understand the very nature of where the Process of Motivation can lead to. If we are called to meet the challenge to expose these Mechanisms for what they are, it now falls upon us to seek venues to at least create awareness for the implications these shared expressions of Collective Coping lead us to, and, in due course, to address the effects they provoke.

We feel compelled to further investigate these findings, as they will appear in subsequent Volumes of this 'Series on Motivation'. A Postscript to the Epilogue is to cover the sequence to lead us there.

May these insights help us on our way to a better understanding of these expressions that appear to be at the roots of the human condition.

A journey of a thousand miles, begins with a single step...

Leiden, December 31st 2022.

# Postscript

The following titles are expected to appear in the 'Series on Motivation':

Volume 1 - Motivation: Mechanisms of the Mind and their Quest for Expression

Volume 2 - Motivation: Foundations for a Study of the Process of Motivation and on Critical Determinants of Interference

Volume 3 - Motivation: In Search of a Paragon of Human Motivation Theory

Volume 4 - Management of Motivation: The Conditions to Lead Us There

Volume 5 - Management of Motivation: The Competencies We Need and Why They are Essential

Volume 6 - Management of Motivation: The Instruments and Their Workings

Volume 7 - Management of Motivation: An Overview of Empirical Findings

Volume 8 - Trilogy: Journey Along the Abyss of Our Time

Volume 9 - Trilogy: A Manifesto

Volume 10 - Trilogy: A Kingdom of Heaven

# References

Abramson, L.Y., Metalsky, G.I. & Alloy, L.B. (1989). Hopelessness Depression: a Theory-based Subtype of Depression. *Psychological Review, 96,* 358-372. Doi: 10.1037/0033-295X.96.2.358

Abramson, L.Y., Seligman, M.E. & Teasdale, J.D. (1978). Learned helplessness in humans: Critique and reformulation. *Journal of Abnormal Psychology, 87,* 49-74. Doi: 10.1037/0021-843X.87.1.49

Adams, J.S. (1965). Inequity In Social Exchange. *Advances in Experimental Social Psychology, 2.* 267-299. Doi: 10.1016/S0065-2601(08)60108-2

Adams, N., Little, T.D. & Ryan, R.M. (2017). Self-determination theory. In: M.L. Wehmeyer, K.A. Shogren, T.D. Little & S.J. Lopez (Eds.), *Development of self-determination through the life-course* (pp. 47-54). Berlin, Germany: Springer Science & Business Media. Doi: 10.1007/978-94-024-1042-6_4

Ahn, H.S. & Bong, M. (2019). Self-Efficacy in Learning – Past, Present, and Future. In: K.A. Renninger & S.E. Hidi (Eds.) *The Cambridge Handbook of Motivation and Learning* (pp. 63-86). Cambridge, UK: Cambridge University Press.

Ainley, M. & Patrick, L. (2006). Measuring self-regulated learning processes through tracking patterns of student interaction with achievement activities. *Educational Psychology Review, 18,* 267-286. Doi: 10.1007/s10648-006-9018-z

Alivernini, F. & Lucidi, F. (2011). Relationship between social context, self-efficacy, motivation, academic achievement, and intention to drop out of high school: A longitudinal study. *The Journal of Educational Research, 104,* 241-252. Doi: 10.1080/00220671003728062

Allscheid, S.P. & Cellar, D.F. (1996). An interactive approach to work motivation: The effects of competition, rewards, and goal difficulty on task performance. *Journal of Business and Psychology, 11,* 219-237. Doi: 10.1007/BF02193860

Amabile, T.M. (1983). The social psychology of creativity: A componential conceptualization. *Journal of Personality and Social Psychology, 45,* 357-376. Doi: 10.1037/0022-3514.45.2.357

Amabile, T.M. (1996). *Creativity in context: Update to "The Social Psychology of Creativity."* Boulder, CO.: Westview Press.

Amabile, T.M., DeJong, W. & Lepper, M.R. (1976). Effects of externally imposed deadlines on subsequent intrinsic motivation. *Journal of Personality and Social Psychology, 34,* 92-98. Doi: 10.1037/0022-3514.34.1.92

Ames, C. (1992a). Classrooms: Goals, structures, and student motivation. *Journal of Educational Psychology, 84,* 261-271. Doi: 10.1037/0022-0663.84.3.261

Ames, C. (1992b). Achievement goals and classroom motivational climate. In: D.H. Schunk & J.L. Meece (Eds.), *Student perceptions in the classroom* (pp. 327-348). Hillsdale, NJ: Lawrence Erlbaum Associates.

Anderman, E.M. (1998). The Middle School Experience: Effects on the Math and Science Achievement of Adolescents with LD. *Journal of Learning Disabilities, 31,* 128-138. Doi: 10.1177/002221949803100203

Anderman, E.M. (2020). Achievement motivation theory: Balancing precision and utility. *Contemporary Educational Psychology, 61,* Article 101864. Doi: 10.1016/j.cedpsych.2020.101864

Anderman, L.H. & Anderman, E.M. (1999). Social predictors of changes in students' achievement goal orientations. *Contemporary Educational Psychology, 24,* 21-37. Doi: 10.1006/ceps.1998.0978

Anderman, E.M. & Maehr, M.L. (1994). Motivation and schooling in the middle grades. *Review of Educational Research, 64,* 287-309. Doi: 10.2307/1170696

Anderman, E.M. & Midgley, C. (1997). Changes in Achievement Goal Orientations, Perceived Academic Competence, and Grades across the Transition to Middle-Level Schools. *Contemporary Educational Psychology, 22,* 269-298. Doi: 10.1006/ceps.1996.0926

Anderson, C.A. (1983). The causal structure of situations: The generation of plausible causal attributions as a function of type of event situation. *Journal of Experimental Social Psychology, 19,* 185-203. Doi: 10.1016/0022-1031(83)90037-9

Archer, J. (1994). Achievement goals as a measure of motivation in university students. *Contemporary Educational Psychology, 19,* 430-446.

Atkinson, J.W. (1957). Motivational determinants of risk-taking behavior. *Psychological Review, 64,* 359-372. Doi: 10.1037/h0043445

Au, R.C.P., Watkins, D., Hattie, J. & Alexander, P. (2009). Reformulating the depression model of learned hopelessness for academic outcomes. *Educational Research Review, 4,* 103-117. Doi: 10.1016/j.edurev.2009.04.001.

Austin, J. T. & Vancouver, J. B. (1996). Goal constructs in psychology: Structure, process, and content. *Psychological Bulletin, 120,* 338-375. Doi: 10.1037/0033-2909.120.3.338

Bandura, A. (1977). Self-efficacy: Toward a unifying theory of behavioral change. *Psychological Review, 84,* 191-215. Doi: 10.1037/0033-295X.84.2.191

Bandura, A. (1982). Self-efficacy mechanism in human agency. *American Psychologist, 37,* 122-147. Doi: 10.1037/0003-066X.37.2.122

Bandura, A. (1986). *Social foundations of thought and action: A social cognitive theory.* Englewood Cliffs, NJ: Prentice Hall.

Bandura, A. (1989). Human agency in social cognitive theory. *American Psychologist, 44,* 1175-1184. Doi: 10.1037/0003-066X.44.9.1175

Bandura, A. (1991). Social cognitive theory of self-regulation. *Organizational Behavior and Human Decision Processes, 50,* 248-287. Doi: 10.1016/0749-5978(91)

90022-L

Bandura, A. (1993). Perceived self-efficacy in cognitive development and functioning. *Educational Psychologist, 28,* 117-148. Doi: 10.1207/s15326985ep2802_3

Bandura, A. (1997). *Self-efficacy: The exercise of control.* New York, NY.: Freeman.

Bandura, A. (1999). Social cognitive theory of personality. In: L.A. Pervin & O.P. John (Eds.), *Handbook of personality: Theory and research* (pp. 154-196). New York, NY.: Guilford Press.

Bandura, A. (2000). Self-efficacy: The foundation of agency. In: W.J. Perrig & A. Grob (Eds.), *Control of human behavior, mental processes, and consciousness: Essays in honor of the 60th birthday of August Flammer* (pp. 17–33). Mahwah, NJ.: Lawrence Erlbaum Associates Publishers.

Bandura, A. (2001). Social cognitive theory: An agentic perspective. *Annual Review of Psychology, 52,* 1-26. Doi: 10.1146/annurev.psych.52.1.1

Bandura, A. (2002). Social cognitive theory in cultural context. *Applied Psychology: An International Review, 51,* 269-290. Doi: 10.1111/1464-0597.00092

Bandura, A. (2006a). Toward a psychology of human agency. *Perspectives on Psychological Science, 1,* 164-180. Doi: 10.1111/j.1745-6916.2006.00011.x

Bandura, A. (2006b). Guide for constructing self-efficacy scales. In: F. Pajares & T. Urdan (Eds.), *Self-Efficacy Beliefs of Adolescents (p. 307-337).* Greenwich, CT.: Information Age Publishing.

Bandura, A. (2006c). Adolescent development from an agentic perspective. In: F. Pajares & T. Urdan (Eds.), *Self-Efficacy Beliefs of Adolescents (p. 1-43).* Greenwich, CT.: Information Age Publishing.

Bandura, A. (2008). An agentic perspective on positive psychology. In: S.J. Lopez (Ed.), *Positive psychology: Exploring the best in people, Vol. 1: Discovering human strengths* (pp. 167-196). Westport, CT: Praeger/Greenwood.

Bandura, A. (2011). Social cognitive theory. In: P.A.M. van Lange, A.W. Kruglanski & E.T. Higgins (Eds.). *Handbook of social psychological theories.* (pp. 349-373). London, UK: Sage.

Bandura, A. (2018). Toward a psychology of human agency: Pathways and reflections. *Perspectives on Psychological Science, 13,* 130-136. Doi: 10.1177/1745691617699280

Bandura, A. & Cervone, D. (1983). Self-evaluative and self-efficacy mechanisms governing the motivational effects of goal systems. *Journal of Personality and Social Psychology, 45,* 1017-1028. Doi: 10.1037/0022-3514.45.5.1017

Bandura, A. & Locke, E.A. (2003). Negative self-efficacy and goal effects revisited. *Journal of Applied Psychology, 88,* 87-99. Doi: 10.1037/0021-9010.88.1.87

Bandura, A. & Schunk, D. H. (1981). Cultivating competence, self-efficacy, and intrinsic interest through proximal self-motivation. *Journal of Personality and Social Psychology, 41,* 586–598. Doi: 10.1037/0022-3514.41.3.586

Baranik, L.E., Stanley, L.J., Bynum, B.H. & Lance, C.E. (2010). Examining the construct validity of mastery-avoidance achievement goals: A meta-analysis. *Human Performance, 23,* 265-282. Doi: 10.1080/08959285.2010.488463

Barron, K.E. & Harackiewicz, J.M. (2000). Achievement goals and optimal motivation: A multiple goals approach. In: C. Sansone & J.M. Harackiewicz (Eds.), *Intrinsic and extrinsic motivation: The search for optimal motivation and performance* (pp. 229-254). Academic Press. Doi: 10.1016/B978-012619070-0/50031-3

Barron, K.E. & Hulleman, C.S. (2015). Expectancy-value-cost model of motivation. In: J.S. Eccles & K. Salmelo-Aro (Eds.), *International Encyclopedia of Social and Behavioral Sciences: Motivational Psychology* (2nd ed., pp. 503-509). New York, NY.: Elsevier. Doi: 10.1016/B978-0-08-097086-8.26099-6

Bar-Tal, D., Goldberg, M. & Knaani, A. (1984). Causes of success and failure and their dimensions as a function of SES and gender: A phenomenological analysis. *British Journal of Educational Psychology, 54,* 51-61. Doi: 10.1111/j.2044-8279.1984.tb00844.x

Baumeister, R.F., Campbell, J.D., Krueger, J.I. & Vohs, K.D. (2003). Does high self-esteem cause better performance, interpersonal success, happiness, or healthier lifestyles? *Psychological Science in the Public Interest, 4,* 1-44. Doi: 10.1111/1529-1006.01431

Benware, C.A. & Deci, E.L. (1984). Quality of learning with an active versus passive motivational set. *American Educational Research Journal, 21,* 755-765. Doi: 10.2307/1162999

Berry, J.M. & West, R.L. (1993). Cognitive self-efficacy in relation to personal mastery and goal setting across the life span. *International Journal of Behavioral Development, 16,* 351-379. Doi: 10.1177/016502549301600213

Boggiano, A.K. (1998). Maladaptive achievement patterns: A test of a diathesis–stress analysis of helplessness. *Journal of Personality and Social Psychology, 74,* 1681-1695. Doi: 10.1037/0022-3514.74.6.1681

Bong, M. (2001a). Role of self-efficacy and task value in predicting college students' course performance and future enrolment intentions. *Contemporary Educational Psychology, 26,* 553-570. Doi: 10.1006/ceps.2000.1048

Bong, M. (2001b). Between- and within-domain relations of academic motivation among middle and high school students: Self-efficacy, task value, and achievement goals. *Journal of Educational Psychology, 93,* 23-34. Doi: 10.1037/0022-0663.93.1.23

Bong, M. (2009). Age-Related Differences in Achievement Goal Differentiation. *Journal of Educational Psychology, 101,* 879-896. Doi: 10.1037/a0015945

Bong, M. & Clark, R.E. (1999). Comparison between self-concept and self-efficacy in academic motivation research. *Educational Psychologist, 34,* 139-154. Doi: 10.1207/s15326985ep3403_1

Bong, M., Lee, S.K. & Woo, Y.K. (2015). The Roles of Interest and Self-Efficacy in the Decision to Pursue Mathematics and Science. In: K.A. Renninger, M. Nieswandt & S. Hidi (Eds.), *Interest in Mathematics and Science Learning* (pp. 33-48). Washington, DC: American Educational Research Association.

Bong, M. & Skaalvik, E.M. (2003). Academic self-concept and self-efficacy: How different are they really? *Educational Psychology Review, 15,* 1-40. Doi:

10.1023/A:1021302408382

Bradley, G.W. (1978). Self-serving biases in the attribution process: A reexamination of the fact or fiction question. *Journal of Personality and Social Psychology, 36,* 56-71. Doi: 10.1037/0022-3514.36.1.56

Britner, S.L. & Pajares, F. (2006). Sources of science self-efficacy beliefs of middle school students. *Journal of Research in Science Teaching, 43,* 485-499. Doi: 10.1002/tea.20131

Brown, J. & Weiner, B. (1984). Affective Consequences of Ability versus Effort Ascriptions: Controversies, Resolutions, and Quandaries. *Journal of Educational Psychology, 76,* 146-158. Doi: 10.1037/0022-0663.76.1.146

Bruner, J. (1962). *On Knowing: Essays for the left hand.* Cambridge, MA: Belknap Press of Harvard University Press.

Burger, J.M., Cooper, H.M. & Good, T.L. (1982). Teacher attributions of student performance: Effects of outcome. *Personality and Social Psychology Bulletin, 8,* 685-690. Doi: 10.1177/0146167282084013

Burgers, C., Eden, A., van Engelenburg, M.D. & Buningh, S. (2015). How feedback boosts motivation and play in a brain-training game. *Computers in Human Behavior, 48,* 94-103. Doi: 10.1016/j.chb.2015.01.038

Byrne, B.M. (1996). Academic self-concept: Its structure, measurement, and relation to academic achievement. In: B.A. Bracken (Ed.), *Handbook of Self-concept: Developmental, social, and clinical considerations* (pp. 287-316). New York, NY.: Wiley.

Calsyn, R.J. & Kenny, D.A. (1977). Self-concept of ability and perceived evaluation of others: Cause or effect of academic achievement? *Journal of Educational Psychology, 69,* 136-145. Doi: 10.1037/0022-0663.69.2.136

Caprara, G.V., Fida, R., Vecchione, M., Del Bove, G., Vecchio, G.M., Barbaranelli, C. & Bandura, A. (2008). Longitudinal analysis of the role of perceived self-efficacy for self-regulated learning in academic continuance and achievement. *Journal of Educational Psychology, 100,* 525-534. Doi: 10.1037/0022-0663.100.3.525

Carpentier, J. & Mageau, G.A. (2013). When change-oriented feedback enhances motivation, well-being and performance: A look at autonomy-supportive feedback in sport. *Psychology of Sport and Exercise, 14,* 423-435. Doi: 10.1016/j.psychsport. 2013.01.003

Carson, P.P. & Carson, K.D. (1993). Managing Creativity Enhancement Through Goal-Setting and Feedback. *Journal of Creative Behavior, 27,* 36-45. Doi: 10.1002/j.2162-6057.1993.tb01385.x

Cerasoli, C.P., Nicklin, J.M. & Ford, M.T. (2014). Intrinsic motivation and extrinsic incentives jointly predict performance: A 40-year meta-analysis. *Psychological Bulletin, 140,* 980-1008. Doi: 10.1037/a0035661

Cerasoli, C.P., Nicklin, J.M. & Nassrelgrgawi, A.S. (2016). Performance, incentives, and needs for autonomy, competence, and relatedness: A meta-analysis. *Motivation and Emotion, 40,* 781-813. Doi: 10.1007/s11031-016-9578-2

Chen, S., Yeh. Y., Hwang, F. & Lin, S.S.J. (2013). The relationship between academic self-concept and achievement: A multicohort–multioccasion study. *Learning and*

*Individual Differences, 23,* 172-178. Doi: 10.1016/j.lindif.2012.07.021

Conley, A.M. (2012). Patterns of motivation beliefs: Combining achievement goal and expectancy-value perspectives. *Journal of Educational Psychology, 104,* 32-47. Doi: 10.1037/a0026042

Conroy, D.E. (2017). Achievement motives. In: A.J. Elliot, C.S. Dweck & D.S. Yeager (Eds.), *Handbook of Competence and Motivation: Theory and application* (pp. 25-42). New York, NY.: The Guilford Press.

Cooper, H.M. & Burger, J.M. (1980). How teachers explain students' academic performance: A categorization of free response academic attributions. *American Educational Research Journal, 17,* 95-109. Doi: 10.2307/1162511

Cooper-Hakim, A. & Viswesvaran, C. (2005). The Construct of Work Commitment: Testing an Integrative Framework. *Psychological Bulletin, 131,* 241-259. Doi: 10.1037/0033-2909.131.2.241

Dai, D.Y. & Rinn, A.N. (2008). The big-fish–little-pond effect: What do we know and where do we go from here? *Educational Psychology Review, 20,* 283–317. Doi: 10.1007/s10648-008-9071-x

Daniels, L.M., Haynes, T.L., Stupnisky, R.H., Perry, R.P., Newall, N.E. & Pekrun, R. (2008). Individual differences in achievement goals: A longitudinal study of cognitive, emotional, and achievement outcomes. *Contemporary Educational Psychology, 33,* 584-608. Doi: 10.1016/j.cedpsych.2007.08.002

Deci, E.L. (1971). Effects of externally mediated rewards on intrinsic motivation. *Journal of Personality and Social Psychology, 18,* 105-115. Doi: 10.1037/h0030644

Deci, E.L. & Cascio, W.F. (1972). Changes in Intrinsic Motivation as a Function of Negative Feedback and Threats. Paper presented at the Eastern Psychological Association Meeting in Boston, Massachusetts, April 19, 1972.

Deci, E. L. & Flaste, R. (1995). *Why we do what we do: The dynamics of personal autonomy.* (G P Putnam's Sons). New York, NY.: Penguin.

Deci, E.L., Koestner, R. & Ryan, R.M. (1999). A meta-analytic review of experiments examining the effects of extrinsic rewards on intrinsic motivation. *Psychological Bulletin, 125,* 627-668. Doi: 10.1037/0033-2909.125.6.627

Deci, E.L., Koestner, R. & Ryan, R.M. (2001). Extrinsic rewards and intrinsic motivation in education: Reconsidered once again. *Review of Educational Research, 71,* 1-27. Doi: 10.3102/00346543071001001

Deci, E.L. & Moller, A.C. (2005). The Concept of Competence: A Starting Place for Understanding Intrinsic Motivation and Self-Determined Extrinsic Motivation. In: A.J. Elliot & C.S. Dweck (Eds.), *Handbook of Competence and Motivation* (pp. 579-597). New York, NY.: Guilford Publications.

Deci, E.L. & Ryan, R.M. (1985). *Intrinsic motivation and self-determination in human behavior.* Berlin, Germany: Springer Science & Business Media. Doi: 10.1007/978-1-4899-2271-7

Deci, E.L. & Ryan, R.M. (2000). The "what" and "why" of goal pursuits: Human needs and the self-determination of behavior. *Psychological Inquiry, 11,* 227-268. Doi:

10.1207/S15327965PLI1104_01

Denissen, J.J.A., Zarrett, N.R. & Eccles, J.S. (2007). I like to do it, I'm able, and I know I am: Longitudinal couplings between domain-specific achievement, self-concept, and interest. *Child Development, 78*, 430-447. Doi: 10.1111/j.1467-8624.2007.01007.x

Dey, A. & Gottlieb, J. (2019). Attention, Information-Seeking, and Active Sampling: Empirical Evidence and Applications for Learning. In: K.A. Renninger & S.E. Hidi (Eds), *The Cambridge Handbook of Motivation and Learning* (Cambridge Handbooks in Psychology, pp. 183-208). Cambridge, UK: Cambridge University Press. doi:10.1017/9781316823279.010

Diseth, Å. (2015). The advantages of task-based and other-based achievement goals as standards of competence. *International Journal of Educational Research, 72,* 59-69. Doi: 10.1016/j.ijer.2015.04.011

Duchesne, S. & Larose, S. (2018). Academic competence and achievement goals: Self-pressure and disruptive behaviors as mediators. *Learning and Individual Differences, 68,* 41-50. Doi: 10.1016/j.lindif.2018.09.008

Durik, A.M., Vida, M. & Eccles, J.S. (2006). Task values and ability beliefs as predictors of high school literacy choices: A developmental analysis. *Journal of Educational Psychology, 98*, 382-393. Doi: 10.1037/0022-0663.98.2.382

Dweck, C.S. (1986). Motivational processes affecting learning. *American Psychologist, 41,* 1040-1048. Doi: 10.1037//0003-066X.41.10.1040

Dweck, C.S. (1989). Motivation. In: A. Lesgold & R. Glaser (Eds.), *Foundations for a psychology of education* (pp. 87-136). Hillsdale, NJ: Erlbaum.

Dweck, C.S. (2006). *Mindset: The New Psychology of Success.* New York, NY.: Random House.

Dweck, C.S. (2018). *Mindset: The New Psychology of Success – How We can Learn to Fulfill Our Potential (Updated Edition).* New York, NY.: Ballantine Books.

Dweck, C.S. & Leggett, E.L. (1988). A social-cognitive approach to motivation and personality. *Psychological Review, 95,* 256-273. Doi: 10.1037/0033-295X.95.2.256

Eccles, J.S., Adler, T.F., Futterman, R., Goff, S.B., Kaczala, C.M., Meece, J.L. & Midgley, C. (1983). Expectancies, values, and academic behaviors. In: J.T. Spence (Ed.), *Achievement and Achievement Motivation* (pp. 75-146). San Francisco, CA: W.H. Freeman.

Eccles, J.S. & Midgley, C. (1989). Stage/Environment Fit: Developmentally Appropriate Classrooms for Early Adolescence. In: R.E. Ames & Ames, C. (Eds.), *Research on Motivation in Education* (Vol. 3, pp. 139-186). New York, NY.: Academic Press.

Eccles, J.S. & Midgley, C. (1990). Changes in academic motivation and self-perception during early adolescence. In: R. Montemayor, G.R. Adams & T.P. Gullotta (Eds.), *From childhood to adolescence: A transitional period?* (pp. 134–155). London, UK.: Sage Publications.

Eccles J.S., Midgley C., Wigfield A., Buchanan C.M., Reuman D., Flanagan C. & MacIver, D. (1993). Development during adolescence. The impact of stage-environment fit on young adolescents' experiences in schools and in families. *American Psychologist, 48,* pp. 90-101. Doi: 10.1037//0003-066x.48.2.90. PMID: 8442578.

Eccles, J. S. & Wigfield, A. (1995). In the mind of the actor: The structure of adolescents' achievement task values and expectancy-related beliefs. *Personality and Social Psychology Bulletin, 21,* 215–225. Doi: 10.1177/0146167295213003

Eccles, J.S. & Wigfield, A. (2002). Motivational beliefs, values, and goals. *Annual Review of Psychology, 53,* 109-132. Doi:10.1146/annurev.psych.53.100901.135153

Eccles, J., Wigfield, A., Harold, R. & Blumenfeld, P. (1993). Age and gender differences in children's self and task perceptions during elementary school. *Child Development, 64,* 830-847. Doi: 10.2307/1131221

Eccles, J.S., Wigfield, A. & Schiefele, U. (1998). Motivation to succeed. In: W. Damon & N. Eisenberg (Ed.), *Handbook of child psychology: Social, emotional, and personality development* (pp. 1017-1095). New York, NY.: John Wiley & Sons.

Elig, T.W. & Frieze, I.H. (1979). Measuring causal attibutions for success and failure. *Journal of Personality and Social Psychology, 37,* 621-634. Doi: 10.1037/0022-3514.37.4.621

Elliot, A.J. (1997). Integrating the " classic " and " contemporary " approaches to achievement motivation: A hierarchical model of approach and avoidance achievement motivation. In: M.L. Maehr & P.R. Pintrich (Eds.), *Advances in motivation and achievement* (Vol. 10, pp. 143-179). Greenwich, CT: JAI Press.

Elliot, A.J. (1999). Approach and avoidance motivation and achievement goals. *Educational Psychologist, 34,* 169-189. Doi: 10.1207/s15326985ep3403_3

Elliot, A.J. (2005). A conceptual history of the achievement goal construct. In: A.J. Elliot & C.S. Dweck (Eds.), *Handbook of competence and motivation* (pp. 52-72). New York, NY.: Guildford.

Elliot, A.J. & Church, M.A. (1997). A hierarchical model of approach and avoidance achievement motivation. *Journal of Personality and Social Psychology, 72,* 218-232. Doi: 10.1037/0022-3514.72.1.218

Elliot, A.J. & Covington, M.V. (2001). Approach and avoidance motivation. *Educational Psychology Review, 13,* 73-92. Doi: 10.1023/A:1009009018235

Elliot, A.J. & Dweck, C.S. (Eds.). (2005). *Handbook of competence and motivation.* New York, NY.: Guilford Publications.

Elliot, A.J. & Dweck, C.S. (2005). Competence and Motivation: Competence as the Core of Achievement Motivation. In: A.J. Elliot & C.S. Dweck (Eds.), *Handbook of competence and motivation* (pp. 3–12). New York, NY.: Guilford Publications.

Elliot, A.J., Dweck, C.S. & Yeager, D.S. (Eds.). (2017). *Handbook of competence and motivation: Theory and application (2nd ed.).* New York, NY.: The Guilford Press.

Elliot, A.J. & Harackiewicz, J.M. (1996). Approach and avoidance achievement goals and intrinsic motivation: A mediational analysis. *Journal of Personality and Social Psychology, 70,* 461-475. Doi: 10.1037/0022-3514.70.3.461

Elliot, A.J. & Hulleman, C.S. (2017). Achievement goals. In: A.J. Elliot, C.S. Dweck & D.S. Yeager (Eds.), *Handbook of Competence and Motivation: Theory and application* (pp. 43-60). New York, NY.: The Guilford Press.

Elliot, A.J. & McGregor, H.A. (1999). Test anxiety and the hierarchical model of approach and avoidance achievement motivation. *Journal of Personality and Social Psychology, 76,* 628-644. Doi: 10.1037/0022-3514.76.4.628

Elliot, A.J. & McGregor, H.A. (2001). A 2 × 2 achievement goal framework. *Journal of Personality and Social Psychology, 80,* 501-519. Doi: 10.1037/0022-3514.80.3.501

Elliot, A.J., McGregor, H.A. & Gable, S.L. (1999). Achievement goals, study strategies, and exam performance: A mediational analysis. *Journal of Educational Psychology, 91,* 549-563. Doi: 10.1037/0022-0663.91.3.549

Elliot, A.J., McGregor, H.A. & Thrash, T.M. (2002). The need for competence. In: E.L. Deci & R.M. Ryan (Eds.), *Handbook of self-determination research* (pp. 361-387). Rochester, NY.: University of Rochester Press.

Elliot, A.J., Murayama, K. & Pekrun, R. (2011). A 3 x 2 achievement goal model. *Journal of Educational Psychology, 103,* 632-648. Doi: 10.1037/a0023952

Elliott, E.S. & Dweck, C.S. (1988). Goals: An approach to motivation and achievement. *Journal of Personality and Social Psychology, 54,* 5-12. Doi: 10.1037/0022-3514.54.1.5

Erez, M. (1977). Feedback: A necessary condition for the goal setting-performance relationship. *Journal of Applied Psychology, 62,* 624-627. Doi: 10.1037/0021-9010.62.5.624

Flanagan, M.J., Putwain, D.W. & Caltabiano, M.L. (2015). The relationship between goal setting and students' experience of academic test anxiety. *International Journal of School & Educational Psychology, 3,* 189-201. Doi: 10.1080/ 21683603.2015.1060910

Försterling, F. (2001). *Attribution: An Introduction to Theories, Research, and Applications*. Hove, UK: Psychology Press.

Frieze, I.H. (1976). Causal attributions and information seeking to explain success and failure. *Journal of Research in Personality, 10,* 293-305. Doi: 10.1016/0092-6566(76)90019-2

Frieze, I.H. & Snyder, H.N. (1980). Children's beliefs about the causes of success and failure in school settings. *Journal of Educational Psychology, 72,* 186-196. Doi: 10.1037/0022-0663.72.2.186

Frodi, A., Bridges, L. & Grolnick, W. (1985). Correlates of mastery-related behavior: A short-term longitudinal study of infants in their second year. *Child Development, 56,* 1291-1298. Doi: 10.2307/1130244

Garbarino, J. (1975). The impact of anticipated reward upon cross-age tutoring. *Journal of Personality and Social Psychology, 32,* 421-428. Doi: 10.1037/h0077087

Gillet, N., Lafrenière, M.-A.K., Huyghebaert, T. & Fouquereau, E. (2015). Autonomous and controlled reasons underlying achievement goals: Implications for the 3 × 2 achievement goal model in educational and work settings. *Motivation and Emotion, 39,* 858-875. Doi: 10.1007/s11031-015-9505-y

Gillet, N., Vallerand, R.J. & Lafrenière, M.-A.K. (2012). Intrinsic and extrinsic school motivation as a function of age: The mediating role of autonomy support. *Social Psychology of Education: An International Journal, 15,* 77-95. Doi: 10.1007/s11218-011-9170-2

Gonçalves, T., Niemivirta, M. & Lemos, M.S. (2017). Identification of students' multiple achievement and social goal profiles and analysis of their stability and adaptability. *Learning and Individual Differences, 54,* 149-159. Doi: 10.1016/j.lindif. 2017.01.019.

Gordon, T. (1975). *Parent Effectiveness Training: The Proven Program for Raising Responsible Children.* New York, NY.: New American Library.

Gordon, T. (1991). *Discipline That Works: Promoting Self-discipline in Children.* New York, NY.: Plume/Penguin.

Gottlieb, J., Oudeyer, P.-Y., Lopes, M. & Baranes, A. (2013). Information seeking, curiosity and attention: Computational and neural mechanisms. *Trends in Cognitive Science, 17,* 585-596. Doi: 10.1016/j.tics.2013.09.001.

Graham, S. (1991). A review of attribution theory in achievement contexts. *Educational Psychology Review, 3,* 5–39. Doi: 10.1007/BF01323661

Graham, S. (2020). An attributional theory of motivation. *Contemporary Educational Psychology, 61,* 101861. Doi: 10.1016/j.cedpsych.2020.101861

Grant, H. & Dweck, C.S. (2003). Clarifying Achievement Goals and Their Impact. *Journal of Personality and Social Psychology, 85,* 541-553. Doi: 10.1037/0022-3514.85.3.541

Greene, D. & Lepper, M.R. (1974). Effects of Extrinsic Rewards on Children's Subsequent Intrinsic Interest. *Child Development, 45,* 1141-1145. Doi: 10.2307/1128110

Grolnick, W.S. (2009). The role of parents in facilitating autonomous self-regulation for education. *Theory and Research in Education, 7,* 164-173. Doi: 10.1177/1477878509104321

Grolnick, W.S. & Ryan, R.M. (1987). Autonomy in children's learning: An experimental and individual difference investigation. *Journal of Personality and Social Psychology, 52,* 890-898. Doi: 10.1037/0022-3514.52.5.890

Grossnickle, E.M. (2016). Disentangling curiosity: Dimensionality, definitions, and distinctions from interest in educational contexts. *Educational Psychology Review, 28,* 23-60. Doi: 10.1007/s10648-014-9294-y

Hackman, J.R. & Oldham, G.R. (1975). Development of the Job Diagnostic Survey. *Journal of Applied Psychology, 60,* 159-170. Doi: 10.1037/h0076546

Hackman, J.R. & Oldham, G.R. (1976). Motivation through the design of work: Test of a theory. *Organizational Behavior & Human Performance, 16,* 250-279. Doi: 10.1016/0030-5073(76)90016-7

Hackman, J.R. & Oldham, G.R. (1980). *Work Redesign.* Reading, MA: Addison-Wesley Publishing Company.

Haggbloom, S.J., Warnick, R., Warnick, J.E., Jones, V.K., Yarbrough, G.L., Russell, T.M., Borecky, C.M., McGahhey, R. Powell, J.L., Beavers, J. & Monte, E. (2001). The 100 Most Eminent Psychologists of the Twentieth Century. *Review of General Psychology, 6,* 139–152. Doi: 10.1037//1089-2680.6.2.139

Hansford, B.C. & Hattie, J.A. (1982). The relationship between self and achievement/performance measures. *Review of Educational Research, 52,* 123-142. Doi: 10.2307/1170275

Harackiewicz, J.M., Barron, K.E. & Elliot, A.J. (1998). Rethinking achievement goals: When are they adaptive for college students and why? *Educational Psychologist, 33,* 1-21. Doi: 10.1207/s15326985ep3301_1

Harackiewicz, J.M., Barron, K.E., Carter, S.M., Lehto, A.T. & Elliot, A.J. (1997). Predictors and consequences of achievement goals in the college classroom: Maintaining interest and making the grade. *Journal of Personality and Social Psychology, 73,* 1284-1295. Doi: 10.1037/0022-3514.73.6.1284

Harackiewicz, J.M., Barron, K.E., Pintrich, P.R., Elliot, A.J. & Thrash, T.M. (2002). Revision of achievement goal theory: Necessary and illuminating. *Journal of Educational Psychology, 94,* 638-645. Doi: 10.1037/0022-0663.94.3.638

Harackiewicz, J.M., Barron, K.E., Tauer, J.M., Carter, S.M. & Elliot, A.J. (2000). Short-term and long-term consequences of achievement goals: predicting interest and performance over time. *Journal of Educational Psychology, 92,* 316-330. Doi: 10.1037/ 0022-0663.92.2.316

Harackiewicz, J.M., Barron, K.E., Tauer, J.M. & Elliot, A.J. (2002). Predicting success in college: A longitudinal study of achievement goals and ability measures as predictors of interest and performance from freshman year through graduation. *Journal of Educational Psychology, 94,* 562-575. Doi: 10.1037/0022-0663.94.3.562

Hareli, S. & Weiner, B. (2002). Social emotions and personality inferences: A scaffold for a new direction in the study of motivation. *Educational Psychologist, 37,* 183-193. Doi: 10.1207/S15326985EP3703_4

Harlow, H.F., Harlow, M.K. & Meyer, D.R. (1950). Learning motivated by a manipulation drive. *Journal of Experimental Psychology, 40,* 228-234. Doi: 10.1037/ h0056906

Harvey, J.H. & Weary, (1981). (With an invited chapter by Ben Harris). *Perspectives on attributional processes.* Dubuque, IA.: W.C. Brown Co.

Hattie, J. & Marsh, H.W. (1996). The relationship between research and teaching: A meta-analysis. *Review of Educational Research, 66,* 507-542. Doi: 10.2307/1170652

Hayakawa, S.I. (1941). *Language in Action.* New York, NY.: Harcord Brace and Company.

Hayakawa, S.I., Berger, A.A. & Chandler, A. (1978). *Language in Thought and Action.* New York, NY.: Harcourt, Brace, Jovanovich (revised fourth edition).

Hayakawa, S.I. & Hayakawa, A.R. (1990). *Language in Thought and Action.* New York, NY.: Harvest Original, Harcord Inc (revised fifth edition).

Heider, F. (1958). *The psychology of interpersonal relations.* New York, NY.: Wiley.

Heneman, H.G. & Schwab, D.P. (1972). Evaluation of research on expectancy theory predictions of employee performance. *Psychological Bulletin, 78,* 1-9. Doi: 10.1037/h0033093

Hennessey, B.A. (2000). Rewards and creativity. In: C. Sansone & J.M. Harackiewicz (Eds). *Intrinsic and extrinsic motivation: The search for optimal motivation and performance* (pp. 55-78). New York, NY.: Academic Press. Doi: 10.1016/B978-012619070-0/50025-8

Hennessey, B.A. & Amabile, T.M. (1998). Reality, intrinsic motivation, and creativity. *American Psychologist, 53(6),* 674-675. Doi: 10.1037/0003-066X.53.6.674

Hennessey, B.A., Amabile, T.M. & Martinage, M. (1989). Immunizing children against the negative effects of reward. *Contemporary Educational Psychology, 14,* 212-227. Doi: 10.1016/0361-476X(89)90011-8

Hennessey, B.A. & Zbikowski, S.M. (1993). Immunizing children against the negative effects of reward: A further examination of intrinsic motivation training techniques. *Creativity Research Journal, 6(3),* 297-307. Doi: 10.1080/10400419309534485

Herzberg, F.I. (1966). *Work and the nature of man.* Cleveland, OH: World Pub, Co.

Herzberg, F. (1968) One More Time: How Do You Motivate Employees? *Harvard Business Review, 46,* 53-62.

Hewett, R., Shantz, A., Mundy, J. & Alfes, K. (2018). Attribution theories in Human Resource Management research: A review and research agenda. *The International Journal of Human Resource Management, 29(1),* 87-126. Doi: 10.1080/09585192. 2017.1380062

Hidi, S. & Harackiewicz, J.M. (2000). Motivating the academically unmotivated: A critical issue for the 21st century. *Review of Educational Research, 70,* 151-179. Doi: 10.2307/1170660

Higgins, R.L., Snyder, C.R. & Berglas, S. (1990). *Self-handicapping: The paradox that isn't.* New York, NY.: Plenum. Doi: 10.1007/978-1-4899-0861-2

Hiroto, D.S. & Seligman, M.E.P. (1975). Generality of learned helplessness in man. *Journal of Personality and Social Psychology, 31,* 311-327. Doi: 10.1037/h0076270

Hoffman, M. (1976). Empathy, Role-Taking, Guilt, and Development of Altruistic Motives. In: T. Lickona (Ed.), *Moral Development: Current Theory and Research* (pp. 124-143). New York, NY.: Holt, Rinehart & Winston.

Hoffman, M.L. (1982). Affect and moral development. *New Directions for Child Development, 16,* 83-103. Doi: 10.1002/cd.23219821605

Holden, G.W., Moncher, M.S., Schinke, S.P. & Barker, K.M. (1990). Self-efficacy of children and adolescents: A meta-analysis. *Psychological Reports, 66,* 1044-1046. Doi: 10.2466/PR0.66.3.1044-1046

Holt, J. (1964). *How Children Fail.* London, UK.: Pitman Publishing Company.

Honicke, T. & Broadbent, J. (2016). The influence of academic self-efficacy on academic performance: A systematic review. *Educational Research Review, 17,* 63-84. Doi: 10.1016/j.edurev.2015.11.002

Hornstra, L., van der Veen, I., Peetsma, T. & Volman, M. (2013). Developments in motivation and achievement during primary school: A longitudinal study on groupspecific differences. *Learning and Individual Differences, 23,* 195-204. Doi: 10.1016/j.lindif.

2012.09.004.

Hout, M. & Elliott, S.W. (2011). *Incentives and test-based accountability in education.* National Research Council. Washington, DC.: The National Academies Press. Doi: 10.17226/12521

Howard, J.L., Gagné, M. & Bureau, J.S. (2017). Testing a continuum structure of self-determined motivation: A meta-analysis. *Psychological Bulletin, 143,* 1346-1377. Doi: 10.1037/bul0000125

Huang, C. (2011). Self-concept and academic achievement: A meta-analysis of longitudinal relations. *Journal of School Psychology, 49,* 505-528. Doi: 10.1016/j.jsp.2011.07.001

Hull, C.L. (1943). *Principles of behavior: An introduction to behavior theory.* New York, NY.: Appleton-Century-Crofts.

Hull, C.L. (1951). *Essentials of behavior.* New Haven: Yale University Press.

Hull, C.L. (1952). *A behavior system: An introduction to behavior theory concerning the individual organism.* New Haven: Yale University Press, 1952.

Hulleman, C.S. & Harackiewicz, J.M. (2009). Promoting interest and performance in high school science classes. *Science, 326(5958),* 1410-1412. Doi: 10.1126/science.1177067

Hulleman, C.S., Schrager, S.M., Bodmann, S.M. & Harackiewicz, J.M. (2010). A meta-analytic review of achievement goal measures: Different labels for the same constructs or different constructs with similar labels? *Psychological Bulletin, 136,* 422-449. Doi: 10.1037/a0018947

Hunter, J. P. & Csikszentmihalyi, M. (2003). The positive psychology of interested adolescents. *Journal of Youth and Adolescence, 32,* 27–35. Doi: 10.1023/A:1021028306392

Hunter, J.E. & Schmidt, F.L. (2000). Fixed effects vs. random effects meta-analysis models: Implications for cumulative research knowledgge. *International Journal of Selection and Assessment, 8,* 275-292. Doi: 10.1111/1468-2389.00156

Hunter, J.E. & Schmidt, F.L. (2004). *Methods of Meta-Analysis: Correcting Error and Bias in Research Findings.* Thousand Oaks, CA.: Sage.

IPCC, (2021). *Climate Change 2021: The Physical Science Basis. Contribution of Working Group I to the Sixth Assessment Report of the Intergovernmental Panel on Climate Change.* V. Masson-Delmotte, P. Zhai, A. Pirani, S.L. Connors, C. Péan, S. Berger, N. Caud, Y. Chen, L. Goldfarb, M.I. Gomis, M. Huang, K. Leitzell, E. Lonnoy, J.B.R. Matthews, T.K. Maycock, T. Waterfield, O. Yelekçi, R. Yu, and B. Zhou (Eds). Cambridge, UK.: Cambridge University Press. Doi: 10.1017/9781009157896

IPCC, (2022). *Climate Change 2022: Impacts, Adaptation, and Vulnerability. Contribution of Working Group II to the Sixth Assessment Report of the Intergovernmental Panel on Climate Change.* H.-O. Pörtner, D.C. Roberts, M. Tignor, E.S. Poloczanska, K. Mintenbeck, A. Alegría, M. Craig, S. Langsdorf, S. Löschke, V. Möller, A. Okem, B. Rama (Eds). Cambridge, UK.: Cambridge University Press. Doi: 10.1017/9781009325844

Isakson, K. & Jarvis, P. (1999). The adjustment of adolescents during the transition into high school: A short term longitudinal study. *Journal of Youth and Adolescence, 28,* 1-26. Doi: 10.1023/A:1021616407189

Jacobs, J.E., Lanza, S., Osgood, D.W., Eccles, J.S. & Wigfield, A. (2002). Changes in children's self-competence and values: Gender and domain differences across grades one though twelve. *Child Development, 73,* 509–527. Doi: 10.1111/1467-8624.00421

Jagacinski, C.M. & Nicholls, J.G. (1984). Conceptions of ability and related affects in task involvement and ego involvement. *Journal of Educational Psychology, 76,* 909-919. Doi: 10.1037/0022-0663.76.5.909

Jansen in de Wal, J., Hornstra, L., Prins, F.J., Peetsma, T. & van der Veen, I. (2016). The prevalence, development and domain specificity of elementary school students' achievement goal profiles. *Educational Psychology, 36,* 1303-1322. Doi: 10.1080/ 01443410.2015.1035698

Jeong, Y.H., Healy, L.C. & McEwan, D. (2021). The application of Goal Setting Theory to goal setting interventions in sport: a systematic review. *International Review of Sport and Exercise Psychology,* pp.1-26. Doi: 10.1080/1750984X.2021.1901298

Joët, G., Usher, E.L. & Bressoux, P. (2011). Sources of self-efficacy: An investigation of elementary school students in France. *Journal of Educational Psychology, 103,* 649-663. Doi: 10.1037/a0024048

Johnson, M.L. & Kestler, J.L. (2013). Achievement goals of traditional and nontraditional aged college students: Using the 3 × 2 achievement goal framework. *International Journal of Educational Research, 61,* 48-59. Doi: 10.1016/j.ijer. 2013.03.010

Johnson, M.L. & Safavian, N. (2016). What is cost and is it always a bad thing? Furthering the discussion concerning college-aged students' perceived costs for their academic studies. *Journal of Cognitive Education and Psychology, 15,* 368-390. Doi: 10.1891/1945-8959.15.3.368

Jones, E.E., Kanouse, D.E., Kelley, H.H., Nisbett, R.E., Valins, S. & Weiner, B. (1972). *Attribution: Perceiving the Causes of Behavior.* Morristown, NJ.: General Learning Press.

Judge, T.A., Thoresen, C.J., Bono, J.E. & Patton, G.K. (2001). The job satisfaction–job performance relationship: A qualitative and quantitative review. *Psychological Bulletin, 127,* 376-407. Doi: 10.1037/0033-2909.127.3.376

Kanfer, R. & Chen, G. (2016). Motivation in organizational behavior: History, advances and prospects. *Organizational Behavior and Human Decision Processes, 136,* 6-19. Doi: 10.1016/j.obhdp.2016.06.002

Kanfer, R., Chen, G. & Pritchard, R.D. (2008). *Work motivation: Past, present, and future.* New York, NY.: Routledge, Taylor and Francis.

Kanfer, R., Frese, M. & Johnson, R.E. (2017). Motivation related to work: A century of progress. *Journal of Applied Psychology, 102,* 338-355. Doi: 10.1037/ apl0000133

Kaplan, A. & Maehr, M.L. (1999). Achievement goals and student well-being. *Contemporary Educational Psychology, 24,* 330-358. Doi: 10.1006/ceps.1999.0993

Kaplan, A. & Maehr, M.L. (2007). The contributions and prospects of goal orientation theory. *Educational Psychology Review, 19,* 141-184. Doi: 10.1007/s10648-006-9012-5

Kaplan, A., Middleton, M.J., Urdan, T. & Midgley, C. (2002). Achievement goals and goal structures. In.: C. Midgley (Ed.), *Goals, goal structures, and patterns of adaptive learning* (pp. 21-53). Mahwah, NJ.: Erlbaum.

Karabenick, S.A. & Urdan, T.C. (2014). *Motivational Interventions (Advances in Motivation and Achievement, Vol. 18)*, UK.: Emerald Group Publishing Limited. Doi: 10.1108/S0749-742320140000018017

Kaufman, E.K., Israel, G.D. & Rudd, R.D. (2008). Exploring goal-setting as a tool for leadership development. *Journal of Leadership Studies, 1*, 51-61. Doi: 10.1002/jls.20032

Kelley, H.H. (1967). Attribution theory in social psychology. In: D. Levine (Ed.), *Nebraska symposium on motivation* (Vol. 15). Lincoln, NE.: University of Nebraska Press.

Kelley, H.H. & Michela, J.L. (1980). Attribution theory and research. In: M. Rosenweig & L. Porter (Eds.), *Annual Review of Psychology, 31*, 457-501. Doi: 10.1146/ annurev.ps.31.020180.002325

Kenrick, D. T., Griskevicius, V., Neuberg, S. L. & Schaller, M. (2010). Renovating the pyramid of needs: Contemporary extensions built upon ancient foundations. *Perspectives on Psychological Science, 5*, 292-314. Doi: 10.1177/1745691610369469

Klapp, A. (2015). Does grading affect Educational attainment? A longitudinal study. *Assessment in Education: Principles, Policy & Practice, 22*, 302-323, Doi: 10.1080/0969594X.2014.988121

Klassen, R.M. (2004a). A cross-cultural investigation of the efficacy beliefs of South Asian immigrant and Anglo Canadian nonimmigrant early adolescents. *Journal of Educational Psychology, 96*, 731-742. Doi: 10.1037/0022-0663.96.4.731

Klassen, R.M. (2004b). Optimism and realism: A review of self-efficacy from a cross-cultural perspective. *International Journal of Psychology, 39*, 205-230. Doi: 10.1080/00207590344000330

Klassen, R.M. & Usher, E.L. (2010). Self-efficacy in educational settings: Recent research and emerging directions. In: T.C. Urdan & S.A. Karabenick (Eds.), *Advances in motivation and achievement. Volume 16A, the decade ahead: Theoretical perspectives on motivation and achievement* (pp. 1-33). Bingley, UK: Emerald Publishing Group.

Klein, H.J., Wesson, M.J., Hollenbeck, J.R. & Alge, B.J. (1999). Goal commitment and the goal-setting process: Conceptual clarification and empirical synthesis. *Journal of Applied Psychology, 84*, 885-896. Doi: 10.1037/0021-9010.84.6.885

Koestner, R., Ryan, R.M., Bernieri, F. & Holt, K. (1984). Setting limits on children's behavior: The differential effects of controlling vs. informational styles on intrinsic motivation and creativity. *Journal of Personality, 52*, 233-248. Doi: 10.1111/ j.1467-6494.1984.tb00879.x

Koka, A. & Hein, V. (2003). Perceptions of teacher's feedback and learning environment as predictors of intrinsic motivation in physical education. *Psychology of Sport and Exercise, 4*, 333-346. Doi: 10.1016/S1469-0292(02)00012-2

Korzybski, A. (1933). *Science and sanity. An introduction to non-Aristotelian systems and general semantics*. New York, NY.: International Non-Aristotelian Library Publishing

Company.

Kosovich, J.J., Hulleman, C.S., Barron, K.E. & Getty, S. (2015). A practical measure of student motivation: Establishing validity evidence for the Expectancy-Value-Cost Scale in middle school. *The Journal of Early Adolescence, 35,* 790-816. Doi: 10.1177/0272431614556890

Kruglanski, A.W., Friedman, I. & Zeevi, G. (1971). The effects of extrinsic incentive on some qualitative aspects of task performance. *Journal of Personality, 39,* 606-617. Doi: 10.1111/j.1467-6494.1971.tb00066.x

Latham, G.P. (2007). *Work Motivation: History, Theory, Research and Practice.* Thousand Oaks, CA.: Sage.

Latham, G.P. (2012). *Work Motivation: History, Theory, Research, and Practice.* (2nd ed). Thousand Oaks, CA.: SAGE Publications, Inc. Doi: 10.4135/9781506335520

Latham, G.P., Erez, M. & Locke, E.A. (1988). Resolving scientific disputes by the joint design of crucial experiments by the antagonists: Application to the Erez–Latham dispute regarding participation in goal setting. *Journal of Applied Psychology, 73,* 753-772. Doi: 10.1037/0021-9010.73.4.753

Latham, G. P. & Locke, E. A. (1975). Increasing productivity with decreasing time limits: A field replication of Parkinson's law. *Journal of Applied Psychology, 60,* 524-526. Doi: 10.1037/h0076916

Latham, G.P. & Locke, E.A. (1991). Self-regulation through goal setting. *Organizational Behavior and Human Decision Processes, 50,* 212-247. Doi: 10.1016/ 0749-5978(91)90021-K

Latham G.P. & Locke, E.A. (2007) New developments in and directions for goal-setting research. *European Psychologist, 12,* 290-300. Doi: 10.1027/1016-9040.12.4.290

Latham, G.P., Locke, E.A. & Fassina, N.E. (2002). The high performance cycle: standing the test of time. In: S. Sonnentag (Ed.), *The psychological management of individual performance. A handbook in the psychology of management organizations* (pp. 199-228). Chichester, UK.: Wiley & Sons. Doi: 10.1002/0470013419.ch10

Latham, G.P., Winters, D.C. & Locke, E.A. (1994). Cognitive and motivational effects of participation: A mediator study. *Journal of Organizational Behavior, 15,* 49-63. Doi: 10.1002/job.4030150106

Lau, R.R. & Russell, D. (1980). Attributions in the sports pages. *Journal of Personality and Social Psychology, 39,* 29-38. Doi: 10.1037/0022-3514.39.1.29

Lawler, E.E. & Porter, L.W. (1967). The effect of performance on job satisfaction. *Industrial Relations*, 7, 20-28. Doi: 10.1111/j.1468-232X.1967.tb01060.x

Lazowski, R. A. & Hulleman, C. S. (2016). Motivation interventions in education: A meta-analytic review. *Review of Educational Research, 86,* 602–640. Doi: 10.3102/0034654315617832

Lee, C. & Bobko, P. (1992). Exploring the meaning and usefulness of measures of subjective goal difficulty. *Journal of Applied Social Psychology, 22,* 1417-1428. Doi: 10.1111/j.1559-1816.1992.tb00957.x

Lee, J., Bong, M. & Kim, S. (2014). Interaction between task values and self-efficacy on maladaptive achievement strategy use. *Educational Psychology, 34,* 538-560. Doi: 10.1080/01443410.2014.895296

Lee, J., Lee, M. & Bong, M. (2013). High value with low perceived competence as an amplifier of self-worth threat. In: D. McInerney, H. Marsh, R. Craven & F. Guay (Eds.), *Theory driving research: New wave perspectives on self-processes and human development* (pp. 205-231). Charlotte, NC: Information Age.

Lepper, M.R. & Henderlong, J. (2000). Turning "Play" into "Work" and "Work" into "Play": 25 Years of Research on Intrinsic Versus Extrinsic Motivation. In: C. Sansone & J.M. Harackiewicz (Eds.), *Intrinsic and Extrinsic Motivation - The Search for Optimal Motivation and Performance* (pp. 257-307). New York, NY.: Academic Press. Doi: 10.1016/B978-012619070-0/50032-5

Lepper, M.R., Corpus, J.H. & Iyengar, S.S. (2005). Intrinsic and Extrinsic Motivational Orientations in the Classroom: Age Differences and Academic Correlates. *Journal of Educational Psychology, 97,* 184-196. Doi: 10.1037/0022-0663.97.2.184

Lepper, M.R., Greene, D. & Nisbett, R.E. (1973). Undermining children's intrinsic interest with extrinsic reward: A test of the "overjustification" hypothesis. *Journal of Personality and Social Psychology, 28,* 129-137. Doi: 10.1037/h0035519

Lerner, B.S. & Locke, E.A. (1995). The effect of goal setting, self-efficacy, competition, and personal trials on the performance of an endurance task. *Journal of Sport & Exercise Psychology, 17,* 138-152.

Linnenbrink, E.A. (2005). The Dilemma of Performance-Approach Goals: The Use of Multiple Goal Contexts to Promote Students' Motivation and Learning. *Journal of Educational Psychology, 97,* 197-213. Doi: 10.1037/0022-0663.97.2.197

Lin-Siegler, X., Dweck, C.S. & Cohen, G.L. (2016). Instructional interventions that motivate classroom learning. *Journal of Educational Psychology, 108,* 295-299. Doi: 10.1037/edu0000124

Lipsey, M.W. & Wilson, D.B. (2001). *Practical meta-analysis.* Thousand Oaks, CA: Sage Publications.

Liu, W.C., Wang, C.K.J., Tan, O.S., Ee, J. & Koh, C. (2009). Understanding students' motivation in project work: A 2 × 2 achievement goal approach. *British Journal of Educational Psychology, 79,* 87-106. Doi: 10.1348/000709908X313767

Locke, E.A. (1964). The relationship of intentions to motivation and affect. Unpublished doctoral dissertation, Cornell University.

Locke, E.A. (1968). Toward a theory of task motivation and incentives. *Organizational Behavior & Human Performance, 3,* 157-189. Doi: 10.1016/0030-5073(68)90004-4

Locke, E.A. (1991). Goal theory vs. control theory: Contrasting approaches to understanding work motivation. *Motivation & Emotion, 15,* 9-28. Doi: 10.1007/BF00991473

Locke, E.A. (1996). Motivation through conscious goal setting. *Applied & Preventive Psychology, 5,* 117-124. Doi: 10.1016/S0962-1849(96)80005-9

Locke, E.A. (2000). *Handbook of principles of organizational behavior.* Oxford, UK.: Blackwell Publishers.

Locke, E.A. & Latham, G.P. (1984). *Goal setting: A motivational technique that works.* Englewood Cliffs, NJ.: Prentice Hall.

Locke, E.A. & Latham, G.P. (1990). *A theory of goal-setting and task performance.* Englewood Cliffs, NJ.: Prentice Hall.

Locke, E.A. & Latham, G.P. (2002). Building a practically useful theory of goal setting and task motivation: A 35-year odyssey. *American Psychologist, 57,* 705-717. Doi: 10.1037/0003-066X.57.9.705

Locke, E.A. & Latham, G.P. (2005). Goal setting theory: Theory building by induction. In: K.G. Smith & M.A. Hitt (Eds.), *Great minds in management: The process of theory development.* Oxford, UK: Oxford University Press.

Locke, E.A. & Latham, G.P. (2009). Has goal setting gone wild, or have its attackers abandoned good scholarship? *Academy of Management Perspectives, 23,* 17-23. Doi: 10.5465/AMP.2009.37008000

Locke, E.A. & Latham, G.P. (2013) Goal setting theory. In: E.H. Kessler (Ed.). *Encyclopedia of Management Theory.* Thousand Oaks, CA: Sage.

Locke, E.A & Latham, G.P. (2019) The development of goal setting theory: A half century retrospective. *Motivation Science, 5,* 93-105. Doi : 10.1037/mot0000127

Locke, E.A., Shaw, K.N., Saari, L.M. & Latham, G.P. (1981). Goal setting and task performance: 1969–1980. *Psychological Bulletin, 90,* 125-152. Doi: 10.1037/0033-2909.90.1.125

Lopez, S.J. (Ed.). (2008). *Positive psychology: Exploring the best in people, Vol. 1. Discovering human strengths.* Westport, CT: Praeger/Greenwood.

Loveland, K.K. & Olley, J.G. (1979). The Effect of External Reward on Interest and Quality of Task Performance in Children of High and Low Intrinsic Motivation. *Child Development, 50,* 1207-1210. Doi: 10.2307/1129350

Lowry, R.J. (Ed.) (1979). The Journals of A.H. Maslow – Volumes I and II (with assistance of Maslow, B.G.). Monterey, CA.: Brooks Cole.

Luo, W., Paris, S.G., Hogan, D. & Luo, Z. (2011). Do performance goals promote learning? A pattern analysis of Singapore students' achievement goals. *Contemporary Educational Psychology, 36,* 165-176. Doi: 10.1016/j.cedpsych.2011.02.003

Maehr, M.L. & Midgley, C. (1991). Enhancing student motivation: A schoolwide approach. *Educational Psychologist, 26,* 399-427. Doi: 10.1207/s15326985ep2603&4_9

Malle, B.F. (2006). The actor-observer asymmetry in attribution: A (surprising) meta-analysis. *Psychological Bulletin, 132,* 895-919. Doi: 10.1037/0033-2909.132.6.895

Markus, H.R. & Kitayama, S. (1991). Culture and the self: Implications for cognition, emotion, and motivation. *Psychological Review, 98,* 224-253. Doi: 10.1037/ 0033-295X.98.2.224

Marsh, H.W. (1986). Verbal and math self-concepts: An internal/external frame of reference model. *American Educational Research Journal, 23,* 129-149.

Marsh, H.W. (1987). The big-fish-little-pond effect on academic self-concept. *Journal of Educational Psychology, 79*(3), 280-295. Doi: 10.1037/0022-0663.79.3.280

Marsh, H.W. (1990a). The causal ordering of academic self-concept and academic achievement: A multiwave, longitudinal panel analysis. *Journal of Educational Psychology, 82,* 646-656. Doi: 10.1037/0022-0663.82.4.646

Marsh, H.W. (1990b). A multidimensional, hierarchical model of self-concept: Theoretical and empirical justification. *Educational Psychology Review, 2,* 77-172. Doi: 10.1007/BF01322177

Marsh, H.W. (1991). Failure of high-ability high schools to deliver academic benefits commensurate with their students' ability levels. *American Educational Research Journal, 28,* 445-480. Doi: 10.2307/1162948

Marsh, H.W. (1992). The content specificity of relations between academic achievement and academic self-concept. *Journal of Educational Psychology, 84,* 35-42. Doi: 10.1037/0022-0663.84.1.35

Marsh, H. W. (1993). Academic self-concept: Theory measurement and research. In: J. Suls (Ed.), *Psychological perspectives on the self* (Vol. 4, pp. 59-98). Hillsdale, NJ: Erlbaum.

Marsh, H.W. (2008). A multidimensional, hierarchical model of self-concept: An important facet of personality. In: G. J. Boyle, G. Matthews & D. H. Saklofske (Eds.), *The SAGE handbook of personality theory and assessment, Vol. 1: Personality theories and models* (pp. 447-469). Thousand Oaks, CA: Sage Publications. Doi: 10.4135/ 9781849200462

Marsh, H.W., Byrne, B.M. & Shavelson, R.J. (1988). A multifaceted academic self-concept: Its hierarchical structure and its relation to academic achievement. *Journal of Educational Psychology, 80,* 366-380. Doi: 10.1037/0022-0663.80.3.366

Marsh, H.W., Byrne, B.M. & Yeung, A.S. (1999). Causal ordering of academic self-concept and achievement: Reanalysis of a pioneering study and revised recommendations. *Educational Psychologist, 34,* 155-167. Doi: 10.1207/s15326985ep3403_2

Marsh, H.W., Chessor, D., Craven, R.G. & Roche, L. (1995). The effects of gifted-and-talented programmes on academic self-concept: The big fish strikes again. *American Educational Research Journal, 32,* 285-319. Doi: 10.2307/1163433

Marsh, H.W. & Craven, R. (1997). Academic self-concept: Beyond the dustbowl. In: G.D. Phye (Ed.), *Handbook of classroom assessment: Learning, achievement, and adjustment* (pp. 131–198). New York, NY.: Academic Press.

Marsh, H.W. & Craven, R.G. (2002). The pivotal role of frames of reference in ASC formation: The big fish little pond effect. In: F. Pajares & T. Urdan (Eds.) *Adolescence and education* (Vol. 2, pp. 83-123). Greenwich, CT: Information Age Publishing.

Marsh, H. W. & Craven, R. G. (2005). A reciprocal effects model of the causal ordering of self-concept and achievement : new support for the benefits of enhancing self-concept. In: H.W. Marsh, R.G. Craven & D.M. Mclnerney (Eds). *New Frontiers for Self Research - Volume 2: International advances in self research* (pp. 17-51). Greenwich, CT: Information Age Publishing.

Marsh, H.W. & Craven, R.G. (2006). Reciprocal effects of self-concept and performance from a multidimensional perspective: Beyond seductive pleasure and unidimensional perspectives. *Perspectives on Psychological Science, 1,* 133-163. Doi : 10.1111/j.1745-6916.2006.00010.x

Marsh, H.W. & Hattie, J. (1996). Theoretical perspectives on the structure of self-concept. In: B.A. Bracken (Ed.), *Handbook of self-concept: Developmental, social, and clinical considerations* (pp. 38–90). New York, NY.: John Wiley & Sons.

Marsh, H.W. & Hau, K.-T. (2003). Big-Fish--Little-Pond effect on academic self-concept: A cross-cultural (26-country) test of the negative effects of academically selective schools. *American Psychologist, 58,* 364–376. Doi: 10.1037/0003-066X. 58.5.364

Marsh, H.W., Hau, K.-T. & Kong, C.-K. (2002). Multilevel causal ordering of academic self-concept and achievement: Influence of language of instruction (English compared with Chinese) for Hong Kong students. *American Educational Research Journal, 39,* 727-763. Doi: 10.3102/00028312039003727

Marsh, H.W., Köller, O. & Baumert, J. (2001). Reunification of East and West German school systems: Longitudinal multilevel modeling study of the big-fish-little-pond effect on academic self-concept. *American Educational Research Journal, 38,* 321-350. Doi: 10.3102/00028312038002321

Marsh, H.W. & O'Mara, A. (2008). Reciprocal effects between academic self-concept, self-esteem, achievement, and attainment over seven adolescent years: Unidimensional and multidimensional perspectives of self-concept. *Personality and Social Psychology Bulletin, 34,* 542-552. Doi: 10.1177/0146167207312313

Marsh, H.W. & O'Mara, A.J. (2010). Long-term total negative effects of school-average ability on diverse educational outcomes: Direct and indirect effects of the big-fish-little-pond effect. *Zeitschrift für Pädagogische Psychologie / German Journal of Educational Psychology, 24,* 51-72. Doi: 10.1024/1010-0652.a000004

Marsh, H.W. & O'Neill, R. (1984). Self Description Questionnaire III: The construct validity of multidimensional self-concept ratings by late adolescents. *Journal of Educational Measurement, 21,* 153-174. Doi: 10.1111/j.1745-3984.1984.tb00227.x

Marsh, H.W. & Parker, J.W. (1984). Determinants of student self-concept: Is it better to be a relatively large fish in a small pond even if you don't learn to swim as well? *Journal of Personality and Social Psychology, 47,* 213-231. Doi: 10.1037/0022-3514.47.1.213

Marsh, H.W., Parker, P.D. & Pekrun, R. (2019). Three paradoxical effects on academic self-concept across countries, schools, and students: Frame-of-reference as a unifying theoretical explanation. *European Psychologist, 24,* 231-242. Doi: 10.1027/ 1016-9040/a000332

Marsh, H.W. & Seaton, M. (2015). The big-fish–little-pond effect, competence self-perceptions, and relativity: Substantive advances and methodological innovation. In: A.J. Elliott (Ed.), *Advances in Motivation Science, 2,* 127-184. New York, NY.: Elsevier. Doi: 10.1016/bs.adms.2015.05.002

Marsh, H. W., Seaton, M., Dicke, T., Parker, P. D. & Horwood, M. S. (2019). The centrality of academic self-concept to motivation and learning. In: K.A. Renninger & S.E. Hidi (Eds.), *The Cambridge handbook of motivation and learning* (pp. 36-62). Cambridge,

UK.: Cambridge University Press. Doi: 10.1017/9781316823279.004

Marsh, H.W., Seaton, M., Trautwein, U., Lüdtke, O., Hau, K.T., O'Mara, A.J. & Craven, R.G. (2008). The big-fish-little-pond-effect stands up to critical scrutiny: Implications for theory, methodology, and future research. *Educational Psychology Review, 20,* 319-350. Doi: 10.1007/s10648-008-9075-6

Marsh, H.W. & Shavelson, R. (1985). Self-concept: Its multifaceted, hierarchical structure. *Educational Psychologist, 20,* 107-123. Doi: 10.1207/s15326985ep2003_1

Marsh, H. W., Trautwein, U., Lüdtke, O., Baumert, J. & Köller, O. (2007). The big-fish-little-pond effect: Persistent negative effects of selective high schools on self-concept after graduation. *American Educational Research Journal, 44,* 631-669. Doi: 10.3102/0002831207306728

Marsh, H.W., Trautwein, U., Lüdtke, O., Köller, O. & Baumert, J. (2005). Academic self-concept, interest, grades, and standardized test scores: Reciprocal effects models of causal ordering. *Child development, 76,* 397-416. Doi: 10.1111/j.1467-8624.2005.00853.x

Marsh, H.W., Trautwein, U., Lüdtke, O., Köller, O. & Baumert, J. (2006). Integration of multidimensional self-concept and core personality constructs: Construct validation and relations to well-being and achievement. *Journal of Personality, 74,* 403-456. Doi: 10.1111/j.1467-6494.2005.00380.x

Marsh, H.W. & Yeung, A.S. (1997). Causal effects of academic self-concept on academic achievement: Structural equation models of longitudinal data. *Journal of Educational Psychology, 89,* 41-54. Doi: 10.1037/0022-0663.89.1.41

Martin, A.J., Marsh, H.W. & Debus, R.L. (2001). Self-handicapping and defensive pessimism: Exploring a model of predictors and outcomes from a self-protection perspective. *Journal of Educational Psychology, 93,* 87-102. Doi: 10.1037/0022-0663.93.1.87

Martin, A.J., Marsh, H.W. & Debus, R.L. (2003). Self-handicapping and defensive pessimism: A Model of self-protection from a longitudinal perspective. *Contemporary Educational Psychology, 28,* 1-36. Doi: 10.1016/S0361-476X(02)00008-5

Martin, A.J., Marsh, H.W., Williamson, A. & Debus, R.L. (2005). Fear of failure in students' academic lives: Exploring the roles of self-handicapping and defensive pessimism from longitudinal, multidimensional, and qualitative perspectives. In: H.W. Marsh, R.G. Craven & D.M. McInerney (Eds.), *New Frontiers for Self Research - Volume 2: International advances in self research* (pp. 357-385). Greenwich, CT: Information Age.

Martinko, M.J. & Mackey, J.D. (2019). Attribution theory: An introduction to the special issue. *Journal of Organizational Behavior, 40,* 523-527. Doi: 10.1002/job.2397

Mascret, N., Elliot, A.J. & Cury, F. (2015). Extending the 3 × 2 achievement goal model to the sport domain: The 3 × 2 achievement goal questionnaire for sport. *Psychology of Sport and Exercise, 17,* 7–14. Doi: 10.1016/j.psychsport.2014.11.001

Maslow, A.H. (1943). A theory of human motivation. *Psychological Review, 50,* 370-396. Doi: 10.1037/h0054346

Maslow, A.H. (1954). *Motivation and personality.* New York, NY.: Harper & Row.

Maslow, A.H. (1970). *Motivation and personality.* (Second Edition) New York, NY.:

Harper & Row.

Maslow, A.H. (1971). *The farther reaches of human nature.* New York, NY.: Viking.

Mathieu, J.E. & Hamel, K. (1989). A causal model of the antecedents of organizational commitment among professionals and nonprofessionals. *Journal of Vocational Behavior, 34,* 299-317.Doi: 10.1016/0001-8791(89)90022-5

Mathieu, J.E. & Zajac, D.M. (1990). A review and meta-analysis of the antecedents, correlates, and consequences of organizational commitment. *Psychological Bulletin, 108,* 171-194. Doi: 10.1037/0033-2909.108.2.171

McClelland, D.C. (1961). *The achieving society.* Princeton, NJ. : Van Nostrand.

McClelland, D.C. (1978). Managing motivation to expand human freedom. *American Psychologist, 33,* 201-210. Doi: 10.1037/0003-066X.33.3.201

McClelland, D.C., Atkinson, J.W., Clark, R.A. & Lowell, E.L. (1953). *The achievement motive.* New York, NY.: Appleton-Century-Crofts. Doi: 10.1037/11144-000

McGraw, K.O. & McCullers, J.C. (1979). Evidence of a detrimental effect of extrinsic incentives on breaking a mental set. *Journal of Experimental Social Psychology, 15,* 285-294. Doi: 10.1016/0022-1031(79)90039-8

McGregor, D.M. (1960). *The human side of enterprise.* New York, NY.: McGraw-Hill.

McGregor, H.A. & Elliot, A.J. (2002). Achievement goals as predictors of achievement-relevant processes prior to task engagement. *Journal of Educational Psychology, 94,* 381-395. Doi: 10.1037/0022-0663.94.2.381

Meece, J.L. & Holt, K. (1993). A pattern analysis of students' achievement goals. *Journal of Educational Psychology, 85,* 582-590. Doi: 10.1037/0022-0663.85.4.582

Meece, J.L. & Miller, S.D. (2001). A longitudinal analysis of elementary school students' achievement goals in literacy activities. *Contemporary Educational Psychology, 26,* 454-480. Doi: 10.1006/ceps.2000.1071

Meece, J.L., Wigfield, A. & Eccles, J.S. (1990). Predictors of math anxiety and its consequences for young adolescents' course enrollment intentions and performances in mathematics. *Journal of Educational Psychology, 82,* 60-70. Doi: 10.1037/0022-0663.82.1.60

Mennes, M.A. (2016). *De Theatro Motivarum, Motivation: In Search of Essentials. Research on a Theoretical Model of the Process of Motivation and on Critical Determinants of Interference.* Doctoral thesis. Amsterdam, The Netherlands: Amsterdam University Press.

Mento, A.J., Locke, E.A. & Klein, H.J. (1992). Relationship of goal level to valence and instrumentality. *Journal of Applied Psychology, 77,* 395-405. Doi: 10.1037/0021-9010.77.4.395

Mento, A.J., Steel, R.P. & Karren, R.J. (1987). A meta-analytic study of the effects of goal setting on task performance: 1966–1984. *Organizational Behavior and Human Decision Processes, 39,* 52-83. Doi: 10.1016/0749-5978(87)90045-8

Meyer, J.P. (1980). Causal attribution for success and failure: A multivariate investigation of dimensionality, formation, and consequences. *Journal of Personality and Social Psychology, 38,* 704-718. Doi: 10.1037/0022-3514.38.5.704

Meyer, J.P. & Koelbl, S.L. (1982). Students' test performances: Dimensionality of causal attributions. *Personality and Social Psychology Bulletin, 8,* 31-36. Doi: 10.1177/014616728281005

Michela, J.L., Peplau, L.A. & Weeks, D.G. (1982). Perceived dimensions of attributions for loneliness. *Journal of Personality and Social Psychology, 43,* 929-936. Doi: 10.1037/0022-3514.43.5.929

Middleton, M.J, Kaplan, A. & Midgley, C. (2004). The change in middle school students' achievement goals in mathematics over time. *Social Psychology of Education: An International Journal, 7,* 289-311. Doi: 10.1023/B:SPOE.0000037484.86850.fa

Middleton, M.J. & Midgley, C. (1997). Avoiding the demonstration of lack of ability: An underexplored aspect of goal theory. *Journal of Educational Psychology, 89,* 710-718. Doi: 10.1037/0022-0663.89.4.710

Midgley, C. (Ed.) (2002). *Goals, goal structures, and patterns of adaptive learning.* Mahwah, NJ.: Lawrence Erlbaum Associates Publishers.

Midgley, C., Kaplan, A. & Middleton, M. (2001). Performance-approach goals: Good for what, for whom, under what circumstances, and at what cost? *Journal of Educational Psychology, 93,* 77-86. Doi: 10.1037/0022-0663.93.1.77

Miller, D.T. & Ross, M. (1975). Self-serving biases in the attribution of causality: Fact or fiction? *Psychological Bulletin, 82,* 213-225. Doi: 10.1037/h0076486

Mills, J.A. (1998). *Control: A history of behavioral psychology.* New York, NY.: New York University Press.

Miner, J.B. (2003). The Rated Importance, Scientific Validity, and Practical Usefulness of Organizational Behavior Theories: A Quantitative Review. *Academy of Management Learning & Education, 2,* 250-268. Doi: 10.5465/AMLE.2003.10932132

Mitchell, T.R. (1974). Expectancy models of job satisfaction, occupational preference and effort: A theoretical, methodological, and empirical appraisal. *Psychological Bulletin, 81,* 1053-1077. Doi: 10.1037/h0037495

Mitchell, T.R. & Daniels, D. (2003). Motivation. In: W.C. Borman, D.R. Ilgen & R.J. Klimoski (Eds.), *Handbook of psychology: Industrial and organizational psychology,* (Vol. 12, pp. 225-254). New York, NY.: John Wiley & Sons.

Mitchell, T.R. & Nebeker, D.M. (1973). Expectancy theory predictions of academic effort and performance. *Journal of Applied Psychology, 57,* 61-67. Doi: 10.1037/ h0034181

Montessori, M. (1967). *The Discovery of the Child.* New York, NY.: Ballantine Books.

Multon, K.D., Brown, S.D. & Lent, R.W. (1991). Relation of self-efficacy beliefs to academic outcomes: A meta-analytic investigation. *Journal of Counseling Psychology, 1,* 30-38. Doi: 10.1037/0022-0167.38.1.30

Musu-Gillette, L.E., Wigfield, A., Harring, J.R. & Eccles, J.S. (2015). Trajectories of change in students' self-concepts of ability and values in math and college major choice.

*Educational Research and Evaluation, 21,* 343-370. Doi: 10.1080/13803611.2015.1057161

Nagengast, B. & Marsh, H.W. (2012). Big fish in little ponds aspire more: Mediation and cross-cultural generalizability of school-average ability effects on self-concept and career aspirations in science. *Journal of Educational Psychology, 104,* 1033-1053. Doi: 10.1037/a0027697

National Research Council, Commission on Physical Sciences, Mathematics & Applications, Board on Mathematical Sciences, Committee on Applied & Theoretical Statistics, Panel on Statistical Issues & Opportunities for Research in the Combination of Information. (1992). *Combining information: Statistical issues and opportunities for research.* Washington, DC.: National Academy Press.

Nicholls, J.G. (1984). Achievement motivation: Conceptions of ability, subjective experience, task choice, and performance. *Psychological Review, 91,* 328-346. Doi: 10.1037//0033-295X.91.3.328

Nicholls, J.G. (1989). *The competitive ethos and democratic education.* Cambridge, MA.: Harvard University Press.

Nicholls, J.G. & Burton, J.T. (1982). Motivation and equality. *Elementary School Journal, 82,* 367-378.

Nicholls, J.G., Patashnick, M., Cheung, P.C., Thorkildsen, T.A. & Lauer, J.M. (1989). Can achievement motivation theory succeed with only one conception of success? In: F. Halisch & J.H.L. van den Bercken (Eds.), *International perspectives on achievement and task motivation* (pp. 187–208). Lisse, The Netherlands: Swets & Zeitlinger Publishers.

Nichols, S.L. & Berliner, D.C. (2007). *Collateral damage: How high-stakes testing corrupts America's schools.* Cambridge, MA.: Harvard Education Press.

Niemivirta, M. (1998). Individual differences in motivational and cognitive factors affecting self-regulated learning: a pattern-oriented approach. In: P. Nenniger, R.S. Jäger, A. Frey & M. Wosnitza (Eds.), *Advances in motivation* (pp. 23-42). Landau, Germany: Verlag Empirische Pädagogik.

Niemivirta, M. (2002). Motivation and performance in context: the influence of goal orientations and instructional setting on situational appraisals and task performance. *Psychologia: An International Journal of Psychology in the Orient, 45,* 250-270. Doi: 10.2117/psysoc.2002.250

Niemivirta, M. (2004). *Habits of mind and academic endeavors: the correlates and consequences of achievement goal orientations.* Helsinki, Finland: University of Helsinki, Department of Education.

Niemivirta, M., Pulkka, A.-T., Tapola, A. & Tuominen, H. (2019) Achievement Goal Orientations - A Person-Oriented Approach. In: K.A. Renninger & S.E. Hidi (Eds.) *The Cambridge Handbook of Motivation and Learning* (pp. 566-616). Cambridge, UK: Cambridge University Press. Doi: 10.1017/9781316823279.025

Niemivirta, M. & Tapola, A. (2007). Self-efficacy, interest, and task performance: Within-task changes, mutual relationships, and predictive effects. *Zeitschrift für Pädagogische Psychologie, 21,* 241-250. Doi: 10.1024/1010-0652.21.3.241

Nolen, S.B. (1988). Reasons for studying: motivational orientations and study strategies. *Cognition & Instruction, 5,* 269-287. Doi: 10.1207/s1532690xci0504_2

Nolen, S.B. (2019). Conceptualizing Goals in Motivation and Engagement. In: K.A. Renninger & S.E. Hidi (Eds.) *The Cambridge Handbook of Motivation and Learning* (pp. 547–565). Cambridge University Press. Doi: 10.1017/9781316823279.024

Oades-Sese, G.V., Matthews, T.A. & Lewis, M. (2014). Shame and pride and their effects on student achievement. In: R. Pekrun & L. Linnenbrink-Garcia (Eds.). *International Handbook of Emotions in Education* (pp. 246-264). New York, NY.: Taylor and Francis. Doi: 10.4324/9780203148211

O'Donohue, W.T. & Kitchener, R.F. (Eds.). (1999). *Handbook of behaviorism.* San Diego, CA.: Academic Press.

Pajares, F. (1996). Self-efficacy beliefs in academic settings. *Review of Educational Research, 66,* 543-578. Doi: 10.3102/00346543066004543

Pajares, F. (1997). Current directions in self-efficacy research. In: M.L. Maehr & P.R. Pintrich (Eds.), *Advances in motivation and achievement* (Vol. 10, pp. 1-49). Greenwich, CT: JAI Press.

Pajares, F. (2003). Self-efficacy beliefs, motivation, and achievement in writing: A review of the literature. *Reading & Writing Quarterly, 19,* 139-158. Doi: 10.1080/10573560308222

Pajares, F. (2006). Self-efficacy during childhood and adolescence. In: F. Pajares & T. Urdan (Eds.), *Self-Efficacy Beliefs of Adolescents (p. 339-367).* Greenwich, CT.: Information Age Publishing.

Pajares, F. (2007). Motivational Role of Self-Efficacy Beliefs in Self-Regulated Learning. In: B. J. Zimmerman & D. H. Schunk (Eds.), *Motivation and Self-Regulated Learning: Theory, Research, and Applications* (pp. 111-140). New York, NY.: Erlbaum.

Pajares, F., Britner, S.L. & Valiante, G. (2000). Relation between achievement goals and self-beliefs of middle school students in writing and science. *Contemporary Educational Psychology, 25,* 406-422. Doi:10.1006/ceps.1999.1027

Pajares, F. & Schunk, D.H. (2001). Self-beliefs and school success: Self-efficacy, self-concept, and school achievement. In: R.J. Riding & S.G. Rayner (Eds), *International perspectives on individual differences, Volume 2: Self-perception* (pp. 239-265). Westport, CT: Ablex Publishing.

Pajares, F. & Schunk, D.H. (2005). Self-efficacy and Self-concept Beliefs - Jointly Contributing to the Quality of Human Life. In: H.W. Marsh, R.G. Craven & D.M. Mclnerney (Eds). *New Frontiers for Self Research - Volume 2: International advances in self research* (pp. 95-121). Greenwich, CT: Information Age Publishing.

Passer, M.W. (1977). Perceiving the causes of success and failure revisited: A multidimensional scaling approach. Ann Arbor, MI.: ProQuest Dissertations Publishing.

Passer, M.W., Kelley, H.H. & Michela, J.L. (1978). Multidimensional scaling of the causes for negative interpersonal behavior. *Journal of Personality and Social Psychology, 36,* 951-962. Doi : 10.1037/0022-3514.36.9.951

Pastor, D.A., Barron, K.E., Miller, B.J. & Davis, S.L. (2007). A latent profile analysis of college students' achievement goal orientation. *Contemporary Educational Psychology, 32*, 8-47. Doi: 10.1016/j.cedpsych.2006.10.003

Patall, E.A. (2012). The motivational complexity of choosing: A review of theory and research. In: R.M. Ryan (Ed.), *The Oxford handbook of human motivation* (pp. 248-279). Oxford, UK.: Oxford University Press.

Patall, E.A. & Hooper, S.Y. (2019). The promise and peril of choosing for motivation and learning. In: K.A. Renninger & S.E. Hidi (Eds.), *The Cambridge handbook of motivation and learning* (pp. 238–262). Cambridge UK.: Cambridge University Press. Doi: 10.1017/9781316823279.012

Patall, E.A., Cooper, H. & Robinson, J.C. (2008). The effects of choice on intrinsic motivation and related outcomes: A meta-analysis of research findings. *Psychological Bulletin, 134,* 270-300. Doi: 10.1037/0033-2909.134.2.270

Patrick, H., Knee, C.R., Canevello, A. & Lonsbary, C. (2007). The role of need fulfillment in relationship functioning and well-being: A self-determination theory perspective. *Journal of Personality and Social Psychology, 92,* 434-457. Doi: 10.1037/0022-3514.92.3.434

Pekrun, R., Elliot, A.J. & Maier, M.A. (2006). Achievement goals and discrete achievement emotions: a theoretical model and prospective test. *Journal of Educational Psychology, 98,* 583-597. Doi: 10.1037/0022-0663.98.3.583

Pekrun, R., Elliot, A.J. & Maier, M.A. (2009). Achievement goals and achievement emotions: Testing a model of their joint relations with academic performance. *Journal of Educational Psychology, 101,* 115-135. Doi: 10.1037/a0013383

Pekrun, R. & Linnenbrink-Garcia, L. (2012). Academic emotions and student engagement. In: S.L. Christenson, A.L. Reschly & C. Wylie (Eds.), *Handbook of research on student engagement* (pp. 259-282). Berlin, Germany: Springer Science & Business Media. Doi: 10.1007/978-1-4614-2018-7_12

Perry, R.P. & Hamm, J.M. (2017). An attribution Perspective on Competence and Motivation. In: A. Elliot, C. Dweck & D. Yeager (Eds.) *Handbook of Competence and Motivation: Theory and Application* (2nd ed., pp 61-84). New York, NY.: The Guilford Press.

Perry, R.P., Hechter, F.J., Menec, V.H. & Weinberg, L.E. (1993). Enhancing achievement motivation and performance in college students: An attributional retraining perspective. *Research in Higher Education, 34,* 687-723. Doi: 10.1007/BF00992156

Pervin, L.A. (Ed.). (1989). *Goal concepts in personality and social psychology.* Hillsdale, NJ.: Lawrence Erlbaum Associates, Publishers

Peterson, C. (2006). *A primer in positive psychology.* Oxford, UK.: Oxford University Press.

Peterson, C., Maier, S. F. & Seligman, M. E. P. (1993). *Learned helplessness: A theory for the age of personal control.* Oxford, UK.: Oxford University Press.

Pinder, C.C. (1998). *Work Motivation in Organizational Behavior.* Englewood Cliffs, NJ.: Prentice Hall.

Pintrich, P.R. (2000a). The role of goal orientation in self-regulated learning. In: M.

Boekaerts, P.R. Pintrich & M. Zeidner (Eds.), *Handbook of self-regulation: Theory, research and applications* (pp. 451-502). San Diego, CA.: Academic Press.

Pintrich, P.R. (2000b). Multiple goals, multiple pathways: The role of goal orientation in learning and achievement. *Journal of Educational Psychology, 92*, 544-555. Doi: 10.1037/0022-0663.92.3.544

Pintrich, P.R. & Schunk, D.H. (1996). *Motivation in education: Theory, research, and applications.* Englewood Cliffs, NJ: Prentice Hall.

Pinxten, M., De Fraine, B., Van Damme, J. & D'Haenens, E. (2010). Causal ordering of academic self-concept and achievement: Effects of type of achievement measure. *British Journal of Educational Psychology, 80*, 689-709. Doi: 10.1348/000709910X493071

Porter, L.W. & Lawler, E.E. (1968). *Managerial attitudes and performance.* Homewood, Ill.: R. D. Irwin.

Pulfrey, C., Buchs, C. & Butera, F. (2011). Why grades engender performance-avoidance goals: The mediating role of autonomous motivation. *Journal of Educational Psychology, 103,* 683-700. Doi: 10.1037/a0023911

Pulkka, A.-T. & Niemivirta, M. (2013). Adult students' achievement goal orientations and evaluations of the learning environment: A person-centred longitudinal analysis. *Educational Research and Evaluation, 19,* 297-322. Doi: 10.1080/13803611. 2013.767741

Reeve, J. (2002). Self-determination theory applied to educational settings. In: E.L. Deci & R.M. Ryan (Eds.), *Handbook of self-determination research* (pp. 183-203). Rochester, NY.: University of Rochester Press

Reeve, J. (2005). *Understanding motivation and emotion.* New York, NY.: John Wiley & Sons.

Reeve, J., Bolt, E. & Cai, Y. (1999). Autonomy-supportive teachers: How they teach and motivate students. *Journal of Educational Psychology, 91,* 537-548. Doi: 10.1037/0022-0663.91.3.537

Reeve, J., Ryan, R., Deci, E.L. & Jang, H. (2008). Understanding and promoting autonomous self-regulation: A self-determination theory perspective. In: D.H. Schunk & B.J. Zimmerman (Eds.), *Motivation and self-regulated learning: Theory, research, and applications* (pp. 223–244). Mahwah, NJ.: Lawrence Erlbaum Associates Publishers.

Renninger, K.A. & Hidi, S. (2016). Interest, attention, and curiosity. In: K.A. Renninger & S. Hidi (Eds.), *The power of interest for motivation and engagement* (pp. 32-51). New York, NY.: Routledge.

Renninger, K.A. & Hidi, S.E. (2019a). *The Cambridge Handbook of Motivation and Learning* (Cambridge Handbooks in Psychology). Cambridge, UK: Cambridge University Press. Doi:10.1017/9781316823279

Renninger, K.A. & Hidi, S.E. (2019b). Interest Development and Learning. In: K.A. Renninger & S.E. Hidi (Eds.) *The Cambridge Handbook of Motivation and Learning* (pp. 265-290). Cambridge, UK: Cambridge University Press.

Roeser, R.W., Eccles, J.S. & Freedman-Doan, C. (1999). Academic functioning and mental health in adolescence: Patterns, progressions, and routes from childhood. *Journal of Adolescent Research, 14,* 135-174. Doi: 10.1177/0743558499142002

Roeser, R.W., Midgley, C. & Urdan, T.C. (1996). Perceptions of the school psychological environment and early adolescents' psychological and behavioral functioning in school: The mediating role of goals and belonging. *Journal of Educational Psychology, 88,* 408-422. Doi: 10.1037/0022-0663.88.3.408

Roeser, R.W., Strobel, K.R. & Quihuis, G. (2002). Studying early adolescents' academic motivation, social-emotional functioning and engagement in learning: Variable- and person-centered approaches. *Anxiety, Stress & Coping: An International Journal, 15,* 345-368. Doi: 10.1080/1061580021000056519

Rogers, C. (1969). *Freedom to Learn.* Columbus, OH.: Charles E. Merrill.

Rosenzweig, E.Q. & Wigfield, A. (2017). What if reading is easy but unimportant? How students' patterns of affirming and undermining motivation for reading information texts predict different reading outcomes. *Contemporary Educational Psychology, 48,* 133-148. Doi: 10.1016/j.cedpsych.2016.09.002

Rosenzweig, E.Q., Wigfield, A. & Eccles, J.S. (2019). Expectancy-Value Theory and Its Relevance for Student Motivation and Learning. In: K.A. Renninger & S.E. Hidi (Eds.) *The Cambridge Handbook of Motivation and Learning* (pp. 617-644). Cambridge, UK: Cambridge University Press. Doi: 10.1017/9781316823279.026

Rotter, J.B. (1966). Generalized expectancies for internal versus external control of reinforcement. *Psychological Monographs, 80,* 1-28. Doi: 10.1037/h0092976

Rottinghaus, P.J., Larson, L.M. & Borgen, F.H. (2003). The relation of self-efficacy and interests: A meta-analysis of 60 samples. *Journal of Vocational Behavior, 62,* 221-236. Doi: 10.1016/S0001-8791(02)00039-8

Ryan, R.M. (Ed.). (2012). *The Oxford handbook of human motivation.* Oxford, UK.: Oxford University Press.

Ryan, R.M. & Deci, E.L. (2000). Self-determination theory and the facilitation of intrinsic motivation, social development, and well-being. *American Psychologist, 55,* 68-78. Doi: 10.1037/0003-066X.55.1.68

Ryan, R.M. & Deci, E.L. (2002). An overview of self-determination theory. In: E.L. Deci & R.M. Ryan (Eds.), *Handbook of self-determination research* (pp. 3-33) Rochester, NY.: University of Rochester Press.

Ryan, R.M. & Deci, E.L. (2006). Self-Regulation and the Problem of Human Autonomy: Does Psychology Need Choice, Self-Determination, and Will? *Journal of Personality, 74,* 1557-1585. Doi: 10.1111/j.1467-6494.2006.00420.x

Ryan, R.M. & Deci, E.L. (2018). *Self-Determination Theory - Basic Psychological Needs in Motivation, Development, and Wellness.* New York, NY.: The Guilford Press.

Ryan, R.M. & Deci, E.L. (2020). Intrinsic and extrinsic motivation from a self-determination theory perspective: Definitions, theory, practices, and future directions. *Contemporary Educational Psychology, 61,* Article 101860. Doi: 10.1016/j.cedpsych.2020.101860

Ryan, R.M., Deci, E.L. & Grolnick, W.S. (1995). Autonomy, relatedness, and the self: Their relation to development and psychopathology. In: D. Cicchetti & D.J. Cohen (Eds.), *Developmental psychopathology, Vol. 1. Theory and methods* (pp. 618-655). New

York, NY.: John Wiley & Sons.

Sadri, G. & Robertson, I.T. (1993). Self-efficacy and work-related behaviour: A review and meta-analysis. *Applied Psychology: An International Review, 42,* 139-152. Doi: 10.1111/j.1464-0597.1993.tb00728.x

Sansone, C. & Harackiewicz, J.M. (2000a). *Intrinsic and Extrinsic Motivation – The Search for Optimal Motivation and Performance.* New York, NY.: Academic Press.

Sansone, C. & Harackiewicz, J.M. (2000b). Looking beyond Rewards: The Problem and Promise of Intrinsic Motivation. In: C. Sansone & J.M. Harackiewicz (Eds.), *Intrinsic and Extrinsic Motivation – The Search for Optimal Motivation and Performance* (pp. 1-9). New York, NY.: Academic Press.

Sarkisian, C.A., Prohaska, T.R., Davis, C. & Weiner, B. (2007). Pilot test of an attribution retraining intervention to raise walking levels in sedentary older adults. *Journal of the American Geriatrics Society, 55,* 1842-1846. Doi: 10.1111/j.1532-5415.2007.01427.x

Schunk, D.H. (1981). Modeling and attributional effects on children's achievement: A self-efficacy analysis. *Journal of Educational Psychology, 73,* 93-105. Doi: 10.1037/0022-0663.73.1.93

Schunk, D.H. (1995). Self-efficacy and education and instruction. In: J.E. Maddux (Ed.), *Self-efficacy, Adaptation, and Adjustment: Theory, research, and application* (pp. 281-303). New York, NY.: Plenum Press. Doi: 10.1007/978-1-4419-6868-5_10

Schunk, D.H. & Ertmer, P.A. (1999). Self-regulatory processes during computer skill acquisition: Goal and self-evaluative influences. *Journal of Educational Psychology, 91,* 251-260. Doi: 10.1037/0022-0663.91.2.251

Schunk, D.H. & Miller, S.D. (2002). Self-efficacy and adolescents' motivation. In: F. Pajares & T. Urdan (Eds). *Academic Motivation of Adolescents, 2,* (pp. 29-52). Greenwich, CT: Information Age Publishing.

Schunk, D.H. & Pajares, F. (2002). The development of academic self-efficacy. In: A. Wigfield & J.S. Eccles (Eds.), *Development of Achievement Motivation* (pp. 15-31). San Diego, CA: Academic Press. Doi: 10.1016/B978-012750053-9/50003-6

Schunk, D.H. & Pajares, F. (2009). Self-efficacy theory. In: K.R. Wentzel & A. Wigfield (Eds.), *Handbook of Motivation at School* (pp. 35-53). New York, NY.: Routledge/Taylor & Francis Group.

Schunk, D.H., Pintrich, P.R. & Meece, J.L. (2008) *Motivation in Education: Theory.* London, UK.: Pearson Education Inc.

Schuster, B., Forsterlung, F. & Weiner, B. (1989). Perceiving the causes of success and failure: A crosscultural examination of attributional concepts. *Journal of Cross-Cultural Psychology, 20,* 191-213.

Schwinger, M., Steinmayr, R. & Spinath, B. (2016). Achievement goal profiles in elementary school: Antecedents, consequences, and longitudinal trajectories. *Contemporary Educational Psychology, 46,* 164-79. Doi: 10.1016/j.cedpsych. 2016.05.006

Schwinger, M. & Wild, E. (2012). Prevalence, stability, and functionality of achievement goal profiles in mathematics from third to seventh grade. *Contemporary*

*Educational Psychology, 37*, 1-13. Doi: 10.1016/j.cedpsych.2011.08.001

Seaton, M., Marsh, H.W. & Craven, R.G. (2009). Earning its place as a pan-human theory: Universality of the big-fish-little-pond effect across 41 culturally and economically diverse countries. *Journal of Educational Psychology, 101*, 403-419. Doi: 10.1037/a0013838

Seaton, M., Marsh, H.W. & Craven, R.G. (2010). Big-fish-little-pond effect generalizability and moderation - two sides of the same coin. *American Educational Research Journal, 47*, 390-433. Doi: 10.3102/0002831209350493

Seijts, G.H. & Latham, G.P. (2001). The effect of distal learning, outcome, and proximal goals on a moderately complex task. *Journal of Organizational Behavior, 22,* 291-307. Doi: 10.1002/job.70

Selden, S.C. & Brewer, G.A. (2000). Work Motivation in the Senior Executive Service: Testing the High Performance Cycle Theory, *Journal of Public Administration Research and Theory, 10,* 531-550, Doi: 10.1093/oxfordjournals.jpart.a024280

Seligman, M. E. (1972). Learned helplessness. *Annual Review of Medicine, 23,* 407-412.

Seligman, M.E.P. (1975). *Helplessness: On depression, development, and death.* San Francisco, CA.: Freeman.

Seligman, M.E.P. (1998). *Learned optimism.* New York, NY.: Pocket Books.

Seligman, M.E.P. (2002). *Authentic happiness: Using the new positive psychology to realize your potential for lasting fulfillment.* New York, NY.: Free Press.

Seligman, M. (2018). PERMA and the building blocks of well-being. *The Journal of Positive Psychology, 13,* 333-335. Doi: 10.1080/17439760.2018.1437466

Seligman, M.E.P. (2019). Positive Psychology: A Personal History. *Annual Review of Clinical Psychology, 7;15,* 1-23. Doi: 10.1146/annurev-clinpsy-050718-095653.

Seligman, M.E.P. & Csikszentmihalyi, M. (2000). Positive psychology: An introduction. *American Psychologist, 55,* 5-14. Doi: 10.1037/0003-066X.55.1.5

Seligman, M.E.P. & Pawelski, J.O. (2003). Positive psychology: FAQs. *Psychological Inquiry, 14,* 159-163.

Seligman, M.E.P. & Peterson, C. (2001). Learned Helplessness. In: N.J. Smelser & P.B. Baltes (Eds.), *International Encyclopedia of Social & Behavioral Sciences* (pp. 8583-8586). Oxford, UK.: Pergamon Press.

Senko, C. (2016). Achievement goal theory: a story of early promises, eventual discords, and future possibilities. In: K.R. Wentzel & D.B. Miele (Eds.), *Handbook of Motivation of School* (2nd ed., pp. 75-95). New York, NY.: Routledge.

Senko, C., Hulleman, C.S. & Harackiewicz, J.M. (2011). Achievement goal theory at the crossroads: Old controversies, current challenges, and new directions. *Educational Psychologist, 46,* 26-47. Doi: 10.1080/00461520.2011.538646

Shah, J.Y. & Gardner, W.L. (Eds.). (2008). *Handbook of Motivation Science.* New York, NY.: The Guilford Press.

Shavelson, R.J. & Bolus, R. (1982). Self-concept: The interplay of theory and methods. *Journal of Educational Psychology, 74*(1), 3-17. Doi: 10.1037/0022-0663.74.1.3

Shavelson, R.J., Hubner, J.J. & Stanton, G.C. (1976). Self-concept: Validation of construct interpretations. *Review of Educational Research, 46*, 407-441. Doi: 10.2307/ 1170010

Shawn, A. (2007). *Wish I Could Be There: Notes from a Phobic Life.* London, UK.: Penguin Books.

Shim, S.S., Ryan, A.M. & Anderson, C.J. (2008). Achievement goals and achievement during early adolescence: Examining time-varying predictor and outcome variables in growth-curve analysis. *Journal of Educational Psychology, 100,* 655-671. Doi: 10.1037/0022-0663.100.3.655

Sideridis, G.D. (2005). Goal orientation, academic achievement, and depression: Evidence in favor of a revised goal theory framework. *Journal of Educational Psychology, 97,* 366-375. Doi: 10.1037/0022-0663.97.3.366

Skaalvik, E.M. (1997). Self-enhancing and self-defeating ego orientation: Relations with task and avoidance orientation, achievement, self-perceptions, and anxiety. *Journal of Educational Psychology, 89,* 71-81. Doi: 10.1037/0022-0663.89.1.71

Skaalvik, E.M. & Skaalvik, S. (2002). Internal and external frames of reference for academic self-concept. *Educational Psychologist, 37,* 233-244. Doi: 10.1207/ S15326985EP3704_3

Skinner, B.F. (1938). *The behavior of organisms: An experimental analysis.* New York, NY.: Appleton-Century-Crofts.

Skinner, B.F. (1953). *Science and Human Behavior.* New York, NY.: Macmillan.

Skinner, B.F. (1974). *About Behaviorism.* New York, NY.: Vintage.

Smetana, J.G., Campione-Barr, N. & Daddis, C. (2004). Longitudinal development of family decision making: Defining healthy behavioral autonomy for middle-class African American adolescents. *Child Development, 75,* 1418-1434. Doi: 10.1111/j.1467-8624.2004.00749.x.

Smith, M., Duda, J., Allen, J. & Hall, H. (2002). Contemporary measures of approach and avoidance goal orientations: Similarities and differences. *British Journal of Educational Psychology, 72,* 155-190. Doi: 10.1348/000709902158838

Smith, L., Sinclair, K.E. & Chapman, E.S. (2002). Students' goals, self-efficacy, selfhandicapping, and negative affective responses: An Australian senior school student study. *Contemporary Educational Psychology, 27,* 471-485. Doi: 10.1006/ceps.2001.1105

Stajkovic, A.D. & Luthans, F. (1998). Self-efficacy and work-related performances: A meta-analysis. *Psychological Bulletin, 124,* 240-261. Doi: 10.1037/0033-2909.124.2.240

Star, J. (2003). *Lao Tzu: Tao Te Ching – The Definitive Edition.* New York, NY.: Jeremy P. Tarcher/Putnam.

Stipek, D.J. (1983). A developmental analysis of pride and shame. *Human Development, 26,* 42-54. Doi: 10.1159/000272869

Stipek, D. & Mac Iver, D. (1989). Developmental change in children's assessment of intellectual competence. *Child Development, 60,* 521-538. Doi: 10.2307/1130719

Strang, H.R., Lawrence, E.C. & Fowler, P.C. (1978). Effects of assigned goal level and knowledge of results on arithmetic computation: A laboratory study. *Journal of Applied Psychology, 63,* 446-450. Doi: 10.1037/0021-9010.63.4.446

Swann, C., Rosenbaum, S., Lawrence, A., Vella, S.A., McEwan, D. & Ekkekakis, P. (2021). Updating goal-setting theory in physical activity promotion: A critical conceptual review. *Health Psychology Review, 15,* 34-50. Doi: 10.1080/17437199.2019.1706616

Tanaka, K. (2007). Relations between general goal orientations and task-specific self-appraisals. *Japanese Psychological Research, 49,* 235-247. Doi: 10.1111/j.1468-5884.2007.00350.x

Tang, T.L.-P. & Reynolds, D.B. (1993). Effects of self-esteem and perceived goal difficulty on goal setting, certainty, task performance, and attributions. *Human Resource Development Quarterly, 4,* 153-170. Doi: 10.1002/hrdq.3920040206

Tapola, A. & Niemivirta, M. (2008). The role of achievement goal orientations in students' perceptions of and preferences for classroom environment. *British Journal of Educational Psychology, 78,* 291-312. Doi: 10.1348/000709907X205272

Tracy, J.L. & Robins, R.W. (2007). The psychological structure of pride: A tale of two facets. *Journal of Personality and Social Psychology, 92,* 506-525. Doi: 10.1037/0022-3514.92.3.506

Trautwein, U., Marsh, H.W., Nagengast, B., Lüdtke, O., Nagy, G. & Jonkmann, K. (2012). Probing for the multiplicative term in modern expectancy–value theory: A latent interaction modeling study. *Journal of Educational Psychology, 104,* 763-777. doi:10.1037/a0027470

Tuominen, H., Niemivirta, M., Lonka, K. & Salmela-Aro, K. (2020). Motivation across a transition: Changes in achievement goal orientations and academic well-being from elementary to secondary school. *Learning and Individual Differences, 79,* 101854. Doi: 10.1016/j.lindif.2020.101854

Tuominen-Soini, H., Salmela-Aro, K. & Niemivirta, M. (2008). Achievement goal orientations and subjective well-being: A person-centred analysis. *Learning and Instruction, 18,* 251-266. Doi: 10.1016/j.learninstruc.2007.05.003

Tuominen-Soini, H., Salmela-Aro, K. & Niemivirta, M. (2011). Stability and change in achievement goal orientations: A person-centered approach. *Contemporary Educational Psychology, 36,* 82-100. Doi: 10.1016/j.cedpsych.2010.08.002

Tuominen-Soini, H., Salmela-Aro, K. & Niemivirta, M. (2012). Achievement goal orientations and academic well-being across the transition to upper secondary education. *Learning and Individual Differences, 22,* 290-305. Doi: 10.1016/j.lindif.2012.01.002

Turner, J.C., Thorpe, P.K. & Meyer, D.K. (1998). Students' reports of motivation and negative affect: A theoretical and empirical analysis. *Journal of Educational Psychology, 90,* 758-771. Doi: 10.1037/0022-0663.90.4.758

Urdan, T. (1997). Achievement goal theory: Past results, future directions. In: M.L. Maehr & P.R. Pintrich (Eds.), *Advances in motivation and achievement, Volume 10* (pp. 99-141). Greenwich, CT.: JAI Press.

Urdan, T.C. (2004). Predictors of academic self-handicapping and achievement:

examining achievement goals, classroom goal structures, and culture. *Journal of Educational Psychology, 96,* 251-264. Doi: 10.1037/0022-0663.96.2.251

Urdan, T. & Kaplan, A. (2020). The origins, evolution, and future directions of achievement goal theory. *Contemporary Educational Psychology, 61,* Article 101862. Doi: 10.1016/j.cedpsych.2020.101862

Urdan, T. & Midgley, C. (2001). Academic self-handicapping: What we know, what more there is to learn. *Educational Psychology Review, 13,* 115-138. Doi: 10.1023/A:1009061303214

Usher, E.L. & Pajares, F. (2008). Sources of self-efficacy in school: Critical review of the literature and future directions. *Review of Educational Research, 78,* 751-796. Doi: 10.3102/0034654308321456

Utman, C.H. (1997). Performance effects of motivational states: A meta-analysis. *Personality and Social Psychology Review, 1,* 170-182. Doi: 10.1207/s15327957pspr0102_4

Valentine, J.C. (2002). The relation between self-concept and academic achievement: A meta-analytic review (Doctoral dissertation, University of Missouri-Columbia, 2001). *Dissertation Abstracts International, 62,* 4278.

Valentine, J.C. & DuBois, D.L. (2005). Effects of self-beliefs on academic achievement and vice versa: Separating the chicken from the egg. In: H.W. Marsh, R.G. Craven & D.M. McInerney (Eds.), *New Frontiers for Self Research - Volume 2: International advances in self research* (pp. 53-77). Greenwich, CT: Information Age.

Valentine, J.C., DuBois, D.L. & Cooper, H. (2004). The Relation Between Self-Beliefs and Academic Achievement: A Meta-Analytic Review. *Educational Psychologist, 39,* 111-133. Doi: 10.1207/s15326985ep3902_3

Valle, A., Cabanach, R.G., Núñez, J.C., González-Pienda, J., Rodríguez, S. & Piñeiro, I. (2003). Multiple goals, motivation and academic learning. *British Journal of Educational Psychology, 73,* 71-87. Doi: 10.1348/000709903762869923

Vallerand, R.J. & Reid, G. (1984). On the causal effects of perceived competence on intrinsic motivation: A test of cognitive evaluation theory. *Journal of Sport Psychology,* 6, 94-102.

Vallerand, R.J., Pelletier, L.G. & Koestner, R. (2008). Reflections on self-determination theory. *Canadian Psychology / Psychologie Canadienne, 49,* 257-262. Doi: 10.1037/a0012804

Van Eerde, W. & Thierry, H. (1996). Vroom's expectancy models and work-related criteria: A meta-analysis. *Journal of Applied Psychology, 81,* 575-586. Doi: 10.1037/ 0021-9010.81.5.575

Van Petegem, S., Beyers, W., Vansteenkiste, M. & Soenens, B. (2012). On the association between adolescent autonomy and psychosocial functioning: Examining decisional independence from a self-determination theory perspective. *Developmental Psychology, 48,* 76-88. Doi: 10.1037/a0025307

Van Yperen, N.W. (2006). A Novel Approach to Assessing Achievement Goals in the Context of the 2 × 2 Framework: Identifying Distinct Profiles of Individuals with

Different Dominant Achievement Goals. *Personality and Social Psychology Bulletin, 32,* 1432-1445. Doi: 10.1177/0146167206292093

Veermans, M. & Tapola, A. (2004). Primary School Students' Motivational Profiles in Longitudinal Settings. *Scandinavian Journal of Educational Research, 48,* 373-395. Doi: 10.1080/0031383042000245780

Wang, C.K.J., Biddle, S.J.H. & Elliot, A.J. (2007). The 2 x 2 achievement goal framework in physical education context. *Psychology of Sport and Exercise, 8,* 147-168. Doi: 10.1016/j.psychsport.2005.08.012

Wang, M.-T., Chow, A., Hofkens, T. & Salmela-Aro, K. (2015). The trajectories of student emotional engagement and school burnout with academic and psychological development: Findings from Finnish adolescents. *Learning and Instruction, 36,* 57-65. Doi: 10.1016/j.learninstruc.2014.11.004

Watson, J. B. (1925). *Behaviorism.* New York, NY.: WW Norton.

Watt H.M. (2004). Development of adolescents' self-perceptions, values, and task perceptions according to gender and domain in 7th- through 11th-grade Australian students. *Child Development, 75,* 1556-1574. Doi: 10.1111/j.1467-8624.2004.00757.x. PMID: 15369531.

Weiner, B. (1972). *Theories of Motivation: From Mechanism to Cognition.* Chicago, IL.: Markham.

Weiner, B. (1979). A theory of motivation for some classroom experiences. *Journal of Educational Psychology, 71,* 3-25. Doi: 10.1037/0022-0663.71.1.3

Weiner, B. (1980a). A cognitive (attribution)-emotion-action model of motivated behavior: An analysis of judgments of help-giving. *Journal of Personality and Social Psychology, 39,* 186-200. Doi: 10.1037/0022-3514.39.2.186

Weiner, B. (1980b). *Human Motivation.* New York, NY.: Holt, Rinehart and Winston.

Weiner, B. (1982). The emotional consequences of causal ascriptions. In: M.S. Clark & S.T. Fiske (Eds.), *Affect and Cognition: The 17th Annual Carnegie Symposium on Cognition* (pp. 185-200). Hillsdale, NJ.: Erlbaum.

Weiner, B. (1985). An attributional theory of achievement motivation and emotion. *Psychological Review, 92,* 548-573. Doi: 10.1037/0033-295X.92.4.548

Weiner, B. (1986). *An Attributional Theory of Motivation and Emotion.* New York, NY.: Springer-Verlag.

Weiner, B. (1992). *Human Motivation, Metaphors, Theories, and Research.* London, UK: Sage Publications.

Weiner, B. (1995). *Judgements of responsibility: A foundation for a theory of social conduct.* New York, NY.: Guilford Press.

Weiner, B. (2000). Intrapersonal and Interpersonal Theories of Motivation from an Attributional Perspective. *Educational Psychology Review, 12,* 1-14. Doi: 10.1023/A:1009017532121

Weiner, B. (2006). *Social Motivation, Justice, and the Moral Emotions.* Mahwah, NJ: Lawrence Erlbaum Associates.

Weiner, B. (2008). Reflections on the History of Attribution Theory and Research: People, Personalities, Publications, Problems. *Social Psychology. 39.* 151-156. Doi: 10.1027/1864-9335.39.3.151

Weiner, B. (2009). Attribution Theory. In: D. Sander & K.R. Scherer. (Eds.), *The Oxford companion to emotion and the affective sciences* (Series in affective science). Oxford, (p. 62). Oxford, UK.: Oxford University Press.

Weiner, B. (2010). The development of an attribution based theory of motivation: A history of ideas. *Educational Psychologist, 45,* 28-36. Doi: 10.1080/00461520903433596

Weiner, B. (2013). Little-Known Truths, Quirky Anecdotes, Seething Scandals, and Even Some Science in the History of (Primarily Achievement) Motivation. *Personality and Social Psychology Review, 17,* 293-304. Doi: 10.1177/1088868313484587

Weiner, B. (2018). The legacy of an attributional approach to motivation and emotion: A no-crisis zone. *Motivation Science, 4,* 4-14. Doi: 10.1037/mot0000082

Weiner, B. (2019). Wither attribution theory? *Journal of Organizational Behavior, 40,* 603-604. Doi: 10.1002/job.2398

Weiner, B., Frieze, I., Kukla, A., Reed, L., Rest, S. & Rosenbaum, R.M. (1987). Perceiving the causes of success and failure. In: E.E. Jones, D.E. Kanouse, H.H. Kelley, R.E. Nisbett, S. Valins & B. Weiner (Eds.), *Attribution: Perceiving the causes of behavior* (pp. 95–120). Mahwah, NJ.: Lawrence Erlbaum Associates, Inc.

Weiner, B. & Graham, S. (1984). An attributional approach to emotional development. In: C. Izard, J. Kagan & R. Zajonc (Eds.), *Emotion, Cognition and Behavior* (pp. 167-191). Cambridge, MA.: Cambridge University Press.

Weiner, B., Graham, S. & Chandler, C. (1982). Pity, anger, and guilt: An attributional analysis. *Personality and Social Psychology Bulletin, 8,* 226-232. Doi: 10.1177/0146167282082007

Weiner, B., Russell, D. & Lerman, D. (1978). Affective consequences of causal ascriptions. In: J. H. Harvey, W.J. Ickes & R.F. Kidd (Eds.), *New Directions in Attribution Research* (Vol 2. pp. 59-88). New York, NY.: Psychology Press.

Weiner, B., Russell, D. & Lerman, D. (1979). The cognition–emotion process in achievement-related contexts. *Journal of Personality and Social Psychology, 37,* 1211–1220. Doi: 10.1037/0022-3514.37.7.1211

Wells, L.E. & Marwell, G. (1976). *Self Esteem: Its Conceptualization & Measure* (Volume 20 of SAGE Library of Social Research). London, UK: Sage Publications.

White, R.W. (1959). Motivation reconsidered: The concept of competence. *Psychological Review, 66,* 297-333. Doi: 10.1037/h0040934

Whitley, B.E. & Frieze, I.H. (1985). Children's causal attributions for success and failure in achievement settings: A meta-analysis. *Journal of Educational Psychology, 77,* 608-616. Doi: 10.1037/0022-0663.77.5.608

Wicker, F.W., Payne, G.C. & Morgan, R.D. (1983). Participant descriptions of guilt and shame. *Motivation and Emotion, 7,* 25-39. Doi: 10.1007/BF00992963

Wiese, B.S. & Freund, A.M. (2005). Goal progress makes one happy, or does it?

Longitudinal findings from the work domain. *Journal of Occupational and Organizational Psychology, 78,* 287-304. Doi: 10.1348/096317905X26714

Wigfield, A. (1994). Expectancy-value theory of achievement motivation: A developmental perspective. *Educational Psychology Review, 6,* 49-78. Doi: 10.1007/BF02209024

Wigfield, A. & Cambria, J. (2010a). Expectancy-value theory: retrospective and prospective. In: T.C. Urdan & S.A. Karabenick (Eds.), *The Decade Ahead: Theoretical Perspectives on Motivation and Achievement* (Advances in Motivation and Achievement Vol. 16A) (pp. 35-70). London, UK.: Emerald. Doi: 10.1108/S0749-7423(2010)000016A005

Wigfield, A. & Cambria, J. (2010b). Students' achievement values, goal orientations, and interest: Definitions, development, and relations to achievement outcomes. *Developmental Review, 30,* 1-35. Doi: 10.1016/j.dr.2009.12.001

Wigfield, A. & Eccles, J.S. (1992). The development of achievement task values: A theoretical analysis. *Developmental Review, 12,* 265-310. Doi: 10.1016/0273-2297(92)90011-P

Wigfield, A. & Eccles, J.S. (2000). Expectancy-value theory of achievement motivation. *Contemporary Educational Psychology, 25,* 68–81. Doi: 10.1006/ceps.1999.1015

Wigfield, A. & Eccles, J.S. (2002). The Development of Competence Beliefs, Expectancies for Success and Achievement Values from Childhood through Adolescence. In: A. Wigfield & J.S. Eccles (Eds.), *Development of Achievement Motivation. A Volume in the Educational Psychology Series* (pp. 91-120). London, UK.: Academic Press. Doi: 10.1016/B978-012750053-9/50006-1

Wigfield, A., Eccles, J.S., Schiefele, U., Roeser, R.W. & Davis-Kean, P. (2006). Development of achievement motivation. In: N. Eisenberg, W. Damon & R.M. Lerner (Vol. Eds.), *Handbook of Child Psychology: Social, Emotional, and Personality Development: Vol. 3.* (pp. 933–1002). Hoboken, NJ: John Wiley & Sons.

Wigfield, A., Eccles, J.S., Yoon, K.S., Harold, R.D., Arbreton, A.J.A., Freedman-Doan, C. & Blumenfeld, P.C. (1997). Changes in children's competence beliefs and subjective task values across the elementary school years: A three-year study. *Journal of Educational Psychology, 89,* 451-469. Doi: 10.1037/0022-0663.89.3.451

Wigfield, A., Rosenzweig, E.Q. & Eccles, J.S. (2017). Achievement Values – Interactions, Interventions, and Future Directions. In: A.J. Elliot, C.S Dweck & D.S. Yeager (Eds.) *Handbook of Competence and Motivation: Theory and Application* (2nd ed., pp. 116-134). New York, NY.: Guilford Press.

Wigfield, A., Tonks, S.M. & Klauda, S.L. (2009). Expectancy-Value Theory. In: K.R. Wentzel & A. Wigfield (Eds), *Handbook of Motivation at School* (pp. 55-76). New York, NY.: Routledge Taylor Francis Group.

Wigfield, A., Tonks, S.M. & Klauda, S.L. (2016). Expectancy-value theory. In: K.R. Wentzel & D.B. Miele (Eds.), *Handbook of Motivation at School* (2nd ed., pp. 55-74). New York, NY.: Routledge.

Willson, V.L. & Palmer, D.J. (1983). Latent partition analysis of attributions for actual achievement. *American Educational Research Journal, 20,* 581-589. Doi: 10.2307/1162815

Wilson, T.D., Damiani, M. & Shelton, N. (2002). Improving the academic performance of college students with brief attributional interventions. In: J. Aronson (Ed.), *Improving academic achievement: Impact of psychological factors on education* (pp. 89–108). New York, NY.: Academic Press. Doi: 10.1016/B978-012064455-1/50008-7

Wimer, S. & Kelley, H.H. (1982). An investigation of the dimensions of causal attribution. *Journal of Personality and Social Psychology, 43,* 1142-1162. Doi: 10.1037/0022-3514.43.6.1142

Wolters, C.A. (2004). Advancing achievement goal theory: Using goal structures and goal orientations to predict students' motivation, cognition, and achievement. *Journal of Educational Psychology, 96,* 236-250. Doi: 10.1037/0022-0663.96.2.236

Wolters, C.A., Yu, S.L. & Pintrich, P.R. (1996). The relation between goal orientation and students' motivational beliefs and self-regulated learning. *Learning and Individual Differences, 8,* 211-238. Doi:10.1016/S1041-6080(96)90015-1

Wong, Y. & Tsai, J. (2007). Cultural models of shame and guilt. In: J.L. Tracy, R.W. Robins & J.P. Tangney (Eds.), *The self-conscious emotions: Theory and research* (pp. 209–223). New York, NY.: Guilford Press.

Wood, R. & Bandura, A. (1989). Impact of conceptions of ability on self-regulatory mechanisms and complex decision making. *Journal of Personality and Social Psychology, 56,* 407-415. Doi: 10.1037/0022-3514.56.3.407

Wormington, S.V. & Linnenbrink-Garcia, L. (2017). A new look at multiple goal pursuit: The promise of a person-centered approach. *Educational Psychology Review, 29,* 407-445. Doi: 10.1007/s10648-016-9358-2

Wylie, R. C. (1979). *The Self-Concept: Volume 2.* Theory and Research on Selected Topics. Lincoln, NE.: University of Nebraska Press.

Yu, S., Levesque-Bristol, C. & Maeda, Y. (2018). General need for autonomy and subjective well-being: A meta-analysis of studies in the US and East Asia. *Journal of Happiness Studies: An Interdisciplinary Forum on Subjective Well-Being, 19,* 1863-1882. Doi: 10.1007/s10902-017-9898-2

Zeidner, M.H. & Schleyer, E.J. (1999). The big-fish-little-pond effect for academic self-concept, test anxiety, and school grades in gifted children. *Contemporary Educational Psychology, 24,* 305-329. Doi: 10.1006/ceps.1998.0985

Zimmerman, B.J. (2000). Self-efficacy: An essential motive to learn. *Contemporary Educational Psychology, 25,* 82-91. Doi: 10.1006/ceps.1999.1016

Zimmerman, B.J., Bandura A. & Martinez-Pons, M. (1992). Self-motivation for academic attainment: The role of self-efficacy beliefs and personal goal setting. *American Educational Research Journal, 29,* 663-676. Doi: 10.3102/00028312029003663

Zimmerman, B.J. & Cleary, T.J. (2006). Adolescents' development of personal agency: The role of self-efficacy beliefs and self-regulatory skill. In: F. Pajares & T. Urdan (Eds.), *Adolescence and education: Self-efficacy beliefs of adolescents* (pp. 45–69).

Greenwich, CT.: Information Age.

Zimmerman, B.J. & Kitsantas, A. (1997). Developmental phases in self-regulation: Shifting from process goals to outcome goals. *Journal of Educational Psychology*, *89*, 29-36. Doi: 10.1037/0022-0663.89.1.29

Zimmerman, B.J. & Martinez-Pons, M. (1990). Student differences in self-regulated learning: Relating grade, sex, and giftedness to self-efficacy and strategy use. *Journal of Educational Psychology*, *82*, 51-59. Doi: 10.1037/0022-0663.82.1.51

Zuckerman, M. (1979). Attribution of success and failure revisited: or The motivational bias is alive and well in attribution theory. *Journal of Personality, 47,* 245-287. Doi: 10.1111/j.1467-6494.1979.tb00202.x

# Index

## *Abbreviated Subject Index of Main Concepts and Constructs*

## H



## I

## K



## L



## M

## N



## O



## P

## T

# Photo Credits

Page 2 Sangre de Christo National Park, Crestone, CO., USA. Photo by the author.

Page 24 Sintra, Portugal. Photo by the author.

Page 27 Park and Palace of Monserrate, Sintra, Portugal. Photo by the author.
Courtesy of Parques de Sintra, Park and Palace of Monserrate, Sintra, Portugal.

Page 30 Singapore Botanic Gardens, view from Cluny Road, Singapore. Photo by the author.

Page 64 Park and Palace of Monserrate, Sintra, Portugal. Photos by the author.
Courtesy of Parques de Sintra, Park and Palace of Monserrate, Sintra, Portugal.

Page 110 Phoenician glass face bead, 3rd cent BC. Property of the author.
Phoenician polychrome glass figurine, 4th-3rd cent BC. Property of the author.
Photos by the author.

Page 112 Phoenician glass face bead, 3rd cent BC. Property of the author.
Phoenician polychrome glass figurine, 4th-3rd cent BC. Property of the author.
Photos by the author.

Page 114 Phoenician glass face bead, 3rd cent BC. Property of the author.
Phoenician style polychrome glass figurine, contemporary. Property of the author.
Photos by the author.

Page 302 Thong Nhat Park, Ho Chi Minh City, Vietnam. Photo by the author.

Page 306 Phoenician glass face bead, 3rd cent BC. Property of the author.
Phoenician polychrome glass figurine, 4th-3rd cent BC. Property of the author.
Photos by the author.

Page 307, 320 Phoenician glass face bead, 3rd cent BC. Property of the author.
Photo by the author.

Page 319 Phoenician glass face bead, 3rd cent BC. Property of the author.
Photo by the author.

Page 341, 343, 345, 347, 363, 365 Egyptian glass eye inlays, Late Period, 664-332 BC.
Property of the author. Photos by the author.

Page 363 © Geert van Kesteren, 2005. Photo taken at the refugee camp of Médecins Sans Frontières / Doctors Without Borders, Zinder, Niger.
Courtesy of Geert van Kesteren.

# *About the Author*

Dr. Menno A. Mennes first revealed the fundamentals of the Mennes Model of Motivation in his dissertation, which appeared in 2016, after a lifelong period of research in which he made progressive attempts at validating his ideas.

No publications were to appear before completion of his work. The tragic death of his youngest son, on January 1st, 2017, finally made him decide to accept an offer from Amsterdam University Press to publish his ideas and research findings. These are to appear in the present 'Series on Motivation', consisting of ten Volumes, covering successive aspects of his work. The present Volume is to provide a first, comprehensive introduction of his Model.

Dr. Mennes graduated cum laude at Utrecht University, the Netherlands, in clinical psychology. After several years in education, he spent most of his career doing research on motivation in Europe, the United States and South-East Asia. Until his recent retirement, he was Program Director at the Honours Academy of Leiden University, the Netherlands.

Menno Mennes was born in Singapore, and spent most of his youth in Paris, France. Although these formative years remained influential throughout his life, he left for the Netherlands, where he has lived ever since. He is happily married and the proud father of four sons, three daughters-in-law, and (at the time of writing) grandfather of four grandchildren.

Dr. Menno A. Mennes can be reached at following institutes:

- University email address: m.a.mennes@ha.leidenuniv.nl
- Institute for Studies in Motivation and Development of Human Potential: mennes@motivation.institute

For Product Safety Concerns and Information please contact our EU representative GPSR@taylorandfrancis.com Taylor & Francis Verlag GmbH, Kaufingerstraße 24, 80331 München, Germany

**Batch number: 10722122**

Printed by Printforce, the Netherlands